Faith's Reasons
for
Believing

FAITH'S REASONS FOR BELIEVING

An
Apologetic Antidote
to
Mindless Christianity

Robert L. Reymond

MENTOR

Dedication

A patient and careful editor is of priceless value to any writer. After seeing eight previous books of mine through the publishing process it is long overdue that I publicly acknowledge the tremendous contribution the Rev. Dr. Malcolm Maclean, pastor in the Free Church of Scotland, has made to my writing projects.

This I do now by dedicating this book to him.

Thank you, Malcolm, for all you have done to make my books better than they would have been without your sharp eye, kind advice, and red pencil.

© Robert L. Reymond

ISBN 978-1-84550-337-6

10 9 8 7 6 5 4 3 2 1

Published in 2008
in the
Mentor Imprint
by
Christian Focus Publications Ltd.,
Geanies House, Fearn, Ross-shire,
IV20 1TW, Great Britain

Cover design by Moose77.com
Printed by CPD Wales

Contents

Frontispiece   7

Preface   9

1. What is Christian Apologetics?   17

2. Faith's Reasons for Believing in Christian Theology as an Intellectual Discipline   33

3. Faith's Reasons for Believing the Bible is God's Word   69

4. Faith's Reasons for Believing in the Bodily Resurrection and Ascension to Heaven of Jesus Christ   131

5. Faith's Reasons for Believing in the Virgin Birth of Christ   167

6. Faith's Reasons for Believing in Biblical Miracles in General and Jesus' Miracles in Particular   197

7. Faith's Reasons for Believing in Paul's Supernatural Conversion on the Damascus Road   227

8. Faith's Reasons for Rejecting Evidentialism: A Case Study in Apologetic Methodology   243

9. Faith's Reasons for Believing in the God of
   Christian Theism   293

10. Faith's Reasons for Believing the Bible Is Man's
    Only *Pou Stō* for Knowledge and Personal   343
    Significance

11. Faith's Reasons for Believing in the Nature of
    Biblical Truth   371

12. Faith's Reasons for Believing in the Apologetic
    Value of Christian Theistic Ethics   397

13. Faith's Reasons for Believing in the Pauline
    Apologetic for Reaching This Postmodern   431
    Generation

    Epilogue   457

    Subject Index   468

Frontispiece

"...in your light do we see light."
(Psalm 36:9)

"...by faith [in the truth of God's Word, the Bible] we
understand...."
(Hebrews 11:3)

"Faith has its reasons that the world's reason does not know."

Δός μοι ποῦ στῶ καἰ κινῶ τήν γῆν.
(*Dos moi pou stō kai kinō tēn gēn.*)

Archimedes, the Greek mathematician and inventor (287?–212?
B.C.), boasted in conjunction with his experimentation with the
simple machine of the lever: "Give to me [a place] where I may
stand [that is, where I may place my lever's fulcrum, and a lever
long enough] and I will move the earth." He was, of course,
asking for a place *outside* the cosmos by such a request.

Similarly, mankind needs an extra-cosmic "Archimedean
point of reference" *epistemologically* – an extra-cosmic "first
principle" that can and will promote a unified field of knowledge,
the philosopher's dream. This means that only a revelation
from the omniscient God who is transcendentally outside of the
cosmos can provide the ποῦ στῶ (*pou stō*), "the place where

they may stand," that is essential to the justification of human knowledge and ethical predications, since men beginning with themselves can never break out of their finite cosmic perspective and comprehend enough of the particulars of the cosmos to arrive at the universals that give the particulars their meaning, a step that is the necessary prerequisite for understanding with certainty either any single part of the cosmos or the cosmos as a whole, since the latter can be essentially different from the sum total of all its parts. Only an extra-cosmic "first principle" can provide that perspective. It is this matter of one's first principle, then, that is all-important in Christian apologetics.

* * * * *

"The nature of faith is to be certain. Any measure of doubt or uncertainty is not a degree of faith but an assault upon it. Faith, therefore, must rest on something more sure than an inference of probability" (J. I. Packer, *"Fundamentalism" and the Word of God*, 117). Biblical faith is not a leap in the dark; it is not fideism. It is whole-souled commitment to Jesus Christ that the Holy Spirit works in the human heart by and with the proclamation of the objective truth of the self-evidencing Word of God. Such faith has its reasons for believing that the world's reason does not and cannot understand (1 Cor. 2:14).

Preface

I have always tried to give my readers a sense of what lay behind my writing a particular book. In 1976 Presbyterian and Reformed Publishing Company published my small book on apologetics entitled *The Justification of Knowledge*. If my memory serves me correctly this book went through two printings, one revision, and then another printing. Then P&R decided to allow the book to go out of print. P&R never gave me the reason for its decision and I never inquired.

Nevertheless, through the 1990s up to this present day I continued to receive both requests for *JofK* and inquiries concerning where a copy of it might be obtained. I have been no help in either case. A good many people who had read *JofK* urged me to try to get it back into print. (I recently learned that an institution in California has been reproducing it – without my knowledge – and selling it.) But occupied as I was with my teaching responsibilities and with other writing projects I had neither the time nor the inclination to do so, even though I continued to read in the field, since I believed any reprint of it now would require considerable updating.

When Reformed Theological Seminary requested in October 2006, however, that I teach its course on apologetics at its Boca Raton campus I happily agreed to do so and turned my attention once again to the subject of apologetics and prepared the chapters of this book as lectures for that course. That course, by the way, never materialized because of scheduling problems, but through this providential collocation of events I now had in hand the material for a new book that is essentially what you my readers now hold in your hands. These chapters, however, are not *JofK* simply warmed over. While I adapted from *JofK* with a good many revisions this book's Chapters One and Eight, the other eleven chapters are in the main new, some of the material found therein having been adapted with alterations from Chapter Six and Chapter Fifteen of my *A New Systematic Theology of the Christian Faith*. This new material in the first half of the book deals more extensively than did *JofK* with faith's reasons for believing in several of the central historical events of the Faith. In the second half I defend again the apologetic method that I espoused in *JofK*, namely, presuppositionalism, because I believe that of all the apologetic methods that would claim our allegiance it best reflects the mind of the one living and true God who has revealed himself in Holy Scripture. As I wrote in the "Preface" to *JofK* thirty years ago I still recommend the reader to make the effort to read carefully the many biblical references to which I refer, and to think about their apologetic implications. No matter what he finally concludes with regard to apologetics he cannot but be richer for his labors.

An explanation of this book's title is in order. Militant atheist writers are making an all-out assault on the Christian faith today[1] – they speak of ours as a "mindless Christianity" – and as a result many people today, including many scientists and many poorly taught Christians, would think it very strange to talk about faith's *reasons* for believing, for if there is one

---

[1]For example, see Oxford professor Richard Dawkins' *The God Delusion* and Sam Harris' *Letter to a Christian Nation*. While I certainly do not agree with everything they said in their response entitled *The Dawkins Delusion?*, nevertheless Alister McGrath and Joanna Collicutt McGrath addressed Dawkins' arguments so successfully that, after reading their response, Michael Ruse declared: "*The God Delusion* makes me embarrassed to be an atheist." And Douglas Wilson in his *Letter from a Christian Citizen* and Joel McDurmon in his *Return of the Village Atheist* have, in my opinion, more than adequately answered Harris' anti-God tract.

thing not understood today about biblical faith it is that it eschews any and all anti-intellectual, fideistic "leaps" of faith. But according to Scripture "saving faith" is grounded in the knowledge of propositional truths about Jesus Christ. Benjamin B. Warfield explains: "We cannot be said to believe or to trust in a thing or person of which we have no knowledge; 'implicit faith'[2] in this sense is an absurdity."[3] Knowledge (*notitia*) of propositional truths is the cognitive foundation or base of saving faith. The Bible insists that "faith comes by hearing, and hearing through the word of Christ" (Rom. 10:17) and that men must "love the truth in order that they may be saved" (2 Thess. 2:10), and it speaks of "repentance leading to a knowledge [*epignōsin*] of the truth" (2 Tim. 2:25). In sum, saving faith is based upon divine testimony. It knows nothing of the postmodern notion that faith is the enemy of knowledge or that faith repudiates all grounding in propositional truths. This contemporary notion is expressed in such sentiments as "When one does not know then one must believe; if one knows then there is no room for belief," and "It does not matter what one believes as long as one is sincere." To illustrate, A. J. Carlson, an early president of the American Association for the Advancement of Science, declared: "The scientist tries to rid himself of all faiths and beliefs. He either knows or he does not know. If he knows, there is no room for faith or belief. If he does not know he has no right to faith or belief."[4] In these

---

[2]"Implicit faith" (fides implicita) is the Roman Catholic dogma that as long as one accepts as true "what the church teaches," even though one does not know the objective content of that faith, one may regard himself as exercising true faith. The Reformers uniformly rejected this dogma, contending that since knowledge is lacking it is no true faith at all. They referred to such faith as the "faith of colliers" (fides carbonaria), that is, of charcoal burners, on the assumption that the average collier knows little or nothing of Christian doctrine.

[3]Benjamin B. Warfield, "On Faith in Its Psychological Aspects" in *Biblical and Theological Studies* (Philadelphia: Presbyterian and Reformed, 1952), 402-03.

[4]See A. J. Carlson, *Science* (1931), 73:217-25.

words one finds enunciated the total bifurcation of knowledge and faith. A very popular song some years ago expressed the other side of the bifurcation – the presence of faith devoid of knowledge – this way:

> I believe for every drop of rain that falls a flower grows,
> I believe that somewhere in the darkest night a candle glows;
> I believe for everyone who goes astray,
> someone will come to show the way,
> I believe, I believe.
>
> I believe above the storm the smallest prayer will still be heard,
> I believe that someone in the great somewhere hears every word;
> Every time I hear a newborn baby cry,
> or touch a leaf, or see the sky,
> Then I know why I believe.

But the song never made clear beyond its reference to the "someone in the great somewhere" who the one is in whom the singer believed. Is this someone the tooth fairy, Dorothy's fairy godmother, an evil spirit bent on deceiving us, maybe even Satan himself disguised as an angel of light (2 Cor. 11:14)? And what was his authority for believing what he did? What he himself heard, touched, and saw, which just happens to be the least trustworthy authority there is (Prov. 3:5).[5] Such sentimental drivel is simply jabberwocky,[6] irrational

---

[5]People believe what they do on the basis of a book, an institutional tradition, or their own opinion.

[6]"Jabberwocky," written by Lewis Carroll and found in *Through the Looking Glass, and What Alice Found There* (1871), is considered one of the greatest nonsense poems in the English language, about which Alice said: "Somehow it seems to fill my head with ideas – only I don't exactly know what they are." Here is the first of its seven quatrains:

'Twas brillig, and the slithy toves
Did gyre and gimple in the wabe:
All mimsy were the borogroves
And the mome raths outgrabe.

nonsense, absurd inanity. And as far as salvation is concerned it portends a salvation by ignorance and/or by sincerity, which instrumentalities will never save. They amount to having "faith in the power of faith," a sentiment best captured perhaps by Norman Vincent Peale's popular phrase, "the power of positive thinking." Frankly, I find Peale's representation of faith appalling for it fatally wounds Christianity in the heart, while I find Paul's representation of faith appealing for he everywhere glories and delights in revealed knowledge and propositional truth as the foundation of true faith while at the same time characterizing "faith devoid of knowledge" as "believing the lie" that leads to condemnation (2 Thess. 2:11-12). The Bible often highlights this knowledge base of saving faith by employing some form of the construction *pisteuein hoti*[7] ("to believe that"), followed by a propositional truth, to indicate the content of saving faith:

Hebrews 11:6: "...without faith it is impossible to please God, for the one coming to God must *believe that* he exists and is the rewarder of those seeking him."

John 8:24: "...if you do not *believe that* I am, you shall die in your sins."

John 11:42: "...I said this for the benefit of the crowd standing here, in order that they may *believe that* you sent me" (see also John 17:8, 21).

John 14:11: "*Believe me that* I am in [union with] the Father and the Father is [in union] in me."

John 16:27: "For the Father himself loves you, because... you have *believed that* I came out from the Father" (see also John 16:30).

John 20:31: "...these things [that is, the entire Gospel of John] are written that you may *believe that* Jesus is the Christ,

---

[7]I have transliterated all of the Hebrew and Greek words for the benefit of those who have not studied these biblical languages. Horizontal lines over the ā, ē, and ō indicate that they should be vocalized as follows: ā as in "father," ē as the "a" in "fate," and ō as in "know."

the Son of God, and that by believing you may have life in his name."

Romans 10:9: "...if you *believe...that* God raised [Jesus] from the dead [this is not all that one must believe but it is one thing that must be believed], you will be saved."

1 Thessalonians 4:14: "...we *believe that* Jesus died and rose again."

1 John 5:1: "Everyone who *believes that* Jesus is the Christ has been begotten by God."

1 John 5:4: "Who is it who overcomes the world but he who *believes that* Jesus is the Son of God?"

In this feature of saving faith "lies the importance of doctrine respecting Christ. The doctrine defines Christ's identity, the identity in terms of which we entrust ourselves to him. Doctrine consists in propositions of truth."[8] All this simply means that faith must indeed have its reasons for believing. Some of the more significant reasons I intend to provide in this book.

One final comment: For what it is worth to those who may be interested, I required the students in my course in apologetics to read the following books and articles:

Clark, Gordon H., *Three Types of Religious Philosophy* (P&R, 1977) (they read all)

Clark, Gordon H., *Religion, Reason and Revelation* (Trinity Foundation, 1986) (they read all)

Dulles, Avery Cardinal, *A History of Apologetics* (Second edition; Ignatius, 2005) (they read all)

Frame, John M., *Apologetics to the Glory of God: an Introduction* (P&R, 1994) (they read all)

Geehan, E. R. (ed.), *Jerusalem and Athens: Critical Discussions on the Philosophy and Apologetics of Cornelius Van Til*

---

[8]John Murray, "Faith" in *Collected Writings of John Murray* (Edinburgh: Banner of Truth, 1977), 2:258.

(P&R, 1971) (they read "My Credo" and Chapters III, IV, V, XIV, XVI, XIX, XXI, XXIII)

Nash, Ronald H. (ed.), *The Philosophy of Gordon H. Clark: A Festschrift* (P&R, 1968) (they read "Part One: The Wheaton Lectures" and Chapters V and XVII, VI and XVIII, VII and XIX, XI and XXII)

Sproul, R. C., John Gerstner, and Arthur Lindsley, *Classical Apologetics: A Rational Defense of the Christian Faith and a Critique of Presuppositional Apologetics* (Zondervan, 1984) (they read all)

Warfield, Benjamin B., "Apologetics" in *The Works of Benjamin B. Warfield* (Reprint; Grand Rapids: Baker, 1991), IX, 3-21

Warfield, Benjamin B., "Introduction to Francis R. Beattie's *Apologetics*" in *Selected Shorter Writings of Benjamin B. Warfield* (Reprint; Nutley, N. J.: Presbyterian and Reformed, 1973), II, 93-105

Warfield, Benjamin B., "The Real Problem of Inspiration" in *The Inspiration and Authority of the Bible* (Reprint; Philadelphia: Presbyterian and Reformed, 1948)

I also required them to write a book review of *Classical Apologetics,* 1200-1500 words in length, in which they were to pinpoint its major flaw and explain why.

Robert L. Reymond
Christmas 2007

Chapter One

What is Christian Apologetics?

In contrast to Muhammad and the first four caliphates of Islam true Christianity's single "weapon of propagation" is divine truth (Eph. 6:17), *not* the civil magistrate's or the crusader's sword.[1] In its best moments Christianity has made its way in the world by proclaiming and teaching the world's only rational faith. As preeminently the "reasoning religion," Christianity is an apologetical religion, feeling deeply and passionately the burden both to tell humankind *what* they must believe in order to be saved from the guilt and power of sin and to give to humankind the reasons, when sought, *why* they should believe. Quite often Christianity's proclamation will pass into "contention for the faith that was *once for all* [*hapax*] delivered to the saints" (Jude 3).

---

[1]Muhammad's actions prove that he intended the "war verses" of the Koran to be understood militarily as he propagated his religion beginning with his move to Medina in September, A.D. 622. He waged *jihad* ("holy war") in the name of Allah against village after village in Arabia. In sum, virtually from its beginning Islam was spread by the sword. And the first four caliphs (successors) of Muhammad – Abu Bakr, Umar, Othman, and Ali – all drew the sword and conquered one land after another through Palestine and North Africa all the way to Spain. In the last hundred years Muslim expansion goes on apace by warfare. The Muslim Ottoman Turks slaughtered a million and a half Armenians in 1915–1924. Today converts to Christianity are regularly executed in Saudi Arabia and tortured and murdered in Egypt. In the Sudan over two million Christians have been slaughtered and a million Christian children have been sold into slavery, all under the direction of the Islamic General Umar Bashir. In Indonesia Muslims have killed over three hundred thousand East Timorese Catholics since 1975.

Christian apologetics, therefore, is the intellectual discipline wherein the intelligent effort is made carefully to delineate and to contend for the truth claims of the Christian faith before the unbelieving world, specifically, its claim of exclusive true knowledge of the one living and true God, in a manner that is consistent with the teaching of Holy Scripture.

As a term "apologetics" derives from the Greek root *apolog-*, meaning "defense" or "reply to a formal charge" such as Socrates' "apology." This root occurs in either verbal, nominal, or adjectival form some twenty-plus times in the Greek New Testament.[2] Through an evolution occasioned by usage the term has come to refer in its narrowest sense to the individual Christian's defense of his faith and lifestyle though it is perhaps better to speak of such a defense as an "apology" rather than an "apologetic." In a broader sense it is the Christian's answer to the world's attacks directed against the truth claims of Holy Scriptures. And in the fullest sense it is the defense and vindication of the Christian faith against all attacks of doubters and unbelievers that will include the positive presentation of the reasonableness of Christianity's truth claims and its more than ample sufficiency to meet the spiritual needs of humankind. Apologetics in this last sense then is not only a defensive but also an offensive discipline, to be employed not only in defense of the gospel but also in its propagation.

Some Christians opine that they are under no obligation to defend their faith before a hostile world; their responsibility is simply to proclaim the gospel to the world which proclamation is itself a fully adequate defense of the faith. This opinion cannot be sustained on biblical grounds. In addition to the obvious examples of both Jesus and Paul who constantly defended their claims respectively of Messiah (Matt. 22) and apostle (Gal. 1-2; 1 Cor. 9; Acts 22-26) we have the classic Petrine admonition: "...as Lord set apart the Christ in your hearts, always being prepared *to make*

---

[2]Luke 12:11; 21:14; Acts 19:33; 22:1; 24:10; 25:8, 16; 26:1, 2, 24; Romans 2:15; 1 Corinthians 9:3; 2 Corinthians 7:11; 12:19; Philippians 1:7, 16; 2 Timothy 4:16; 1 Peter 3:15; see also Romans 1:20, 2:1.

a defense [*pros apologian*] to anyone who asks you for a reason[3] for the hope that is in you; yet do it with gentleness and respect, having a good conscience…" (1 Pet. 3:15-16a). Even a surface analysis of Peter's statement will show that this text

- commands that we make the Lordship of Christ our ultimate heart-commitment. We should believe him more certainly than we believe anyone else. Since this is so, his Word is the criterion, that is, the ultimate standard of truth, which validates *all* other authorities in *every* area of life. That is to say, our Lord's authority over us is comprehensive; in *all* we do we should seek to please him (1 Cor. 10:31; Col. 3:17, 23). Surely this includes the area of our thinking and knowing. "The fear of the Lord is the beginning of knowledge" (Prov. 1:7; Ps. 111:10);

- assumes a heart stance of faith ("the hope that is in you"), on the one hand a self-conscious commitment to Jesus Christ as Lord on the part of the Christian, on the other the recognition of this commitment on the part of the unbeliever who is asking of the Christian the reason for his hope;

- implies that the Christian's hope is fully capable of a reasonable defense since the apostle would not have commanded the Christian to defend that which is rationally indefensible;

- assumes the possibility of communication between the believer and unbeliever; otherwise, the exhortation would be pointless, the precise basis of this possibility of communication constituting the apologetic problem of the nature of "common ground" or "point of contact" (*Anknüpfungspunkt*) between believer and unbeliever;

- calls upon *every* believer to be ready upon *every* occasion to give to *anyone* who asks the reason for his faith commitment to Jesus Christ as Lord; and

---

[3]The Greek word translated "reason" is *logon* from *logos*, which root regardless of whether one translates it "word," "explanation," "speech," "sentence," etc. implicitly includes the idea of rationality and reasonableness.

- indicates the proper attitude with which the Christian is to make his "apology": It is not to be made with intellectual pride but with gentleness, a good conscience, and respect for the unbeliever who is also an image-bearer of God. Accompanying his defense should be an awareness that he too is a sinner saved by grace, and a pure walk before God. Only so may he expect God's fullest blessing upon his apologetic efforts.

Peter's command should not be construed to mean, however, that the Christian can "reason" men into the kingdom of God. A divinely initiated, regenerating work of almighty grace accompanying the gospel proclamation is alone capable of enabling men to enter the kingdom of heaven. The context of Peter's exhortation makes it clear that Christians who suffer persecution for their godly testimony (see 1 Pet. 1:3-7; James 1:2, 12) will occasionally be questioned by their pagan neighbors concerning their "strange behavior" under such adverse conditions. When in God's providence this happens Christians should be able to articulate the rational ground for their Christian hope, which answer should include a clear statement of God's redemptive activity in the saving work of Jesus Christ.

It is clear then that the Christian cannot avoid the task of making an intelligent defense of the Christian faith if he is obedient to Scripture. So far from being inconsistent with the Christian faith its cogent defense is in fact demanded by it. This does not justify, of course, any and every *method* of apologetics. Obviously we cannot defend our religious convictions by violence. Nor should we devise an apologetic method inconsistent with the very content of the gospel we proclaim. This is just to say that if the Reformed faith is in fact the faith taught in Holy Scripture it is incumbent upon the Reformed apologist to develop and utilize a Reformed apologetic, that is, a Reformed method of defending the Reformed faith. This is only being consistent.

The Place of Apologetics in Theological Encyclopedia

The basic intention of Christian apologetics is the vindication of the propriety of Christian commitment. How this is to be conducted specifically, however, varies from apologist to apologist and largely depends upon the relation the apologist sees apologetics sustaining to theological encyclopedia as a whole. The latter has normally been divided into four disciplines or departments, namely, the exegetical, the historical, the systematic, and the practical, and in that order. F. Schleiermacher, J. H. A. Ebraud, B. B. Warfield and F. R. Beattie all urged, however, that an apologetics department should precede these four as a separate discipline and should do its work first and independently simply because, as a discipline it alone "presupposes nothing." Before any of the other disciplines can achieve their results the apologetics department must establish the existence of God, the religious nature of man, the fact of revelation, the divine origin of Christianity, and the trustworthiness of the Bible. Otherwise, after explicating the Christian system, the systematician, for example, may discover that he has been dealing all along with fancies. Abraham Kuyper, Herman Bavinck, Valentine Hepp, and Louis Berkhof, on the contrary, argued that apologetics should follow upon the work of the systematician. Otherwise, if apologetics is allowed to establish both the possibility and presuppositions of Christian theology the Christian apologist has virtually attributed to unaided fallen man the ability to determine the truth of Christianity apart from revelation, thereby denying by implication the biblical doctrines of man's depravity and inability to know God apart from powerful aid coming to him *ab extra* ("from outside") or *anōthen*, "from above." Furthermore, these theologians insist that one must first determine what kind of God Christianity advances before he can really ask intelligently whether such a God exists. In other words, the apologist must concern himself with the *what* of Christianity, if not before, at least at the same time he concerns himself with the question of whether it is true. Obviously, defining Christian apologetics as I did earlier as the defense of the Christian faith,

I am in agreement with Kuyper *et al.* that apologetics should accompany or follow upon the disciplines that determine the content of the Christian faith. This also seems to be the most reasonable approach since it would seem that one has to know what it is he is defending before he defends it. If and when Reformed apologetics occasionally appears to precede the other disciplines I would argue that it is presupposing the facts of special revelation and the results of systematic theology.

Aspects of the Apologetic Task

As a defense of the Christian faith the aspects of the task confronting Christian apologetics fall under the following four heads:

1. To answer particular objections

The Christian apologist will often find himself confronted with specific objections brought against the Christian faith such as alleged contradictions between scriptural statements. He should resolve such contradictions and remove the objection on the basis of scholarly research and accurate exegesis. This labor will strengthen and support the faithful, remove obstacles standing in the way of further inquiry by the doubter, and disarm the opposition by laying to rest specious objections, misconceptions, and inaccuracies in the doubter's mind about Christianity. This task is not uniquely assignable to the discipline of apologetics alone. Or if one prefers to keep such a task within the discipline of apologetics it should be acknowledged that this is the task of apologetics broadly conceived. For *every* department of theological encyclopedia should engage itself in carrying out this task. Old and New Testament experts will develop apologetic responses to destructive criticism of and hostile theories respecting the biblical text and its teaching. J. Gresham Machen, professor of New Testament at Princeton Theological Seminary, for example, was a persuasive apologist for the Christian faith when he wrote his masterful monographs, *The Virgin Birth of Christ* and *The Origin of Paul's Religion.* As a systematic theologian I will defend in the first half of this book the facticity and historicity of such central events of Christianity as Christ's bodily resurrection on the third day after his crucifixion and his ascension to heaven, his virgin birth, his mighty miracles, and Paul's supernatural conversion on the Road to Damascus. The church historian will take care to assure that any false reading of church history to the detriment of the truthfulness of the Christian faith is detected and corrected.

More than likely, however, such direct responses to specific objections and difficulties raised against the Christian faith are possible only at the beginning of any conversation with the unbeliever; quite likely, the issue will quickly shift to more basic, in fact, to ultimate premises. Then something more is needed. The defense of the faith will then array itself at the deeper level of presuppositions where Christian apologetics as a philosophical and/or epistemological discipline comes into its own. Such matters I will take up in the second half of this book.

2. To give an account of the foundations of the Christian faith
At the deeper level of ultimate premises or foundational issues the Christian apologist will often deal with such questions as the following:

- Does God exist?
- Has he revealed himself? If so, where and how?
- Why do I believe these things?
- How do I know that what I believe is true?

Once it is seen that these questions fall specifically and properly within the domain of Christian apologetics it is clear that Christian apologetics as a discipline often entails an exercise in philosophical theology and takes us into the sphere of epistemology.

In light of this task of apologetics it should be obvious that apologetic dialogue will not always be simply proclamation of gospel content. Of course, the apologist should assume throughout his labor the full trustworthiness of the whole counsel of God in Scripture and will unhesitatingly draw upon its insights along the way. He will refer often to the facts of God, sin, Christ's work, and salvation. Consequently, it will doubtless appear at times to the non-Christian that the apologist is merely "throwing gospel rocks at his head." Of course, in one sense he will be. But a biblical defense of the faith, while it will include gospel content, will also concern itself with the deepest questions of religion and will seek to demonstrate that the Christian faith alone gives rational answers to them.

3. To challenge non-Christian systems

Some of the earliest church fathers after the apostolic age were called Apologists (Justin Martyr, Tatian, Irenaeus, Athenagoras, and Theophilus of Antioch) as they attempted to answer such charges against Christians as cannibalism and immorality, but it gradually became apparent that any defense of the faith must be built upon the positive affirmation of the Christian faith and its implications for non-Christian systems (see Augustine's *The City of God*). In more recent times certain Christian apologists, more perceptive and more consistently Christian in their vision of the apologetic task than others, have not only answered the objections of the unbelievers but have also exposed the irrationality inherent within non-Christian systems of thought and challenged them to justify epistemologically their very existence not to mention their unfounded dogmatic pronouncements. It is this evangelistic offensive, spearheaded by such men as Cornelius Van Til, Gordon H. Clark, Carl F. H. Henry, and Francis Schaeffer, that has challenged many younger theologians to familiarize themselves thoroughly with the drift of modern thought and to expose the inherent inadequacies of and the epistemological nihilism within any system that refuses to place at its base the Word of God coming to them from the unseen spiritual world.

4. To persuade men of the truth claims of the Christian faith

As the natural outcome of the preceding concerns Christian apologetics has for its ultimate goal the persuasion of men of the truth claims of the Christian faith. This aspect of the apologetic task points up the fact that Christian apologetics should not only be concerned with correct epistemological method but at bottom should also be *evangelistic* and *kērygmatic*. Although he fully recognizes the depravity of man and the noetic effects of sin[4] and his own inability to persuade men apart from the regenerating work of the Holy Spirit, the Christian apologist will nonetheless seek to present persuasively the Christian faith in all of its wholeness

---

[4]The fall of man in Genesis 3 from his created stated of integrity (*status integritatis*) into his present state of moral corruption (*status corruptionis*) brought mankind not only into a state of depravity and inability to change this depravity (Rom. 1:18-32; 3:10-18; 5:12-19; 8:7-8; 1 Cor. 2:14; Eph. 4:17-19) but also into a state of real guilt before God because of his sin. A major reason for his inability to alter his condition is the noetic effects of sin upon his thinking in which men "walk in the futility of their mind. They are darkened in their understanding, alienated from the life of God because of the ignorance that is in them, due to their hardness of heart" (Eph. 4:17-18). A profound treatment of the noetic effects of sin can be found in Abraham Kuyper's *Principles of Sacred Theology* (Grand Rapids, Eerdmans, n. d.), 106-14. There he shows that as men construct their sciences they now, because of sin's effects upon the fallen mind, must reckon with the likelihood that falsehood, unintentional mistakes, self-delusion and self-deception, the intrusion of phantasy into the imagination, intentional negative influences of other minds, for example, in education, upon the mind of the scientist, physical weaknesses influencing the total human psyche, the disorganized relationships of life, the effect of misinformation and inaccuracies learned from one realm of life upon ideas from other domains, human self-interest, the weakening of mental energies and the darkness of consciousness, internal disorganizations of life-harmonies, and the loss of the *pou stō* (see the frontispiece for my explanation of this phrase) found only in the revealed knowledge of the transcendent God by which one may understand the cosmos and himself – now men, Kuyper says, must face the likelihood that any and all of these effects of sin can and do bring them in their search for knowledge to ignorance. A classic example of this is Bertrand Russell, philosopher and mathematician and winner of the Nobel Prize for Literature in 1950, who wrote before his death: "All the labor of the ages and all the noonday brightness of human genius are destined

and beauty as a self-consistent, coherent, significant body of truth that alone gives a rational basis for understanding man and his universe. In other words, just as the Christian apologist will incorporate gospel content in any properly conceived apologetic methodology so also will he self-consciously regard his apologetic efforts as simply part of responsible evangelism!

The Major Issue Confronting Christian Apologetics

The most crucial issue facing the Christian apologetist is that of method: Should the apologist in his effort to defend the faith and to persuade the unbeliever of Christianity's truth claims reason to or from special revelation?[5] Said another way, Should the Christian apologist begin his defense of the faith standing within the circle of revelation or with the unbeliever outside the circle of revelation? *Evidential/historical apologetics* undertakes to demonstrate the foundations of faith without assuming special revelation, that is, it attempts to establish by reasons amenable to human reason unaided by the light of special revelation (1) the existence of God and (2) the fact of Christian revelation. In its attempt at such a demonstration it is a form of methodological natural theology.[6] *Presuppositional or dogmatic apologetics* (I prefer to call it simply "scripturalism"), in contrast, takes its stance unabashedly within the circle of special revelation and argues from it (1) the compelling sufficiency, both pistically and

---

to extinction in the vast death of the solar system, and the whole temple of man's achievement must inevitably be buried beneath the debris of a universe in ruins." How tragic! Where did all of Russell's unbelieving brilliance take him? To God and to his eternal consolations? No, he was an avowed atheist. And as an atheist how little did all his learning finally benefit him!

[5]By "special revelation" I refer to the Bible as God's inspired propositional self-revelation. Both the evidentialist and the presuppositional apologist will use the Bible in their approach to the unbeliever, but the former represents the Bible at first simply as generally trustworthy first-century documents whereas the latter uses the Bible at the outset of his arguments as God's inspired Word.

[6]By "methodological natural theology" I intend that theological method whereby a "first story" philosophical prolegomenon is first built by natural reason working independently with what is portrayed as "neutral data"

epistemologically, of the Christian understanding of the world and man and (2) the impossibility of the contrary.

One's response to this basic and crucial issue will figure prominently in all of the other issues of particular concern for Christian apologetics such as the following:

- What is the nature and function of general revelation?
- What is the nature and function of special revelation?
- What significance do the noetic effects of sin carry for man's ability to know God?
- What is the character of faith?
- What is the test of truth?
- What kind of certainty does Christianity offer?
- What is the value of the theistic proofs?
- What is the value of Christian evidences?
- What is the nature of the common ground between believer and unbeliever that affords the point of contact for intelligent conversation?

Major Apologetic Systems

So consistently has the apologist's methodology dictated his responses to the nine questions above, once the crucial question was settled, that apologetic systems have tended to fall by their responses into the following four distinguishable groups:

1. Evidentialism, its methodology often being described by the Latin expression *Intelligo et credo* ("I understand and I believe").

This group stresses some form of methodological natural theology as the point at which apologetics begins. Group characteristics here are (1) a genuine belief in the ability and trustworthiness of human reason in its search for religious knowledge; (2) the effort to ground faith in probability arguments

---

upon which a "second story" set of beliefs derived from special revelation is later placed. In this kind of "natural theology" the Christian revelation, not intended to displace or to function as the ground of the philosophical prolegomenon, presupposes the philosophical prolegomenon and presumably confirms and supplements it.

of empirical and/or historically verifiable facts; and (3) the insistence that religious propositions must be subjected to the same kind of verification, namely, demonstration, that scientific assertions must undergo. The Thomistic Roman Catholic tradition, the inconsistent Reformed evidentialist tradition, and the Arminian tradition are representatives of this group.

2. Presuppositionalism (or Biblical Foundationalism or scripturalism), its methodology often being described by the Latin expression *Credo ut intelligam* ("I believe in order that I may understand").

This group presupposes the primacy of special revelation as providing the ground for the entire theological enterprise. Group characteristics here are (1) the conviction that the fear of the Lord precedes understanding everything else (Prov. 1:7); (2) the conviction that elucidation of the system follows upon and is governed by the faith commitment; (3) the conviction that the religious experience must be grounded in the objective Word of God and the objective work of Christ; (4) the conviction that human depravity has rendered autonomous reason incapable of satisfactorily anchoring its truth claims to anything objectively certain; and (5) the conviction that a special regenerating act of the Holy Spirit is indispensable for Christian faith and enlightenment. The consistent Reformed tradition represents this group.[7]

3. Experientialism, its methodology often being described by the Latin expression *Credo quia absurdum est* ("I believe because it is absurd").

This group, neither evidential nor presuppositional, stresses the inward religious experience as the foundation of the theological structure. Group characteristics here are (1) the

---

[7]The title of this book *Faith's Reasons for Believing* and the title of Reformed evidentialist John H. Gerstner's book *Reasons for Faith* highlight respectively the difference between the consistent and inconsistent Reformed apologetic methodologies by their reversal of words.

insistence upon revelation as non-propositional "encounter"; (2) great stress upon the subjective religious experience as the ground of truth and meaning, truth and meaning being defined in terms of inwardness and subjectivity; (3) the insistence upon the paradoxical character of Christian teaching, that is to say, Christian truth is not capable of rational analysis; and (4) a strong emphasis upon the "otherness," the transcendence, and hiddenness of God in the religious experience. The Neo-orthodox tradition and the "I was there when it happened and therefore I know though no one else may know" people are representative of this group.

4. Autonomous humanism, its methodology often being described by the Latin expression *Intelligo ut credam* ("I understand in order that I may believe").

The first three groups, in addition to their attempts to persuade each other, are seeking to convince this fourth group of thinkers, who make no pretense of being even religious, of their respective claims. Group characteristics here are (1) a total denial of any need for God and divine revelation as essential to understanding the world and the nature of man; (2) complete confidence in the human rational process and its sciences to discover all knowledge; (3) the conviction that only that is to be believed as true that satisfies the demands of autonomous reason; and (4) the rejection of biblical or supernatural Christianity. This is nothing more or less than anti-supernaturalistic humanism and the signers of *Humanist Manifesto I* and *Humanist Manifesto II* are representative of this group. Unfortunately, in their attempt to reach this group some Christian apologists unwittingly grant the legitimacy of much that characterizes and supports humanists in their rebellion against God.

These remarks will suffice as an introduction to our subject. I have defined Christian apologetics as the defense of the Christian faith but a defense that will often assume the initiative and challenge opposing systems of thought to justify their own existence epistemologically. This definition presupposes that the exegetical, historical, and systematic departments of theology have done their work and that the Christian truth system has been sufficiently extracted from Scripture and articulated. Apologetics is then called upon to defend that system. This means that the Reformed apologist will not be content to defend simply pieces of the picture on the "puzzle box" of the Christian faith such as the bodily resurrection of Christ or the conversion of the apostle Paul on the Damascus Road. He will conduct such defenses, and we will do this as well. But the Reformed apologist, convinced as he is that the Bible teaches a *total theism*, that is, a system of truth encompassing all of life as a world and life view, a *Weltanshauung*, believes that the Christian faith in its *systemic entirety* must finally be defended. For it must not be forgotten that the events of the Christian *kērygma* did not occur in isolation from the larger metanarrative[8] of Scripture and that they will surely be misinterpreted unless they are kept within that metanarrative. With Cornelius Van Til I believe that we "must set the message of the cross into the framework [of Scripture as a whole]. If we do not do this, then we are not really and fully preaching Jesus and the resurrection. The facts of Jesus and the resurrection are what they are only in the framework of the doctrines of creation, providence and the consummation of history in the final judgment."[9] But this means that "if we would really defend Christianity as an historical religion we must at the same time defend the theism upon which it is based."[10]

One more thing must be said before I conclude this introductory chapter. As a Reformed theologian I am convinced that the Reformed faith is the most consistent theological expression of biblical Christianity. I regard it as a solemn obligation to defend the Reformed faith in a manner consistent

---

[8]If metaphysics is a sort of "big physics" that explains all the other branches of physics, similarly metanarrative is the "big story" that provides the context of all the "lesser stories."

[9]Cornelius Van Til, *Paul at Athens* (a pamphlet published by Lewis J. Grotenhuis; Phillipsburg, New Jersey, n. d.), 13.

[10]Cornelius Van Til, *The Defense of the Faith* (Philadelphia: Presbyterian and Reformed, 1955), 24.

with that faith. In other words, a Reformed theologian should be a Reformed apologist; he should not become Arminian in his defense of the Faith. He should seek always to be *epistemologically self-conscious* as he works out his defense, that is to say, he should not forget who he is by faith and what he believes. This is just to say that in determining both the content of the Reformed faith and the proper method of defending that faith he should be *radically biblical*. He must guard against a method of defending the faith that would undercut even the slightest portion of the content of that faith.

We will illustrate what we mean in the following chapters as we address, first, the justification of the Christian faith as a whole (Chapter Two), then of the Bible as the Word of God (Chapter Three), then we will take up the evidence[11] for the facticity and historicity of four of the Christian faith's central events – the bodily resurrection of Jesus Christ (Chapter Four), his virgin birth (Chapter Five), his mighty miracles (Chapter Six), and Paul's conversion on the Damascus Road (Chapter Seven). In the next two chapters (Chapters Eight and Nine respectively) we will discuss the apologetic methodology of Benjamin B. Warfield (sometimes designated "the Old Princeton apologetic") and the apologetic method of presuppositionalism (I prefer the designation "scripturalism"). Then we will treat some of the latter's implications for faith and life such as the Bible as the only sufficient basis for knowledge and personal significance (Chapter Ten), the nature of biblical truth (Chapter Eleven) and the apologetic value of Christian theistic ethics (Chapter 12).

---

[11]By these four chapters I hope to dispel the misconception of evidential apologists that presuppositionalists (or "scripturalists") have no interest in the evidences for the Christian faith, for this simply is not true. Presuppostionalists regularly employ the evidences for the Christian faith in their apologetic endeavors. They do not, however, employ them in probability constructs that allow the unbeliever to conclude that the evidence proves at best that Christianity is only *probably* true. This was a major mistake of the Old Princeton apologetic and continues to be a major mistake of evidential apologetics today. The chief error of such apologetics is to presume that the unbeliever is honest enough to examine the evidence fairly.

We will conclude by arguing that we should employ the Pauline apologetic method as we seek to reach people for Christ in this postmodern generation (Chapter Thirteen), and close with an Epilogue.

Chapter Two

Faith's Reasons for Believing in Christian Theology as an Intellectual Discipline

I want to begin with a touch of personal history; you will quickly see my reason for this. For a good many years now when signing my books for those who request it of me I have placed under my signature the biblical reference Psalm 71:17-18 that reads:

> O God, you have taught me from my youth, and until now I have proclaimed your wondrous deeds. Now during old age and graying hair, O God, do not forsake me until I have proclaimed your might to the next generation, your power to the whole of it.

I have thought for some time that the Psalmist's words could describe me in a measure. They certainly express the desire of my heart. You see, for ninety-five semesters now, not counting winter and summer terms, and in five American and about a dozen international seminaries I have taught and proclaimed the Reformed faith. But I have not taught and proclaimed it simply because it is a hobby of mine. No, I have not been riding a hobby these last forty-seven years. Rather, the wondrous, dread, and awesome Reformed faith, while I admit it is the love of my spiritual and professorial life, is also, I am convinced, the teaching of the Lord God himself and therefore its propagation is for me, by God's grace, both a *passion* and a *mission*. I view the five great *solas* of the Magisterial Reformation – *Grace* alone, *Christ* alone, *Faith* alone, *Scripture* alone, to the *Glory* of God alone – as matters of eternal life and eternal death for the peoples of this world. Agreeing with the Magisterial Reformers I came to understand early on in my seminary days and professorial career, by the grace of God, of course, the following truths:

- The *only* man with whom the infinitely holy God can have *direct* fellowship is Jesus Christ, the only mediator "between God and man" (1 Tim. 2:5), and it is only as sinful people such as you and I place their trust in Christ's saving cross-work and are thereby regarded by God as no longer "in Adam" but "in Christ" that the triune God can have any fellowship with them (this is the *solus Christus* or "Christ alone" principle of salvation).

- The only way to protect the *solus Christus* and the *sola gratia* ("grace alone") of salvation is to insist upon *sola fide* ("faith alone") as the instrumental means of justification, and the only way to protect *sola fide* as the instrumental means of justification is to insist upon the *solus Christus* and the *sola gratia* of salvation.

- The only way to protect both the *solus Christus* and the *sola gratia* of salvation and the *sola fide* of justification is to insist upon *sola Scriptura* ("Scripture alone") as the church's sole authority in such matters.

- Justification by faith is not to be set off over against justification by works as such but over against justification by *our* works, for justification is indeed grounded in Christ's alien preceptive and penal obedience in our stead, whose obedience we receive through faith alone.

- Saving faith is to be directed solely to the doing and dying of Christ alone and never in any sense to the good works or inner experience of the believer.

- The Christian's righteousness before God today is *in heaven* at the right hand of God in Jesus Christ and *not on earth* within the believer.

- The ground of our justification is the vicarious work of Christ *for* us, not the gracious work of the Spirit *in* us.

- The faith-righteousness of justification is
  - not personal but vicarious,
  - not infused but imputed,
  - not experiential but forensic,
  - not psychological but legal,
  - not our own but Christ's alien righteousness, and
  - not earned but graciously given through faith in Christ, which faith in Christ is itself a gift of grace. I learned too that

- The salvation of the elect is to be credited to God's grace alone (*sola gratia*) to whom alone belongs all the praise for their salvation (*soli Deo gloria*).

But because I was seriously challenged many years ago to do so, I also came to understand early on in my career that these great Reformation truths and the Reformation *solas* require that the entire Christian system of which they are a central part must be defended as an intellectual discipline before a critical world. Thus I was forced to face the more ultimate issue of the need to justify the Christian theological enterprise as such, including my involvement in it. But how was I to do this? I realized that an appeal to extra-biblical data that I am very willing to use in *ad hominem* arguments in accordance with Proverbs 26:5, "Answer a fool according to his folly lest he be wise in his own eyes," to show the non-Christian that he cannot consistently live with his world-and-life-view[1] could never in itself make the justification of Christian theology as such logically or apodictically demonstrative. I knew that such an appeal would at best advance only possibilities, including the possibility that my conclusions were themselves in error, and would end up suffering the fate of total and unrelenting skepticism. So I sought the justification of Christian theology as an intellectual discipline, including my

---

[1] See Addendum A, "Answering the Biblical 'Fool.'"

engagement in it, where there could be no question regarding its validity or certitude – an Archimedean point of reference, so to speak, outside the universe. And where was *that*? In the data of God's inspired, inerrant Word to us from another world and by good and necessary inferences therefrom.

As we begin our study of apologetics it is this issue of justifying our theology as such that I want to develop, for it is both appropriate and needful to explain why we believe we may legitimately do what we do in our Reformed seminaries and why we offer academic training in Christian theology. As we begin let us face some hard questions. Many seminary students through the years have wondered: "What am I doing here at Seminary? Why should I study theology? Am I wasting my time and money studying *Christian* theology? Does Christian theology serve any useful purpose in today's world? Was moving my family here a rash act? And why should I make the arduous sacrifice that I am asking of myself and of my family in order to attend seminary?"

Such questions, I would argue, are not a waste of time to consider since we must admit that Christian theology has fallen upon hard times in our generation. Let me make clear what I mean by recounting two events, one borrowed and one personally experienced.

First, the borrowed event: In one of Dr. Martyn Lloyd-Jones' books he tells of a large religious conference he attended which was being held in the city of Glasgow in Scotland. As is often done, for some extraordinary reason when such conferences are held, the Lord Provost of the City had been invited to attend the inaugural meeting and to welcome and address the conference for a few minutes. As reported by the "Doctor," here is the essence of what he said:

> All of you men assembled here today are very learned theologians, and confessedly I am not. I am a plain man. I am a man of affairs and I do not understand your theology and all these church things. In fact, I am not interested in your theology, and personally I believe you are wasting a lot of time when

you argue among yourselves about your theology. What *I* want to know – in fact, what a lot of people like me want to know – is simply this: How can I love my neighbor? That is what we want to know from you. We are not interested in your great theology. We just want to know – indeed, the common man simply wants to know – How can I love my neighbor?

Now if one has had a course in Christian personal and social ethics in a good Reformed seminary he will immediately recognize that man's total doctrinal illiteracy, for he knows that the Bible and theology are directly related to his interest in love for one's neighbor. In fact, he knows that unless a transcendent and absolute Authority requires us to love our neighbors and to do so in such a way that we will do it even to our own hurt, no other reason can possibly be given to obligate any of us to do anything at all for anyone else other than for ourselves. But this is not the reason behind my citing this illustration at this moment. It is to illustrate my present point. For this man, the church with its Bible and its theology was completely irrelevant unless it could address what *he* wanted to know, that is, what for him was the wholly secular matter of "how to live at peace with one's neighbor."

Now the second and directly personal event: Several years ago one weekend my wife and I decided we would drive down to Key West for a day or two of relaxation. The Orthodox Presbyterian Church has a church on a Key close by, and its preacher, Bill Welzien, a chalk-talk artist, goes to Mallory Pier on the west side of the island each evening on Monday, Wednesday, and Friday (he has trained a church member to go on Tuesday, Thursday, and Saturday, but quite often on these evenings he also goes) when the hundreds of tourists gather to watch the sun set in the West, attracts a crowd with his artistry, and preaches the gospel as he limns his drawing. Knowing this, we made it a point to be there on Friday evening and we stood in the crowd and prayed for him as he drew his picture and proclaimed the gospel to the crowd. In the middle of his presentation, a man who was pushing through the crowd in his attempt to get to an attraction farther down the pier yelled to this preacher with a great deal of huff: "What do you think you are doing here? Why don't you go out and get yourself a real job?" I hope you see my point: This man's remarks dripped with stinging sarcasm. To this man, and to many people like him, Pastor Welzien was an irrelevancy. He was suggesting that Bill would have spent his time much more profitably studying to become a doctor, an engineer, a school or business administrator, a chef, an environmental designer, an educator – yes, even a lawyer – than studying to enter the Christian ministry.

Then there is Søren Kierkegaard's lampooning definition of a theologian as "a professor of the fact that *Another* [that is, Someone else] has suffered" but not he,[2] while Jaroslav Pelikan reminds us that the nearest equivalents to the term "theologian" in the New Testament are "scribes and Pharisees."[3] Such reminders do not make the work of the theologian very appealing either to the church or to the world at large. Indeed, as the Western world has become increasingly a "secular city" more and more men and women within as well as outside the church argue that it is impossible even to say anything meaningful about God. Accordingly, Gordon H. Clark began his book *In Defense of Theology* with the following assessment:

> Theology, once acclaimed "the Queen of the Sciences," today hardly rises to the rank of a scullery maid; it is often held in contempt, regarded with suspicion, or just ignored.[4]

If Clark's judgment is correct seminary students might well conclude that they should be done with Christian theology as an intellectual discipline altogether and devote their time to some mental pursuit holding out promise of greater esteem among men. But I hope to show that such a conclusion would be

---

[2]Søren Kierkegaard, *Journals*, edited and translated by Alexander Dru (Oxford: University Press, 1938), no. 1362.

[3]Jaroslav J. Pelikan, "The Function of Theology" in *Theology in the Life of the Church*, edited by Robert M. Bertram (Philadelphia: Fortress, 1963), 3.

[4]Gordon H. Clark, *In Defense of Theology* (Milford, Michigan: Mott, 1984), 3.

singularly wrong-headed. The issue before us can be pointedly framed: How are Christian theology, construed as an intellectual discipline that deserves the church's, and the world's, highest interest and respect, and our lifelong occupation as preachers and teachers of that theology to be justified? Still more pointedly: Why should *you* as a Christian engage yourself for a lifetime in scholarly reflection on the content and proclamation of the Christian message? And why should you engage yourself in the particular way that the church in her best moments, in my opinion, has worked out her theology in the past, namely, by means of the historical/grammatical/theological canons of interpreting the Scriptures of the Old and New Testaments? I offer the following five pillars upon which, in my opinion, the justification of Christian theology as an intellectual discipline securely rests, pillars that lead me to conclude that we all should continue in our engagement in the theological enterprise.

Christ's Own Theological Method

The first pillar upon which the justification of Christian theology as an intellectual discipline rests is Christ's own theological method. Because of the significance of his testimony I will treat this pillar more extensively than the others.

All four Evangelists depict Jesus Christ who after rising bodily from death on the third day after his crucifixion showed himself alive by "many convincing proofs" (Acts 1:3), and upon whose earthly ministry God the Father placed his *imprimatur* by raising him from the dead (Gal. 1:1; Rom. 8:11), thereby both declaring him powerfully to be the divine Son of God (Rom. 1:4) and vouchsafing to us his Son's every word as true – all our Evangelists, I say, depict the divine Christ as being deeply engaged throughout his earthly ministry in heart and mind with the Old Testament Scriptures.[5]

---

[5]Even critical scholars acknowledge that their so-called original sources of the four Gospels, *Ur-Markus*, Q, M, L, and John represent Jesus as teaching with utter seriousness the reliability, authority, and inspiration of the Old Testament.

Jesus' attitude toward the historicity of the Old Testament

It is popular to criticize the historicity of the Old Testament today and to reconstruct it along critical lines. Martin Noth, for example, contended that nothing can be known with certainty of Israel's past prior to her entrance by various stages into Canaan.[6] John Bright, though more moderate in his reconstruction of Old Testament history than Noth, nonetheless questions the historicity of the pre-patriarchal period of biblical history.[7] But this was not Jesus' attitude toward the historicity of the Old Testament. In fact, J. W. Wenham has observed: "Curiously enough, the narratives that proved least acceptable to what was known a generation or two ago as 'the modern mind' are the very ones that [Jesus] seemed most fond of choosing for His illustrations."[8] For example, if we consider only Matthew's Gospel Jesus refers therein to the following historical events and in every instance it is plain that he viewed their historicity as unimpeachable:

- The creation of Adam and Eve by a direct act of God (Matt. 19:4-5)
- The murder of Abel (Matt. 23:23)
- The times of Noah and the Genesis flood (Matt. 24:37)
- The destruction of Sodom and Gomorrah (Matt. 10:15)
- The word of God coming to Moses (Matt. 22:32)
- David's eating the bread of the presence (Matt. 12:3-4)
- The queen of Sheba's visit to Solomon (Matt. 12:3-4)
- The stoning of Zechariah (Matt. 23:35)
- The great fish's swallowing of Jonah (Matt. 12:40)
- Jonah's preaching and Ninevah's repentance (Matt. 12:41)
- Allusions to other Old Testament characters such as Abraham, Isaac, Jacob, Isaiah, and Daniel (Matt. 8:11; 13:14; 15:7-8; 24:15)[9]

---

[6] Martin Noth, *The History of Israel* (New York: Harper & Row, 1960).

[7] John Bright, *A History of Israel* (Philadelphia: Westminster, 1959).

[8] J. W. Wenham, *Our Lord's View of the Old Testament* (London: Tyndale, 1953), 9.

[9] I must address here a matter that has troubled many people about Jesus' full endorsement of the historicity of the events of the Old Testament: Did

Jesus' attitude toward the inspiration of the Old Testament
There are several indications in Matthew's Gospel that Jesus believed and taught that the Old Testament Scriptures were the very words of God. In Matthew 19:5 Jesus taught that words spoken in Genesis 2:24 by either Adam or Moses (probably the latter) proceeded more ultimately from God ("God created...and said...."). In his argument with the Sadducees regarding the resurrection of the body (Matt. 22:31-32) Jesus asked them:

not the God of the Old Testament demand of his people the same thing that Christians find so repulsive today in Islam's Allah – the killing for religious reasons of other human beings who were their enemies? I could say much more about this so-called "moral problem" of the Old Testament (for help here see James Orr, *The Problem of the Old Testament*), but I will say this here: Even if there were no other differences (and there are many), the God of the Old Testament and Islam's Allah certainly differ in this respect: The God of the Christian Scriptures moved in the progressiveness of his verbal revelation from calling in the Old Testament for the occasional destruction of his people's enemies when it was necessary to preserve them, to the demand for non-violence against their enemies in the New whereas Islam's Allah is depicted as moving from his demand for non-violence toward his enemies in the 90 suras written at Mecca to his call for violence against them in the remaining 24 suras written at Medina. This movement suggests that the Allah of *mature* Islam is *militant* and *jihadic* while the biblical God is not. So the parallel between them fails here. Critics may still insist, even so, that the Old Testament God did call upon Israel at times to destroy its enemies, whatever the reason. How could he do this if he is a God of love? And are not the imprecatory Psalms (better "imprecations in the psalms") (5:10; 10:15; 55:15; 69:22-25; 109:9-13) of the same spirit? If Jesus endorsed the historicity of the Old Testament did he not endorse such activity?

It is true that in the Old Testament God occasionally called for the destruction of a city in accordance with the Old Testament *ḥerem* ("devoted" to the Lord and hence "banned") principle. For example, in conquering Sihon, king of the Amorites, Israel "took all his towns and completely destroyed them – men, women and children. We left no survivors" (Deut. 2:34), "destroying [*haḥᵃrēm*] every city – men, women, and children" (Deut. 3:6). Why? Even though Moses had promised that Israel "would not turn aside into any field or vineyard, or drink water from any well. We will travel along the king's highway until we have passed through your territory" (Num. 21:22), Sihon had refused to grant Israel passage across his domain, had instead mustered his entire army, and had fought against Israel (Num. 21:23), thereby posing a threat to the continuation of the people of God and the fulfillment of

"...have you not read what was said *to you* [*humin*] by God: 'I am the God of Abraham, and the God of Isaac, and the God of Jacob'?" He then cited words that God addressed *to Moses* (Exod. 3:6). Thus Jesus regarded these words of Scripture as the Word of God addressed both to Moses and to

---

the Abrahamic promise. So we see Israel carrying out the ḥerem principle – the irrevocable giving over of persons and things to the Lord, often by killing them. Liberal theologians and free thinkers, of course, have found this principle exceedingly distasteful and repugnant, and accordingly have concluded that the God of the Old Testament is barbaric in the extreme, governed by a sub-Christian ethic, and is in no way to be identified with the loving "God and Father of our Lord Jesus Christ."

But Meredith Kline rightly declares in his *Treaty of the Great King* (Grand Rapids: Eerdmans, 1963), 68 (emphasis supplied):

> Actually, the offense taken is taken at the theology and religion of the Bible as a whole. The New Testament, too, warns men of the realm of the everlasting ban where the reprobate, devoted to wrath, must magnify the justice of God whom they have hated. *The judgments of hell are the [OT] ḥerem principle come to full and final manifestation....*

As for the imprecations in some psalms one cannot and should not dismiss them as simply reflecting a low Old Testament morality, especially when one recalls that the Old Testament itself forbids vengeance (Lev. 19:17-18), teaches that the Lord hates violence (Ps. 5:6), and insists that vengeance must be left to him (Ps. 7:4). When one takes note that all the imprecations are prayers that commit the psalmist's problem to God and that leave vengeance to him and are *not* declarations of intent on the psalmist's part, they show an obedient faith toward God and a non-retaliatory intent toward man, express holy indignation concerning their enemies' flaunting of God's holy name, cry out for the vindication of God's name, and express hatred of their enemies not with an imperfect but with a *perfect*, that is, a morally pure, hatred (Ps. 139:21-22). Moreover, Jesus too endorsed capital punishment for the one who cursed his parents (Matt. 15:3) and pronounced maledictions against his enemies (Matt. 23:13ff.) while Paul invoked God's curse upon those who distorted his gospel (Gal. 1:8-9; see also Rev. 6:10; 19:20). So the morality of the Old and the New Testaments is of one piece here: Both Testaments simply reflect the truth that God will judge his enemies in certain and just retribution both to some degree in this life and fully in the life that is to come. See Louis Berkhof, *Principles of Biblical Interpretation* (Grand Rapids: Baker, 1966), 157.

his own contemporaries. Moreover, Jesus hung his case for the resurrection of the body on the present tense of the verb "to be": "I *am* [*eimi*] the God of Abraham," not "I was the God of Abraham," implying thereby, first, that Abraham was still alive and would be resurrected someday from death and, second, that the words of Scripture were so carefully superintended by God that one can hang an argument on the tense of a verb. In Matthew 22:43-45 Jesus based his argument that he is the Son of God on David's calling his son according to the flesh his Lord "by the Spirit." That is to say, the words of Psalm 110, although penned by David, originated from the Spirit of God, thereby highlighting the remarkable concurrence of God and man in the production of Scripture (see 2 Pet. 1:20-21). And again Jesus' argument here hung on one word – David's employment of the word "Lord" (*'adhōn*) to describe his son.

Jesus' attitude toward the authority of the Old Testament

No one can seriously question that the Old Testament was for Jesus authoritative in all that it affirmed. In his Sermon on the Mount Jesus taught his disciples: "Do not think that I have come to destroy the Law or the Prophets. I have not come to abolish them but to fulfill them. For truly I say to you, until heaven and earth pass away, not an iota, not a dot, will pass from the Law until all is accomplished" (Matt. 5:17-18). In Luke 16:17 he also declared that the tiniest portion of the written letters of Scripture would never fail. Again and again he refers to "the Law and the Prophets" (Matt. 5:17; 7:12; 11:13; 22:40), often citing them to settle an issue (Matt. 12:5; 15:3-6; 21:31, 42; 22:42-43). He implies by this phrase a fixed canon of authoritative material, intending by it the entire Old Testament. In Matthew 4:4-10 he repulsed the Tempter by citing Deuteronomy 8:3, 6:16, and 6:13 in that order, each time demonstrating his belief in the finality of the Old Testament's authority by prefacing his citation by the Greek perfect (or its Aramaic "force equivalent"): "It has been written [and continues to stand so]" (see also Matt. 11:10; 21:13; 26:24, 31). Setting "the Word of God" off over against

Jewish tradition in Mark 7:13 Jesus implied that God was the authority behind the entire Old Testament. Repeatedly he asked his interrogators: "Have you not read?" (Matt. 12:3; 19:4; 21:16; 22:31). He ordered the cleansed leper to obey the Mosaic legislation pertaining to cases of cleansing (Matt. 8:4). He charged the Sadducees with error concerning the resurrection of the body because they did not know the Scriptures (Matt. 22:29). He approved the scribes' and Pharisees' obedience to the law of the tithe though he denounced them for neglecting the weightier matters of the Law – justice, mercy, and faith (Matt. 23:23). In Matthew 26:53-56 Jesus revealed his great esteem for the prophetic Scripture when he declined the aid of more than twelve legions of angels to deliver him from the cross, saying: "Do you think that I cannot appeal to my Father, and he will send me more than twelve legions of angels? But how then should the Scriptures be fulfilled, that it must be so?" And at his death his thoughts were centered on Scripture, for he cited Psalm 22:1 just moments before he died (Matt. 27:46). This Matthean material – and the other three Gospels make the same case – proves beyond all controversy that for Jesus the Old Testament was unimpeachably authoritative.

Jesus' attitude toward the predictive character of Old Testament prophecy

Jesus constantly emphasized the predictive nature of Old Testament prophecy. In Matthew 11:10 he taught that John the Baptizer's ministry fulfilled Malachi 3:1. He warned that Daniel's prophecy concerning the abomination of desolation would soon be fulfilled (Matt. 4:15). His own death he viewed as the inaugurating event fulfilling Jeremiah's prophecy of the "new covenant" (Matt. 26:28). But most significantly Jesus drew from the Old Testament Scriptures fascinating theological deductions about himself. On forty-nine different occasions by my count, discounting Gospel parallels, Jesus in the Gospels cited or referred to the Old Testament and many of these citations he applied to himself as evidenced by the following examples:

According to Luke 4:16-21 Jesus "came to Nazareth, where he had been brought up, and as was his custom, he went to the synagogue on the Sabbath day, and he stood up to read. And the scroll of the prophet Isaiah was given to him. He unrolled the scroll and found the place where it was written: 'The Spirit of the Lord is upon me, because he has anointed me to proclaim good news to the poor. He has sent me to proclaim liberty to the captives and recovering of sight to the blind, to set at liberty those who are oppressed, to proclaim the year of the Lord's favor.' And he rolled up the scroll and gave it back to the attendant and sat down. And he began to say to them: 'Today this Scripture has been fulfilled in your hearing.'" Here Jesus claimed to be the Old Testament Messiah.

According to John 5:46-47 Jesus expressly affirmed to the Jewish religious leadership of his day on another occasion: "If you believed Moses, you would believe me, for he wrote of me. But if you do not believe his writings, how will you believe my words?" Here Jesus claimed to be the Prophet like Moses. And in John 10:35 Jesus declared after citing Psalm 82:6 in defense of his claim to divine Sonship: "…the Scripture cannot be broken," that is, because it is unchangeable it cannot be nullified – a striking declaration regarding the extent to which Jesus thought Scripture spoke truth concerning him.

According to Luke 18:31-33 on still another occasion Jesus informed his disciples: "See, we are going up to Jerusalem, and everything that is written about the Son of Man by the prophets will be accomplished…." He also taught in Matthew 26:24, 31, 53-56: "The Son of Man goes as it is written of him…You will all fall away because of me this night, for it is written, 'I will smite the shepherd and the sheep of the flock will be scattered'…Do you think that I cannot appeal to my Father, and he will at once send me more than twelve legions of angels? But how then should the Scriptures be fulfilled, that it must be so?"

According to Luke 22:37 on yet another occasion Jesus, citing Isaiah 53:12: "And he was numbered with the transgressors," declared: "...this Scripture must be fulfilled in me.... For what is written about me will have its fulfillment." Here Jesus claimed to be the suffering Servant of the so-called Fourth Servant Song of Isaiah.

Then according to Luke 24:26-27 on the Road to Emmaus on the evening of his bodily resurrection from the dead Jesus "beginning with Moses and all the Prophets,...explained to [two of his disciples] what was said in all the Scriptures concerning himself" (see also John 13:18; 19:24, 28, 36-37; 20:9). Such an extensive engagement of his mind in Scripture exposition involved our Lord in theological activity in the highest conceivable sense. I would say in passing that Christians have often expressed the wish that they could have heard Jesus' Emmaus Road discourse. They can be assured, however, that both the apostles' sermons recorded in Acts and their apostolic letters bear the stamp of the major features of Christ's exposition in the way in which they interpret the Old Testament christologically. So we know essentially what Jesus said, and our hearts should burn within us, as the hearts of those two disciples did, as his Spirit opens the Scriptures about him to us. Then according to Luke 24:44 that same evening Jesus declared to the disciples who had gathered in the upper room along with others with them: "This is what I told you while I was still with you. Everything must be fulfilled that is written about me in the Law of Moses, the Prophets and the Psalms."[10] By these claims Jesus taught that the entire

---

[10]The tripartite division of the Old Testament to which Jesus alludes here reflects the Old Testament canon of Palestinian Judaism. The Palestinian Jews never accepted the Apocryphal books, their canon being the same as the Protestant Old Testament (see Josephus, *Against Apion*, 1.41; *Babylonian Talmud*, Yomah 9b, Sota 48 b, Sanhedrin 11a). Nor did Jesus or the New Testament writers ever cite these books. When Paul declared then that the Jews possessed "the oracles of God" (Rom. 3:2) he was implicitly excluding the Apocrypha from those "oracles." Merrill F. Unger, *Introductory Guide to the Old Testament* (Grand Rapids: Zondervan, 1956), 81-114, treats the phenomena of the Apocrypha that make it evident that these books are not products of the Holy Spirit's inspiration. See also R. Laird Harris,

Old Testament spoke about him as the Seed of the Woman, the unique Seed of Abraham, Moses' Prophet, David's Priest after the order of Melchizedek, Isaiah's virgin-born Immanuel, his Child of the four exalted titles "Wonderful Counselor," "Mighty God," "Everlasting Father," and "Prince of Peace," and his Suffering Servant, Jeremiah's Branch, Daniel's Son of Man, Malachi's Messenger of the Covenant, and in sum God's Messiah, all which meant that for him, and therefore for us, the Old Testament, if read aright, *must* be read in light of his ministry as the prophetic fulfillment of the Old Testament age of prophetic promise.[11]

Jesus' pre-authentication of the New Testament writers
Finally, Christ pre-authenticated his apostles as authoritative teachers of doctrine when he declared to them: "The Counselor, the Holy Spirit, whom the Father will send in my name, will teach you all things and bring to your remembrance everything I have said to you" (John 14:26), and then he taught them: "I still

---

Inspiration and Canonicity of the Bible (Grand Rapids: Zondervan, 1957), Chapters 6, 8, and Roger Beckwith, *The Old Testament Canon of the New Testament Church and Its Background in Early Judaism* (Grand Rapids: Eerdmans, 1986), 338-437.

[11]I should say in passing that world Jewry's rejection today of Jesus as the Christ is precisely the reason that it does not understand its own Scriptures correctly. Paul declared in 2 Corinthians 3:7-16 that an unlifted "veil" (*kalumma*) covers the hearts of unbelieving Jews when they read Moses, that is, the old covenant, a veil that can only be removed by Christ. The blindness that Israel experienced when beholding the radiant face of Moses, Paul writes, continues "to this day" as a veil over their hearts when they read the old covenant, so the Jewish people do not today and never will read aright the Old Testament as long as they read it apart from its fulfillment in Jesus Christ and his saving work. They do not understand that the glory of God that they seek in Torah has been surpassed by the greater glory found in Christ who is the image of God, and that therefore the Old Testament must be read christologically, that is, from the present perspective of its fulfillment in Christ. The real truth of the matter is that no one – neither Jew nor Gentile – who has heard of the Messiah and his atoning work and then rejects him understands the Old Testament.

have many things to say to you, but you cannot bear them now. When the Spirit of truth comes, he will guide you into all the truth, for he will not speak on his own authority, but whatever he hears he will speak, and he will declare to you the things that are to come [here Christ pre-authenticates the prophecies of the New Testament]. He will glorify me, for he will take what is mine and declare it to you" (John 16:12-14).[12]

It is Christ himself then who established for his church the pattern and end of all proper theologizing. The *pattern*? What should it be? To make sound exposition of Scripture the basis of our theologizing. And the *end* of all our theological labors? What should it be? To arrive by our exegetical labors finally at him![13]

---

[12]Christ also instructed his disciples "not to be anxious how you are to speak or what you are to say" when they were arrested and brought before courts of law, governors, and kings. "For what you are to say will be given you in that hour. For it is not you who speak, but the Spirit of your Father speaking through you" (Matt. 10:19-20; Mark 13:11). Jesus also promised them in those situations: "I will give you a mouth and wisdom, which none of your adversaries will be able to withstand or contradict" (Luke 21:15).

[13]All this means, since the only Christ about whom one knows anything with confidence is the Christ about whom the Old and New Testament Scriptures inform us, that one must never separate the testimony of the Old and New Testament Scriptures about him from the testimony of the divine Christ concerning them or the testimony of the divine Christ concerning them from the testimony of the Old and New Testament Scriptures about him. They authenticate each other.

Of course, there are other authenticating lines of evidence in addition to Christ's divine testimony concerning Holy Scripture by which it "doth *abundantly evidence itself* to be the word of God" – what Benjamin B. Warfield calls the Scripture's own intrinsic divine *indicia* – such as "the heavenliness of the matter, the efficacy of the doctrine, the majesty of the style, the consent of all the parts, the scope of the whole (which is to give all glory to God), the full discovery [disclosure] it makes of the only way of man's salvation, the many other incomparable excellencies, and the entire perfection thereof" (*Westminster Confession of Faith*, I/v, emphasis supplied). That is to say, the Bible is self-evidencingly, self-validatingly, self-authenticatingly the Word of God. For one to disagree with this statement he would need to possess some authoritative source of information about God other than the Bible. Take, for example, the Bible's doctrine of the atonement.

Christ's Mandate to His Church
to Disciple and to Teach the Nations

The second pillar upon which the justification of Christian theology as an intellectual discipline rests is the risen Christ's mandate to his church to disciple and to teach the nations. After determining for his church the pattern and end of all proper theologizing the glorified Christ commissioned his church to disciple the nations, baptizing and teaching his followers to obey everything that he had commanded them (Matt. 28:18-20). And his promise to be with his disciples "always, to the

---

If one does not have another authoritative source of information about it, how could one know that the Bible's teaching is wrong? But someone may ask: "How does one know that the Bible's doctrine is right?" The first answer the *Confession* gives is as follows: "The authority of the Holy Scripture, for which it ought to be believed and obeyed, dependeth not upon the testimony of any man or church, but wholly upon God (who is truth itself), the author thereof; and, therefore, it is to be received, because it is the word of God" (I/iv). Its second answer, in the following article, is as follows: "Our full persuasion and assurance of the infallible truth and divine authority [of the Old and New Testaments] is from the inward work of the Holy Spirit, bearing witness by and with the word in our hearts." That is to say, it is God himself who causes one to believe that the Bible is his Word. This faith he works in the hearts of his elect, and by this faith "a Christian believeth to be true whatsoever is revealed in the word, for the authority of God himself speaking therein" (*Confession*, XIV.2). The Psalmist declared: "Blessed is the one you choose and bring near, to dwell in your courts" (Ps. 65:4). Gordon H. Clark correctly notes in his *What Do Presbyterians Believe?* (Philadelphia: Presbyterian and Reformed, 1965), 18:

> Logically the infallibility of the Bible is not a theorem [a proposition deduced from other propositions; a demonstrable truth] to be deduced from some prior axiom [a self-evident truth accepted as the basis for deductions]. The infallibility of the Bible is the axiom from which the several doctrines are themselves deduced as theorems. Every religion and every philosophy must be based on some first principle. And since a first principle is first, it cannot be "proved" or "demonstrated" on the basis of anything prior.

The first principle of Christianity is this: God is there and he has spoken infallibly to us in and by his Word.

consummation of the age" implies that he expected this mandate to continue in force beyond the lives of his contemporaries. Thus Christ's Great Commission placed upon his church three continuing *intellectual* requirements, namely, the *evangelistic* requirement to reach effectively every generation and every culture with its message about Christ, the *didactic* requirement to correlate the manifold data of Scripture into a coherent system and to apply this systematized knowledge to all phases of humankind's thinking and conduct in order to fulfill the cultural mandate, and the *apologetic* requirement both to justify before this hostile world the existence of Christianity as alone the revealed religion of God and to protect its message from adulteration and distortion (see Titus 1:9).

To meet these concrete requirements of the Great Commission – no small task I assure you – Christian theology as an intellectual discipline arose in and has continued throughout the life of the church. I will mention here only a few people who responded to Christ's command, namely, the "triple-A's" of the ancient church, the *Apostolic Fathers* (Barnabas of Alexandria, Hermes, Clement of Rome, Polycarp, Papias of Hierapolis, and Ignatius of Antioch), the *Apologists* (Justin Martyr, Tatian, Irenaeus, Athenagoras, and Theophilus of Antioch), and the *Antignostic Fathers* (Irenaeus and Tertullian), who were followed by Origen of Alexandria, Athanasius, the "three great Cappadocians," Basil and the two Gregories, and Augustine of Hippo. Then in *the Middle Ages* came the Augustinians Gottschalk and Thomas Bradwardine, followed in the *fourteenth* and *fifteenth* centuries by the pre-Reformers John Wycliffe and Jan Hus. Then appeared in the *sixteenth* century the great Reformers Martin Luther, Philip Melanchthon, William Farel, John Calvin, Martin Bucer, Ulrich Zwingli, Johann Heinrich Bullinger, Theodore Beza, John Knox, Casper Olevianus and Zacharias Ursinus. In the *seventeenth* century appeared Francis Turretin, Johannes Cocceius, and Herman Witsius, in the *eighteenth* century Jonathan Edwards who dominated the American theological scene, in the *nineteenth* century James Bannerman, James Buchanan, William

Cunningham, Robert Lewis Dabney, James Henley Thornwell, Charles and A. A. Hodge, and in the *twentieth* and *twenty-first* centuries Abraham Kuyper, Herman Bavinck, B. B. Warfield, Geerhardus Vos, Gerrit C. Berkouwer, Louis Berkhof, John Murray, Lorraine Boettner, Gordon H. Clark, Carl F. H. Henry, Roger Nicole, James Packer, Henri Blocher, Gerald Bray, Donald A. Carson, and O. Palmer Robertson.

Time would fail me were I to mention more than a handful of the deserving thousands of pastor-theologians such as Charles Spurgeon, Martyn Lloyd-Jones, James Montgomery Boice, and Peter Masters as well as the untold numbers of missionaries who responded to Christ's Commission during the modern missionary movement in the nineteenth century such as William Carey and the Baptists in England, Henry Venn and the Church of England, Adoniram Judson, Hudson Taylor, David Livingstone and the Church of Scotland, and in our day D. James Kennedy, founder of Evangelism Explosion, most of whom, by the way, were Calvinistic in their theology as well as being great soul winners.

Who would be so brash as to suggest that these theological giants ignorantly wasted their time and talents as servants of Christ? So standing on the shoulders of these people in continuing obedience to Christ's Commission we today must acquire, explicate, proclaim, propagate, and defend in a logical and coherent manner the truth that God has revealed in Holy Scripture about himself, the world he has created, and the people who inhabit it. And doing this is doing Christian theology.

The Apostolic Model

The third pillar on which the justification of Christian theology as an intellectual discipline rests is the apostolic model. Such activity as eventually led to the church's engagement in theology is found not only in the teaching and example of Jesus Christ and in his Great Commission to his church but also throughout the *entirety* of the New Testament. The apostles all theologized. Peter inferred from his vivid memory of the risen Christ breathing upon his disciples fifty days earlier in the upper room that it was the ascended Christ who had breathed by his Holy Spirit upon his church on the day of Pentecost. Paul wasted no time after his baptism but set out immediately to "prove" from the Old Testament to his fellow Jews that Jesus is the Son of God and the Old Testament Messiah (Acts 9:20-22). Later, as a seasoned missionary he entered the synagogue in Thessalonica and on three Sabbath days he "reasoned" with them *from the Scriptures*, explaining and proving that the Messiah had to suffer and rise from the dead (Acts 17:2-3). The learned Apollos vigorously refuted the Jews in public debate, proving *from the Scriptures* that Jesus was the Messiah (Acts 18:18).

Nor was Paul's evangelistic theologizing limited to the synagogue. While waiting for Silas and Timothy in Athens Paul "reasoned" not only in the synagogue with the Jews and God-fearing Greeks but also in the marketplace with all those who happened to be there about Jesus and his resurrection (Acts 17:17-18). This got him an invitation to address the Areopagus, which he did in a "big picture" way that could be understood by the Epicurean and Stoic philosophers gathered there but without any accommodation of his message to what they were prepared to believe. Then, in addition to that three-month period at Ephesus during which he spoke boldly in the synagogue, arguing persuasively about the kingdom of God (Acts 19:8) Paul dialogued daily in the lecture hall of Tyrannus, not hesitating as he would say later to the Ephesian elders at Miletus either from preaching everything that was helpful to them or teaching them publicly and from house to house the whole counsel of God, declaring to both Jews and Greeks that they must turn to God in repentance and to Jesus Christ in faith (Acts 20:20-21). Paul was clearly not just an apostle but a missionary theologian as well.

We also see in Paul's letter to the Romans both his theological exposition of the doctrine of justification by faith alone and the theologizing method that he employed. Note should be taken of the brilliant "theological flow" of his letter to the Roman church, how he moved logically and systematically from the dire plight of the human condition (Rom. 1:18-3:20), employing the Old Testament to drive home his point (Rom. 3:10-18), on to God's provision of salvation in Christ, namely, justification by faith alone in Christ apart from works of law (Rom. 3:21-31) in connection with which he used Abraham as the best Old Testament example (Rom. 4); then, in turn, to the results of justification (Rom. 5) and to the two major objections he constantly faced regarding his doctrine of justification, namely, that his doctrine of justification by faith alone granted men license to sin (Rom. 6–8) and that his doctrine of justification by faith alone nullified the promises God made to Israel as a nation (Rom. 9–11), both of which he addressed through his exposition of Old Testament scripture, and finally on to the Christian ethic that flows out of this central doctrine of the Christian faith (Rom. 12–16).

It detracts in no way from Paul's "inspiredness" (see 1 Thess. 2:13; 2 Tim. 3:16; 2 Pet. 3:15-16) to acknowledge that he reflected upon and bolstered his theological conclusions along the way by appeals to earlier conclusions, Old Testament history, and even his own personal relationship to Christ as he laid out his doctrinal perceptions of the gospel of God under the Spirit's superintendence. One finds these theological reflections and logical deductions embedded in Romans in the very heart of some of the apostle's most radical assertions. For example, ten times, after reaching a specific point in his argument's development, Paul asks: "What shall we conclude then?" (Rom. 3:5, 9; 4:1; 6:1, 15; 7:7; 8:31; 9:14, 30; 11:7), and he then proceeds to deduce by good and necessary inference theological conclusions that he desires his readers to adopt. Also in Romans 4 he draws the theological conclusion that circumcision is unnecessary to the blessing of justification and that Abraham is the spiritual father of the uncircumcised Gentile believer from the simple observation based on Old Testament history that "Abram believed the Lord, and he credited it to him as righteousness" (Gen. 15:6) some fourteen years *before* he was circumcised (Gen. 17:24) – *striking* theological deductions to draw in his particular religious and cultural milieu simply from the "before and after" relationship between two historical events! Then, to prove that "at the present time there is a [Jewish] remnant chosen by grace" (Rom. 11:5) Paul simply appeals to his own status as a Christian Jew (Rom. 11:1), again a striking theological assertion to derive from the simple fact of his personal faith in Jesus.

This apostolic model of theological exposition of, theological reflection upon, and theological deduction from Scripture supports our current need for engagement in the theological enterprise. If we are to help our generation understand the Scriptures and their saving message we too must arrange and deduce theological conclusions from what we gain from our exegetical labors in Scripture interpretation, frame them both didactically and sermonically, and be ready to "dialogue" theologically with this generation. When we do these things we are doing theological work!

The Apostolically Approved Example and Activity of the New Testament Church

The fourth pillar upon which the justification of Christian theology as an intellectual discipline rests is the apostolically approved example and activity of the New Testament church in its creation of extra-biblical, uninspired confessions and creedal statements. The New Testament by its descriptive terms and phrases such as "the traditions" (2 Thess. 2:15), "the pattern of doctrine" (Rom. 6:17), "the faith once for all delivered to the saints" (Jude 3), "the deposit" (1 Tim. 6:20), and the five "faithful sayings" of Paul's pastoral letters (1 Tim. 1:15; 3:1; 4:7-9; 2 Tim. 2:11-13; Titus 3:4-8) indicates that already in the days of the apostles the theologizing activity had begun of reflecting upon and comparing Scripture with Scripture, collating, deducing, and framing doctrinal statements into creedal formulae approaching the character of later church confessions. Examples of these early Christian creedal formulae may be seen in the following verses:

- Romans 1:3-4: "…concerning his Son, who was descended from David according to the flesh, who was powerfully declared to be the Son of God according to the Spirit of holiness by his resurrection from the dead, Jesus Christ our Lord."

- Romans 10:9: "…if you confess with your mouth that Jesus is Lord and believe in your heart that God raised him from the dead you will be saved."

- 1 Corinthians 12:3: "Jesus is Lord."

- 1 Corinthians 15:3-5: "that Christ died for our sins according to the Scriptures, and that he was buried, and that he was raised on the third day according to the Scriptures, and that he appeared to Cephas, then to the Twelve."

- 1 Timothy 3:16: "Great indeed, we confess, is the mystery of godliness who was manifested in the flesh, vindicated by the Spirit, seen by angels, proclaimed among the nations, believed on in the world, taken up in glory."

- 1 Timothy 1:15: "*The saying is trustworthy and deserving of full acceptance*, that Christ Jesus came into the world to save sinners."

- 1 Timothy 3:1: "*The saying is trustworthy*: If anyone aspires to the office of overseer, he desires a noble task."

- 1 Timothy 4:7-9: "…train yourself for godliness; for while bodily training is of some value, godliness is of value in every way, as it holds promise for the present life and also for the life to come. *The saying is trustworthy and deserving of full acceptance*."

- 2 Timothy 2:11-13: "*The saying is trustworthy*, for if we have died with him, we will also live with him; if we endure, we will also reign with him; if we deny him, he also will deny us; if we are faithless, he remains faithful – for he cannot deny himself."

- Titus 3:4-8: "…when the goodness and loving kindness of God our Savior appeared, he saved us, not because of works done by us in righteousness, but according to his own mercy, by the washing of regeneration and renewal of the Holy Spirit, whom he poured out on us richly through Jesus Christ our Savior, so that being justified by his grace we might become heirs according to the hope of eternal life. *The saying is trustworthy*, and I want you to insist on these things."[14]

All of these extra-canonical creedal formulae the New Testament church developed with the full knowledge and approval of Christ's inspired apostles who cite these creeds. Indeed, the apostles were personally involved in this "creedalizing" activity. For example, at the Jerusalem Council in Acts 15:1–16:5 – that I believe may be justifiably designated the "first General Assembly of the Presbyterian Church on Earth" – the apostles, laboring not as apostles but as elders together with other elders, prepared for the church's guidance through the activity of deliberation and debate an uninspired written conciliar response that addressed the issue they were confronting at that time, namely, whether the church would require of Gentiles for church membership faith in Christ alone or faith in Christ plus circumcision and observance of the law of Moses. "It seemed good to the Holy Spirit and to us," they wrote, to opt for the former position.[15] Clearly, then, the church did not err when it wrote creeds; it errs when it ceases to write them.

---

[14]An excellent survey of this material may be found in J. N. D. Kelly, "Creedal Elements in the New Testament," in *Early Christian Creeds* (London: Longmans, Green, 1950).

[15]The council's "It seemed good…" statement does not mean that the letter it wrote was a divinely inspired document. It means that what it wrote was in accord with the will of God the Spirit. It is certainly evident that their conclusions "seemed good" to the assembly delegates themselves, but how did they know that their conclusions "seemed good" to the Holy Spirit as well? Because the speeches at the assembly had made it abundantly clear to those there that the Holy Spirit had placed his divine *imprimatur* upon the conclusions they had reached. The Spirit's endorsement of their conclusions may be seen in his threefold, collectively incontrovertible, objective involvement in

Thus when we today, under the guidance of the Spirit of God and in faith, come to Holy Scripture and, working with our best intellectual tools and the canons of grammatical/ historical exegesis, make the effort to explicate the Bible's propositions and precepts by our exegetical theology, trace their workings in the world by our historical theology, systematize them into creeds and confessions by our systematic theology, and propagate and defend their systematized message to the world by our practical theology we are standing squarely in the theologizing process already present in and conducted by the church of the apostolic age under the sanctions of the apostles themselves.

The Very Nature of Holy Scripture as the Revealed Word of God

The fifth pillar upon which the justification of Christian theology as an intellectual discipline rests is a particularly striking one, namely, a good and necessary inference from the very nature of Holy Scripture as the revealed Word of God (2 Tim. 3:16-17; 2 Pet. 1:20-21). I have presumed throughout this address that the Bible is the revealed Word of God. However, I have presumed this because, among other reasons that could also be adduced, the divine Christ himself, the Lord of the church, regarded it as such and gave his church ample reason as well so to regard it. This means that the triune God about whom the Bible speaks is "really

---

(1) the conversion of the uncircumcised Cornelius and all the other Gentiles who had heard Peter's sermon on that occasion (see Acts 10:19, 44-47), to which Peter later referred both in Jerusalem on an earlier occasion and now at the assembly (11:12, 15-17; 15:8);

(2) the Spirit-mandated (13:1) and Spirit-validated ministry of Barnabas and Paul (13:9 [see Gal. 3:5]; 14:27; 15:3) and their later evidentiary description at the assembly of his validation of their ministry by the signs and wonders (*sēmeia kai terata*) that he had empowered them to perform among the Gentiles (15:12); and

(3) the Spirit-inspired Scripture of Amos 9:11-12, that James cited, that prophetically endorsed the mission activities of Peter in the Cornelius incident and of Barnabas and Paul among the Gentiles (15:13-19).

there and he has spoken." Now if this God is really there and if he has spoken to us in Holy Scripture as Christ and his inspired apostles taught, then he is someone about whom mankind *ought* to want to know. This fact alone provides sufficient warrant to study the Old and New Testaments. It is as simple as this: *If the one living and true God has revealed propositional truth about himself, about us, and about the relationship between himself and us in Holy Scripture alone, then we ought to want to know, indeed, we must know Holy Scripture.* If we take seriously the biblical truth that only in the light of God's Word will we come to understand for sure anything as we should (Ps. 36:9), then we *must* study his propositional revelation to us, or what amounts to the same thing, we *must* engage our minds in the pursuit of theological truth exegetically drawn from the written Oracles of God.

Now I am going to say something that may shock. Here it is: *Not to be intensely interested – and this is true for clergy and laity alike – I repeat, not to be intensely interested in the study of Holy Scripture if the one living and true God has revealed himself therein is the height of spiritual folly, indeed, such disinterest is a form of insanity.* I characterize such disinterest this way with no hesitation because Jesus taught it before I did. In his parable of the prodigal son Jesus taught that the son in the far country away from his father's house, representing all of us in our raw natural state, was not just in great physical need; *he was mad!* This is clear from Jesus' statement that the son, destitute in the far country and in great peril, finally "came to himself" and said: "I will arise and go to my father" (Luke 15:17). Jesus' descriptive expression "came to himself" means literally, "came to his senses," which means that the prodigal son was *out of his mind* to think that he could find lasting fulfillment and live happily out of fellowship with his father. Paul affirms the same thing when he states in 2 Timothy 2:22-26 that the servant of the Lord must "in humility teach those who oppose him, that God may grant them 'a change of mind' with reference to a knowledge of the truth, that *they may regain their senses and escape* from the snare of the devil."[16] Indeed, because of fallen mankind's refusal to retain God in their knowledge, declares Paul, God abandoned the peoples of this world in their rebellion against him to a debased mind (Rom. 1:28) and they are "darkened in their understanding, alienated from the life of God because of the ignorance that is in them, due to their hardness of heart" (Eph. 4:18). And God himself implies that there is something epistemically bizarre about mankind's rebellion against him for even brute beasts he declares – the dumb ox and the ass – know their owners and their masters' cribs but "My people do not know or understand [who it is who made them, who owns them, and who daily feeds them]" (Isa. 1:3). Now *that* is grotesque ignorance, to say the very least! So I say again, for a person to have no interest in what the one living and true God thinks and says about him and no interest in discovering the remedy that God has provided to reverse the human plight reflects the fact that his is a criminal insanity of the first order. He is, spiritually speaking, deranged!

This pillar stands even if one is not sure that the Bible is the Word of God, for if the Bible even *might be* the Word of God, as Christ and his apostles declare that it is, then the obligation is upon the doubter to determine whether it is or not. If he refuses to study the evidence that supports the divine nature of the Bible or if after considering the evidence he wrongly rejects it, well, he will remain in the far country of his spiritual insanity at the peril of his soul. But if, by the grace of God, his study leads him to conclude rightly that the Bible is God's Word, then he will want to know everything he can about what God thinks about him as taught therein and he will engage himself in the theological enterprise. But *to possess no interest in the teaching of Holy Scripture whatsoever is simply sheer spiritual madness.*

---

[16]See Addendum B, "A Brief Exposition of 2 Timothy 2:23-26," for a brief exposition of this passage.

Theology an Act of Worship

Well, there you have it: Christian theology as an intellectual discipline supported by five unassailable pillars provided by Holy Scripture – the intellectual discipline that supports in turn the great salvific *solas* of the Reformation faith that the Reformers derived from careful Scripture exposition and then proclaimed to their world.

So why should *we* engage in Christian theology today? Because Christ the Lord of the church did so, because Christ's Great Commission mandates it, because the apostles did so, because the New Testament church under the sanctions of the apostles did so, and because the very nature of Holy Scripture as God's revealed Word lays the burden upon people to do so. I commend these five pillars to you for your careful consideration and submit that they provide more than ample justification for the church to remain committed to the theological enterprise as an intellectual discipline. And it can remain so committed with the full assurance that its labors will not be a waste of time and energy. And these pillars give you who have involved yourselves in theological training the same assurance that your labors will not be in vain in the Lord. I will even state categorically that no intellectual pursuit will prove more rewarding ultimately to you than your acquisition of a knowledge of God and of his ways and works based upon Holy Scripture. So clear is the Bible's mandate for the theological enterprise, since the Lord of the church and his apostles leave us with no other viable option, that actually the church's primary question should not be whether or not it should engage itself in the theological task. *Of course it should*, and it will if it is faithful to Christ and his apostles as authoritative teachers of doctrine. Rather, what should ever be of even greater concern to the church than the engagement itself is *whether in its engagement in theology as an intellectual discipline it is listening as intently and submissively as it should to its Lord's voice speaking to his church in Holy Scripture.* And in light of these pillars I have delineated your *primary* concern should be, not whether you should engage yourself in the theological enterprise – of course you should – but whether the theology you are acquiring is correct? Is it orthodox? Better still, is it *biblical*? And this is where we Reformed seminary faculty members come into the picture. We annually renew by sacred vow what we believe is our divine calling to do all we can to make certain that our students acquire both a theology that will pass biblical muster and "a mind for truth, a heart for God." We take that vow very seriously *ex animo*. And we urge you to join us in that theological task as we seek to rekindle the Reformation in our time with its five great *sola*s. I urge you to dedicate yourself to the oft-times arduous study that the acquisition and defense of a great theology that is worthy of God will demand of you, for make no mistake about this: Your theology and your defense of it are acts of worship whatever else they may be. As I close this chapter I will ask you two questions:

- Is your God worthy of your theology and your defense of it? He will be only if he is the sovereign triune God of Holy Scripture; no other God is worthy of your efforts.

- Is your theology and your defense of it worthy of your God? They will be only if you ground them upon Holy Scripture alone; no other ground is worthy of the one living and true God.

You must always remember that you are laboring to hear your blessed Savior say to you someday: "Well done, good and faithful servant. You have been faithful over a little; I will set you over much. Enter into the joy of your Master" (Matt. 25:21). Moreover, "you have done your best to present yourself to God as one approved, a worker who has no need to be ashamed, rightly handling the word of truth" (2 Tim. 2:15). May he express these sentiments to each of us in the great and final Judgment Day.

Addendum A: Answering the Biblical "Fool"

"Do not answer a fool according to his folly,
lest you become like him yourself."
"Answer a fool according to his folly,
lest he be wise in his own eyes." (Prov. 26:4-5)

Holy Scripture has a lot to say about the "fool" or the "foolish man" and by extension about the foolish woman. The first thing we must do is to determine who this fool is according to Scripture. He is *not* necessarily a shallow-minded or illiterate ignoramus; to the contrary, he can be quite educated and highly sophisticated in social reckoning and in the ways of the world. Why then does the Bible describe him as fool? Because in his fallen state (see Rom. 1:18-32; 3:10-18; 5:12-19; 8:7-8; 1 Cor. 2:14; Eph. 4:17-19) he has forsaken the source of true wisdom in God – never forget that the fear of the Lord is the beginning of wisdom and knowledge (Prov. 1:7; 4:7) – in order to rely on his own self-sufficient intellectual powers. In short, the biblical fool is simply the unbeliever who consciously determines that he can live his life by his own intellectual resources and without God, and who as a result, though he may not admit it or realize it, has abandoned the only *pou stō*, upon which he may come to certain knowledge about anything. Does Scripture bear out this understanding of who the "fool" is? Is he simply the unbeliever who has chosen to live his life without God? Consider the following verses:

- Job 2:9-10: "[Job's] wife said to him: '…curse God and die!' He replied: 'You are talking like a foolish woman.'"

- Psalm 14:1: "The fool says in his heart: 'There is no God.' They are corrupt, their deeds are vile; there is no one who does good." Note that the fool denies God a place in his life, with his resultant idolatry leading him to immorality.

- Psalm 74:22: "Arise, O God, defend your cause; remember how the foolish scoff at you all the day."

- Proverbs 1:7: "The fear of the Lord is the beginning of knowledge; fools despise wisdom and instruction." Note that the fool refuses to place God's wisdom at the beginning of all his thinking.

- Proverbs 12:15: "The way of a fool is right in his own eyes, but a wise man listens to advice."

- Proverbs 12:23: "A prudent man conceals knowledge, but the heart of a fool proclaims folly."

- Proverbs 13:16: "In everything the prudent acts with knowledge, but a fool flaunts his folly."

- Proverbs 13:19: "A desire fulfilled is sweet to the soul, but to turn away from evil is an abomination to fools."

- Proverbs 14:7: "Leave the presence of a fool, for there you do not meet words of knowledge."

- Proverbs 14:16: "One who is wise is cautious and turns away from evil, but a fool is reckless and careless." Note that the fool is contrasted with the wise man who fears and shuns evil. The implication is that the fool with reckless impetuosity continues down his path to ruin, convinced that his *pou stō* is adequate to address every emergency.

- Proverbs 15:5: "A fool despises his father's instruction; but whoever heeds reproof is prudent." The fool here wants to do his own thing, to go his own way.

- Proverbs 18:2: "The fool takes no pleasure in understanding, but only in expressing his opinion."

- Proverbs 19:1: "Better is a poor person who walks in his integrity than one who is crooked in speech and is a fool."

- Proverbs 24:9: "The devising of folly is sin, and the scoffer is an abomination to mankind."

- Proverbs 28:26: "Whoever trusts in his own mind is a fool, but he who walks in wisdom will be delivered."

- Jeremiah 4:22: "My people are foolish; they know me not. They are stupid children; they have no understanding. They are wise – in doing evil! But how to do good they know not." Note that fools are expressly said here not to know God, to have no spiritual understanding, to be ignorant of the way of righteousness.

- Jeremiah 5:21-23: "Hear this, O foolish and senseless people, who have eyes but see not...Do you not fear me? declares the Lord.... But this people has a stubborn and rebellious heart; they have turned aside and gone away."

- Matthew 7:26: "Everyone who hears these words of mine and does not do them will be like a foolish man who built his house on the sand."

- Luke 12:20: "God said to him: 'Fool! This night your soul will be required of you, and the things you have prepared, whose will they be?' So is the one who lays up treasure for himself and is not rich toward God."

- Romans 1:21-23: "For although they knew God, they did not honor him as God or give thanks to him, but they became futile in their thinking, and their foolish hearts were darkened. Claiming to be wise, they became fools, and exchanged the glory of the immortal God for images resembling mortal man and birds and animals and reptiles."

- 1 Corinthians 1:18-24: "...the word of the cross is folly to those who are perishing, but to us who are being saved it is the power of God. For it is written: 'I will destroy the wisdom of the wise, and the discernment of the discerning I will thwart.' Where is the one who is wise? Where is the scribe? Where is the debater of this age? Has not God made foolish the wisdom of the world? For since, in the wisdom of God, the world did not know God through wisdom, it pleased God through the folly of what we preach to save those who believe. For Jews demand signs and Greeks seek wisdom, but we preach Christ crucified, a stumbling block to Jews and folly to Gentiles, but to those who are called, both Jews and Greeks, Christ [is] the power of God and wisdom of God."

- Ephesians 5:17: "...do not be foolish, but understand what the will of the Lord is."

These Scripture verses make it plain that the biblical fool is the man or woman who does not make God and his Word the *pou stō* for all of his or her thinking. In sum, the fool is a covenant creature who has not yet been delivered from his sin and who accordingly remains a covenant breaker. As a result he conducts all of his intellectual enterprises from the perspective of his fallen *pou stō* and accordingly views the Christian faith as foolishness.

Having shown that the biblical fool is simply the unbeliever, that is, one who refuses to entrust his life to the teaching of God's Word, we must now determine how the covenant keeper who has freely and willingly placed his life on the bedrock of the Word of God as his *pou stō*, and who lives and moves and has his being within the circle of special revelation, is to answer the covenant breaker with regard to the latter's claims that it is he who has true understanding of the nature of things and that the Christian needs to wake up, to stop smelling the roses, and to begin to live in the "real world." The two proverbs cited at the very beginning of this word study provide us with the procedure we should follow in seeking to win the unbeliever to the Christian faith.

The first of these proverbs – "Do not answer a fool according to his folly, lest you become like him yourself" – means that the Christian is not to attempt to provide ultimate answers to the unbeliever in terms of the unbeliever's misguided *pou stō*. To do so will only lead to apologetic futility. Greg Bahnsen writes:

...the apologist should defend his faith by working within his own presuppositions [that is, working within the circle of special revelation]. If he surrenders to the assumptions of the unbeliever, the believer will never effectively set forth a reason for the hope that is in him. He will have lost the battle from the outset, constantly being trapped behind enemy lines. Hence Christianity's intellectual strength and challenge will not be set forth.[17]

In sum, this proverb demands that the Christian respond to the biblical fool's assertions and questions with "truth rejoinders" and "truth arguments." These truth rejoinders and arguments will appeal to different things. For example, as Paul did in 1 Corinthians 5:3-8 the Christian will appeal (1) to Scripture truths (see his "according to the Scripture"), (2) to historical data such as Christ's appearances to certain people who then became eyewitnesses to the fact of his resurrected state and to the order of the external world (Acts 14:17), and (3) to his own personal experience (see Paul's "last of all, he appeared to me" and to his accounts of his conversion experience in Acts 22 and 26). But regardless of the nature of his appeal, what the Christian says by way of positive rejoinder and argument must always be true and accord with the revelation of God in Holy Scripture.

The second of these proverbs – "Answer a fool [one who is trying to live independently from God] according to his folly [his philosophy of independence], lest he be wise in his own eyes." – means that the Christian may find it necessary at times, with the use of *ad hominem* arguments, to assume the unbeliever's position with him and, from his [the Christian's] enlightened position, force the unbeliever to see that his starting point will logically lead him to epistemological nihilism, a philosophical stance with which he himself cannot live (and is not living) if he would avoid suicide. Again, Bahnsen writes, by doing so the Christian

> ...aims to show the unbeliever the outcome of [his self-proclaimed, misguided] assumptions. Pursued to their

---

[17]Greg Bahnsen, *A Biblical Introduction to Apologetics* (unpublished syllabus), 28.

consistent end the presuppositions of unbelief render man's reasoning vacuous and his experience unintelligible; in short, they lead to the destruction of knowledge, the deadend of epistemological futility, to utter foolishness. By placing himself on the unbeliever's position and pursuing it to its foolish undermining of facts and laws, the Christian apologist prevents the fool from being wise in his own conceit.[18]

Francis Schaeffer, insisting that every unbeliever is living in tension somewhere on the continuum between God, the real world (the world that God says is there), and what he himself really is (a person created in God's image), on the one hand and the logical conclusions of his non-Christian presuppositions (the world and he himself as ultimately products of an impersonal beginning plus time plus chance) on the other, follows this procedure, designating this pushing of the unbeliever toward the logical conclusions of his unbelief as "removing the roof" that he has built over himself to protect himself against the "blows" of his real and final environment, namely, the God who is really there.[19] Martin Luther would have perhaps called this procedure simply "preaching the law" but the Bible, I would submit, would see this as one of the entailments in what it demands of sinners in its summons to men to repent of their autonomy and to turn back to God.

Addendum B: A Brief Exposition of 2 Timothy 2:23-26

The foolish and ignorant discussions avoid, knowing that they breed quarrels. And the Lord's servant must not be quarrelsome but be kind to everyone, able to teach, patient, humbly instructing the ones who oppose him that God may grant to them "a change of mind" with respect to knowledge of truth that they may regain their senses and escape from the snare of the devil, having been captured by him to do his will.

---

[18]Bahnsen, *A Biblical Introduction to Apologetics* (unpublished syllabus), 28.

[19]Francis Schaeffer, *The God Who Is There*, 127-30.

About those who oppose the faith Paul states in this passage that they are by implication "ignorant of the truth," that they have "lost their senses," that they have been "ensnared by the devil," and that they are doing Satan's will. What is equally of interest is that to justify their condition, he says, these unbelievers mount "foolish and ignorant" discussions that the Lord's servant is to avoid because such discussions are governed by the presuppositions of the biblical fool. What those ignorant of the truth need, declares Paul, is "knowledge of truth" in order that they may regain their senses and escape from the snare of the devil. This means that they must be given a new mindset (*pou stō*) oriented toward God. And this the Lord's servant may be instrumental in giving them by "instructing them [in the truth], that God may grant them a 'change of mind,'" but he cannot change their minds; he cannot give them this new orientation. As Proverbs 27:22 states: "Though you grind a fool in a mortar, grinding him like grain in a pestle, you will not remove his folly from him." This is God's doing who uses the truth that the believer gives to the unbeliever in order to grant him repentance. This means that the Christian must recognize that his "apologetic successes" ultimately depend upon and come from God.

Chapter Three

Faith's Reasons for Believing the Bible is God's Word

The true Christian church believes that the Bible is a word revelation from another world, even from the triune God of heaven. The evidence in Holy Scripture is pervasive and persistent for its revealedness, its divine origination, and its inerrancy and infallibility. In Chapter Two I outlined Jesus' teaching with respect to the Bible's supernatural origin and his teaching is, of course, of paramount importance. In this third chapter I want to set forth more of the Bible's witness – its witness to itself – that shows that it is indeed God's revealed and inspired Word. We shall see that, though written entirely by men, the Bible represents itself also as entirely the Word of the living God because the Spirit of the living God inspired men to write it in the whole and in the part. The relation between the Bible writers on the one hand and the Spirit of God on the other, however, was not one of simple cooperation or co-authorship. Men could not (and would not) have written the Bible apart from the Spirit's superintending activity. The Holy Spirit is the Author of Scripture in a more profound and original sense than the human writers ever could (or would) have been. God is the primary author of Holy Scripture (*auctor primarius Scripturae sacrae*) with the human writers being the authors of Scripture only insofar as the Spirit mandated, initiated, and provided their impulse to write (*mandatum aut impulsum scribendi*). Never did the Bible, either in the whole or in the part, exist for a moment apart from its Spirit-mandated and inspired character. Consequently, to regard the Bible as only a library of generally reliable ancient documents (How would anyone know this?) composed by human authors, as some evangelical apologists are willing to do (at least at first) as part of their apologetic strategy,[1] is to ignore the most fundamental fact about the Bible and the Bible's major claim about itself.

The church's conviction that the Holy Spirit is the primary author of Scripture entails another conviction, namely, that the Spirit's superintending influence upon the minds of the Bible writers insured that they would write precisely what God wanted them to say. That is to say, since the God of truth by his Spirit of truth inspired the Bible writers to write what he wanted them to write, the final effect was an *inerrant* autograph or original. To say the least, the person who believes that the God of truth inspired the Bible but that the Bible was not inerrant in the autographs has a major epistemological problem on his hands. Moreover, if we fail to recognize within the Scriptures our Master's voice speaking his infallible truth to us from his world into ours, we destroy ourselves not only epistemically but also personally, for in doing so we abandon our only foundation for the certainty of knowledge and the only "meaning base" by which we may truly know the one infinite, personal God and thereby ourselves as persons of dignity and worth.[2] Now why should Christians believe all this? Why should you and I believe it?

---

[1]See Benjamin B. Warfield, *The Inspiration and Authority of the Bible* (Philadelphia: Presbyterian and Reformed, 1948), 210; John Warwick Montgomery, *History and Christianity* (Downers Grove, Illinois: Inter-Varsity Press, 1972), 25-26; R. C. Sproul, John Gerstner, and Arthur Lindsley, *Classical Apologetics* (Grand Rapids: Zondervan, 1984), 137-55.

[2]See my *The Justification of Knowledge* (Phillipsburg, N. J.: Presbyterian and Reformed, 1976), where I have argued that the Bible is man's only foundation for the certainty of knowledge. Part of and essential to my total argument there is that the Bible as divine revelation is necessarily *self-validating* or *self-authenticating*, carrying as it does within itself its own divine *indicia* (15-16; see in this regard *Westminster Confession of Faith*, I/v). I would also insist that the Bible by its doctrine of creation provides man with the only foundation for justifying his personal meaning and value. But more on this later.

More Evidence that the Bible is the Word of God

More – indeed, much more – can be said beyond what we saw earlier was Jesus' view of the origin and nature of the Bible in the second chapter. So the first thing we will do in this chapter is to consider exegetically more of the evidence concerning what the Bible says about itself since we certainly do not want to claim for the Bible anything that it does not claim for itself. We will consider in turn 1 Corinthians 2:6-14, 2 Peter 3:15-16, 2 Timothy 3:16-17, 1 Peter 1:10-12, and 2 Peter 1:20-21. We will then consider an argument for the Bible's inspiration given by Gordon H. Clark. Then we will discuss the Spirit's witness to the Bible's truthfulness in the hearts of God's elect. Finally, we will conclude with a discussion of New Testament canonicity.

1 Corinthians 2:6-14

In this passage that Charles Hodge describes as "the most formal didactic passage in the whole Bible" on the doctrines of revelation and inspiration,[3] Paul affirmed about himself as an apostle of Christ:[4] "we also are speaking [*the thoughts freely given to us by God*], *not in 'taught by human wisdom words'*, *but in 'taught by the Spirit [words]'*, *with the Spirit's [words] explicating the Spirit's thoughts*" (1 Cor. 2:13).[5]

---

[3]Charles Hodge, *Systematic Theology* (Grand Rapids: Eerdmans, n.d.), I, 165.

[4]We should not forget that what Paul wrote he wrote as the inspiring Christ's inspired mouthpiece. Biblical evidence shows that Paul regarded himself as an apostle of Christ, that he was so regarded by Jesus' intimate friends, that he had abundant sources of information about Jesus, that he shared with Jesus the same "already, not yet" view of the Kingdom of God, the same doctrine of the Fatherhood of God, the same doctrines of salvation by God's free grace, a final judgment, the ethic of love as the fulfilling of the law, and most significant of all, the same religion of redemption in and by the death and resurrection of Jesus. He also had Jesus' promise that he would teach him what to say as his apostle (Acts 9:15-16; 13:2; 13:46-47; 18:9; 22:14-15; 26:16-18). This is just to say that to believe Paul is to believe Christ, to disagree with Paul is to disagree with Christ whose inspired apostle Paul was.

[5]Hodge, *Systematic Theology*, I, 162, translates the last phrase: "...clothing the truths of the Spirit in the words of the Spirit."

In the preceding passage Paul had asserted that, proclaiming Christ crucified (that is, the gospel) as he was, he was speaking God's "secret wisdom", wisdom that none of the "rulers" of his age (which classification includes wise men, scholars, and philosophers; see 1:20) understood. He describes this message as "secret" wisdom (2:7), for what he was proclaiming, he says, "no [human] eye has seen, no [human] ear has heard, no [human] mind has conceived" (2:9). In response to the anticipated question, "If your message is inaccessible to men as you say it is [2:9], how did *you* come to be in possession of it?" Paul states: "God *revealed* it to us by his Spirit" (2:10a). The reason, Paul says, that the Spirit can reveal the mind of God to men is because, being God himself, the Spirit of God knows the thoughts of God (2:11b).

The reason, Paul then states, that he as an apostle could speak what the Spirit of God knows is because he had received the Spirit of God (2:12) who *taught* him not only the thoughts of God but also the *very words* with which to frame them: "The things that God has freely given us, [by the Spirit]" (2:12b), he says, "we speak, not in 'taught by human wisdom words,' but in 'taught by the Spirit [words],' with the Spirit's [words] explicating the Spirit's 'thoughts'"(2:13). Even the words Paul employed to express the Spirit's revealed thoughts, Paul says, were from the Spirit. Here is *verbal* inspiration, indeed, *plenary* verbal inspiration. For we may be certain that the Spirit did not inspire any word by accident. Every word he inspired he deliberately chose and it is there for a specific purpose. So we must never wish that the Spirit had not inspired a biblical writer to say what he did or that he should have inspired the writer to say what he did say differently with other words.

Finally, Paul writes that one has to receive the Spirit of God if he would comprehend "the things taught by the Spirit," because "the man without the Spirit [that is, the fallen man whose understanding of spiritual things is darkened by sin] does not accept the things that come from the Spirit of God, for they are foolishness to him, and he cannot understand them, because they are spiritually discerned [that is, they are discerned through the Spirit's enabling]" (2:14).

In sum, Paul affirmed that, in his capacity as an apostle, both the *thoughts* he proclaimed (see his *laloumen*; lit., "we are speaking") and the *words* by which he expressed his thoughts were not ultimately his but were more originally the Spirit's thoughts and words. Paul's statement here shows that it is not only appropriate but also actually *necessary* to speak of "*verbal* inspiration" if one would be biblical. And again, one may justly infer from this that if Paul recorded these thoughts in written form, framing them by these Spirit-taught words, what he wrote in inscripturated form would equally be the Spirit's thoughts and words.

2 Peter 3:15-16

Do we find a statement anywhere in the New Testament to the effect that what Paul *wrote* as an apostle was the Word of God? Yes, we do – in the passage that George E. Ladd refers to as the "earliest reference to the fact that the apostolic church regarded the Pauline letters – or at least some of them – as Scripture."[6] In 2 Peter 3:15-16 Peter declares: "Our beloved brother Paul, *according to the wisdom given him*, wrote to you, as also *in all his letters*, *speaking* in them of…things…that the untaught and unstable distort, as they do *also the rest of the Scriptures* [*kai tas loipas graphas*], to their own destruction." We may observe four things about this statement.

First, Peter declares that what Paul wrote, not just to his (Peter's) readers but also in all his letters, he wrote according to the wisdom given to him. Here is Peter's inspired affirmation that Paul's letters contain divine wisdom since the wisdom by which he wrote God had given to him. Second, Peter places Paul's letters on a par with and altogether within the venue of divinely inspired Scripture by his particular turn of phrase "as also the rest of the Scriptures." Third, their divine authority is

---

[6]George E. Ladd, *A Theology of the New Testament* (Grand Rapids: Eerdmans, 1974), 605.

seen in Peter's statement that when the untaught and unstable distort the meaning of Paul's letters, they do so to their own destruction. Finally, Peter says these things about Paul's letters even though he himself received a sharp rebuke in one of them for his inconsistent practice at Antioch (Gal. 2:11), showing thereby that he was willing to place himself under the authority of the apostolic word given by Paul.

Peter vouches then for both the intrinsic divine origin and the authority of Paul's letters, which is precisely what one might expect in light of the statements that Paul himself makes about the *ab extra* origin of his message (Gal. 1:11-12).

2 Timothy 3:16

What about Peter's expression, "the rest of the Scriptures"? Are we assuming something about them that we should not assume, namely, their divine origin and "revealedness," when we said what we just did above? Not if we believe Paul. Paul declares in 2 Timothy 3:16 that "*all Scripture is Godbreathed [pasa graphē theopneustos].*"[7] To grasp fully his meaning, we must understand first what he intended as the referent to the phrase "all Scripture" and then what he meant by "Godbreathed."

At the very least Paul meant by "all Scripture" the Scriptures of the Old Testament. This is apparent from his statement to Timothy in the immediately preceding verse: "From childhood you have known *the sacred writings [[ta] hiera grammata]*,"

---

[7]The 1901 Revised Version's rendering of Paul's statement by "Every scripture inspired of God is also profitable..." necessitates two comments.

First, it makes little difference whether *pasa graphē*, is translated "every Scripture [passage]" or "all Scripture" in the sense of "the whole [or entirety] of Scripture." The end result, in my opinion, is essentially the same. Nigel Turner (*A Grammar of New Testament Greek*, edited by James H. Moulton [Edinburgh: T. & T. Clark, 1963], III, 199) states that *pas* before an anarthrous noun means "every" in the sense of "any": "not every individual...but any you please." Accordingly, he translates *pasa graphē*, "whatever is Scripture." But he goes on to say that the "anarthrous *pas* also means *all, the whole of,* just as it does when it has the article." Therefore, Turner could just as readily have translated *pasa graphē*, "all Scripture", meaning by this term the same Old Testament that we possess today. This much is indisputable. But there is sound reason to believe that Paul would have been willing to include, and almost certainly did include, within the technical category of "all Scripture" the New Testament documents, including his own, as well. For when Paul wrote what he did in 1 Corinthians 7, he

---

in the sense of "the whole of Scripture." Indeed, in light of the context that favors the notion that Paul is thinking of the Old Testament in its entirety, I would submit that this is more likely his intended meaning. Paul virtually says this in Romans 15:4 when he states that *"everything that was written in the past [hosa proegraphē]* was written to teach us, so that through endurance and the encouragement *of the Scriptures [graphōn]* we might have hope" (*hosos*, according to BAGD, section 2, 586, when used absolutely as it is here, means "everything that"). C. F. D. Moule (*An Idiom Book of New Testament Greek* [Cambridge: University Press, 1953], 95) concurs. He urges that *pasa graphē* "most unlikely" means "every inspired Scripture," and "much more probably means *the whole of Scripture.*"

Second, with respect to the Revised Version's rendering as a whole, Merrill F. Unger, in his *Introductory Guide to the Old Testament* (Grand Rapids: Zondervan, 1956), 25-26, has correctly seen that it is (1) *exegetically weak* since one does not have to be told the obvious, namely, that every Scripture inspired of God is also profitable; (2) *syntactically objectionable* since the RV renders the same construction (a subject followed by two predicate adjectives joined by the conjunction *kai*) in 1 Corinthians 11:30, 2 Corinthians 10:10, 1 Timothy 4:4 and Hebrews 4:12-13 straightforwardly as two coordinate predicate adjectives; (3) *critically precarious* since very few scholars have approved such a rendering; and (4) *doctrinally dangerous* since it suggests that some Scripture may not be the product of the divine breath. See also J. N. D. Kelly's similar comments in his *A Commentary on the Pastoral Letters* (New York: Harper & Row, 1964), 203. Commenting on this matter in the late nineteenth century, Robert Watts (*The Rule of Faith and the Doctrine of Inspiration* [London: Hodder and Stoughton, 1885], 142) observed:

> …it cannot be for a moment imagined that, after passing such high eulogium upon the Holy Scriptures which Timothy, and his mother, and grandmother, had held in such veneration, the Apostle would at once proceed to inculcate an indefinite theory of inspiration, which, from its indefiniteness, could serve no other end than to perplex those who would attempt to apply it, and must, in the end, lead to skeptical views on the whole subject of the claims of the sacred record.

affirmed sarcastically to those who were claiming to have the Spirit's approval to do otherwise than he had directed: "And I think I also have the Spirit of God" (7:40). Paul expresses here his awareness that what he wrote as an apostle, he wrote under the Spirit's superintendence. Again, Paul expressed an awareness of the Spirit's superintending influence upon him when he wrote in 1 Corinthians 14:37: "If anybody thinks he is a prophet or spiritually gifted, let him acknowledge that *what I am writing to you* is the Lord's command." Then in 1 Timothy 5:18 Paul writes: "*The Scripture* [*hē graphē*] says," and then he proceeds to cite both Deuteronomy 25:4 and Luke 10:7. This can only mean that Luke's Gospel was already in Paul's possession and that Paul regarded it as inspired Scripture on a par with Deuteronomy. From this data it is clear that Paul would have included within his expression, "all Scripture," any and every written document that was from God and thus of the nature of "sacred writings." This means that he included within this term not only the Old Testament but those portions of the New Testament that were already written and whatever portions of the New Testament that were yet to be written. In sum, for Paul, whatever imbibed of the character of "Scripture" according to his consistent usage of the word, about that writing Paul was willing to assert that it was "Godbreathed." Indeed, as we shall now argue, precisely because it is "Godbreathed," it is "sacred Scripture."

What specifically did Paul mean when he asserted that all Scripture is "Godbreathed" (*theopneustos*)? The Greek word occurs only here, but A. T. Robertson identifies it as a verbal adjective based upon an old passive participle form.[8] Its closest New Testament analogue (*theo-*, prefix and the *os*, ending) is *theodidaktos*, that means "God-taught" (note the passive voice idea) in 1 Thessalonians 4:9. This meaning supports the idea

---

[8]A. T. Robertson, *A Grammar of the Greek New Testament in the Light of Historical Research* (Nashville, Broadman, 1934), 1095-97. See also Warfield's lengthy examination of the voice of *theopneustos* in his article, "God-Inspired Scripture" in *The Inspiration and Authority of the Bible*, 245-96. He concludes as well that its voice is passive.

of passive voice action in *theopneustos*, hence our translation "Godbreathed." But what does this mean? Does it mean that God breathed something into the Scriptures, or does it mean that God "breathed out' the Scriptures? After extensive research Benjamin B. Warfield concluded that it means the latter – that God "breathed out" the Scriptures from himself, and his conclusion has generally carried the field of scholarly opinion. Stating that "inspired" is "a distinct and even misleading mistranslation," he offers as his reason for this conclusion the following:

> ...the Greek word in this passage – θεόπνευστος, *theopneustos* – very distinctly does not mean "inspired of God." This phrase is rather the rendering of the Latin, *divinitus inspirata*, restored from the Wyclif ("Al Scripture of God ynspyrid is...") and Rhemish ("All Scripture inspired of God is...") versions of the Vulgate. The Greek word does not even mean, as the Authorized Version translates it, "given by inspiration of God," although that rendering (inherited from Tyndale: "All Scripture given by inspiration of God is..." and its successors; cf. Geneva: "The whole Scripture is given by inspiration of God and is...") has at least to say for itself that it is a somewhat clumsy, perhaps, but not misleading, paraphrase of the Greek term in the theological language of the day. The Greek term has, however, nothing to say of *in*spiring or of *in*spiration: it speaks only of a "spiring" or "spiration." What it says of Scripture is, not that it is "breathed into by God" or is the product of the Divine "inbreathing" into its human authors, but that it is breathed out by God, "Godbreathed," the product of the creative breath of God. In a word, what is declared by this fundamental passage is simply that the Scriptures are a Divine product without any indication of how God has operated in producing them.[9]

When Paul declared, then, that God "breathed [out]" the Scriptures, he was asserting "with as much energy as he could employ that Scripture is the product of a specifically Divine

---

[9]Benjamin B. Warfield, "The Biblical Idea of Inspiration" in *The Inspiration and Authority of the Bible*, 132-33; see also 154.

operation."[10] Said another way, he was asserting the divine origin of the entirety of Scripture, in the whole and in the part, as surely as if he had written *pasa graphē ek theou* ("all Scripture is from God"). Stated differently, he was asserting that the Bible is divine revelation. James S. Stewart does not overstate the case when he asserts that Paul as a Pharisee and later as a Christian believed that every word of "breathed out" Scripture was "the authentic voice of God."[11]

Moreover, when he characterized the Scriptures as "theopneustic," that is, as being of the character of the very "breath of God breathed out," he was asserting something about its nature. Just as God's "breath" (that is, his word) created all the host of heaven (Ps. 33:6), just as his "breath" gave physical life to Adam and to all mankind (Gen. 2:7; Job 33:4), just as his "breath" gave spiritual life to Israel, the "valley of dry bones" (Ezek. 37:1-14), so also his powerful "breath," in its word-form, is "living and active, sharper than any two-edged sword, piercing to the division of soul and of spirit, of joints and of marrow, and discerning the thoughts and intentions of the heart" (Heb. 4:12), is imperishable and abiding (1 Pet. 1:23), and God's Spirit, working by and with it in the soul, imparts new life to the soul that needs rebirth. As Peter writes in 1 Peter 1:23-25: "You have been born again not of seed that is perishable but imperishable, that is, *through the living and abiding word of God.* For, 'all flesh is like grass, and all its glory like the flower of grass. The grass withers, and flower falls off, but the word of the Lord abides forever.' *And this is the word that was preached to you.*"

Paul concluded his description of "all Scripture" by saying that it is "profitable for teaching, for reproof, for correction, for training in righteousness, that the man of God may be *fully*

---

[10]Warfield, "The Biblical Idea of Inspiration" in *The Inspiration and Authority of the Bible*, 133.

[11]James S. Stewart, *A Man in Christ* (London: Hodder and Stoughton, 1935), 39.

qualified, having been thoroughly equipped for *every* good
work" (2 Tim. 3:16-17).[12] Here Paul asserts both the sufficiency
and the finality of Scripture insofar as the godly man's need for
a word-revelation from heaven is concerned.

1 Peter 1:10-12

> The prophets, who *prophesied* [*prophēteusantes*] of the
> grace that was to come to you [Peter declares], searched
> intently and with the greatest care, trying to find out the
> time and circumstances to which the Spirit of Christ in them
> was pointing when *he predicted* [*promarturomenon*] the
> sufferings of Christ and the glories that would follow. *It was
> revealed* [*apekaluphthē*] to them that they were not serving
> themselves but you when they spoke of the things that have
> now been told you by those who preach the gospel to you by
> the Holy Spirit sent from heaven.

Here is an unmistakable affirmation that when the prophets, said
here to have been recipients of divine revelation, prophesied
concerning future things, it was the Spirit of Christ in them who
was predicting these things.

The Doctrinal Statement of Dallas Seminary bases its
statement that the Old Testament saints "did not understand the
redemptive significance of the prophecies and types concerning
the sufferings of Christ" on this passage. But Peter does not teach
this idea in these verses. Rather, he states that it was "the time
and circumstances," *not* the "who"[13] (*tina ē poion kairon*;
literally, "what sort of or what kind of time"), surrounding the
Messiah's suffering, *not* his suffering *per se*, and the glories

---

[12]I would submit that "every good work" includes the work of apologetics
and would urge that apologetics, when rightly done, will presuppose the
revealed truth of Holy Scripture and will base its argumentation on the
teachings of the Bible as incontrovertible *evidence* for the truthfulness of
Christian theism in the whole and in the part.

[13]The NASB and the ETV offer a terribly misleading translation here
by their "what person or time." Peter's "or" is not disjunctive as if two
contrasting questions are referred to but conjunctive, that is, only one

that would follow that they were investigating intently and with great care. I say again, Peter does not say that the Old Testament prophets were ignorant of the Messiah's suffering as such. This fact is borne out by Peter's description of God's revelation that came in response to the prophets' intense searching into the revelation that they already possessed about him. God revealed to them, not *whose* sufferings about which they were speaking – this they clearly knew already – but *when* the Messiah's sufferings were to occur. His sufferings, God informed them, were to occur not in their own time, that is, not in the age of the prophets, but in the age following the age of the prophets, namely, in the age of fulfillment, that is, in this present age, the age in which men would preach the gospel by the Holy Spirit sent from heaven.

Surely, in light of all these great affirmations we have been considering, we must conclude that the Bible speaks of a God who revealed himself propositionally through chosen vessels, and that the Bible represents itself as God's word-revelation or message to needy men.

2 Peter 1:20-21

How did God give his word-revelation to men? Does the Bible give us an answer to this question? Indeed it does. Peter writes: "No prophecy of scripture arose from [the prophet's] own [private] interpretation. For prophecy was never brought by the will of man, but, by the Holy Spirit being borne along, men spoke from God" (2 Pet. 1:20-21).

The first thing we must do is to consider the context in which these statements occur. In 2 Peter, because false teachers, probably (pre-?) Gnostic enthusiasts, in propagating their *gnōsis* theology throughout the Roman Empire, were claiming

---

question concerned them, the question of time, which could be asked either way: "In what sort of or what kind of time period do his sufferings occur?" Either way the issue with which they were concerned was the issue of the *time* of the Messiah's sufferings, not *whether* he would suffer. That they already knew.

to have a new word from God that superseded the authoritative word of the Old Testament prophets and the New Testament apostles, Peter felt it necessary to respond to their claim before they could infect his flock. He first described their "knowledge" as "sophisticated myths" (2 Pet. 1:16) and "made-up stories" (2:3). Then he argued that his eye- and ear-witness experience of Jesus' majestic transfiguration – itself the fulfillment of Old Testament Scripture – "*confirmed* the prophetic word" (1:19a),[14] which word, he counseled his readers, "you will do well to pay attention to, as to a light shining in a dark place, until the Day dawns and the morning star rises in your hearts" (1:19b). Then Peter concluded his response with his classic statement on inspiration:

> ...*knowing* this first [note his use of the word "knowing" in which the Gnostic prided himself], that *no prophecy of scripture arose from [the prophet's] own interpretation. For prophecy was never brought by the will of man, but by the Holy Spirit being borne along, men spoke from God* (2 Pet. 1:20-21).

In this remarkable statement Peter first asserts two negatives about the prophecy of Scripture, that is, *inscripturated* prophecy:

- No prophecy of Scripture originated in ("arose, came from," *ginetai*) the prophet's estimate of the current political state of affairs or in his prognosis about the future, that is, no prophecy of Scripture emerged from his own understanding.

---

[14]The AV translates *bebaioteron* by the phrase "more sure" – "We have also a *more sure* word of prophecy" – leaving the impression with many Christian readers that the written Word is more certain than the "voice from the Majestic Glory" or the eye- and ear-witness testimony of Peter to that Voice. This is unfortunate, for it is the same voice that speaks and the same authority that obtains in both cases. It is true that *bebaioteron* is a comparative adjective, but here is an instance when the comparative adjective stands in for its superlative counterpart – a common occurrence in Greek – and is to be translated accordingly – "most sure." The thought intended is that the prophetic written Word that spoke of Messiah's glory was rendered "*most* sure," that is, "was confirmed," by the Transfiguration.

He was not simply a man of political genius with unusual insight into his times' civic and world affairs.

- No prophecy of Scripture was motivated by the human will, that is, no prophecy of Scripture came from mere human impulse.

By these two negatives Peter totally excludes the human element as the originating cause of Scripture in any ultimate sense. This is striking in the extreme.

Peter then asserts two affirmatives about Scripture prophecy, setting them off over against his previous negatives by the strong adversative *alla* ("but" or "to the contrary"). And these affirmatives are as intriguing as the negatives.

- The prophets spoke from God. This means at the very least that what they spoke did not originate in them (see again 1:20) but was given to them by God. This affirmation also means, since for Peter what the prophets "spoke" included what they "wrote" (for recall that Peter is describing "prophecy of *scripture*"), that the prophetic Scriptures themselves came to them from God. As further evidence that Peter included within the category of their "speaking" what the prophets "spoke" in and by their writings, one may note what he writes in 2 Peter 3:15-16: "Our beloved brother Paul *wrote* [*egrapsen*] to you, as also in all his *letters* [*epistolais*], *speaking* [*lalōn*] in them concerning these things."

- The reason the prophets were able to speak from God as they did was that they were being continually borne along (*pheromenoi*, present passive participle) by the Holy Spirit as they spoke or wrote. That is, they were under the Spirit's direct superintending influence the entire time they spoke or wrote as prophets. Peter's thought here is beautifully illustrated from Acts 27:15 where we read that "when the ship was caught [in the violent wind], and could not face the wind, we gave way to it, and *we were driven along* [*epherometha*]." Just as the ship, knowing no will of its own, was "driven" along by the "will" of the wind, so also the prophets, Peter tells us, knowing no will of their own in any ultimate sense in the production of the prophetic Scriptures, were "driven" along (same verb root) by the will of the Holy Spirit. And as he drove them along, that is, as he superintended them, they spoke from God. Warfield comments:

What this language of Peter emphasizes – and what is emphasized in the whole account which the prophets give of their own consciousness – is, to speak plainly, the passivity of the prophets with respect to the revelation given through them. This is the significance of the phrase: "it was as borne by the Holy Spirit that men spoke from God." To be "borne" (*pherein*) is not the same as to be led (*agein*), much less to be guided or directed (*hodēgein*): he that is "borne" contributes nothing to the movement induced, but is the object to be moved. The term "passivity" is, perhaps, however, liable to some misapprehension, and should not be overstrained. It is not intended to deny that the intelligence of the prophets was active in the reception of their message; it was by means of their active intelligence that their message was received: their intelligence was the instrument of revelation. *It is intended to deny only that their intelligence was active in the production of their message: that it was creatively as distinguished from receptively active.* For reception itself is a kind of activity. What the prophets are solicitous that their readers shall understand is that they are in no sense co-authors with God of their messages. Their messages are given them, given them entire, and given them precisely as they are given out by them. God speaks through them: they are not merely his messengers, but "his mouth."[15]

Does this mean that the prophets were simply secretarial robots through whom the divine Oracle spoke? Against the objection that "in the interest of [the prophets'] personalities, we are asked not to represent God as dealing mechanically with them, pouring his revelations into their souls to be simply received as in so many buckets, or violently wresting their minds from

---

[15]Warfield, "The Biblical Idea of Revelation" in *The Inspiration and Authority of the Bible*, 91.

their own proper actions that he may do his own thinking with them" – the objection that would insist that all revelations must be "psychologically mediated" and first made their recipients' "own spiritual possession" in such a sense that the prophets in a real sense are the true and final authors – Warfield reminds his reader of two things. First, the mode of the communication of the prophetic messages that the objection prefers is directly contradicted by the prophets' own representations of their relations to the revealing Spirit: "In the prophets' own view they were just instruments through whom God gave revelations which came from them, not as their own product, but as the pure word of Jehovah."[16] Let us hear Warfield out on this matter in his own words:

> ...the plausibility of such questionings [should not] blind us to their speciousness. They exploit subordinate considerations, which are not without their validity in their own place and under their own limiting conditions, as if they were the determining or even the sole considerations in the case, and in neglect of the really determining considerations. God is Himself the author of the instruments He employs for the communication of His messages to men and has framed them into precisely the instruments He desired for the exact communication of His message. There is just ground for the expectation that He will use all the instruments He employs according to their natures; intelligent beings therefore as intelligent beings, moral agents as moral agents. But there is no just ground for asserting that God is incapable of employing the intelligent beings He has Himself created and formed to His will, to proclaim His messages purely as He gives them to them; or of making truly the possession of rational minds conceptions which they have themselves had no part in creating. And there is no ground for imagining that God is unable to frame His own message in the language of the organs of His revelation without its thereby ceasing to be, because expressed in a fashion natural to these organs, therefore purely His message. One would suppose it to lie in the very nature of the

---

[16]Warfield, "The Biblical Idea of Revelation" in *The Inspiration and Authority of the Bible*, 92.

case that if the Lord makes any revelation to men, He would do it in the language of men; or, to individualize more explicitly, in the language of the man He employs as the organ of His revelation; and that naturally means, not the language of his nation or circle merely, but his own particular language, inclusive of all that gives individuality to his self-expression. We may speak of this, if we will, as "the accommodation of the revealing God to the several prophetic individualities." But we should avoid thinking of [this "accommodation"] externally and therefore mechanically, as if the revealing Spirit artificially phrased the message which He gives through each prophet in the particular forms of speech proper to the individuality of each, so as to create the illusion that the message comes out of the heart of the prophet himself. Precisely what the prophets affirm is that their messages do not come out of their own hearts and do not represent the workings of their own spirits…. It is vain to say that the message delivered through the instrumentality of [the human] tongue is conditioned at least in its form by the tongue by which it is spoken, if not, indeed, limited, curtailed, in some degree determined even in its matter, by it. Not only was it God the Lord who made the tongue, and who made this particular tongue with all its peculiarities, not without regard to the message He would deliver through it; but His control of it is perfect and complete, and it is as absurd to say that He cannot speak His message by it purely without that message suffering change from the peculiarities of its tone and modes of enunciation, as it would be to say that no new truth can be announced in any language because the elements of speech by the combination of which the truth in question is announced are already in existence with their fixed range of connotation. The marks of the several individualities imprinted on the messages of the prophets, in other words, are only a part of the general fact that these messages are couched in human language, and in no way beyond that general fact affect their purity as direct communications from God.[17]

Why did God have to "bear them along" as they spoke? As an elaboration upon the conception of the revelatory organs'

---

[17]Warfield, "The Biblical Idea of Revelation" in *The Inspiration and Authority of the Bible*, 92-94.

preparation for the prophetic task to which he alluded in the
above comments, Warfield writes:

> Representations are sometimes made as if, when God wished
> to produce sacred books which would incorporate His will
> – a series of letters like those of Paul, for example – He was
> reduced to the necessity of going down to earth and painfully
> scrutinizing the men He found there, seeking anxiously for the
> one who, on the whole, promised best for His purpose; and then
> violently forcing the material He wished expressed through
> him, against his natural bent, and with as little loss from his
> recalcitrant characteristics as possible. Of course, nothing of
> the sort took place. If God wished to give His people a series
> of letters like Paul's, He prepared a Paul to write them, and
> the Paul He brought to the task was a Paul who spontaneously
> would write just such letters.
>
> If we bear this in mind, we shall know what estimate to
> place upon the common representation to the effect that the
> human characteristics of the writers must, and in point of fact
> do, condition and qualify the writings produced by them, the
> implication being that, therefore, we cannot get from a man a
> pure word of God. As light that passes through the colored glass
> of a cathedral window, we are told, is light from heaven, but is
> stained by the tints of the glass through which it passes; so any
> word of God which is passed through the mind and soul of a
> man must come out discolored by the personality through which
> it is given, and just to that degree ceases to be the pure word of
> God. But what if this personality has itself been formed by God
> into precisely the personality it is, for the express purpose of
> communicating to the word given through it just the coloring
> which it gives? What if the colors of the stained-glass window
> have been designed by the architect for the express purpose of
> giving to the light that floods the cathedral precisely the tone
> and quality it receives from them? What if the word of God
> that comes to His people is framed by God into the word of
> God it is, precisely by means of the qualities of the men formed
> by Him for the purpose, through which it is given? When [the
> long providential process of preparing the men who produced
> Scripture is taken into account], we can no longer wonder that

the resultant Scriptures are constantly spoken of as the pure word of God. We wonder, rather, that an additional operation of God – what we call specifically "inspiration," in its technical sense – was thought necessary…. When we give due place in our thoughts to the universality of the providence of God, to the minuteness and completeness of its sway, and to its invariable efficacy, we may be inclined to ask what is needed beyond this mere providential government to secure the production of sacred books which should be in every detail absolutely accordant with the Divine will.

The answer is, Nothing is needed beyond mere providence to secure such books – provided only that it does not lie in the Divine purpose that these books should possess qualities which rise above the powers of men to produce [such as knowledge of the divine purpose, infallibility], even under the most complete Divine guidance. For providence is guidance; and guidance can bring one only so far as his own power can carry him. If heights are to be scaled above man's native power to achieve, then something more than guidance, however effective, is necessary. This is the reason for the superinduction, at the end of the long process of the production of Scripture, of the additional Divine operation which we call technically "inspiration." By it, the Spirit of God, flowing confluently in with the providentially and graciously determined work of men, spontaneously producing under the Divine directions the writings appointed to them, gives the product a Divine quality unattainable by human powers alone. Thus these books become not merely the word of godly men, but the immediate word of God Himself, speaking directly as such to the mind and heart of every reader.

…It lies equally on the face of the New Testament allusions to the subject that its writers understood that the preparation of men to become vehicles of God's message to man was not of yesterday, but had its beginnings in the very origin of their being. The call by which Paul, for example, was made an apostle of Jesus Christ was sudden and apparently without antecedents; but it is precisely this Paul who reckons this call as only one step in a long process, the beginnings of which antedated his own existence: "But when it was the good pleasure of God,

who separated me, even from my mother's womb, and called
me through his grace, to reveal his Son in me" (Gal. i. 15.16;
cf. Jer. i. 5; Isa. xlix. 1.5).[18]

Herein lies the answer to the question, Why did the Spirit of God
"bear" the prophets along as they wrote? He superintended them
in their writing specifically and precisely, not only in order to
guarantee to the books written under his superintendency their
revelatory character, that is to say, not only in order to impart
to them the ability to reveal such things as the divine purpose
that would otherwise have been beyond their ken (see "spoke
from God, as they were being borne along"), but also to insure to
their writings their entire *divine* quality and thus their infallible
trustworthiness.

Beyond all controversy, we may conclude that Peter's perception
of the matter was that the prophets of God spoke and wrote, *as
prophets*, solely by and under the superintending influence of
the Holy Spirit. The prophets, in sum, were organs of revelation.
What they wrote was pure Spirit-inspired revelation.

Does the Spirit's superintendency imply scriptural inerrancy?
Many theologians (for example, Emil Brunner, Karl Barth,
Ernst Käsemann) claim not only that the Bible is anything but
non-contradictory in its teachings – it is filled, they say, with
errors and contradictions – but also that God, who "delights in
surprising us" and who (they say) can "draw a straight line with
a crooked stick," even speaks to us through its contradictions.
So the question naturally arises: Has the evangelical Christian,
when he insists upon the inerrancy of Holy Scripture, foisted
upon Scripture a demand for a doctrinal consistency that
Scripture itself does not require? Henri Blocher has quite
properly observed:

> At all stages of biblical history, coherence is highly valued, and
> ascribed to whatever teaching is believed to have come from

---

[18]Warfield, "The Biblical Idea of Inspiration" in *The Inspiration and
Authority of the Bible*, 155-58, 159.

God. Truth…rhymes with eternity, immutable permanence (Ps. 119:160). The law of the Lord is pure, that is, perfectly homogeneous, more thoroughly purged of dross than refined silver and gold; all his ordinances go together as one in their rightness (Ps. 19:9). No miracle may authorize unorthodox prophecies (Deut. 13:1ff.). In spite of God's freedom to display new things in history, failure to harmonize with the dominant tone of earlier revelations raises doubts on the authenticity of a message (Jer. 28:7ff.). Paul exhorts his readers to be of one mind (Phil. 2:2, etc.); they are to grow into the unity of faith (Eph. 3:13), since there is only, under one Lord, one faith and one baptism (v. 5). His preaching is not 'Yes' and 'No' (2 Cor. 1:18), an echo of Jesus' famous words…. Paul insists that his message is identical with that of the other apostles (1 Cor. 15:11)…. In the face of misinterpretations, 2 Peter 3:16 reaffirms this accord. John highlights the three witnesses' agreement (1 John 5:8), and the Fourth Gospel puts forward a theme of 'repetition', not parrot-like indeed, but meeting a concern for identity of substance (John 8:26, 28; 16:13). Discord is a symptom of untruth, as it was in the case of the false witnesses of Jesus' trial (Mark 14:56, 59). Contradictors are to be refuted (Rom. 16:17; Titus 1:9): it could never be done if the standard itself embraced several conflicting theologies. As a matter of fact, the whole logic of our Lord's appeal to Scripture in argument (and similarly of his apostles') would instantly collapse if the presupposition of scriptural coherence were taken away. Even against the Tempter, Jesus relies on the internal consistency of his Father's Word, quoting Scripture to rebuff a twisted use of Scripture. "It is written" would no longer settle an issue if it were conceded that several contradictory views compete with each other on the pages of the Book. The authority of the Word of God would no longer function as it does in Scripture in that case…. The men of God who had a part in writing the Bible prized consistency; they ascribed it axiomatically to divine revelation; it belonged to the collection of sacred texts which had been handed down to them and was enlarged through their own ministry.[19]

---

[19]Henri Blocher, "The 'Analogy of Faith' in the Study of Scripture" in *The Challenge of Evangelical Theology* (Edinburgh: Rutherford House, 1987), 29-31.

So I must say again that the theologian who says, on the one hand, that he believes the Bible is God's inspired Word but, on the other, that it contained errors in the autographs has a major epistemological and theological problem to explain.

Then there are the two very interesting classes of New Testament passages, each of which,

> when taken separately, throws into the clearest light [the New Testament writers'] habitual appeal to the Old Testament text as to God Himself speaking, while, together, they make an irresistible impression of the absolute identification by their writers of the Scriptures in their hands with the living voice of God. *In one of these classes of passages the Scriptures are spoken of as if they were God; in the other, God is spoken of as if He were the Scriptures*; in the two together, God and the Scriptures are brought into such conjunction as to show that in point of directness of authority *no distinction was made between them.*[20]

The reader should reflect carefully and thoughtfully on Warfield's exposition:

> Examples of the first class of passages are such as these: Gal. iii. 8, "The Scripture, foreseeing that God would justify the heathen through faith, preached before the gospel unto Abraham, saying, In thee shall all the nations be blessed" (Gen. xii. 1-3); Rom. ix. 17, "The Scripture saith unto Pharaoh, Even for this purpose have I raised thee up" (Exod. ix. 16). It was not, however, the Scripture (which did not exist at the time) that, foreseeing God's purposes of grace in the future, spoke these precious words to Abraham, but God Himself in His own person: it was not the not yet existent Scripture that made this announcement to Pharaoh, but God Himself through the mouth of His prophet Moses. These acts could be attributed to "Scripture" only as the result of such a habitual identification, in the mind of the writer, of the text of Scripture with God as speaking, that it became

---

[20]Benjamin B. Warfield, "'It Says:' 'Scripture Says:' 'God Says'" in *The Inspiration and Authority of the Bible*, 299, emphasis supplied.

natural to use the term "Scripture says," when what was really intended was "God, as recorded in Scripture, said."

Examples of the other class of passages are such as these: Matt. xix. 4, 5, "And he answered and said, Have ye not read that he which made them from the beginning made them male and female, and said, For this cause shall a man leave his father and mother, and shall cleave to his wife, and the twain shall become one flesh?" (Gen. ii. 24); Heb. iii. 7, "Wherefore, even as the Holy Ghost saith, Today if ye shall hear his voice," etc. (Ps. xcv. 7); Acts iv. 24, 25, "Thou art God, who by the mouth of thy servant David hast said, Why do the heathen rage and the people imagine vain things" (Ps. ii. 1); Acts xiii. 34, 35, "He that raised him up from the dead, now no more to return to corruption,...hath spoken in this wise, I will give you the holy and sure blessings of David" (Isa. lv. 3); "because he saith also in another [Psalm], Thou wilt not give thy holy one to see corruption" (Ps. xvi. 10); Heb. i. 6, "And when he again bringeth in the first born into the world, he saith, And let all the angels of God worship him" (Deut. xxxii. 43); "and of the angels he saith, Who maketh his angels wings, and his ministers a flame of fire" (Ps. civ. 4); "but of the Son, *He saith*, Thy Throne, O God, is for ever and ever," etc. (Ps. xlv. 7); and, "Thou, Lord, in the beginning," etc. (Ps. cii. 26). It is not God, however, in whose mouth these sayings are placed in the text of the Old Testament: they are the words of others, recorded in the text of Scripture as spoken to or of God. They could be attributed to God only through such habitual identification, in the minds of the writers, of the text of Scripture with the utterances of God that it had become natural to use the term "God says" when what was really intended was "Scripture, the Word of God, says." The two sets of passages, together, thus show an absolute identification, in the minds of these writers, of "Scripture" with the speaking God.[21]

Beyond all controversy, then, the Bible claims for itself that it is the Word of God. This fact, assured by exegesis, must be taken into account and never avoided when we face the question of

---

[21]Warfield, "'It Says:' 'Scripture Says:' 'God Says'" in *The Inspiration and Authority of the Bible*, 299-300.

why we believe the Bible is God's Word. We believe it because this is what it claims for itself. I am indebted to E. Calvin Beisner for calling my attention to Gordon H. Clark's similar developed argument for believing the Bible is the Word of God. His argument is quite simple and, I think, has merit, although Clark would be the first to affirm that by itself it can and will convert no one.

Gordon H. Clark's Argument for the Bible's Inspiration

Gordon H. Clark makes the following argument in the first chapter of *God's Hammer: The Bible and Its Critics* for believing that the Bible is God's Word.

- The Bible claims to be the Word of God.
- All alternative explanations concerning the Bible's claim that it is the Word of God, other than its truthfulness, are untenable.
- All attempts to refute the Bible's claim that it is the Word of God by pitting against it specific so-called errors have failed.
- Therefore, we may believe that the Bible is the Word of God.

These four statements require some elucidation so let us take them up one by one.

"The Bible claims to be the Word of God."

Clark observes that this is not arguing in a circle; it would be simply gratuitous to claim that the Bible is the Word of God if it did not claim to be or if it denied that it was the Word of God. He writes: "...what the Bible claims [about itself] is an essential part of the argument. The Christian is well within the boundaries of logic to insist that the first reason for believing the inspiration of the Bible is that it makes this claim."[22]

---

[22]Gordon H. Clark, *God's Hammer: The Bible and Its Critics* (Hobbs, New Mexico: Trinity Foundation, 1982), 3.

"All alternative explanations concerning the Bible's claim that it is the Word of God, other than its truthfulness, are untenable."
Consider the three following alternative explanations. The first alternative explanation is that the Bible's claim that it is the Word of God is only occasional and accidental and therefore should not be taken seriously. But an examination of the biblical data demonstrates that this claim is pervasive[23] and crucial to much of the rest of the program of Scripture. The claim is therefore not accidental and cannot be trivialized or ignored. More than thirty-eight hundred times in the Old Testament its writers introduce their messages with such statements as "The mouth of the Lord has spoken this," "The Lord says," "The Lord spoke," "Hear the word of the Lord," "Thus has the Lord shown to me," and "The word of the Lord came to me, saying" (see also Luke's employment of this Old Testament terminology in Luke 3:3: "the word of God came to John").

The second alternative explanation says that the Bible's claim that it is the Word of God is one among many other claims by the biblical writers that provide reason for skepticism about their credibility and therefore the claim under discussion lacks *a priori* credibility. But again, a careful examination of their writings indicates the opposite: The biblical writers were quite credible on other matters and made this claim in complete awareness of what they were saying; therefore, the claim's falsehood is unlikely *a priori*.

The third alternative explanation is that though the biblical writers may have made the claim that the Bible is the Word of God, Jesus, the most important person in the Bible, did not or, if he did, he was only accommodating himself to the prevailing "erroneous view" of the biblical writers in order to gain a hearing for his own teaching. But once again – and I laid out the evidence for this in Chapter Two – Jesus did make this claim and he made it pervasively and with full self-awareness as he

---

[23]Clark, *God's Hammer*, 3-13.

did so.[24] And there is no reason to think that he made it merely as an accommodation to the biblical writers' "erroneous view" in order to gain a hearing for his own teaching for we know that he quite often contradicted contemporary views that he considered erroneous. And nowhere do we read that Jesus tipped off his followers privately that his statements about Scripture were only an accommodation to the erroneous view held by the biblical writers. Moreover, if the biblical writers' claim is false and Jesus supported it,

> such a Jesus would be no more worthy of an attribution of deity than the Jesus who was mistaken about the Bible's reliability. For a Jesus who would let the end justify the means, allow His followers to be deceived on such a vital religious question (the extent of revelational reliability), and promote confusion and unnecessary strife in the subsequent history of the church through his equivocation, could hardly stand as a divine model for man's ethical emulation.[25]

Yet everywhere else Jesus' credibility is otherwise impeccable. Therefore, Jesus' otherwise impeccable credibility gives his claim concerning the Bible *a priori* credibility.

A fourth alternative that Bultmannians advance, namely, that the supernaturalism of the Bible is simply mythology, I will show in the next four chapters is wrong. Therefore, if these four alternative explanations are untenable, then it follows that the biblical writers' claim remains unrefuted and is to be affirmed.

"All attempts to refute the Bible's claim by pitting against it specific so-called errors have failed."
The list of alleged errors in the Bible is embarrassingly archaic. They have been shown to be themselves erroneous again and

---

[24]The second and third alternatives are treated by Clark, *God's Hammer*, 13-16.

[25]John Warwick Montgomery, "Biblical Inerrancy: What is at Stake" in *God's Inerrant Word*, edited by John Warwick Montgomery (Minneapolis: Bethany, 1974), 29.

again. John W. Haley's *Alleged Discrepancies of the Bible* and Gleason L. Archer's *Encyclopedia of Biblical Difficulties* have both demonstrated that none of the claims of error has any real merit. I am reminded of John Clifford's poem that captures the fact of the Bible's irrefragibility this way:

> I paused last eve before the blacksmith's door,
> and heard the anvil ring, the vesper's chime,
> And looking in I saw upon the floor
> old hammers, worn with beating years of time.
> "How many anvils have you had," said I,
> "to wear and batter all these hammers so?"
> "Just one," he answered. Then with twinkling eye:
> "The anvil wears the hammers out, you know."
> And so, I thought, the anvil of God's Word
> for ages skeptics' blows have beat upon,
> But though the noise of falling blows was heard,
> the anvil is unchanged, the hammers gone.

I say this facetiously, of course, but one could almost wish that Bible critics would allege a new error if for no other reason than to give the Bible's defenders something to do.

"Therefore, we may believe that the Bible is the Word of God." Not to feel the force of this argument is inexcusable. It is not circular; it addresses the critics' objections, and it is so simple that a high school student can follow the argument. Clark argues, however, that until the Holy Spirit illumines a person's mind he cannot and will not believe that the Bible is God's Word.[26]

The Witness of the Holy Spirit in Regeneration to the Bible's Truthfulness

My last comment brings me to the question of why some people believe the Bible's witness to itself while others do not. Why do I believe this while Rudolf Bultmann believed the Bible is

---

[26]Clark argues this in *God's Hammer*, 16-23.

myth? He knew what the Bible teaches as well as I do. The answer I will state in the most fragile of words: Because I am a regenerate Christian and he was not. While the historical and archeological evidence for the Bible's full truthfulness is of great interest to me and of great embarrassment to unbelievers, my conviction that the Bible is God's Word is not ultimately based on such evidence. My confidence in Holy Scripture was produced by the Holy Spirit who by grace bore witness in my heart at my regeneration to the truthfulness of God's Word that was being proclaimed to me. I am saying nothing here that has not been argued many times before. I am only laying out in some detail the apologetic approach that is in line with the teaching of Scripture itself, with the Reformed faith, and with the Westminster Standards. Let me illustrate that I am not speaking in isolation from the Reformed church's testimony when I say this. John Calvin in his *Institutes of the Christian Religion*, 1.7.4-5 writes (emphasis supplied):

> …credibility of doctrine is not established until we are persuaded beyond doubt that God is its Author. Thus, the highest proof of Scripture derives in general from the fact that God in person speaks in it. The prophets and apostles do not boast either of their keenness or of anything that obtains credit for themselves as they speak; nor do they dwell upon rational proofs. Rather, they bring forward God's holy name, that by it the whole world may be brought into obedience to him. Now we ought to see how apparent it is not only by plausible opinion but by clear truth that they do not call upon God's name heedlessly or falsely. If we desire to provide the best way for our consciences – that they may not be perpetually beset by the instability of doubt or vacillation, and that they may not also boggle at the smallest quibbles – *we ought to seek our conviction in a higher place than human reason, judgments, or conjectures, that is, in the secret testimony of the Spirit.* True, if we wished to proceed by arguments, we might advance many things that would easily prove – if there is any God in heaven – that the law, the prophets, and the gospel come from him. Indeed, ever so learned men, endowed with the highest judgment, rise up in opposition and

bring to bear and display all their mental powers in this debate. Yet, unless they become hardened to the point of hopeless impudence, this confession will be wrested from them: that they see manifest signs of God speaking in Scripture. From this it is clear that the teaching of Scripture is from heaven. And a little later we shall see that all the books of Sacred Scripture far surpass all other writings. Yea, if we turn pure eyes and upright sense toward it, the majesty of God will immediately come to view, subdue our bold rejection, and compel us to obey.

Yet they who strive to build up firm faith in Scripture through disputation are doing things backward. For my part, although I do not excel in great dexterity or eloquence, if I were struggling against the most crafty sort of despisers of God, who seek to appear shrewd and witty in disparaging Scripture, I am confident it would not be difficult for me to silence their clamorous voices. And if it were a useful labor to refute their cavils, I would with no great trouble shatter the boasts they mutter in their lurking places. But, even if anyone clears God's Sacred Word from man's evil speaking, he will not at once imprint upon their hearts that certainty that piety requires. Since for unbelieving men religion seems to stand by opinion alone, they, in order not to believe anything foolishly or lightly, both wish and demand a rational proof that Moses and the prophets spoke divinely. But I reply: *the testimony of the Spirit is more excellent than all reason.* For as God alone is a fit witness of himself in his Word, so also the Word will not find acceptance in men's hearts before it is sealed by the inward testimony of the Spirit. *The same Spirit, therefore, who has spoken through the mouths of the prophets must penetrate into our hearts to persuade us that they faithfully proclaimed what had been divinely commanded....* Some good folk are annoyed that a clear proof is not ready at hand when the impious, unpunished, murmur against God's Word. As if the Spirit were not called both "seal" and "guarantee" [2 Cor. 1:22] for confirming the faith of the godly; because until he illumines their minds, they ever waver among many doubts.

Let this point therefore stand: that *those whom the Holy Spirit has inwardly taught truly rest upon Scripture*, and that Scripture is self-authenticated; hence, it is not right to subject it to proof and reasoning. And the certainty it deserves with us, it attains by the testimony of the Spirit. For even if it wins reverence for itself by its own majesty, it seriously affects us only when it is sealed upon our hearts through the Spirit. Therefore, illumined by his power, we believe neither by our own nor by anyone else's judgment that Scripture is from God; but above human judgment we affirm with utter certainty (just as if we were gazing upon the majesty of God himself) that it has flowed to us from the very mouth of God by the ministry of men. We seek no proofs, no mark of genuineness upon which our judgment may lean; but we subject our judgment and wit to it as to a thing far beyond any guesswork! This we do, not as persons accustomed to seize upon some unknown thing, which, under closer scrutiny, displease them, but fully conscious that we hold the unassailable truth! Nor do we do this as those miserable men who habitually bind over their minds to the thralldom of superstition; but we feel that the undoubted power of his divine majesty lives and breathes there. By this power we are drawn and inflamed, knowingly and willing, to obey him, yet also more vitally and more effectively than by mere human willing and knowing!

...Such, then, is a conviction that requires no reasons; such, a knowledge with which the best reason agrees – in which the mind truly reposes more securely and constantly than in any reasons; such, finally, a feeling that can be born only of heavenly revelation. I speak of nothing other than what each believer experiences within himself – though my words fall far beneath a just explanation of the matter.

...Let us, then, know that only true faith is that which the Spirit of God seals in our hearts. Indeed, the modest and teachable reader will be content with this one reason: Isaiah promised all the children of the renewed church that "they would be God's disciples" [Isa. 54:13; see also John 6:45]. God deems worthy of singular privilege only his elect, whom he distinguishes from the human race as a whole. Indeed, what is the beginning of true doctrine but a prompt eagerness to hearken to God's voice?...Isaiah, warning that the prophetic teaching would be beyond belief, not only to foreigners but also to the Jews who wanted to be reckoned as members of the Lord's household, at the same time adds the reason: "The arm of the Lord will not be revealed to all" [Isa. 53:1]. Wherever, then, the fewness of believers disturbs us, let the converse come to mind, that only those to whom it is given can comprehend the mysteries of God [Matt. 13:11].

In agreement with Calvin's words the Reformed church has insisted in the words of the *Westminster Confession of Faith*, I.4-5 (emphasis supplied):

The authority of the Holy Scripture, for which it ought to be believed and obeyed, dependeth not upon the testimony of any man or Church; but *wholly upon God* (who is truth itself) the author thereof; and therefore it is to be received, because it is the Word of God.

We [Christians] may be moved and induced by the testimony of the Church to an high and reverent esteem of the Holy Scriptures. And the heavenliness of the matter, the efficacy of the doctrine, the majesty of the style, the consent of all the parts, the scope of the whole (which is, to give all glory to God), the full discovery it makes of the only way of man's salvation, the many other incomparable excellencies, and the entire perfection thereof, are *arguments whereby it abundantly evidences itself to be the Word of God*: yet notwithstanding, *our full persuasion and assurance of the infallible truth and divine authority thereof, is from the inward work of the Holy Spirit bearing witness by and with the Word in our hearts.*

Note carefully what I am not saying here by any of this, and neither did Calvin nor does the *Westminster Confession of Faith*:

- I am not saying that Christians should not bother to argue with those with whom they may have some common ground such as with Jehovah's Witnesses who believe fervently, as they do, that the Bible is the Word of God. They should endeavor to show the JWs from the Scriptures, our shared common authority, that Jesus is divine, the second person of the Godhead, and that he made full atonement for the sins of his elect.

- I am not saying that Christians should just ignore historical evidence for the truthfulness of the Bible though I would remind everyone that premises established by historical evidence, being *at best* only probable, cannot validly yield universal conclusions.

- I am not saying that Christians should not argue from the hundreds of fulfilled prophecies of Scripture for the truthfulness of Scripture and for Jesus Christ's messianic status. Indeed, I will do precisely that in Chapter Five in connection with the virgin birth of Jesus Christ for I believe that fulfilled prophecy is a prime example of the "consent of all the parts" of Scripture, that is, the consistency of Scripture, as Old Testament shadow gives place to New Testament substance, as Old Testament prediction comes to fruition in New Testament fulfillment, as Old Testament type yields to New Testament antitype. Habakkuk 2:2-3 is highly significant in this regard for what it teaches us about the nature of Biblical prophecy:

> Then the Lord replied:
> "Write down the revelation [*ḥāzōn*]
> and make it plain on tablets
> so that a herald may run with it.
> For the revelation [*ḥāzōn*] awaits an appointed time;
> it speaks of the end
> and will not prove false.
> Though it linger, wait for it;
> it will certainly come and will not delay.

The first thing we should note here is that *true prophecy is revelation*, for twice the content of Habakkuk 2 is referred to by the word *ḥāzōn* (literally, "vision"). This means that true prophets were not simply men who were rare political thinkers with profound sagacity and intuitive, instinctive insights into national or world affairs. Rather, they were men who spoke as the Holy Spirit "carried them along." Second, we are assured that prophecy can include the *foretelling of future events*, for God states that "the revelation awaits an appointed time," that "it speaks of the end," and that what it foretells "*will* come."

Third, the divine Oracle declares that the vision is *certain of fulfillment*: God declares that the prophecy "will not prove false" and that it "will *certainly* come." In sum, what God was predicting, he was certainly going to fulfill, God himself declaring in Isaiah 41:22-23, 25-27; 42:8-9; 43:11-12; 44:7-8, 24-28; 45:18-21; 46:10-11; 48:3-7 that one distinction between himself and all the false gods of this world is his infallible ability to predict the future and to bring his predictions to fulfillment. Fourth, the prophet is instructed to "*write* the revelation down and make it plain upon tablets." Clearly, biblical prophecy could and did assume *the concrete form of Scripture*. (In this immediate context the revelation refers to the information God gave the prophet in Habakkuk 2.) Fifth and finally, its inscripturated character insures its preservation, thereby enabling the "herald" (*qōrē'*, lit, "one who reads" the tablet) to run with its message to others.

As for Jesus Christ he wore so many prophesied identity markers during his earthly ministry that no "teacher in Israel" should have failed to see them. I will cite just six of the three hundred and thirty-two distinct Old Testament predictions that Canon H. P. Liddon declares were literally fulfilled in Christ:[27] He was born of a virgin (Isa. 7:14), born in Bethlehem (Micah 5:2), conducted his ministry in Galilee (Isa. 9:1), was crucified (Ps. 22:16), fulfilled by his death Isaiah 53,[28] and

---

[27]The mathematical probability that these would all be fulfilled in one person is one over eighty-four followed by ninety-seven zeros! This is surely an incredibly strong reason to inform the unbeliever about biblical prophecy.

[28]Consider just this one prophecy: A careful reading by the unbiased student will show, *first*, that the servant of the Lord portrayed in Isaiah's Fourth Servant Song is divine (see "the arm of the Lord," 53:1), is a human personality (52:14; 53:2-3), is an innocent, indeed, sinless sufferer (53:4, 5, 8d, 9c-d, 12d), is a voluntary sufferer (53:7a), and is an obedient, humble, and silent sufferer (53:7), and *second*, that his suffering springs from his love for sinners including his executioners who act in ignorance (53:4c-d, 7, 12), is ordained by God in love and fulfills the divine will and purpose (53:10), deals with sin in all its aspects (see the word "sin," that is, specific acts of missing the mark, 53:12; "transgressions," that is, willful acts of rebellion, 53:5; "iniquities," that is, moral evil, 53:5), is vicarious (53:4a-b, 5a-b, 6c, 8-9d, 10b, 11d, 12e), is redemptive and spiritual in nature (53:5c-d, 11d), ends in his death (53:8a, c-d, 10a, 12c) that leads to his being buried with

bodily rose after death on the third day (Ps. 16:10). So by all means we should urge the critic and the ordinary unbeliever to consider fulfilled prophecy as extraordinarily strong evidence for the Bible as the Word of God.

- I am not saying that Christians should not bother to argue with unbelievers. Indeed, I insisted in Chapter One that we must always be ready to give an answer to the unbeliever for the hope that we have, and I will do this myself in the next four chapters.

- I am not saying that Christians should not bother to point out to unbelievers their own inconsistencies. Indeed, I urged in Addendum A to Chapter Two that we must "answer the

---

the rich (53:9-10) which condition gives way to his resurrection (53:10b-d, 11), leads the straying people for whom he died to confession and repentance (53:4-6), and finally, as his redemptive work, in implementing a divine plan in which suffering, humiliation, and death are central, inaugurates a fruitful and victorious life for endless ages (53:10c-d, 11a-b, 12a-b). Find such a person as this Song alone describes and one finds the Servant/Messiah. When the passage is applied to Jesus of Nazareth, he and he alone meets all the demands of the details of this prophetic Song. This assertion is clearly substantiated by the following New Testament data: First, Jesus was both a historical human person, born in lowliness (Matt. 2:1; Luke 2:1-2), but also divine (Rom. 9:5; Titus 2:13; Heb. 1:8; 2 Pet. 1:1; John 1:1, 18; 20:28; 1 John 5:20); second, he was an innocent person (John 8:46), third, he was despised and rejected by men and was unjustly executed as a felon (Luke 23:13-15); fourth, he was a voluntary sufferer (John 10:17-18; Gal. 2:20); fifth, he was an obedient, humble, and silent sufferer (Matt. 27:12, 14; Phil. 2:8; 1 Pet. 2:23); sixth, he suffered out of love for others (Luke 23:34); seventh, he suffered in order to fulfill the divine plan and will (Eph. 3:11); eighth, he suffered vicariously for his people (1 Pet. 2:24); ninth, he suffered in order to provide a redemptive intervention in the course of history leading to the justification of the believing evildoer from his sin (1 Cor. 1:30; 1 Pet. 1:18-19); tenth, he suffered to the point of death (Matt. 27:50); eleventh, his death gave way to the resurrection (1 Cor. 15:4); and twelfth, he ascended, after his resurrection from the dead, to heaven and is now highly exalted, sitting on the right hand of God (Phil. 2:9-11). Only Jesus' life comports with the demanding details of this Song. No one can validly write a name under the Song's verbal portrait other than that of Jesus of Nazareth. Jesus himself said as much in Luke 22:37 (see also Acts 8:36-35). I will say more about this in Chapter Five.

fool according to his folly lest he be wise in his own eyes" (Prov. 26:5). Christians must show unbelievers that they cannot live consistently with their world and life view. Finally,

- I am not saying that all that Christians need to do in response to the critics' objections is to urge them to read the Bible. Christians should do all they can to remove their objections by careful exegesis of the biblical text and by answering their questions. But since the Bible carries within itself its own divine *indicia*, I will urge the critic to read the Bible and I will pray that the Holy Spirit will witness to the truthfulness of Scripture as the critic does so.

God's Providence the Ultimate Guiding Force behind the Canonization Process of the New Testament

We argued in the last chapter that the church inherited the Old Testament canon of Palestinian Judaism and treated that ancient canon in its entirety, as Jesus taught, as "the oracles of God" (Rom. 3:2). We also argued there that Jesus preauthenticated the writers of the New Testament as teachers of doctrine with the result that the apostolic church added to that canon the writings of the apostles and regarded them as well to be the Word of God. This much is borne out by the Scriptures themselves and is indisputable.

But the church's coming to an understanding of *which* books were to comprise the New Testament canon was a slow, almost imperceptible, process. Herman N. Ridderbos writes:

> There was never any discussion [among the Apostolic Fathers before around 170 A.D.] of the "canonicity" of the majority [and at first of none] of the New Testament writings. The church never regarded those writings as being anything but the authoritative witness to the great time of redemption.... Uncertainty about *some* of [its] writings...only arose later, as a result of certain actions that occurred within or against the church.[29]

---

[29]Herman N. Ridderbos, *Redemptive History and the New Testament Scriptures* (Second revised edition; Phillipsburg, N. J.; Presbyterian and

By his last comment Ridderbos is alluding to the time around 160 A.D. when Marcion, the Gnostic heretic, repudiated the entire Old Testament canon and accepted only a mutilated Luke/ Acts and ten "corrected" letters of Paul as his rule of authority. Thus the question of the New Testament canon became a matter of concern in some regions of the church. And it seems that this regional uncertainty "damaged the authority a document had from the beginning and destroyed the original certainty of the church" about some New Testament books.[30] Even so, according to the Muratorian Fragment dated around 175 A.D. there seems to have been no doubt on the part of the church at large concerning the canonical status of the four Gospels, Acts, thirteen letters of Paul, 1 Peter, and 1 John. The canonical status of the remaining seven books continued to be a concern in some regions of the church for about two centuries. But as the several regions of the church grew in their ecumenical bonds with one another it became increasingly evident that the doubts concerning these writings were only regional and never universal and that these regional doubts contradicted what the larger church had for a long time believed about these matters. Accordingly, the seven books slowly gained ground in the churches apart from any commission of theologians or a deliverance of a church council[31] until they finally found

---

Reformed, 1988), 40. F. F. Bruce, *The Canon of Scripture* (Downers Grove, Ill.: Inter-Varsity, 1958), 255, wrote virtually the same thing thirty years earlier: "The earliest Christians did not trouble themselves about criteria of canonicity; they would not have readily understood the expression. They accepted the Old Testament scriptures as they had received them: the authority of those Scriptures was sufficiently ratified by the teaching and example of the Lord and his apostles. The teaching and example of the Lord and his apostles, whether conveyed by word of mouth or in writing, had axiomatic authority for them."

[30]Ridderbos, *Redemptive History*, 44.

[31]The Roman Catholic Church has long claimed that it created the New Testament canon. There is no historical data to support this claim. To the contrary, the New Testament canon created the church, not the other way around.

a fixed and permanent place in the larger church's New Testament canon. Accordingly, in A.D. 397 the Third Council of Carthage demanded that nothing be read in the church under the title of divine Scripture except the "canonical books," and it then affirmed precisely the collection of twenty-seven New Testament books as the New Testament canon.

Long have Christian scholars, after the fact, debated about what criteria the early church employed during these early centuries to determine a given book's canonicity: apostolicity, antiquity, orthodoxy, catholicity, lection, and inspiration all having been suggested. Richard B. Gaffin, Jr., has convincingly argued, however, and I think correctly, that scholarship has not been able to establish a set of criteria for canonicity that does not at the same time threaten to undermine the New Testament canon as it has come down to us. The problems with these criteria are as follows:

- The criterion of apostolicity does not account for Mark, Luke-Acts, perhaps Hebrews, Jude, and most likely James being included. This criterion fails to provide the reason some of Paul's other letters (1 Cor. 5:9; 2 Cor. 2:4, 9; Col. 4:16) were not included.

- The criterion of antiquity is a variation of the preceding criterion and it too fails to explain why Paul's "previous letter" (1 Cor 5:9) that was earlier than Hebrews was not included while Hebrews was included.

- The criterion of lection cannot explain why documents such as the Shepherd of Hermes and the Didache that were occasionally read in public worship were finally rejected while 2 Peter, 2 John, 3 John, and Jude were included for which there is little to no evidence that they were read.

- The criterion of inspiration, while certainly necessary for canonicity, cannot explain the reason that Paul's letter to the Laodiceans (Col. 4:16), also apostolic, inspired, and to be read in the churches, was not included.

Gaffin also contends that all attempts to demonstrate these criteria subject the absolute authority of the canon to the relativity of historical study and fallible human insight.[32] Ridderbos also observes in this connection:

> ...no matter how strong the evidence for apostolicity (and therefore for canonicity) may be in many instances and no matter how forceful the arguments in favor of apostolicity of certain other writings may be,[33] historical judgments cannot be the final and sole ground for the church's accepting the New Testament as canonical. To accept the New Testament on that ground would mean that the church would ultimately be basing its faith on the results of historical investigation.[34]

---

[32]Richard B. Gaffin, Jr., "The New Testament as Canon" in *Inerrancy and Hermeneutics*, edited by Harvey M. Conn (Grand Rapids: Baker, 1988), 168-70.

[33]But see addendum at the end of this chapter.

[34]Ridderbos, *Redemptive History*, 32-33. R. C. Sproul, *Essential Truths of the Christian Faith* Wheaton, Ill.: Tyndale, 1992) declares, precisely because of the reason stated by Ridderbos, that our New Testament is "a *fallible* collection of infallible books" (22, emphasis supplied). Of course, given Sproul's reasons for asserting that the New Testament is a "fallible collection," he ought also to assert that it is a fallible collection of "fallible books" as well, for he employs the same basic procedure to establish the authority of the individual books of the New Testament. Suffice it to say, I strongly disagree with him. I believe that he is wrong and that the New Testament is an *infallible* collection of *infallible* books but for reasons he does not share with me. Of course, he is only being consistent as an evidentialist when he asserts what he does about the canon, and I regret that more evidentialists do not see as clearly as he that his opinion is the only consistent conclusion that evidentialists may hold. But if our New Testament is, at best, a fallible collection of infallible books, as he suggests, then it follows that perhaps our New Testament failed to include some "infallible" book that it should have included or may have included a book that God did not intend should become a part of the church's witness to redemption and part of the only rule for faith and life throughout this age. I deeply regret that Sproul espouses this view for it casts a shadow over the infallible authority of the entire New Testament.

If this were the case, one would never know for certain, apart from a direct statement from God on the matter, that it was only these twenty-seven books that God intended should be the New Testament canon. One would never know for certain whether the New Testament includes a book that should not have been included or does not include a book that should have been included.

If then historical research and fallible human investigation do not and cannot provide the ultimate ground for the canonicity of the twenty-seven books of the New Testament, what was the driving force behind their canonicity? To such a question one can never give an answer that will satisfy the mind that insists on thinking autonomously from Scripture. The Christian, however, will accept by faith that the church, providentially guided by the Spirit of God, got the number of books and the list right. All that we know for certain about the history of the first four centuries of the church suggests that God's Spirit providentially led the church – not by the vote of a particular church council but imperceptively and inexorably – when it asked its questions, whatever they were, to adopt the books that the Godhead had determined would serve as the foundation of the church's doctrinal teaching and thus bear infallible witness throughout the Christian era to the great objective central events of redemptive history, and that this "apostolic tradition" *authenticated and established itself* over time in the minds of the people of God as just this infallible foundation and witness. In sum, the formation of the twenty-seven-book New Testament canon, after all is said and done, appears ultimately to have been the work, neither of men nor of the institutional church, but of God's Spirit alone as he bore testimony in the hearts of God's people and brought them to a universal consciousness that these were the books they were to listen to as their authority. Martin H. Franzmann states in this connection that before 170 A.D. none of the Apostolic Fathers

> …explicitly asks or answers the question, "Which books are to be included in the list of those which are normative for the

church?" What we do find in the writings of the so-called Apostolic Fathers...is, first, a witness to the fact that the books destined to become the New Testament canon are *there*, at work in the church from the first....

Secondly, we find a witness to the fact that the thought and life of the church were being shaped by the content of the New Testament writings from the first.... Only a God who is really Lord of all history could risk bringing His written word into history in the way the New Testament was actually brought in. Only the God who by His Spirit rules sovereignly over His people could lead His weak, embattled, and persecuted churches to ask the right questions concerning the books that made their claim upon God's people and to find the right answers; *to fix with a Spirit-guided instinct* on that which was genuinely apostolic and therefore genuinely authoritative... only the Spirit of God could make men see that a word which commands the obedience of God's people thereby established itself as God's word and must inevitably remove all other claimants from the scene.

This the 27-book canon did. *It established itself* in the early centuries of the church and *maintained itself* in the continued life of the church.... And it will maintain itself henceforth.... The 27 books are there in the church, at work in the church. They are what Athanasius called them, "the wellsprings of salvation" for all Christendom.[35]

F. F. Bruce notes in this same regard:

Certainly, as one looks back on the process of canonization in early Christian centuries, and remembers some of the ideas of which certain church writers of that period were capable, it is easy to conclude that in reaching a conclusion on the limits of the canon *they were directed by a wisdom higher than their own.* It may be that those whose minds have been largely formed by scripture as canonized find it natural to make a judgment of this

---

[35]Martin H. Franzmann, *The Word of the Lord Grows* (St. Louis, Concordia, 1961), 287-88, 294-95 (emphasis supplied).

kind. But it is not mere hindsight to say, with William Barclay, that "the New Testament books became canonical because no one could stop them doing so" or even, in the...language of Oscar Cullmann, that "the books which were to form the future canon forced themselves on the church by their intrinsic apostolic authority, as they do still, because the *Kyrios* Christ speaks in them."[36]

D. A. Carson, Douglas J. Moo, and Leon Morris agree:

...it is important to observe that although there was no ecclesiastical machinery like the medieval papacy to enforce decisions, nevertheless the worldwide church almost universally came to accept the same twenty-seven books. *It was not so much that the church selected the canon as that the canon selected itself.* This point has frequently been made, and deserves repeating.

> The fact that substantially the whole church came to recognize the same twenty-seven books as canonical is remarkable when it is remembered that the result was not contrived. All that the several churches throughout the Empire could do was to witness to their own experience with the documents and share whatever knowledge they might have had about their origin and character. When consideration is given to the diversity in cultural backgrounds and in orientation to the essentials of the Christian faith within the churches, their common agreement about which books belonged to the New Testament serves to suggest that *this final decision did not originate solely at the human level.*[37]

---

[36]F. F. Bruce, *The Canon of Scripture* (Downers Grove, Ill.: Inter-Varsity, 1988), 282 (emphasis supplied).

[37]D. A. Carson, Douglas J. Moo, and Leon Morris, *An Introduction to the New Testament* (Grand Rapids: Zondervan, 1992), 494 (emphasis supplied). Their citation is from Glenn W. Barker, William L. Lane, and J. Ramsey Michaels, *The New Testament Speaks* (San Francisco: Harper & Row, 1969), 29 (emphasis supplied). One could also cite Harold Lindsell and Charles J. Woodbridge, *A Handbook of Christian Truth* (Revell, 1953), 21: "Gradually,

In response then to the "bottom line" question, why of all the literary claimants to canonicity and of all the inspired apostolic writings did the current twenty-seven books of the New Testament finally become the New Testament canon, we can only conclude with Gaffin:

> ...just these twenty-seven books are what God has chosen to preserve, and he has not told us why....
>
> In the matter of the New Testament as canon, too, until Jesus comes "we walk by faith, not by sight" (2 Cor. 5:7 RSV). But that faith, grounded in the apostolic tradition of the New Testament, is neither arbitrary nor blind. It has its reasons, its good reasons. It is in conflict only with the autonomy of reason.[38]

*   *   *   *   *

I have provided ample reasons in the last two chapters for believing that the Bible is God's inspired Word.[39] I now want to apply this truth by saying that the pastor who will preach the Bible with conviction and power and who will apply with boldness and courage that sharp two-edged sword to his parishioners' lives in all its searing but healing painfulness and in all its soothing and comforting healing balm and so bind up their wounds and lead them in paths of righteousness – *that* pastor will be a true undershepherd of the Good Shepherd. And he will see living consequences of God's declaration about his Word: "...as the rain and the snow come down from heaven and do not return there but water the earth, making it bring forth and sprout, giving seed to the sower and bread to the eater, so shall my word be that goes out of my mouth; it shall not return to me

---

not by the vote of any particular church council, but by the consent of the 'universal church consciousness' that these books, and these alone, were the inspired Word of God, the New Testament canon emerged as we have it today. We have here a magnificent example of the preserving and superintending power of the Holy Spirit."

[38]Gaffin, "The New Testament as Canon," 181.

[39]I am indebted to E. Calvin Beisner's lecture notes on apologetics for several of the thoughts in this and the following paragraph.

empty, but it shall accomplish that which I purpose, and shall succeed in the thing for which I sent it" (Isa. 55:10-11).

The candidate for Christian ministry who does not believe the Bible is God's inspired Word should not enter the ministry. He does not belong there. If he is already in the ministry he should either quit because he should never have entered it or at the very least he should tell his congregation that he does not believe the Bible is God's inspired Word so that those who have the sense not to submit to his authority, stripped bare as it is of the authority of God's Word, can leave and listen to a pastor who does believe it, because all the other doctrines of the true Faith are derived from the divinely inspired Bible and rest upon it for their authority. The doctrine of inspiration is the bedrock – the mother and guardian – of all the other doctrines of Scripture! It is that important!

Louis Gaussen illustrated how vitally important the doctrine of plenary inspiration is to the Christian ministry, to the individual Christian, to the common man, and to the nations of the world by contrasting two persons, the first of whom (Gaussen himself) holds the orthodox view of Scripture as "Godbreathed" with every word "profitable for teaching, for reproof, for correction, and for training in righteousness" (2 Tim. 3:16) while the second holds the Bible to be anything less than the very Word of God – a book of high human wisdom, perhaps, or of base mythology and folklore – whatever, so long as it is not the Word of God. He writes:

> Were it the case…that all in the Bible is not important, does not bear upon the faith, and does not relate to Jesus Christ; and were it the case, taking another view, that in that book there is nothing inspired except what, *in your opinion*, is important, does bear upon the faith, and does relate to Jesus Christ; then your Bible is quite a different book from that of the Fathers, of the Reformers, and of the Saints of all ages. It is fallible; theirs was perfect….
>
> But there is much more than this in the difference between us; for not only, according to your reply, we shall have two Bibles, but also no one can know what your Bible really is.

It is human and fallible, say you, only in a certain measure; but who shall define the measure?....

But this is not all; what follows is of graver import still. According to your reply, it is not the Bible only that is changed, – it is you.

Yes, even in the presence of the passages which you have most admired you will have neither the attitude nor the heart of a believer! How can that be, after you have summoned these along with the rest of the Scriptures before the tribunal of your judgment, there to be pronounced divine, or not divine, or semi-divine? What authority for your soul can there be in an utterance which for you is infallible only in virtue of yourself? Had it not to present itself at your bar, along with the other sayings of the same book, which you have pronounced to be wholly or partly human? Will your mind, in that case, put itself into the humble and submissive posture of a disciple, after having held the place of its judge? This is impossible. The deference you show to it will be that perhaps of acquiescence, never that of faith; of approval, never of adoration. Do you tell me that you will believe in the divinity of the passage? But then it is not in God that you will believe, but in yourself....

According to the answer which you...make to it, the arm of the Lord is palsied for you; the sword of the Spirit has become blunted – it has lost its temper and its power to pierce. How could it henceforth penetrate your joints and marrow? How could it become stronger than your lusts, than your doubts, than the world, than Satan? How could it give you energy, victory, light, peace?...It possibly may happen, at wide intervals..., by a pure effect of God's unmerited favour, that, in spite of this dismal state of the soul, a divine utterance may come and seize it unawares; but it does not remain the less true, that this disposition which judges the Scriptures, and doubts beforehand of their universal inspiration, is one of the greatest obstacles that we can oppose to their acting with effect. It will thus be seen, that [inspiration] is of immense importance in its bearing upon the vitality of our faith.[40]

---

[40]Louis Gaussen, "Prefatory Observations" in *Theopneustia: The Plenary Inspiration of the Holy Scriptures*, translated by David Scott (Revised edition; Chicago: Bible Institute Colportage, n.d.), 5-22 (emphasis supplied).

Addendum A: The Canonicity of the "Disputed Books"

Lest we appear to be giving too much credence to what G. E. Lessing (1729–1781) termed the "ugly big ditch of history," that is, that because the past by its very nature is at best only indirectly available to later generations, religious certainty cannot be based upon the shaky foundation of historical research (with which basic position I concur), something still can and should be said here in behalf of the historical evidence for the canonicity of the seven so-called "disputed books" of the New Testament. I offer this material without intending in any way to undercut the basic position that I espoused earlier in this chapter, namely, that divine providence was the ultimate guiding force in the process of New Testament canonization.

Though he rightly discounts them as the ultimate reason for the church's faith Ridderbos does refer to "the evidence for apostolicity (and therefore for canonicity)" of some writings and "arguments in favor of apostolicity of certain other writings." With reference to the seven so-called "disputed books" of the New Testament he would doubtless have had in mind such "evidence" and "arguments" as the following:

The Letter of James

James the Just, half-brother of our Lord, most likely authored the New Testament letter bearing the name "James." When we ask ourselves which of the four men named James in the New Testament could and would expect his authorship of the letter to be recognized when he identified himself simply as "James, a servant of God and of the Lord Jesus Christ" (James 1:1) and could speak with such massive authority to Jewish Christianity as he does in this letter, reflection on what we know of the other three – which is virtually nothing – should convince us that James, the Lord's half-brother, alone attained such special leadership authority among Jewish Christians generally that could justify its author making the broad appeal that we find in this letter.

Since this seems indisputable, when one then recalls, first, that one of Jesus' appearances after his resurrection was specifically to James (1 Cor. 15:7), at which time presumably he called his half-brother to faith in him and to a lifetime of service in the Jerusalem church, second, that James certainly moved in apostolic circles (Acts 15; Gal. 2:9) and accordingly could have carried "apostolic endorsement" when he spoke or wrote, third, that Paul speaks of James as an "apostle" and a "pillar" in the church (Gal. 1:19; 2:9), and fourth, that James played a dominant role at the Jerusalem Council attended by Peter and Paul, summarizing the apostolic argument and preparing the Council's decree probably himself (Acts 15:13-21), can one doubt that the other apostles clearly recognized James' authority as a witness to Jesus' resurrection and as a spokesman to the church of the circumcision? The Lord of the church accordingly led his church to recognize the intrinsic canonicity of James' letter.

The Letter to the Hebrews

About the only thing one hears expressed about the question of the authorship of Hebrews today is Origen's opinion to the effect that God alone knows the real truth of the matter. It is not so commonly recognized that the context of his remark suggests that in his opinion the letter was Pauline – certainly in content if not by the actual pen of Paul. He writes: "If I gave my opinion, I should say that *the thoughts are those of the apostle*.... Therefore, if any church holds that this Epistle is by Paul, *let it be commended* for this. For *not without reason* have the ancients handed it down as Paul's" (cited by Eusebius, *Ecclesiastical History*, 6.25.14).

The letter, admittedly, is anonymous. But it is clear that the letter's original recipients knew who the author was, for he calls upon them to pray that he would be restored to them shortly (13:18-24). Could Paul be the author? In Egypt and North Africa Paul's authorship seems never to have been a matter of serious dispute; in Italy and particularly in Rome it was. As evidence of the former, while it is true that Paul in every other instance that we know of indicated his authorship by name, Eusebius (*EH*, 6.14) informs us that Clement of Alexandria (155–215) declared that Paul wrote the letter to Hebrew Christians in Hebrew and that Luke had carefully translated it into Greek and published it among Greek-speaking Christians, and that Paul had omitted his name out of deference to his Lord whom he looked upon as the real Apostle to the Hebrews (3:1; see Rom. 15:8) and also to avoid Jewish prejudice against the letter that would have surely come were they to know that he had authored it. Although it is omitted from the Muratorian Canon (due perhaps to the corrupt state of the text of that Canon), Eusebius himself grouped it with the "fourteen" epistles of Paul (*EH*, 3.3), this striking notice no doubt reflecting an earlier opinion such as is found (1) in P[46] (c. 200) that places the letter to the Hebrews between Romans and 1 Corinthians, (2) in the ancestor of Vaticanus that places it between Galatians and Ephesians, and (3) in the majority of ancient Greek copies that place it after 2 Thessalonians, all three positions implying Pauline authorship. Furthermore, both Jerome (Jerusalem) and Augustine (North Africa) cite it as Paul's. Internal evidence also supports the legitimacy of suggesting that Paul could have been the author. It is certainly a Paulinism to call upon his readers to pray for him (see 1 Thess. 5:25; Rom. 15:30-31; Eph. 6:19-20). Moreover, the author's reference to "our brother Timothy" (13:23) surely has a "Pauline ring" about it (see 1 Thess. 3:2; 2 Cor. 1:1; Col. 1:1; Philem. 1). Furthermore, there is a definite affinity of language between the letter and the recognized Pauline letters. Consider the following comparisons:

- Hebrews 1:4: "…the name he has inherited is more excellent than theirs…," and Philippians 2:9: "God has… bestowed on him the name that is above every name";

- Hebrews 2:2: "…the message [that is, the law] declared by angels…," and Galatians 3:19: "[the law] was put in place through angels…";

- Hebrews 2:10: "...he, for whom and by whom all things exist...," and Romans 11:36: "...from him and through him and to him are all things...";

- Hebrews 7:18: "...a former commandment is set aside because of its weakness...," and Romans 8:3: "...the law, weakened by the flesh...";

- Hebrews 7:27: "...he offered up himself...," and Ephesians 5:2: "...he gave himself up for us, a fragrant offering...";

- Hebrews 8:13: "In speaking of a new covenant he makes the first one obsolete...," and 2 Corinthians 3:11: "[the law] was being brought to an end [by the new covenant]";

- Hebrews 10:1: "...the law [was] but a shadow of the good things to come...," and Colossians 2:17: "[The ritual law was] a shadow of the things to come...";

- Hebrews 10:33: "...sometimes being publicly exposed to reproach and affliction...," and 1 Corinthians 4:9: "...we have become spectacles to the world...";

- Hebrews 11:13: "...they were strangers and exiles on the earth ...," and Ephesians 2:19: "...you are no longer strangers and aliens...";

- Hebrews 12:18-22: "...you have not come to [Mount Sinai]... But you have come to Mount Zion..., the heavenly Jerusalem...," and Galatians 4:25, 26: "...Hagar is Mount Sinai... But the Jerusalem above is our mother...."

Finally, the person and work of Christ are central here as in the Pauline epistles.

In my opinion, far too much weight has been given to the statement in 2:3 ("...so great salvation, that having first been spoken by the Lord, was confirmed to us by the ones who heard [him]") as being "the most significant point" *against* Pauline authorship.[41] The statement, by this construction, supposedly teaches that the author was a "second-generation" Christian who had heard the gospel from the Apostles and who was converted as a result of their preaching, thus precluding Paul as the author because he claims in Galatians 1:12 that he received his gospel directly from Christ (see Acts 9:1-9). But Hebrews 2:3 does not say what this construction contends that it says. It does not say that the author had first *heard* the gospel from the Apostles and was converted thereby. Rather, it says that the message of salvation was *confirmed* (*ebebaiōthē*) to him by those who had heard the Lord, implying thereby that the author was already in possession of it at the time of its confirmation to him, an activity that the Apostles could have done for Paul on the occasion of his second visit to Jerusalem about which he speaks in Galatians 2. Certainly the actions of the Apostles, as described by Paul in Galatians 2, give the appearance of being a "confirming activity."

As for its style and grammar (I have carefully worked through the entire letter in the original Greek on several occasions) and its doctrinal content, I grant that these matters are markedly different in some respects from Paul's other letters to specific churches and individuals, but the letter's specific recipients, its subject matter, its purpose, and Paul's use of an amanuensis (very likely Luke) could have had much to do with regard to the style and vocabulary of the letter. There is nothing in the content of the letter that Paul could not have written. And it is difficult to comprehend why the letter would have been received by the early church as canonical if the Lord had not led his church finally to conclude that it had been written by the inspired apostle.[42]

---

[41]Simon J. Kistemaker, *Exposition of the Epistle to the Hebrews* (Grand Rapids: Baker, 1984), 7.

[42]I would recommend that the reader consult R. Laird Harris, *Inspiration and Canonicity of the Bible* (Grand Rapids: Zondervan, 1957), 263-70, who neatly surveys the patristic evidence and concludes that Hebrews is "a genuine Epistle of Paul using Barnabas as his secretary" (269) though he concedes that another person may have served Paul as an amanuensis (Luke is, in my opinion, the strongest possibility here). Some think that Barnabas

The Letter of Jude

There is little reason to doubt the authenticity of the letter as from the pen of Jude, James' brother and younger half-brother of Jesus himself, inasmuch as it is improbable, as Salmond writes, that "any forger would have selected a name comparatively so obscure as that of Jude under which to shelter himself."[43] Jude's blood relationship to Jesus and to James, while such a relationship would not insure the letter's canonical character in and of itself, doubtless contributed to his letter's acceptance. Eusebius lists it among the books "spoken against" because not many of the earlier Fathers had mentioned it. He admits, however, that some had done so. Jerome reports that it was questioned in some quarters because it seems to quote from the book of Enoch, "nevertheless, it has acquired authority by antiquity and use, and is reckoned among the sacred Scriptures" (see his *Catalog of Ecclesiastical Writers*, chap. 4). It is not certain, however, that Jude cites Enoch, having perhaps relied upon the same Jewish tradition that the book of Enoch did. Besides, other biblical writers, whose "inspiredness" and authority is unquestioned, also cite uninspired sources without jeopardizing the canonicity of their writings.[44] Therefore, these facts must not be used to declare against the canonicity of Jude. One must conclude that God providentially led his church to acknowledge its canonical status as an inspired witness to the "once for all delivered unto the saints faith." Thus the Councils of Laodicea in 363 and 397 included it in the accepted New Testament canon of the day.

---

could have been the *original* author, for as a Levite (Acts 4:36) he would have been acquainted with the temple ritual, and as "a son of consolation" (Acts 4:36) he might have written just such a "word of consolation" (13:22). But Donald Guthrie properly concludes that any solid data for Barnabas' authorship is "practically non-existent" (*New Testament Introduction* [Fourth edition; Downers Grove, Ill.: Inter-Varsity Press, 1990], 675).

[43]S. D. F. Salmond, "The General Epistle of Jude" in *The Pulpit Commentary* (Grand Rapids: Eerdmans, 1950), 22, vi.

[44]Paul cites Aratus of Cilicia (Acts 17:28), Epimenides of Crete (Titus 1:12) and Menander, author of the Greek comedy *Thais* (1 Cor. 15:35).

Peter's Second Letter

The author identifies himself as "Simon Peter, a servant and apostle of Jesus Christ" (1:1), declares that the Lord had spoken to him about his death (1:14; see John 21:18-19), claims to have been an eye- and ear-witness of Christ's transfiguration (1:16-18), claims to have written his readers a previous letter (3:1), and implies that he knows "our dear brother Paul" (3:15-16). All of this provides exceptionally solid internal evidence for accepting the Petrine authorship of 2 Peter. Nevertheless, 2 Peter was probably the most controverted New Testament book throughout the first three centuries of the Christian era. While there is no evidence that any part of the early church ever rejected the letter as "spurious,"[45] it is true that Eusebius (*EH*, 3.3), while he makes it clear that the "majority [of scholars] accepted the Epistle as authentic,"[46] classified it among his list of "disputed" books (the Antilegomena) because it had not been quoted by "the ancient presbyters," by which he may have meant "quoted by name."

How are we to account for its paucity of quotations by the church fathers? Why was 2 Peter not expressly quoted more than it was during the first centuries of the Christian era? Several things may be said in response. First, the nature and shortness of the letter may partly account for the paucity of quotations from it. As Charles Bigg writes: "It contains very few quotable phrases. It is probably very seldom quoted even in the present day."[47] Second, the church was flooded during the second and third centuries with numerous pieces of pseudonymous Petrine literature. Some questions would naturally a rise about any epistle claiming to be Petrine.[48] Third, as E. H. Plumptre suggests: "The false teachers condemned in the epistle would

---

[45]Donald Guthrie, *New Testament Introduction* (Third edition; Downers Grove, Ill., Inter-Varsity, 1970), 819.

[46]Guthrie, *New Testament Introduction*, 817.

[47]Charles Bigg, *Epistles of St. Peter and St. Jude* (ICC; Edinburgh: T. & T. Clark, 1902), 211.

[48]Guthrie, *New Testament Introduction*, 818.

make an effort to discredit and suppress it as far as lay in their power."[49] Finally, as Everett F. Harrison suggests, because it was a general epistle, that is, because it was not addressed to one specific congregation, "no single congregation was committed to preserving it and making it more widely known."[50] These reasons could account for the hesitancy in some church regions in accepting it.

It should be noted, however, that there is reason to believe that Jude used material from it, treating it as though it were authoritative. Furthermore, Justin Martyr quoted it in such a way as to prove that he esteemed it authoritative; Melito of Sardis shows dependence on 2 Peter 3:5-7, 10-12; Theophilus of Antioch in his *Ad Autolycum* (Second Book, 13) alluded to 2 Peter 1:19; Irenaeus in his *Against Heresies* (Third Book, 1; Book Four, 36.4; Book Five, 28.3) alluded to the letter; Clement of Alexandria, who declared that he held to "only those books which he had found everywhere clung to as those which had come down from the apostles,"[51] wrote a commentary on 2 Peter; Firmilian in Asia Minor quoted it as an authoritative letter of Peter, "the blessed apostle," when writing to Cyprian in North Africa, suggesting by the locale of the writer and its recipient the universality of accord on its authorship; Origen cited it at least six times as Peter's and as Scripture; the two great third-century Egyptian versions of the New Testament, the *Bohairic* and the *Sahidic*, included it; P[72] accepted it as Scripture; Jerome

---

[49]E. H. Plumptre, *The General Epistles of St. Peter and St. Jude* (Cambridge: University Press, 1879), 81.

[50]Everett F. Harrison, *Introduction to the New Testament* (Grand Rapids: Eerdmans, 1971), 415.

[51]Benjamin B. Warfield, "The Canonicity of Second Peter" in *Selected Shorter Writings of Benjamin B. Warfield*, edited by John Meeter (Nutley, N. J.; Presbyterian And Reformed, 1973), II, 51. I recommend Warfield's article, E. M. B. Green's *Second Peter Reconsidered* (London: Tyndale, 1961), an admirable monograph of original scholarship which ably combats the contention that 2 Peter is a spurious "pious forgery" (he argues, I think wrongly, for the priority of Jude over 2 Peter), and Gleason L. Archer, Jr.'s brief but substantive defense of the Petrine authorship of 2 Peter in his *Encyclopedia of Bible Difficulties* (Grand Rapids: Zondervan, 1982), 425-27.

admitted it into the Vulgate, and the church fathers Athanasius, Epiphanius, Ambrose, Cyril of Jerusalem, Hillary of Poitiers, Gregory of Nazianzus, Basil the Great, and Augustine, bishop of Hippo, all received the letter both as the Apostle Peter's and as a canonical letter.

John's Second Letter

John's second letter is the next to the shortest letter in the New Testament and in content, speaking comparatively, it is a rather insignificant letter, being probably a "cover letter" written to the church ("the elect lady") to whom he sent his Gospel and his longest First Letter. Even though Eusebius (*EH*, 3:25) lists it among the Antilegomena, the external evidence for 2 John as having been written by the Apostle John is weighty. Irenaeus (c. 140–203) in his *Against Heresies* (1.16.3; 3.16.8) quotes it twice. Clement of Alexandria (c. 155–c. 215) in his *Stromata* (2:15) speaks of "John's longer letter," showing that he recognized that John had at least one other letter and that a shorter epistle. The Muratorian Canon (c. 170), after referring to 1 John in connection with the Fourth Gospel, speaks of "two epistles of the John who had been mentioned before," showing that 2 John and 3 John were known at Rome before the end of the second century. Cyprian, bishop of Carthage (c. 200–258), in his *Concerning the Baptism of Heretics* recounts that Aurelius, bishop of Chullabi, quoted 2 John 10-11 at the Council of Carthage in 256, and the Third Council of Carthage of 397 definitely recognized its canonicity. Alfred Plummer justifiably observes: "…precisely these witnesses who are nearest to S. John in time are favourable to the Apostolic authorship [of 2 John], and seem to know of no other view."[52]

John's Third Letter

Third John is the shortest letter in the New Testament. It was written to Gaius, probably the pastor of the church that received John's Gospel and his First Letter. It was intended

---

[52]Alfred Plummer, *The Epistles of St. John* (Cambridge: University Press, 1889), 53.

as a private note of counsel and greeting with the main body of John's teaching contained in his Gospel and 1 John. Edgar J. Goodspeed held that all three Johannine letters originally circulated as a corpus and that consequently the ancient church referred to them differently as either one, two, or three letters.[53] He too viewed 2 John and 3 John as "cover letters" for John's Gospel and 1 John that John sent respectively to the church and the pastor who were to receive his Gospel and 1 John. Its brevity and the relative unimportance of its content, as well as the fact that it was a private letter, caused it not to be widely read in the churches. Nevertheless, 3 John did become widely known and by divine providence attained canonical ranking, testifying to the soundness of the tradition that had from earliest times assigned it to the Apostle John.

The Revelation of John
Owing both to the enigmatic symbolism and obscurity of its content and to the dogmatic antichiliastic considerations expressed in some regions of the church the Revelation of John came to be listed among the ancient church's Antilegomena, but Papias commented on Revelation 12; Justin Martyr (c. 100–165) in his *Dialogue with Trypho*, 81, written around 155–60, stated that the Apostle John received this prophecy from Christ; Irenaeus (d. 202) in his *Against Heresies* cited from virtually every chapter of the book, accepted it as canonical Scripture, and attributed the book to "John, the Lord's disciple" (4:11; 5.26.1); Tertullian (c. 150–c. 225) frequently quoted it and accepted it as the work of the Apostle John; Clement of Alexandria (155–215) and Origen (185–253) also accepted the Revelation as inspired Scripture written by the Apostle John; and the Muratorian Canon (c. 170) mentions it as a universally recognized book at Rome. After 215 no serious question concerning its canonicity existed in the western church. And by the end of the fourth century the eastern church's resistance to it had disappeared.

---

[53]Edgar J. Goodspeed, *An Introduction to the New Testament* (Chicago: University Press, 1937), 324.

From this data one can see that there are good reasons, humanly speaking, that can be offered in behalf of the "apostolicity" and thus the canonicity of all of these so-called "disputed" books of the New Testament. Of course, in the final analysis the Christian will not rest his faith ultimately on these data but will rest confidently in the assumption that God led his church in the first four centuries to recognize those books that he intended should be included in the New Testament canon, namely, the twenty-seven commonly received books – books that were inspired by him, books that could bear witness to the central redemptive-historical events of the Christian faith, and books that he desired the church to preserve for its continuing spiritual health.

Addendum B: John Calvin's View of Scriptural Inerrancy

Throughout Chapter Three I argued for the inerrancy of the autographs of Holy Scriptures. Some critical scholars argue that the distinction between inerrant autographs and errant apographs is of fairly recent vintage. Indeed, they argue that the distinction is an evangelical ploy to minimize the impact of the "assured results" of textual criticism. This is erroneous. Augustine, who represents generally the opinion of the Patristic Age, drew this same distinction in *Epistle 82* to Jerome:

> I have learned to defer this respect and honor to the canonical books of Scripture alone, that I most firmly believe that no one of their authors has committed any error in writing. And if in their writings I am perplexed by anything that seems to me contrary to truth, I do not doubt that it is nothing else than either that the [copied] manuscript is corrupt, or that the translator has not followed what was said, or that I have myself failed to understand it.

As a second case in point I want to bring John Calvin, because of his incomparable value as a magisterial witness at the dawn of the Reformation, to bear witness to the Bible's autographs as inerrant in all that they taught. Now in spite of Calvin's careful exegesis of Scripture in his commentaries, Calvin scholars today hotly debate whether Calvin held that the autographs were inerrant. Benjamin Warfield contended:

> Calvin held [the sixty-six books of canonical Scripture] to be the very Word of God. This assertion he intended in its simplest and most literal sense. He was far from overlooking the fact that the Scriptures were written by human hands: he expressly declares that, though we have received them from God's own mouth, we have nevertheless received them "through the ministry of men" (1.7.5). But he was equally far from conceiving that the relation of their human authors to their divine author resembled to any degree that of free intermediaries, who, after receiving the divine word, could do with it what they listed. On the contrary, he thought of them rather as notaries (4.8.9), who set down in authentic registers (1.6.3) what was dictated to them. They wrote, therefore, merely as the organs of the Holy Ghost.... The diversity of the human authors thus disappears for Calvin before the unity of the Spirit, the sole responsible author of Scripture, which...is *a Deo*; it has "come down to us from the very mouth of God" (1.7.5). It has "come down to us from heaven as if the living words of God themselves were heard in it" (1.7.1); and "we owe it therefore the same reverence which we owe to God Himself, since it has proceeded from Him alone, and there is nothing human mixed with it" (commentary on 2 Timothy 3:16). According to this declaration the Scriptures are altogether divine, and in them, as he puts it energetically in another place, "it is God who speaks with us and not mortal men" (commentary on 2 Pet. 1:20). Accordingly, he cites Scripture everywhere not as the word of man but as the pure word of God.[54]

While he did not accept the inerrancy of the Bible's autographs himself, Edward A. Dowey, Jr., acknowledged that Calvin not only "conceived the Scriptures as literally dictated by God"[55] but

---

[54]Benjamin Warfield, "Calvin's Doctrine of the Knowledge of God" in *The Works of Benjamin B. Warfield* (Reprint; Grand Rapids: Baker, 1991), V, 60-62.

[55]Edward A. Dowey, Jr., *The Knowledge of God in Calvin's Theology* (Reprint; Grand Rapids: Eerdmans, 1994), 99.

also as inerrant in the autographs: "There is no hint anywhere in Calvin's writings that the original text contained any flaws at all...according to Calvin the Scriptures were so given that – whether by 'literal' or 'figurative' dictation – the result was a series of documents errorless in their original form."[56]

Kenneth S. Kantzer argued as well that the evidence supporting the view that Calvin held to the "rigidly orthodox verbal type of inspiration...is so transparent that any endeavor to clarify his position seems almost to be a work of supererogation":

> The merest glance at Calvin's commentaries will demonstrate how seriously the Reformer applied his rigid doctrine of verbal inerrancy to his exegesis of Scripture...attempts to discover a looser view of inspiration in Calvin's teaching fall flat upon examination.[57]

John Murray further corroborated this conclusion:

> [Calvin] affirms most explicitly that the Scripture is from God, that it comes to us from the very mouth of God, and that in believing the Scripture we feel the firmest conviction that we hold an invincible truth. To insinuate that this conviction has respect simply to the heavenly doctrine, as distinct from Scripture as the depository, is to interject a distinction of which there is no suggestion in the relevant passages. In other words, Calvin identifies the doctrine of which he speaks with the Scripture itself...his jealousy for the original text cannot be dissociated from his estimate of Scripture as the oracles of God, that Scripture has nothing human mixed with it, and in all its parts it is as if we heard the mouth of God speaking from heaven.[58]

---

[56]Dowey, *The Knowledge of God in Calvin's Theology*, 100-02.

[57]Kenneth S. Kantzer, "Calvin and the Holy Scriptures" in *Inspiration and Interpretation*, edited by John F. Walvoord (Grand Rapids: Eerdmans, 1957), 137, 142ff.

[58]John Murray, "Calvin's Doctrine of Scripture" in *Calvin on Scripture and Divine Sovereignty* (Philadelphia: Presbyterian and Reformed, 1960), 21, 28.

James I. Packer also affirmed: "The attribution to [Calvin] of a willingness to admit error in Scripture rests on a superficial mis-reading of what he actually says."[59]

Other American scholars, however, such as Charles Augustus Briggs of Union Seminary, New York,[60] have urged that, while Calvin believed that the Bible is the authoritative Word of God, his view of inspiration "was not the high doctrine of plenary, verbal inspiration, espoused by the Reformed dogmaticians of the seventeenth century,"[61] more specifically, he did not espouse the inerrancy of the Bible's original autographs. John T. McNeill writes: "The authority of the Bible as God's Word and the source of indisputable truth is never called in question by Calvin.... Yet he is not concerned to assert what in later controversy has been spoken of as 'verbal inerrancy.'"[62] Jack B. Rogers and Donald K. McKim urge the same view.[63] This latter contention is based not on remarks in Calvin's *Institutes* but on statements Calvin makes in his commentaries. But if these scholars who say that Calvin occasionally admitted the presence of errors in the autographs – which I deny he did – are correct, they should, at least, acknowledge that these admissions were a case of "Homer nodding" (Packer) since it is apparent that over his long career Calvin uncompromisingly and everywhere argued to the contrary for biblical inerrancy. His classic statements in this regard deserve extended quotation:

---

[59]James I. Packer, "Calvin's View of Scripture" in *God's Inerrant Word*, edited by John Warwick Montgomery (Minneapolis, Minnesota: Bethany Fellowship, 1974), 105.

[60]Charles Augustus Briggs, *The Bible, Church, and Reason* (New York: Scribners, 1892), 110ff., 219ff.

[61]John Murray, "Calvin's Doctrine of Scripture" in *Calvin on Scripture and Divine Sovereignty*, 11. Murray, as we noted, does not share this view.

[62]John T. McNeill, "Introduction" to Ford Lewis Battles' translation of Calvin's *Institutes*, volume XX *in The Library of Christian Classics* (Philadelphia: Westminster, 1967), liv.

[63]Jack B. Rogers and Donald K. McKim, *The Authority and Interpretation of the Bible* (New York: Harper and Row, 1979), 89-116.

...where it pleased the Lord to raise up a more visible form of the church, he willed to have his Word [in the context he is referring to the Law] set down and sealed in writing...he commanded that the prophecies also be committed to writing and be accounted part of his Word. At the same time, histories were added to these, also the labor of the prophets, but composed under the Holy Spirit's dictation.[64] I include the psalms with the prophecies, since what we attribute to the prophecies is common to them.

Therefore, that whole body, put together out of law, prophecies, psalms, and histories, was the Lord's Word for the ancient people...*all perfection was contained in it.*

Let this be a firm principle: No other word is to be held as the Word of God, and given place as such in the church, than what is contained first in the Law and the Prophets, then in the writings of the apostles [who] were to expound the ancient Scripture and to show that what is taught there has been fulfilled in Christ. Yet they were not to do this except from the Lord, that is, with Christ's Spirit as precursor in a certain measure dictating the words [*verba quodammodo dictante Christi Spiritu*; the adverb *quodammodo* would be better translated "in a certain sense"[65]]. [The apostles] were sure and genuine scribes of the

---

[64]Calvin's occasional references to the Spirit's "dictating" Scripture and using the biblical writers as his "amanuenses" should be viewed as a theological metaphor meaning simply that what is written in Scripture bears the same relation to the mind of God, its ultimate source, as a letter written by a good secretary bears to the mind of the person from whom he or she took it (Packer), for Calvin did not deny the variations of style among the penmen themselves.

[65]McNeill, basing his remarks on material supplied primarily by Dowey and Battles, with incidental contributions from other sources, in his comment on Calvin's phrase in the *Institutes* (Battles' translation) on page 1156, footnote 7, goes beyond the evidence when he states that the adverb is a "*deliberate* qualification, *discounting* any doctrine of exact verbal inspiration. The context has reference to teaching, not words merely, showing that Calvin's point is not verbal inerrancy, but the authoritative message of Scripture" (emphasis supplied).

McNeill will not face the fact that a biblical document's authority depends upon its inerrant truthfulness. Anyone who affirms on the one hand that the Bible is God's authoritative Word and on the other that its autographs

Holy Spirit [*certi et authentici Spiritus sancti amanuenses*[66]],
and their writings are therefore to be considered the oracles of
God; and the sole office of others is to teach what is provided
and sealed in the Holy Scriptures." (4.8.6, 8, 9)

Commenting on 2 Timothy 3:16 he writes:

> [Paul] commends the Scripture, first, on account of its authority,
> and, second, on account of the utility that springs from it. In
> order to uphold the authority of Scripture, he declares it to
> be divinely inspired [*divinitus inspiratam*]: for if it be so,
> it is beyond all controversy that men should receive it with
> reverence.... Whoever then wishes to profit in the Scriptures,
> let him first of all lay down as a settled point this – that the law
> and the prophecies are not teaching delivered by the will of
> men, but dictated [*dictatam*] by the Holy Spirit.... Moses and
> the prophets did not utter at random what we have from their
> hand, but, since they spoke by divine impulse, they confidently
> and fearlessly testified, as was actually the case, that it was the
> mouth of the Lord that spoke [*os Domini loquutum esse*].... We
> owe to the Scripture the same reverence that we owe to God,
> because it has proceeded from him alone, and *has nothing of
> man mixed with it* [*nec quicquam humani habet admixtum*].

Scholars who deny that Calvin held to the inerrancy of the
autographs do so, as I have already stated, on the basis of certain

---

contained errors has a major epistemological problem on his hands, namely,
to explain how the Spirit of truth, in order to provide mankind with guidance
into all truth, could move men to write propositions in Scripture that contain
errors, the very opposite of truth.

[66]McNeill affirms on page 1157, footnote 9 of the Battles translation of
the *Institutes*: "This passage has been held to support the view that Calvin's
doctrine of the inspiration of Scripture was one of verbal inerrancy. Yet he has
no explicit support of such a view anywhere else, and here he immediately
makes it clear that his interest is in the teaching rather than in the form of
expression." But Murray is correct when he observed above: "To insinuate
that [Calvin's assertions have] respect simply to the heavenly doctrine,
as distinct from Scripture as the depository, is to interject a distinction of
which there is no suggestion in the relevant passages. In other words, Calvin
identifies the doctrine of which he speaks with the Scripture itself...."

remarks that he makes in his commentaries on Genesis 1:16; Matthew 8:23-27 [compare Mark 4:35-41, Luke 8:22-25]; Matthew 27:9; Acts 7:14-16; Romans 3:4; 9:10; 11:12; 14:1; Ephesians 4:8; and Hebrews 11:21. But Kantzer in his essay, "Calvin and the Holy Scriptures," Murray in his essay, "Calvin's Doctrine of Scripture," and J. I. Packer in his essay, "Calvin's View of Scripture," all address every one of these remarks and demonstrate that they do not undermine Calvin's high view of Scripture's inerrancy for the biblical autographs. The minute handful of passages in his commentaries – like "a few raindrops in the oceans of the world" (Packer) – where negative questions have been raised may be divided into the following categories:

- Some are simply places where God has "accommodated" himself to ordinary forms of human language and is not concerned to speak with the degree of accuracy that goes beyond what these forms of speech would naturally require.

- Some show signs of having been altered in the course of transmission. In Matthew 27:9, for instance, Calvin tells us that "by mistake" Jeremiah's name has somehow "crept in [*obrepserit*]."

- Some deal with cases where apostolic writers quote Old Testament texts loosely or paraphrastically in order to bring out the true sense and to make their application.

- Some constitute what we might call only "formal but not real inaccuracies" in which, since no assertion is intended, therefore no real error can fairly be said to have been made. For example, Calvin denies that the Evangelists meant at every point to write narratives that are chronologically ordered. Therefore, since they did not *intend* to connect everything in precise chronological order but on occasion preferred to follow a topical or theological principle of arrangement, they cannot be said to contradict each other when they narrate the same event in a different sequence.[67]

It will be apparent to and acknowledged by every fair-minded interpreter that in every one of these cited cases Calvin's concern was to show that the biblical writers did *not* commit error. In conclusion, we must in fairness to Calvin declare that he stood with the Church of all ages and did in fact believe that the Bible's original autographs were inerrant. Murray quite properly declares:

> In Calvin we have a mass of perspicuous statement and of lengthened argument to the effect that Scripture is impregnable and inviolable, and it would be the resort of desperation to take a few random comments, wrench them from the total effect of Calvin's teaching, and build upon them a thesis which would run counter to his own repeated assertions respecting the inviolable character of Scripture as the oracles of God, and as having nothing human mixed with it.[68]

---

[67]See Murray, "Calvin's Doctrine of Scripture" in *Calvin on Scripture and Divine Sovereignty*, 12-31, and J. I. Packer, "Calvin's View of Scripture" in *God's Inerrant Word*, 95-114.

[68]Murray, "Calvin's Doctrine of Scripture" in *Calvin on Scripture and Divine Sovereignty*, 31.

Chapter Four

Faith's Reasons for Believing
in the Bodily Resurrection and Ascension
to Heaven of Jesus Christ

Having justified the Christian's faith both in Christian theology as an intellectual discipline and in the Bible as the Word of God I will now defend, as I said I must do in Chapter One, certain historical phenomena of the Christian faith, each of which in its own way proving that Jesus was and is the supernatural Christ. In this chapter I will defend the central historical event of Christianity, namely, the historicity of Christ's bodily resurrection from the dead and its corollary, namely, his bodily ascension to heaven. In the three that follow I will defend his virginal conception in the womb of the Virgin Mary, his mighty miracles, and Paul's conversion on the Damascus Road in precisely the way Luke reported it in his Acts. Why these doctrines, the reader may ask? Well, let us go back into Presbyterian church history a little less than a century ago and see why.

In 1924 the General Assembly of the Presbyterian Church in the United States of America (PCUSA) adopted *The Auburn Affirmation*, signed by 1274 of its ordained ministers. This document addressed the five-point doctrinal deliverances of the 1910, 1916, and 1923 General Assemblies that had affirmed that the inerrancy of the Bible, Christ's virgin birth, his substitutionary atonement, his bodily resurrection, and his mighty miracles were each "an essential doctrine of the Word of God." These three five-point deliverances represented the conservative effort within the PCUSA to maintain at least some semblance of the true faith in a church that was slowly but steadily moving away from the so-called "fundamentals of the faith." Now while the signatories of the 1924 *Affirmation* declared that they held "most earnestly to these great facts and doctrines" they also declared:

> Some of us regard the particular theories contained in the deliverance of the General Assembly of 1923 as satisfactory explanations of these facts and doctrines. But we are united in believing that *these are not the only theories allowed by the Scriptures* and our standards as explanations of these facts and doctrines of our religion, and that all who hold to these doctrines, *whatever theories they may employ to explain them*, are worthy of all confidence and fellowship. (emphasis supplied)

Of course, one would be hard-pressed to provide alternative explanatory "theories" concerning these doctrines as they were traditionally and historically explained that did not at the same time either deny them outright or damn them with a thousand qualifications. For example, what would another explanatory theory of Jesus' bodily resurrection from the dead be that did not deny it? Although there should have been, in my opinion, a major investigation, if not a mass heresy trial, of the signatories and many in the broad middle group of the Assembly who supported them, because the conservatives in the church were so weak in number and because the spirit of postwar pacifism at that time was so widespread in the country and in the church the PCUSA simply did not have the stomach for church "warfare." Consequently, the conservatives who had espoused these five "fundamentals of the faith" failed in their valiant effort to bring the PCUSA back from the slippery slope into unbelief on which it had been sliding for a good many years and eventually some of them bore testimony against the PCUSA's apostasy[1] by withdrawing from that church as they believed 2 Corinthians 6:14-18 instructed them to do and forming

---

[1]As one indication of the PCUSA's continuing apostasy its 217th General Assembly meeting in Birmingham, Alabama, in the summer of 2006

the Orthodox Presbyterian Church. They did this because they believed that these doctrines as the church had traditionally and historically understood them are essential not just to the church's well-being but also to the *being* of the church.

We have already considered the doctrine of the inerrancy of Scripture about which doctrine, by the way, the *Auburn Affirmation* declared,

- first, that the Bible no where asserts that its writers were kept "from error,"

- second, that the *Westminster Confession of Faith* does not make this assertion,[2] and

- third, that the doctrine of inerrancy "in fact *impairs* [the Bible's] supreme authority for faith and life, and *weakens* the testimony of the church to the power of God unto salvation through Jesus Christ,"[3] which assertion, were it true, would mean that the doctrine of biblical inerrancy is a positive evil!

"received" on a vote of 282-212 a study document that notes that the so-called traditional language of the church concerning the Trinity (that just happens to be the biblical language) portrays God as male and therefore implies that men are superior to women (for which "distortion," the report states, "we repent") and that allows individual churches to decide for themselves whether they prefer to speak of the so-called "three embodiments" of God as Compassionate Mother, Beloved Child, and Life-Giving Womb, *or* Lover, Beloved, and Love that Binds Lover and Beloved Together, *or* Rainbow of Promise, Ark of Salvation, and Dove of Peace, *or* Rock, Cornerstone, and Temple, *or* Sun, Light, and Burning Ray, *or* Speaker, Word, and Breath.

[2]It does speak, however, about the "infallible truth" of Scripture in I.5 and declares that "the infallible rule of interpretation of Scripture is the Scripture itself" in I.9, a "rule" that it could not be if it contained errors.

[3]The *Affirmation* offers no plausible explanation why the doctrine of inerrancy impairs the Bible's authority or weakens the church's testimony to the gospel. I suppose the *Affirmation* means that the doctrine of biblical inerrancy shifts attention away from the "living Word" (Christ) to the "written Word" (the Bible). In fact, just the opposite is true: If we take a lesser view of the Bible, we are not making Christ more important; we are making him less important because we are discounting his testimony. Moreover, an errant, fallible Bible would impair the Bible's authority and *weaken* its

These are amazing assertions all! I will only say that the major reason for accepting biblical inerrancy is *plain loyalty to Jesus*. Therefore, I will take up the remaining doctrines in turn and defend them and show that each is an aspect of the *sine qua non* ("without which nothing") of Christianity.

The Bodily Resurrection of Jesus Christ

We begin with the doctrine of Jesus' bodily resurrection from the dead, one major event among many that sets him apart from every other religious figure of the past. Among the other religious leaders of the past stands one common denominator: They all died and remained dead. Jesus Christ alone rose from the dead. Surely this should mean something to the world! In his treatment of Christ's resurrection in 1 Corinthians 15 Paul expressly draws out in verses 14-19 seven implications for the church if God has not bodily raised Christ from the dead:

> ...if Christ has not been raised, then [1] *our preaching is in vain* and [2] *your faith is in vain* [that is, fallacious; *kenē*]. [3] *We [apostles] are even found to be misrepresenting God*, because we testified about God that he raised Christ.... And if Christ has not been raised [4] *your faith is futile* [that is, ineffective; *mataia*] and [note carefully: he does not say "and therefore there is no God so you have nothing to worry about when you die"; he says, rather] [5] *you are still in your sins*. Then [6] *those also who have fallen asleep in Christ have perished*. [7] If in this life only we have hope in Christ, we are of all people most to be pitied.

This passage alone shows the significance for the Christian faith of Christ's bodily resurrection from the dead. So it is important that we give a significant place to its defense. I will begin with some basic biblical facts.

Jesus was crucified as an insurrectionist by Roman authorities at the instigation of the Jewish religious leaders. (Few, if any, would

---

testimony to Christ the living Word. I can only conclude that the liberal mind is a confused mind.

deny this today, which is the reason that world Jewry was incensed by Mel Gibson's *Passion of the Christ*, declaring it to be anti-Semitic.[4]) But in Paul's words, he "was raised on the third day according to the Scriptures" (1 Cor. 15:4).[5] This quotation highlights the major teaching of both the New Testament and church proclamation.

---

[4]It is often mistakenly affirmed that the Roman authorities, namely, Pilate and Herod, were responsible for the crucifixion of Jesus Christ with the Jewish religious leadership being at most only complicit actors in the event. The facts of the matter are the reverse: The Roman authorities had no interest in Jesus before the Jewish religious leadership forced them to take up his case. Even then, both Roman authorities found Jesus to be innocent of the Jewish charges against him, but the Jewish religious leadership was relentless in its antagonism to the Romans freeing him and demanded that he be crucified. True, Rome provided the "knife" in Jesus' crucifixion, namely, the mode of execution, but the Jewish religious leadership was the "hand that drove the knife." It was the Jewish religious leadership that instigated the crucifixion of Christ and it was Rome that played the part of the complicit actor.

[5]The phrase "on the third day" requires comment. Where does the Old Testament teach that Jesus would rise from the dead on the third day after death? Andrew Thiselton in his commentary *The First Epistle to the Corinthians* (NIGTC; Grand Rapids: Eerdmans, 2000), 1196-97, argues that the phrase "according to the Scriptures" does not modify "on the third day" but only the phrase "he was raised." But Jesus himself declared in Luke 24:44-46 that the Old Testament testified that the Messiah would suffer death and rise on the third day. Scholars have long pondered this question because there are not a lot of Old Testament texts from which to choose. Most frequently, Hosea 6:2 is chosen and sometimes Jonah 1:17 and 2 Kings 20:5 are proffered. The problem with Hosea 6:2 is that it speaks of *our* resurrection, not the Messiah's. The problem with Jonah 1:17 is that it requires Matthew 12:40 to make the connection. And the problem with 2 Kings 20:5 is that it does not speak of resurrection at all. I would suggest that the Moriah event in Genesis 22, only rarely considered, is quite likely the best choice when all things are considered. Abraham's statement in Genesis 22:5 clearly implies that Abraham believed that Isaac would be resurrected from death on the third day after God commanded him to sacrifice Isaac, during which period of time Abraham viewed Isaac as good as dead, and the Author of Hebrews expressly states that Abraham "symbolically speaking" received Isaac back from death at that time. One has only to comprehend Isaac's *symbolic* "death and resurrection" as a type of Christ's *actual* death and resurrection to comprehend how Paul could write that Christ was "raised on the third day according to the Scriptures."

Christians must admit, given the first-century Jewish milieu in which Christ's resurrection occurred, that it was not at all what the nation of Israel expected. I do not mean to suggest by this comment either that the Old Testament had no doctrine of the resurrection for it surely did (see Isa. 26:19; Dan. 12:2), or that Jews of the first century did not believe in the resurrection of the dead for it is a well-known fact that many Jews did indeed believe in the resurrection (see Acts 23:6-8). But they believed that the resurrection of the dead would occur in the future at the end of time (see John 11:24). But suddenly here was a small group of men proclaiming, not in some out-of-the-way place like Azotus but in Jerusalem itself – the politico-religious center of the nation – that God had raised Jesus from the dead. Not only was this very strange teaching to the Jewish ear but it was also exceedingly offensive teaching to the Jewish religious leadership, including Saul of Tarsus, because Jesus had been executed as a blasphemer on a Roman cross, which meant he had died under the curse of God (Deut. 21:23), with the sanction of the nation's highest court, the Sanhedrin.

The disciples of Jesus believed, however, that there were compelling reasons for such a proclamation, for in spite of threats, bodily persecution, and martyrdom, they continued to preach that he had risen bodily from the dead. What are these reasons? I would submit that two great interlocking strands of evidence convinced them beyond all reasonable doubt that Jesus had risen from the dead just as he said he would in a real body that had new spiritual qualities that enabled him to pass through closed doors. These strands of evidence are the empty tomb and the fact and character of his numerous post-crucifixion physical appearances. Each of these calls for some comment.

The first great strand of evidence: the empty tomb

All four Gospels report that on the third day after Jesus had been crucified and entombed his disciples discovered that his body had disappeared from the tomb in which it had been placed and that his tomb was empty (Matt. 28:6; Mark 16:5-6;

Luke 24:3, 6, 22-24; John 20:5-8). Almost immediately, as we have already noted, the disciples began to proclaim their conviction that Jesus had risen from the dead. Now if the tomb, in fact, had still contained his body – the women and later Peter and John all having gone to the wrong tomb (a most unlikely eventuality in light of Matthew 27:61; Mark 15:47; Luke 23:55) – we may be sure that the authorities, both Jewish and Roman, would have corrected the disciples' error by directing them to the right tomb and to the fact that the tomb still contained Jesus' physical remains.

Many critical scholars over the years who have not accepted the historicity of Jesus' bodily resurrection have felt it necessary to concede that the tomb was undoubtedly empty, but they have blunted the edge of their concession at the same time by advancing such theories as the stolen body theory and the swoon theory to explain why it was empty.

The stolen body theory

Regarding this theory we may safely conclude that if human hands had removed Jesus' body from the tomb they were the hands either of his disciples, his enemies, or professional grave robbers. Now if his disciples had stolen his body which was the explanation first concocted to explain his body's disappearance (Matt. 28:12-15), one must still face the question how his disciples could have gotten past the Roman guards (who, according to Matthew 27:62-66, had been posted there for the express purpose of preventing his disciples from stealing his body) and how they could have rolled the stone away without being detected. The only possible explanation is that the entire Roman watch must have fallen asleep, which again was the first explanation offered.

But it is most unlikely that disorganized, fearful disciples would have even attempted such an exploit. And it is even more unlikely that all the Roman guards would have fallen asleep at the same time while on duty since to do so would have meant certain and severe punishment. Nevertheless, both of these "unlikelihoods" would have to have occurred simultaneously if this explanation for the fact of the empty tomb is to be sustained. Furthermore, with respect to this first explanation that was offered, it should be patently clear that any tough-minded hearer would have immediately rejected the guards' explanation concerning what happened to Jesus' body, for if in fact they all had fallen asleep they would not have known *who* had stolen the body (see Matt. 28:13). Then there is one more problem that this proffered solution must face: If Jesus' disciples had been responsible for his body's disappearance – a most unlikely prospect in light of their reaction to everything that had just happened to Jesus (see John 20:19), we must believe that they then went forth and proclaimed as historical fact a mere fiction that they knew they had contrived, and when faced by persecution and threats of execution as many of them were, not one of them, even when facing martyrdom, revealed that it was all a hoax. I would submit that this scenario is not only improbable but that it is *highly* improbable; liars and hypocrites are not the stuff from which martyrs are made.

Then if Jesus' enemies (the Jewish religious leadership) arranged for his body's removal, one must surely wonder why they did the one thing that would have contributed as much as anything else to the very idea that they were solicitous to prevent from happening (see Matt. 27:62-66). And if they, in fact, had his body in their possession or knew of its whereabouts, one must wonder why they did not produce either it or reliable witnesses who could explain the body's disappearance and prove the disciples wrong when they began to proclaim that Jesus had risen from the dead.

Finally, to attribute the fact of the empty tomb to grave robbers is the least likely possibility of all. For it is to intrude into the report of the event an explanation for which there is not a grain of evidence. Moreover, not only would thieves have been prevented from doing so by the Roman guards but also, even if they could have somehow avoided detection and had proceeded to plunder the tomb, they would have hardly, having first unwrapped it, taken the *nude* body of Jesus with them, leaving his grave wrappings behind and essentially intact (John 20:6-7).

The swoon theory

As for the swoon theory, if we may accept Albert Schweitzer's judgment (see his *Vom Reimarus zu Wrede* [1906], entitled *The Quest of the Historical Jesus* in the English translation), David Strauss dealt the "death-blow" to this view over one hundred and fifty years ago even though one occasionally hears it advanced as a possibility in popular discussions today. This discredited theory maintains that Jesus had not actually died on the cross but had only slipped into a coma-like state, and that in the tomb he revived and somehow on the first day of the week made his way past the guards to his disciples in the upper room who then concluded that he had risen from the dead. He died shortly thereafter.

But to believe this pushes the limits of credibility beyond all legitimate boundaries. It requires one to believe that those responsible for his execution by crucifixion (not to mention his friends who later prepared his body for burial) were woefully incompetent both as executioners and as judges of the state of their crucified victims when they performed the *crurifragium* (the breaking of the legs) on them (see John 19:31-33). It also requires one to believe that Jesus – though suffering from the excruciating pain of wounded hands and feet not to mention the loss of blood, the physical weakness and the shock to his entire system that would have naturally ensued from the horrible ordeal of the crucifixion itself and the lack of human care and physical nourishment – somehow survived the wound in his side and the cold of the tomb without human aid or succor and then pushed the huge stone away from the entrance of the tomb with wounded hands and made his way on wounded feet past Roman guards into the city to the place where his disciples were hiding and there he convinced his followers that he – the emaciated shell of a man – was the Lord of life! Such a scenario is surely beyond all possibility and is undeserving of any thinking man's assent. Such books as Hugh Schonfield's *The Passover Plot* and Donovan Joyce's *The Jesus Scroll* are only variations on this theme and are not taken seriously by the scholarly community.

But if some critical scholars have acknowledged the fact of the empty tomb and have attempted (unsuccessfully) to offer explanations for it, others have simply declared that the empty tomb was not an essential part of the original resurrection story, that the church only later created the "fact" in order to fortify its stories of the resurrection appearances. This is not true. The empty tomb was part of the church's proclamation from the outset (see Acts 2:31; 1 Cor. 15:4). And it is simply erroneous teaching that asserts that the first disciples believed that one can have a real resurrection without an empty tomb. G. C. Berkouwer has correctly observed:

> Not the empty grave but the resurrection of Christ is the great soteriological fact, but as such the resurrection is inseparably connected with the empty tomb and unthinkable without it. It is absolutely contrary to Scripture to eliminate the message of the empty tomb and still speak of the living Lord. The Gospels picture his resurrection in connection with historical data, moments, and places of his appearance. Scripture nowhere supports the idea of his living on independently of a corporeal resurrection and an empty tomb.[6]

The conclusion is self-evident: The theologian who dismisses the empty tomb as irrelevant to the Christian message but who still speaks of "the resurrection of Jesus" does not mean by his "resurrection" what the New Testament means or what the church has traditionally meant by it. It has become more a saving "idea" than a saving event. But such a view of the resurrection of Jesus would have been rejected out of hand by the early church as no resurrection at all (see 2 Tim. 2:14: "Hymenaeus

---

[6]G. C. Berkouwer, *The Work of Christ*, translated by Cornelius Lambregste (Grand Rapids: Eerdmans, 1965), 184.

and Philetus…have swerved from the truth, saying that the resurrection has already happened.").

We have defended to this point the fact of the empty tomb. But now we must point out that such a description is not entirely accurate since the tomb was not completely empty. For not only did angels appear to the women in the tomb and announce to them that Jesus had risen (Mark 16:5-7; Luke 24:3-7), but also both Luke (24:12) and John (20:5-7) mention the presence of his empty grave clothes. The strips of linen in which Jesus' body had been wrapped were still there, with the cloth that had been around his head folded and lying by itself, separate from the linen. The empty grave linens suggest that not only had Jesus' body not been disturbed by human hands (for it is extremely unlikely that friends or foe would have first unwrapped the body before taking it away), but also that the body that had been bound within the wrappings had simply disappeared, leaving the wrappings behind like an empty chrysalis. It is highly significant, according to John's own testimony (John 20:3-9), that it was when he saw the empty grave wrappings within the empty tomb that he himself came to understand that Jesus had risen from the dead.

The second great strand of evidence: Jesus' numerous post-crucifixion appearances

The second great strand of evidence, after the fact of Jesus' empty tomb, is the many post-crucifixion appearances that our Lord made to his disciples under varying circumstances and in numerous places. The New Testament records at least eleven such appearances, five of them occurring on that first "Easter," and the remaining five occurring during the following forty days leading up to and including the day of his ascension, and his appearance to Saul (Acts 9:1-5).

He appeared first to the women who had left the tomb (Matt. 28:8-10),[7] and then to Mary Magdalene who had returned

---

[7]Mark 16:9 states that Jesus "appeared first to Mary Magdalene" and this may well be the case. But appearing as this statement does in the long

to the tomb after telling Peter and John what she and the other women had seen (John 20:10-18). Then he appeared to Cleopas and the other unnamed disciple on the road to Emmaus (Luke 24:13-35), and then to Peter, no doubt sometime that same afternoon (Luke 24:34; 1 Cor 15:5). His last appearance on that historic day was to the "Twelve" (actually ten in number since Judas and Thomas were not present) in the upper room (Luke 24:36-43; John 20:20-28; 1 Cor. 15:5). What is of great significance on this last occasion is the fact that Jesus invited the disciples to touch him in order to satisfy themselves that it was really he who stood among them, and he ate a piece of broiled fish in their presence as proof that his body was materially real and not merely a phantasm.

A week later he appeared again to his disciples, Thomas this time being present with the other ten disciples (John 20:26-29). In the vignettes concerning Thomas in the Fourth Gospel (11:16; 14:5; 20:24) John limned for us a picture of Thomas as a somewhat pessimistic, theologically dull, hard-boiled skeptic who was willing to face head-on the significance of the facts that Jesus had been crucified and lay at that moment, so he believed, in Joseph's tomb. He was certainly not gullible, a person who would believe or who could be persuaded to believe just anything. At this time Thomas was the skeptic who was convinced that the game was over, that it had been a "nice ride" while it lasted, but that now they all should move on to something less discouraging and that promised more success! He must have asked himself more than once: "Why can the others not see all this as plainly as I do?" Hence the epithet "doubting Thomas" that Christian tradition has pinned on him – indeed, one well earned but in actuality not so unlike what

---

ending of Mark 16, there is some question as to its authenticity and veracity. The appearance accounts, in my opinion, are more easily harmonized if one has Jesus appearing first to the women as they hurried away from the tomb (Matt. 28:8-9), and then to Mary who followed Peter and John back to the tomb after informing them that the tomb was empty (see John 20:1-18). But a harmonization is still possible even if Jesus appeared first to Mary Magdalene.

all of the other disciples who were normal, rational, sane men had also been just a few days earlier! Again Jesus encouraged confidence in the reality and factuality of his resurrection by inviting Thomas to do precisely what the doubting disciple had said earlier would be necessary if he was ever to believe that Jesus had risen bodily from the dead, namely, to put his fingers into the wounds in Jesus' hands and side: "Put your finger here; see my hands. Reach out your hand and put it into my side. *Stop doubting and believe!*" John does not tell us whether Thomas did these things or not. I am inclined to believe that he did not for such a test was really unnecessary. Had not the risen Christ indicated by his very words that he knew about Thomas' required tests before Thomas could ask a thing? Thus Jesus proved in *his* way, not Thomas', that it was really he. Thomas was doubtless smitten by something else in that moment: The wounds of the risen Christ of Calvary (John 20:29) powerfully spoke to him and his doubts immediately all vanished away. And Thomas gave instantaneous utterance to one of the great professions of Scripture, certainly the greatest of any in the Gospels: "[You are] my Lord and my God!" Note Thomas' precise words: not just "'[You are] Lord and God" but "[You are] *my* Lord and *my* God." It was now not enough for Thomas that Jesus be both sovereign and divine. He was now to be these things for Thomas *personally*! Then Jesus appeared to seven disciples (Thomas among them) by the Sea of Galilee – the third time Jesus appeared to his disciples – and he prepared and ate breakfast with them (John 21:1-22). Then he appeared to the Eleven on a mountain of Galilee (Matt. 28:16-20), this occasion quite possibly being the same occasion when he appeared to more than five hundred disciples at one time, many of whom were still alive at the time Paul wrote 1 Corinthians (1 Cor. 15:6). Then he appeared to unbelieving James (John 7:5), his half-brother, converting him to the Faith (1 Cor. 15:7), and finally to the Eleven again on the occasion of his ascension into heaven (Luke 24:44-52; Acts 1:4-9; 1 Cor. 15:7). Then some years later he appeared to the church's arch-foe Saul of Tarsus, converting him to the Faith (Acts 9:1-5), and possibly too to Ananias (Acts 9:10).

Viewed as "evidence," it is true that the fact of the empty tomb alone does not prove that Jesus rose from the dead, but it does indicate that something had happened to his body after his entombment. The numerous post-crucifixion appearances of Jesus best explain what had happened to his body: *He had risen bodily from the dead.* For when a dead man's tomb is later found empty and he is appearing all over the place to different people the best explanation is that one has a bodily resurrection from the dead on his hands! And the fact that the appearances occurred (1) to individuals (Mary, Peter, James), to a pair of disciples, to small groups, and to large assemblies, (2) to women and to men, (3) in public and in private, (4) at all hours of the day – in the morning, during the day, and at night, and (5) both in Jerusalem and in Galilee, removes any and all likelihood that these appearances were simply hallucinations. An individual may have a hallucination, but it is highly unlikely, if not impossible, that entire groups and large companies of people would have the same hallucination at the same time!

One more highly significant feature about the Gospel accounts of the appearances of Jesus must be noted – they lack the smooth artificiality that always results when men of guile have conspired to make a contrived story plausible. One immediately encounters difficulty in harmonizing the four accounts of the several post-crucifixion appearances. Furthermore, according to the Gospel record it was women who first discovered the empty tomb and it was to women that Jesus first appeared after his resurrection. Given the fact that the testimony of women was virtually worthless in that day and time in a court of law, it is highly unlikely, if the disciples had conspired together to concoct the stories of the empty tomb and Jesus' several post-crucifixion appearances, that they would have begun their account with a significant detail that almost certainly would have discredited it at the outset. So in spite of the fact that it might have been more desirable from the disciples' point of view – in order to make their proclamation more plausible – to be able to say that men had first discovered the empty tomb and that it was to men that Jesus had first appeared, this feature as it stands in the Gospel accounts compels the conclusion that it simply did not happen that way and, concerned to report what in fact had happened because they were honest men, the disciples reported the event accordingly, refusing to embellish or to change their story as classical writers would have done. This feature of the Gospel record gives the account the ring of truth.

These two great strands of New Testament data – the empty tomb and Jesus' numerous post-crucifixion appearances – put beyond all legitimate doubt, I would urge, the facticity and the historicity of Jesus' bodily resurrection from the dead.

In addition to these two lines of argument, one may mention for their inferential value for the historicity of Jesus' bodily resurrection, third, the disciples' transformation from paralyzing discouragement immediately after his death to faith and certainty three days later, fourth, the later conversion of James and of Saul of Tarsus, and fifth, the visible institution in this world, even the church of Jesus Christ, whose members from the beginning worshiped Jesus Christ as God on the first rather than the seventh day of the week.[8] Each of these facts requires

---

[8]Regarding the church's shift in days for Sabbath observance from the seventh to the first day of the week I would assert that there were only two *essential* elements in the Old Testament Sabbath regulation: First, that it should be a day in which one rests from his labors, and second, that it should be devoted to the worship of God and the service of religion. All else was circumstantial and variable. Even the particular day of the week was variable and might be changed, if changed (1) for sufficient reason, and (2) by competent authority. Indeed, where these two factors would present themselves, the change would be obligatory. Were these two factors present in the first century, thereby legitimatizing the changing of the day of Sabbath observance from the seventh to the first day of the week? Indeed they were! A *sufficient reason* was patently present – the momentous event of Jesus' resurrection from the dead on the first day of the week! And *competent authority* was also patently present – the example and words of Christ himself, the Lord of the Sabbath, and his apostles (John 20:1, 19, 26; Acts 20:7; 1 Cor. 16:2; Heb. 10:25; Rev. 1:10).

for its explanation just such an event behind it as is provided by the bodily resurrection of Christ.

Now one might concede that everything said thus far is admittedly a strong case for Christ's bodily resurrection for those who believe the Bible is the Word of God since the entire discussion centered upon and derived its substance from the teaching of Scripture about this event. But, one might continue, the argument carries no weight for those who do not believe the witness of Scripture. What can I say in rejoinder? Well, I would note that those who are unimpressed by this argument have an entity that is not the Bible that they must explain, even the existence of the visible, extra-biblical institutional entity known as the church of Jesus Christ that has worshiped Christ as God from its beginning. What is more, the church for some reason just happens to worship Christ as such publicly on the first day of the week. How are these facts to be explained? How and why did the church of Jesus Christ appear in the world? What force

---

The inevitable conclusion that the Christian church reached was that the change of days was not only appropriate but also had Christ's and the apostles' manifest sanction. For the church to continue to observe the seventh-day Sabbath would by implication either have asserted that the *typical* redemptive event of the Exodus with its "seventh day" commandment *vis à vis* the antitypical redemptive work of Christ was the more important redemptive event whereas in fact the Exodus was only the foreshadowing of the redemptive work of Christ or would have denied the fact of the resurrection of Christ altogether. Second, such observance would have meant the rejection of the authority of Christ and his apostles (not to mention the Old Testament prophetic scriptures as well) over the church. Which is just to say that for the church to continue to observe the seventh-day Sabbath would have been to ignore the progressive nature of revelation that was here governing the situation. Geerhardus Vos in his *Biblical Theology* (Grand Rapids: Eerdmans, 1954), 158 (emphasis supplied), elucidates my point:

Inasmuch as the Old Covenant was still looking forward to the performance of the Messianic work, naturally the days of labor to it come first, the day of rest falls at the end of the week. We, under the New Covenant, look back upon the accomplished work of Christ. We, therefore, first celebrate the rest in principle procured by Christ, although the Sabbath also still remains a sign looking forward to the final

lay behind its origination? Why does it worship Christ, and why does it worship him publicly on the first day of the week? The unbeliever cannot and must not ignore these questions; he must squarely face them and provide an explanation that is as plausible as the one the Bible provides. But this he cannot do. Every naturalistic attempt to explain the emergence of the church in the world apart from the bodily resurrection of Jesus Christ lacks plausibility and has been found wanting. As N. T. Wright states: "All the alternative explanations [for the empty tomb and the "meetings with Jesus"] fail, and they were bound to do so."[9] In sum, the historical event of the bodily resurrection of Jesus Christ on the first day of the week provides the reason that the church not only worships Christ as God but also worships him on the first day of the week.

All this shows the blasphemous vacuity of Toronto filmmaker Simcha Jacobovici's 2007 so-called "documentary," *The Last Tomb of Jesus*, in which he tries to make the case that ten small ossuaries discovered in 1980 in a Jerusalem suburb may have held the bones of Jesus and his family. Completely apart from the fact that inspired Scripture witnesses to the contrary, the

---

eschatological rest. The O.T. people of God had to typify in their life the future development of redemption. Consequently, the precedence of labor and the consequence of rest had to find expression in their calendar. The N.T. Church has no such typical function to perform, for the types have been fulfilled. But it has a great historic event to commemorate, the performance of the work by Christ and the entrance of Him and His people through Him upon the state of never-ending rest. We do not sufficiently realize the profound sense the early Church had of the epoch-making significance of the appearance, and especially the resurrection, of the Messiah. The latter was to them nothing less than the bringing in of a new, the second, creation. And they felt that this ought to find expression in the placing of the Sabbath with reference to the other days of the week. Believers knew themselves [to be] in a measure partakers of the Sabbath fulfillment. *If the one creation required one sequence, then the other required another.*

[9]Nicholas T. Wright, *The Resurrection of the Son of God* (Minneapolis, 2003), 717.

odds in favor of these ossuaries containing Jesus' bones are infinitesimally small to non-existent. It is truly sad to see the imbecilic lengths to which some people are willing to go to rob mankind of its *only* hope, for without the bodily resurrection of Jesus Christ mankind has *no* hope of redemption and are yet in their sin.

I say again, the disciples were absolutely convinced by the fact of his empty tomb and by his many post-crucifixion appearances that Jesus Christ rose bodily from death on the third day after his crucifixion and were willing to endure persecution and to die for their conviction. If their testimony was a contrived fiction it is difficult to explain why not one of them, even when facing martyrdom, revealed that their story was a fabricated hoax.

Critical views answered

For many critical scholars today the appearance stories recorded in the Gospels are legends. But what is intriguing is that while these same scholars are not prepared to admit that Jesus actually rose bodily from the dead, most by far, if not all of them, will acknowledge the historicity of Jesus' death by crucifixion under Pontius Pilate, the subsequent despair of his disciples, their "Easter" experiences that they understood to be appearances to them by the risen Jesus, their resultant transformation, and the later conversion of Saul. In short, for many scholars today, while the resurrection of Jesus is not to be construed as a *historical event*, the disciples, they will admit, had some *subjective experiences* on the basis of which they proclaimed that Jesus had risen from the dead and had appeared to them. How should we respond to this?

Regarding the contention that the appearance stories are late legendary creations of the early church it is significant that New Testament scholars in increasing numbers are advocating that Paul's statements in 1 Corinthians 15:3-5 (the first written account of the resurrection appearances, since 1 Corinthians was written prior to the canonical Gospels) reflect the contents of a quasi-official early Christian creed much older than 1 Corinthians itself (which letter was written probably in the spring of A.D. 56 from Ephesus) which circulated within the *Palestinian* community of believers.[10] This assertion is based upon (1) Paul's references to his "delivering" to the Corinthians what he had first "received," terms suggesting that we are dealing with a piece of "tradition," (2) the stylized parallelism of the "delivered" material itself (see the four *hoti* clauses and the repeated *kata tas graphas* phrases in the first and third of them), (3) the Aramaic "Cephas" for Peter, suggesting an earlier Palestinian milieu, not a later Graeco-Roman milieu, for this tradition, (4) the traditional description of the disciples as "the Twelve," and (5) the omission of the appearances to the women from the list. If Paul, in fact, had "received" some of this "tradition," for example, that concerning Jesus' appearances to Peter and to James (referred to in 15:5, 7; see also Acts 13:30-31) directly from Peter and James themselves during his first visit to Jerusalem three years after his conversion (see Acts 9:26-28; Gal. 1:18-19), which is quite likely, then this pericope reflects what those who were the earliest eye-witnesses to the events that had taken place in Jerusalem were teaching on *Palestinian* soil within days after the crucifixion. This clearly implies that the material in 1 Corinthians 15:3b-5 is based on *early, Palestinian* eyewitness testimony and is hardly the reflection

---

[10]Günther Bornkamm, for example, refers to Paul's enumeration of the appearances of the risen Christ in 1 Corinthians 15:3-7 as "the oldest and most reliable Easter text...formulated long before Paul." He says of this "old form" that it "reads almost like an official record" (*Jesus of Nazareth* [New York: Harper and Brothers, 1960], 182). See also Wolfhart Pannenberg, *Jesus – God and Man* (Philadelphia: Westminster, 1968), 90-91. Excellent treatments of this generally accepted view may be found in George E. Ladd, "Revelation and Tradition in Paul," in *Apostolic History and the Gospel*, eds. W. Ward Gasque and Ralph P. Martin (Exeter: Paternoster, 1970), 223-30, particularly 224-25; Grant R. Osborne, *The Resurrection Narratives: A Redactional Study* (Grand Rapids: Baker, 1984), 221-25; and Gary R. Habermas, *Ancient Evidence for the Life of Jesus* (Nashville: Thomas Nelson, 1984), 124-27.

of legendary reports arising much later within the so-called Jewish Hellenistic or Gentile Hellenistic communities of faith. There simply was not enough time, with the original disciples still present in Jerusalem to correct false stories that might arise about Jesus, for legendary accretions of this nature to have risen and to have become an accepted feature of the "tradition." The presence of this "early confession" raises serious questions in turn concerning whether the appearance stories in the canonical Gospels are "legendary" stories based upon non-Palestinian sources, as many Bultmannian scholars have insisted. The facts strongly suggest otherwise – that the appearance stories in the Gospels are not legendary accounts as these Bultmannians contend.

Now it is significant that virtually all critical scholars today, as we have already noted, are prepared to admit that the disciples very shortly after Jesus' death – for some reason – underwent a remarkable emotional transformation, with confidence and certainty suddenly and abruptly displacing their earlier discouragement and despair. Even Bultmann admits the historicity of their "Easter" experience[11] and concedes that it was this newborn confidence that created the church as a missionary movement. What effected this transformation? If one replies as some scholars do that it was their belief that they had seen Jesus alive that effected this transformation from fear

---

[11]Rudolf Bultmann writes: "The resurrection itself is not an event of past history. All that historical criticism can establish is the fact that the first disciples came to believe in the resurrection" ("New Testament and Mythology" in *Kērygma and Myth*, ed. Hans-Werner Bartsch [London: SPCK, 1972], I, 42). Donald Guthrie, however, is quite right to insist at this point upon an explanation for their "Easter faith": "The more pressing need at once arises for an explanation of the 'event of the rise of the Easter faith.' The fact is that the skepticism of Bultmann over the relevance of historical enquiry into the basis of the Christian faith excludes the possibility of a satisfactory explanation of any event, whether it be the actual resurrection or the rise of Easter faith. The one is in no different position from the other. The rise of faith demands a supernatural activity as much as the resurrection itself, especially since it arose in the most adverse conditions" (*New Testament Theology* [Leicester: Inter-Varsity, 1981], 183).

to confidence, I must point out that this is tautological: One in the final analysis is simply saying that their *belief* that they had seen Jesus alive gave rise to their *faith* in Jesus' resurrection. We are still left with the question: What gave rise to their belief that they had seen Jesus alive and in person? Some prior event had to effect their belief that they had seen the risen Lord. What was it? If one replies that a visionary experience, that is, a hallucination, was the event that gave rise to their Easter faith, it must be asked what caused this visionary experience? Opinions vary, of course. Some scholars (Lampe, Schweizer, and Bornkamm, for example) have held that the resurrection appearances were mental images that the spiritual ego of the disembodied Jesus actually communicated back to his disciples from heaven, that the resurrection appearances, in other words, were real activities on the part of a "spiritualized" Jesus by which he entered into genuine personal intercourse with his disciples. Others have held that the experience of seeing Jesus after his crucifixion was a purely natural phenomenon – simply the work of autosuggestion. Bultmann, for example, suggests that Jesus' "personal intimacy" with them during the days of his ministry among them began to nourish such fond memories in them that they began to experience "subjective visions" of him and to imagine that they saw him alive again.[12] Michael Goulder, in the first of his two contributions to *The Myth of God Incarnate*, traces belief in Jesus' resurrection back to Peter who, being psychologically a "mumpsimus" whose beliefs are rather strengthened than weakened the more apparently refuted they are,[13] underwent a "conversion experienced in the

---

[12]Bultmann's actual words are as follows: "The historian can perhaps to some extent account for that faith from the personal intimacy which the disciples had enjoyed with Jesus during his earthly life, and so reduce the resurrection appearances to a series of subjective appearances" (*Kērygma and Myth*, 42).

[13]A "mumpsimus" is one who sticks obstinately to his opinion in spite of the clearest evidence that he is wrong. This word is first recorded in 1530 in William Tyndale's *The Practice of Prelates*. It seems that a medieval British monk persisted in employing a phrase in the Latin Eucharist wrongly, either

form of a vision" and imagined that he saw Jesus on that first Easter morning. That night he told the other disciples of his experience, and

> ...so great is the power of hysteria within a small community that in the evening, in [the hypnotic spell (?) of] the candlelight, with [the highly charged emotional situation of] fear of arrest still a force, and hope of resolution budding in them too [but on what ground?], it seemed as if the Lord came through the locked door to them, and away again. So [now note how effortlessly Goulder moves to his conclusion]...the experience of Easter fused a faith that was to carry Jesus to divinity, and his teachings to every corner of the globe.[14]

Gerd Lüdemann regards the resurrection story as a fantasy brought on by the grief and guilt of the apostles.[15] But really now, are these plausible explanations for the existence of the church and its faith? Hardly. In addition to the fact that all such views (1) leave the fact of the empty tomb unexplained (it is not too much to say that they are scuttled on the "rock" of the empty tomb, and (2) fail to come to terms with the variety of objective details in the several accounts of the appearances themselves. George E. Ladd has quite correctly pointed out that

> ...visions do not occur arbitrarily. To experience them requires certain preconditions on the part of the subjects concerned, preconditions that were totally lacking in the disciples of Jesus.

---

because he was illiterate or because his copy of the rite had been transcribed incorrectly. Instead of *quod in ore sumpsimus* that means "that we have taken into the mouth" he would say *quod in ore mumpsimus*, a phrase that is just plain nonsense. What makes his mistake memorable is what he said when his Latin was corrected. According to Richard Pace in 1517, later Dean of Saint Paul's Cathedral in London, the monk said: "I have said the Eucharist this way for forty years. I will not change my old *mumpsimus* for your new *sumpsimus*."

[14]Michael Goulder, "Jesus, The Man of Universal Destiny" in *The Myth of God Incarnate*, edited by John Hick (Philadelphia: Westminster, 1977), 59.

[15]Gerd Lüdemann, *The Resurrection of Jesus: History, Experience, Theology*, translated by John Bowden (Minneapolis, 1994).

To picture the disciples nourishing fond memories of Jesus after his death, longing to see him again, not expecting him really to die, is contrary to all the evidence we possess. To portray the disciples as so infused with hope because of Jesus' impact on them that their faith easily surmounted the barrier of death and posited Jesus as their living, risen Lord would require a radical rewriting of the Gospel tradition. While it may not be flattering to the disciples to say that their faith could result only from some objectively real experience, this is actually what the Gospels record.[16]

A number of Bultmann's students, including Gerhard Ebeling, Ernst Käsemann, Günther Bornkamm, and Ernst Fuchs, have rejected their teacher's dissolution of the bonds between faith and scientific history on the ground that it makes the Christian faith indistinguishable from commitment to a mythical Lord. Bornkamm, one of Bultmann's most influential students, admits that "the miracle of the resurrection does not have a satisfactory explanation in the inner nature of the disciples":

The men and women who encounter the risen Christ [in the Gospels] have come to an end of their wisdom. Alarmed and disturbed by his death, mourners, they wander about the grave of their Lord in their helpless love, trying with pitiable means – like the women at the grave – to stay the process and odor of corruption, disciples huddled fearfully together like animals in a thunderstorm (John xx.19 ff.). So it is, too, with the two disciples on the way to Emmaus on the evening of Easter day; their last hopes, too, are destroyed. One would have to turn all the Easter stories upside down if one wanted to present these people in the words of Faust: "They are celebrating the resurrection of the Lord, for they themselves are resurrected." No, they are not themselves resurrected. What they experience is fear and doubt, and what only gradually awakens joy and jubilation in their hearts is just this: They, the disciples, on this

---

[16]George E. Ladd, "The Resurrection of Jesus Christ" in *Christian Faith and Modern Theology*, edited by Carl F. H. Henry (Grand Rapids: Baker, 1964), 270-71.

Easter day, are the ones marked out by death, but the crucified and buried one is alive.[17]

Bornkamm goes on to say that by no means was "the message of Jesus' resurrection…only a product of the believing community," and he concludes that "it is just as certain that the appearances of the risen Christ and the word of his witnesses have in the first place given rise to this faith."[18] I concur, and would insist that the "objectively real experience" of the disciples, of which Ladd spoke earlier, came to them as the result of the "many convincing proofs" (Acts 1:3) of his bodily resurrection afforded them by Jesus' numerous post-crucifixion appearances to them. Nothing less than his actual bodily resurrection from the dead can explain both the empty tomb and the disciples' transformation from doubt and gloom to faith and the martyr's joy. Neither should we nor need we look for another explanation as the ground of their Easter faith.

The significance of Christ's bodily resurrection in the early Christian proclamation

The early church employed the truth of Jesus' bodily resurrection from the dead as the "doorway" into the good news of the gospel. A survey of the sermons in Acts 2:14-39; 3:13-26; 4:10-12; 5:30-32; 10:36-43; 13:17-41; 17:22-31 and the teachings in the New Testament letters (Rom. 1:2-4; 2:16; 8:34; 9:5; 10:8-9; 1 Cor. 15:3-4) make it clear that the apostles' use of Jesus' bodily resurrection as the "doorway" to the gospel was not an anomaly at all. They used it for its shock value! Indeed, *the stress in the primitive kērygma* ("proclamation") *was always on Christ's bodily resurrection from the dead.* In none of these recorded preachments does the preacher stop to elucidate for his auditors the saving significance of the death

---

[17]Bornkamm, *Jesus of Nazareth*, 184-85.

[18]Bornkamm, *Jesus of Nazareth*, 183. The reader should recall, however, that Bornkamm espouses the view that Jesus' resurrection appearances were visions sent from heaven and not physical in nature.

of Christ. Rather, they all stress that God reversed the verdict of men by raising bodily from the dead a certain man – even Jesus of Nazareth – who had been crucified as a criminal by the Roman authorities at the instigation of the Jewish Sanhedrin. Wilbur M. Smith asserts: "The Book of Acts testifies to the fact that it was by the preaching of the resurrection of Christ [not the cross, that] the world was turned upside down."[19] More accurately, it was the *implications* that the Apostles drew from that momentous event that stirred the first-century Roman world to its very roots, namely, that

- Christ's bodily resurrection from the dead showed him to be divine (Rom. 1:3-4);
- [20]

- Christ's bodily resurrection from the dead was the means to his enthronement in heaven as the Lord of men (Acts 2:36; 10:42; Rom. 14:9);

- Christ's bodily resurrection from the dead showed him to be the only Savior of men (Acts 4:12) and by implication gave evidence that all the other religions of the world are false and unworthy of men's devotion;

- Christ's bodily resurrection from the dead showed that God had set his seal of approval on Christ's atoning work (Rom. 4:25; Heb. 9:24-25; 13:20);

---

[19]Wilbur M. Smith, "Resurrection" in *Baker's Dictionary of Theology* (Grand Rapids: Baker, 1960), 453. In Luke's Acts Christ's "blood" is mentioned one time and that to the Ephesian elders (20:28). The fact that Christ was "killed" is mentioned only one time (3:15). The fact that he was "crucified" is mentioned twice (2:36; 4:10). The "tree" upon which he died is mentioned three times (5:30; 10:39; 13:29) while his "cross" is not mentioned at all! But his "resurrection" is mentioned ten times. The fact that he had been bodily "raised" from the dead is mentioned fourteen times. And the apostolic witness to the fact of his bodily resurrection is mentioned ten times. The emphasis in the primitive *kērygma* is clearly on the fact of Christ's bodily resurrection from the dead and its implications.

[20]See my exposition of this passage in my *Jesus, Divine Messiah: the New and Old Testament Witness* (Ross-shire, Scotland: Mentor, 2003), 372-84.

- Christ's bodily resurrection from the dead made him the true "temple site" at which men are to find and worship God (John 2:19, 21; Mark 14:58);

- Christ's bodily resurrection from the dead is an essential aspect of the faith that saves sinners (Rom. 10:9).

- Christ's bodily resurrection from the dead assures Christians of the truthfulness of his teaching (Matt. 16:21) and becomes their encouragement to be faithful to him when persecuted for their faith (2 Tim. 2:8);

- Christ's bodily resurrection from the dead, as the "first-fruits of those who sleep," assures both Christians and by implication all other people that the eschatological resurrection of the dead has already begun and therefore that someday they too will be raised bodily from death, some to weal and some to woe (John 5:28-29; Acts 24:15; Rom. 8:19ff.; 1 Cor. 15:20ff.; 1 Thess. 4:14; 1 Pet. 1:3-4);

- Christ's bodily resurrection from the dead and subsequent ascension to Lordship has established him as the Judge of all men (Acts 17:31); and

- The church was to celebrate the fact of Christ's bodily resurrection from the dead by assembling together every first day of the week throughout the year until the end of the world! The church must never allow mankind to forget the reason for the shift of the Sabbath from the seventh to the first day.

While one might legitimately remain unimpressed by the announcement that someone claiming to be the Jewish Messiah had been crucified on a Roman cross since thousands of people had so died, one cannot remain neutral regarding the announcement that God had raised this Jesus bodily from the dead. One cannot yawn and say, "How nice," and shake my hand and turn away with impunity! But Christ's resurrection was and is a miracle! It either occurred or it did not occur!

There is no room for neutrality here! This aspect of the primitive proclamation arrested the hearer's attention and demanded an intellectual decision from him. If he rejected it, he did so at the peril of his soul for he was denying the exalted Lord who would someday judge him. If he accepted it he was in the process of turning to the only Savior of mankind who had died for his sins. And when Paul explained that "good news" to him he explained it, please note, in terms of justification by faith alone!

This "doorway" into the early church's gospel presentation I have for years pointed out in my classroom lectures. While students have always been impressed at the time by this fact, not one of them to my knowledge has ever gone out and put the early church's approach to evangelizing the biblically illiterate into practice. I can only pray that someday one of them will. Who knows? Perhaps he will again turn the world upside down as they did!

Jesus' Ascension to Heaven

If Jesus rose bodily from the dead where is he today? He is not walking the streets of the great cities of the world and preaching in their public parks and marketplaces as he once did. All of the above implications of his bodily resurrection assume that Jesus forty days after his resurrection ascended to heaven as Luke reports. Indeed, in one sense one can say that Jesus' bodily resurrection was simply the means to the greater end of his ascension to messianic glory. So it is necessary, when one argues the case for Jesus' bodily resurrection, that he also deal with the historicity and the significance of its corollary, namely, Jesus' ascension to heaven.

The biblical data

Both in his Gospel and in his Acts Luke records that Jesus, upon completing his forty-day pre-ascension ministry, bodily "ascended into heaven." He employs three verbs to describe this momentous event: *anephereto*, "was led up" (Luke 24:51), *anelēmphthē*, "was taken up" (Acts 1:2, 11; see *analēmpseōs* in Luke 9:51), and *epērthē*, "was lifted up" (Acts 1:9). Of the four Gospel writers, Luke alone records the historical account of Jesus' ascension,[21] but he is by no means the only New Testament writer who refers to the event. Peter, Luke reports, referred to it in the upper room shortly after it occurred (Acts 1:22) and mentioned it in his sermons later (2:33-35; 3:21; 5:31); he also writes of it directly in 1 Peter 3:22. Stephen's statement in Acts 7:56 presupposes the past occurrence of it. Paul presupposes its historical actuality in his references to Christ's session at the Father's right hand in Romans 8:34 and Colossians 3:1, alludes to it in his words of Ephesians 1:20-22, 2:6, and Philippians 2:9-11, and expressly mentions it in Ephesians 4:8-10 and 1 Timothy 3:16. The Author of Hebrews presupposes it in 1:3, 13, 2:9, 8:1, 10:12, and 12:2, and expressly refers to it in 4:14, 6:20, and 9:24. John informs us that Jesus himself often alluded to it (John 3:13; 6:62; 7:33-34; 8:21; 13:33; 14:2, 28; 16:7-10; 20:17), and that he "knew that…he had come from God and was returning to God" (13:3). Finally, it is clear that Jesus presupposed it in his testimony before the Sanhedrin at his trial when he said: "…you will see the Son of Man sitting at the right hand of the Mighty One" (Matt. 26:64; Mark 14:62; Luke 22:69).

The Bultmann school of interpretation, not surprisingly, relegates Christ's ascension to the realm of legend, Bultmann himself writing:

> According to 1 Cor. 15:5-8, where Paul enumerates the appearances of the risen Lord as tradition offered them, the resurrection of Jesus meant simultaneously his exaltation; not until later was the resurrection interpreted as a temporary return to life on earth, and this idea then gave rise to the ascension story.[22]

---

[21]The long ending of Mark (16:9-20) records that Jesus "was taken up [*anelēmphthē*] into heaven and he sat at the right hand of God." This section is textually suspect, but it does reflect a tradition that accords with the Lukan report. It appears, in fact, to have been based mainly on the Lukan testimony.

[22]Rudolf Bultmann, *Theology of the New Testament*, translated by Kendrick Grobel (London: SCM, 1971), 1, 45.

This construction reflects his overarching aversion to the "intrusion" of the supernatural into the realm of space-time history, the ascension particularly mirroring for him the so-called "mythological" (non-scientific) "three-story universe" concept of the ancient world. But as Donald Guthrie states, this is not the construction that should be placed on the ascension data:

> The upward movement [of Jesus' physical figure] is almost the only possible method of pictorially representing complete removal. The OT instances of Enoch and Elijah present certain parallels. Inevitably a spatial notion is introduced, but this is not the main thrust of the Acts description. The focus falls on the screening cloud, precisely as it does in the transfiguration account.... The reality of the ascension is not seen in an up-there movement, so much as in the fact that it marked the cessation of the period of confirmatory appearances.[23]

B. F. Westcott, likewise, aids us by sensitively commenting on the nature of the ascension in these words:

> [Jesus] passed beyond the sphere of man's sensible existence to the open Presence of God. The physical elevation was a speaking parable, an eloquent symbol, but not the Truth to which it pointed or the reality which it foreshadowed. The change which Christ revealed by the Ascension was...a change of state, not local but spiritual. Still from the necessities of our human condition the spiritual change was represented sacramentally, so to speak, in an outward form.[24]

In other words, the "heavenly places" of Scripture expression are not to be conceived in spatio/temporal dimensions as "up

---

[23]Donald Guthrie, *New Testament Theology* (Leicester: Inter-Varsity, 1981), 395. See also Gordon H. Clark, "Bultmann's Three-Storied Universe," *A Christianity Today Reader*, ed. Frank E. Gabelein (New York: Meredith, 1966), 173-76.

[24]B. F. Westcott, *The Revelation of the Risen Lord* (London: Macmillan, 1898), 180.

there," but in spiritual dimensions to which Jesus' *glorified* corporeal existence was capable of adapting without ceasing to be truly human as evidenced by his activity described in Luke 24:31, 36, and John 20:19, 26. Therefore, Berkouwer quite properly declares:

> Only severe Bible criticism can lead one to a denial of the ascension and even to its complete elimination from the original apostolic *kērygma*.... To the Church it has always been a source of comfort to know that Christ is in heaven with the Father. And over against the denial of both the *ascensio* and *sessio* as being contrary to the "modern world conception," the Church may continue on the basis of Holy Scripture to speak of these facts in simplicity of faith.[25]

Still other critical scholars contend that the earliest ascension tradition in the church had Christ ascending to heaven directly from the cross with no intervening resurrection and pre-ascension ministry. Traces of this are purportedly found in the early Christian hymn cited by Paul in Philippians 2:6-11, for there Christ's humiliation and exaltation are contrasted with no mention of his burial and resurrection. John's Gospel also is supposed to reflect this "ascension from the cross" teaching – with no room for the resurrection or pre-ascension ministry – in such verses as 12:23 and 13:21 where John quotes Jesus to the effect that his hour of death would also mean his glorification. The author of Hebrews is also said to have favored the idea that Jesus ascended to heaven from the cross because of such statements as the one in 10:12: "But when this priest had offered for all time one sacrifice for sins, he sat down at the right hand of God." Again, the point is made, there is no mention here of Christ's resurrection or pre-ascension ministry.

Several things may be said about this effort to explain the ascension in non-literal, non-historical terms. First, apparently the operative (but erroneous) canon of exegesis here is this: if

---

[25]Gerritt C. Berkouwer, *The Work of Christ*, 206, 234.

a New Testament writer does not mention Christ's bodily resurrection in every context where he mentions Christ's exaltation or his session at the right hand of his Father, one may conclude that either he was unaware of the resurrection and the subsequent pre-ascension ministry or that the tradition he is citing was unaware of these events. But this is a *non sequitur*, and it imposes the highly artificial requirement upon the New Testament writer, if he believed in them, always to mention the bodily resurrection, pre-ascension ministry, and ascension whenever he mentions Christ's session at the right hand of God. Second, such a contention completely ignores the fact that all of these New Testament writers refer elsewhere – indeed, in the very works where the so-called "ascension from the cross" is supposedly taught – to the post-crucifixion resurrection of Christ: by *Paul*, for instance, in Galatians 1:1, 1 Thessalonians 1:10, 4:14, Acts 17:31, 26:23, 1 Corinthians 15:4, 12-20, Romans 1:4, 4:25, 6:4, 5, 9, 7:4, 8:11, 34, Ephesians 1:20, Philippians 3:10, Colossians 1:18, 2:12, 3:1, 2 Timothy 2:8; by *John* in John 2:19-21, 20:1-29, 21:1-22; and by the *author of Hebrews* in Hebrews 13:20. Moreover, Paul will make mention of the "many days" intervening between Christ's resurrection and ascension (Acts 13:31). Third, what Berkouwer says in defense of the Author of Hebrews, namely, that the only way these critical scholars can interpret the work in this way is to proceed with the following formula: "The glory of Christ in Hebrews minus Hebrews 13:20 equals the ascension 'from the cross,'"[26] may be said in defense of all of the New Testament writers: the only way they can be used to support the idea that Christ ascended to heaven from the cross and not some weeks later is to ignore all of the references in their writings to Christ's bodily resurrection, his post-crucifixion appearances, and his pre-ascension ministry.

One can only conclude that these scholars have very little confidence in the trustworthiness of the Gospels and epistles. For myself, I am aware of no reason advanced to date that can justify the wholesale abandonment of Luke's account of the

---

[26]Berkouwer, *The Work of Christ*, 208.

ascension. Accordingly, I will turn to the significance of Christ's ascension both for men and for himself.

Its significance

The ascension of Christ meant, of course, for those first disciples and also for every other disciple since then, in a word, his *separation* from them, not "with respect to his Godhead, majesty, grace and Spirit" (*Heidelberg Catechism*, Ques. 47; see also Ques 46), of course, for his spiritual communion with them remains unbroken and undisturbed as a genuine and even enhanced spiritual reality, but only with respect to his physical presence among them. This separation Christ himself spoke about in such places as Luke 5:35; John 7:33; 12:8; 13:33; 14:30; and 16:10 (see also 1 Pet. 1:8; 1 John 3:2).[27]

With respect to Christ himself, the Scriptures virtually exhaust available "triumphalist" language, images, and metaphors, to describe the significance of Christ's ascension for him. At this time I can only enumerate some of these descriptions. As his resurrection was the means to his ascension, and so a significant aspect of his total exaltation, so his ascension in turn was the means to his climactic exaltation and enthronement (*sessio*) at the Father's right hand as Holy One, Lord, Christ, Prince, and Savior of the world (Acts 2:27, 33-36; 5:31; Rom. 8:34; Col. 3:1; Phil. 2:9-11; Heb. 1:3). And what an exalted enthronement it is! If his ascension was "in [*en*] glory" (1 Tim. 3:16), exalting him thereby "higher than all the heavens" (Eph. 4:10; Heb. 7:26), he is also now "crowned with glory and honor" (*doxēi kai timēi estephanōmenon*, Heb. 2:9), "with angels, authorities, and powers in submission to him" (1 Pet. 3:22), with "everything under his feet," the Father alone excepted (1 Cor. 15:26; Eph. 1:22a), sitting "far above all rule

---

[27]The trained theologian will recognize by my formulation here that I am following the Reformed rather than the Lutheran tradition, which latter tradition maintains, because of its peculiar doctrine of the *communicatio idiomatum*, that Christ is, by virtue of the union of the two natures in the one person of Christ, *physically* ubiquitous and therefore physically present "in, with, and under" the elements of the Lord's Supper.

and authority, power and dominion, and every title that can be given, not only in the present age but also in the one to come" (Eph. 1:21). God has also "given" (*edōken*) him to be "head-over-everything for the church, which is his body, the fullness of him who fills everything in every way" (Eph. 1:22-23), indeed, who fills "the whole universe" (*ta panta*) with his power and lordship (Eph. 4:10). In sum, he now occupies the "highest place" (Phil. 2:9) of glory and honor (Heb. 2:9) which heaven can afford, and to him belongs *de jure* and *de facto* the titles "Lord of all" (Acts 10:36; Rom. 10:12) and Lord above all other lords (Acts 2:36; Phil. 2:9b; Rev. 19:16), "that at the name of Jesus, every knee should bow in heaven and on earth and under the earth, and every tongue confess that Jesus Christ is Lord" (Phil. 2:10-11a). The nature of his lordship entitles him sovereignly to bestow gifts of whatever kind he pleases upon men (Eph. 4:7-8, 11).

There can be no question, in light of such undeniably transparent language, that upon his resurrection and ascension (these two events may be construed quite properly together, even though the former preceded the latter by forty days, as the collective two-stage means to his exaltation to lordship), as the fruit and reward for his labors on earth, Jesus as the Messiah was granted supreme lordship and universal dominion over men. This is also suggested (1) by his own statement in Matthew 28:18: "All authority in heaven and on earth has been given to me," where he speaks of that messianic lordship which he received *de jure* at his resurrection but which he actually began to exercise *de facto* universally from heaven upon his ascension and present session at the Father's right hand (I would suggest that his references in Matthew 11:27 and John 17:2 to a possessed "delegated" dominion should be understood against the background of the covenant of redemption in the councils of eternity); (2) by Peter's statement "God made [*epoiēsen*: "appointed," "constituted"] him both Lord and Christ" (Acts 2:36) following upon his resurrection and ascension – another declaration, surely, of his *de facto* assumption of mediatorial reign as the God-man, since Jesus was obviously both Lord and Messiah by divine appointment from the moment of his incarnation; and (3) by Paul's statement: "because of which [*dio kai*] [earthly work] God exalted him to the highest place and gave him the name, the 'above everything' name," that is, the name of "Lord" (Phil. 2:9).

It would be a fatal mistake theologically to deduce from any of this that Jesus as the Son of God, who (though in union with our flesh) continued infinitely to transcend all creaturely limitations, became "Lord" only at his exaltation and acquired *as God's Son* only then *de jure* and *de facto* universal dominion. We must never forget that, for Peter, it was "our God and Savior Jesus Christ" who "sprinkles us with his blood" (2 Pet. 1:1; 1 Pet. 1:2). For Paul, likewise, it was "the Lord of Glory" (*ho kyrios tēs doxēs*), this expression meaning "the Lord to whom glory belongs as his native right," who was also just both "God over all" (Rom. 9:5) and "our great God" (Titus 2:13), who was crucified for us (1 Cor. 2:8). As God the Son, then, Jesus, of course, continued as he always had done to uphold all things by the word of his power (Heb. 1:3) and to exercise the powers and lordly rights which were intrinsically his as the divine Being (see Calvin, *Institutes*, 2.13.4). Consequently, when these apostles tell us that Christ Jesus was "appointed" Lord or was "exalted" and "given" authority and the title of "Lord" at his ascension, it is necessary that we understand that these things were said of him in his mediatorial role as the Messiah. It is appropriate to say these things about him but only because he, "the Son," who is intrinsically and essentially "rich," who is "Lord" by right of nature, had *first* deigned to take into union with himself our "flesh," becoming thereby "poor" (2 Cor. 8:9). It was as the divine-human Messiah, then, that he "acquired" or "was given" at his ascension *de facto* authority to exercise mediatorial dominion. It was not then the exaltation but the prior "humiliation" that was the "strange experience"[28] to the Son *as*

---

[28]Warfield, *The Lord of Glory* (Reprint; Grand Rapids: Baker, 1974 reprint), 225.

God. Conversely, it was not the humiliation but the "exaltation" that was the "new experience" to the Son *as the divine-human Messiah.* If we are to take history and specifically redemptive history seriously we must say this. We must be willing to say that, in a certain sense, the exaltation entailed for the Son an experience that had not been his before. This "new experience" was universal dominion, not as God *per se,* of course, but as the divine-*human* Messiah and as the divine-*human* Mediator between God and man. There Jesus as the exalted Lord is our Advocate in the presence of the Father (Rom. 8:34; Heb. 7:25; 1 John 2:1), and there we have our flesh in heaven: As the Scottish theologian John "Rabbi" Duncan said: "The dust of the earth is on the throne of the majesty on high." And from there he baptizes his people and engifts them with spiritual gifts. We learn elsewhere (1 Cor. 15:24-28) that this mediatorial dominion is a temporarily delegated authority. When he and his Father have subjugated finally all his and our enemies, then he will yield up, not his sonship,[29] but his delegated authority as the Messiah to God, even the Father, and his special mediatorial dominion will be "absorbed" into the universal and eternal dominion of the triune God.

In sum, the ascension meant for the Son, as the divine-human Messiah, the assumption of the prerogatives of the messianic investiture on a universal scale, rights that were already his by right of nature as God the Son, but that he "won" or was "awarded" as the incarnate Son for fulfilling the obligations pertaining to the estate of humiliation intrinsic to the messianic investiture.

It was this risen, glorified Christ, in precisely the terms of this his glorious lordship, who was made central to all early

---

[29]Herman Ridderbos, *Paul: An Outline of His Theology*, translated by John Richard DeWitt (Grand Rapids: Eerdmans, 1975) observes that "where there is a mention of the consummation of Christ's work of redemption, in the words of 1 Corinthians 15:28 (when the Son has subjected all things to the Father, then will he himself be subject to him, that God may be all in all), this cannot mean the end of the Sonship. One will rather have to judge the 'post-existence' of the Son intended here in the light of what is elsewhere so clearly stated of his pre-existence" (69).

apostolic preaching. The apostles were solicitous to draw out the implications of Christ's exclusive lordship over the world for their audiences. None of the modern clamor for religious pluralism was present in their preaching. For them there was an exclusivity and finality about God's revelation to men in Jesus Christ (Matt. 21:37; Mark 12:6; Heb. 1:1). For them, because of who Christ is, the work he did, the place he presently occupies, and the titles he bears, "salvation is in no one else, for there is no other name given among men by which we must be saved" (Acts 4:12). For them, as Jesus said, he alone is the way, the truth and the life (John 14:6). For them, he is the only mediator between God and man (1 Tim. 2:5). He is also the One who, as Lord, will judge the living and the dead at his appearing (Acts 10:42; 17:31; Rom. 14:9; 2 Tim. 4:1). And he is the one whose once-for-all offering up of himself as a sacrifice to satisfy divine justice is alone acceptable to God the Father, the "legal" representative of the Godhead, in the "great transaction" of redemption and the canceling of sin (Heb. 9:24-26), and whose high priestly intercession alone meets with the Father's approval (Rom. 8:34; Heb. 7:24-25; 1 John 2:1). In light of their exclusive claims for him, it is not surprising that the blessing and power of God rested upon the Apostles' evangelistic efforts.

Chapter Five

Faith's Reasons for Believing
in the Virgin Birth of Christ

In accordance with popular usage I am using the term "virgin birth" throughout this chapter to refer both to the virginal conception of Jesus Christ by Mary his mother without benefit of sexual intercourse with Joseph or any other human male and to the fact that she remained a virgin "until she had given birth to a son." This doctrine is the composite teaching of Isaiah 7:14, Matthew 1:18-25, and Luke 1:26-38. Admittedly, we are talking about a miracle here. We will consider these passages in turn.

Isaiah 7:14: an Exclusive Prophecy of Jesus Christ's Virginal Conception

A major aspect of an apologetic for the Christian faith that will pass biblical muster, I said earlier, is the argument for Christianity's truth claims based on the fulfillment of biblical prophecy. Isaiah 7:14-16 is one such prophecy, indeed, a major one, among over three hundred and thirty prophecies about Christ that are present in the Old Testament.

The historical setting of the prophecy
The historical setting of Isaiah 7:14-16 is well known. During the reign of King Ahaz of Judah, probably around 734 B.C., Rezin, king of Syria, and Pekah, king of Israel, formed an alliance against Ahaz of Judah to dethrone him and to install in his place the son of Tabeel as a puppet king who would do their

bidding and bring Judah into their coalition against Assyria.[1]
News of their alliance produced great anxiety throughout the
southern kingdom of Judah, so God sent Isaiah to Ahaz to
assure him that the plot against him would come to nought.
But as a warning to Ahaz not to rely on an alliance of his own
with Assyria (see 7:9), God informed him that within sixty-five
years the northern kingdom, in spite of its Syrian alliance, would
be "broken." We may note here that, historically, the alliance
was "broken" in three stages: Assyria overran Damascus and
despoiled the northern kingdom in 732 B.C. (2 Kings 15:29),
then Samaria fell to the Assyrians in 722 B.C., and finally, with
the Assyrians' deportation of the Israelite population and the
colonization of the land with non-Israelites (see 2 Kings 17:24ff.
and Ezra 4:2, 10), by 669 B.C. (sixty-five years from 734 B.C.),
when Ashurbanipal began to reign over Assyria, Ephraim's
destruction became complete.[2]

To give a pointed lesson to the faithless Ahaz that he should
put his confidence in God and not in Assyria, and also to
encourage him to do so, God graciously invited Ahaz to ask
him for a "sign" as a confirmation or attestation of his power to
save Judah. Ahaz was informed, in so many words, that he was
not to feel the slightest restriction in what he could request, for
he was granted unfettered latitude of request "whether in the
deepest depth or in the highest heights." Any righteous request
within the bounds of this antonymic venue, which is just to say
any righteous request at all, was permissible.

Since it has often been suggested that the word "sign" in 7:14
does not mean that the thing it signified should be understood
as necessarily entailing something out of the ordinary, I think

---

[1]See Edward J. Young, "The Immanuel Prophecy" in *Studies in Isaiah*
(London: Tyndale, 1954), 145-48, for a reconstruction of the historical
background to the prophecy in which reconstruction he harmonizes the details
of 2 Kings 15:37; 16:1-9; 2 Chronicles 28:5-21; and Isaiah 7:1-9.

[2]This is essentially the view of Gleason L. Archer, Jr., as well. See his
"Isaiah" in *The Wycliffe Bible Commentary*, edited by C. F. Pfeiffer and E.
F. Harrison (Chicago: Moody, 1962), 617.

it important to stress here that at least in Isaiah 7:11 it is quite apparent that it was precisely the "extraordinary" or the "miraculous" that God had in mind when he extended to Ahaz his invitation. And had Ahaz requested of him a miracle, God was prepared to perform one. This is evident from the proximate purpose that the sign was to serve (a proof that God was able to deliver and to keep his people) and from the unrestricted latitude in the invitation that was extended to Ahaz. It is not too much to say that upon this occasion God was "thinking miracle" and was ready to perform one as a sign to Ahaz of the certainty of his promise. So while it does not prove that the sign spoken of in verses 14-16 must be construed as entailing the miraculous, the fact that the referent of the word "sign" in verse 11 clearly is of that order lends strong credence to the presumption that, when God declared in verse 14 that he himself would give a "sign" since Ahaz had refused to ask for one, the words that then followed upon his declaration that he would give a "sign" also entailed the miraculous.

Ahaz, because he had doubtless already determined to rely upon a coalition with Assyria (see 2 Kings 16:5-9), feigned great piety and refused God's gracious invitation, hypocritically declaring that to ask for a sign was to test God (an appeal to Deut. 6:16). At this, God declared that he himself would give a sign – not only to Ahaz but also to the whole House of David – implying by this latter statement that the sign carried implications for the entire nation and for its future. God's sign is then stated in these verses (7:14-16):

> Behold, the *'almāh*, ["virgin," that is, the specific one before the prophet's mind in his vision] is [or, will be] with child and will give birth to a son and will call[3] his name Immanuel.

---

[3] I regard the verb *weqārā'th*, of the Massoretic Text as a *third* feminine singular ("and *she* will call") (supported by the *kalesei* in א) in spite of the fact that it has the appearance of a *second* feminine singular (supported by the *kaleseis* in A and B). Walter C. Kaiser, Jr., *Toward an Old Testament Theology* (Grand Rapids: Zondervan, 1978), 208, stresses that the verb should be construed as a second feminine singular ("and *you*, the *'almāh*, will call")

Curds and honey he will eat when he knows enough to reject the wrong and choose the right. For before the child knows enough to reject the wrong and choose the right, the land which you dread will be forsaken of her two kings.

The meaning and referent of the Hebrew word *'almāh*

What does the Hebrew word *'almāh* mean here, and to whom does it refer? These questions have received many responses. The consensus of modern Old Testament scholarship contends that the word simply means "young woman of marriageable age" who may or may not be married, a word that carries no implication either way regarding her virginity. But two studies of this word were conducted by Robert Dick Wilson and Edward J. Young respectively, in which the nine occurrences of the word in the Old Testament (five times in the plural – Song of Solomon 1:3; 6:8; Ps. 46, superscription; 68:25 (MT, v 26); 1 Chron. 15:20; four times in the singular – Gen. 24:43; Exod. 2:8; Prov. 30:19; Isa. 7:14) were investigated (1) contextually, (2) against their historical background, and (3) in the versions, including in the case of Young's study a consideration of the Ras Shamra material from ancient Ugarit. Both came to the same conclusion: *Never is the word employed to describe a married woman.* Their conclusions are worthy of quotation. Robert Dick Wilson, who could speak forty-five different languages and dialects, wrote:

> ...two conclusions from the evidence seem clear; first, that *'alma,* so far as known, never meant "young married woman";

that indicates that the *'almāh* was standing before the prophet as he spoke. But *Gesenius' Hebrew Grammar* (Corrected second English edition; Oxford: Clarendon, 1910) explains this particular form as a "rarer form" of the *third* feminine singular in *lamedh 'aleph* verbs (see 120, par. 44f, 206, par. 74g). Besides, Matthew's citation of Isaiah 7:14 reads *kalesousin* ("and *they* will call"), the third common *plural* form, suggesting, to say the least, that in the final analysis precisely who it was who would actually do the "naming" of the child apparently is of no great moment. The verb form simply cannot support the exegetical freight that Kaiser wants it to carry.

and secondly since the presumption in common law and usage was and is, that every *'alma* is virgin and virtuous, until she is proven not to be, we have a right to assume that Rebecca and the *'alma* of Is. vii. 14 and all other *'almas* were virgin, until and unless it shall be proven that they were not.[4]

Wilson's first point is based on the usage of the word. His second point simply means that a gentleman will give a young woman the benefit of the doubt as to whether she is virtuous or not until proven otherwise, which is just to say that scholars who do not believe that *'almāh* means "virgin" are not gentlemen. E. J. Young's conclusion is similar to Wilson's:

We are far from asserting that this word is the precise equivalent of the English "virgin." It rather seems to be closer to words such as "damsel" or "maiden", words which most naturally suggest an unmarried girl. In fact the Hebrew word *'almah* would seem to be a shade stronger than the English words "maiden" and "damsel", since there is no evidence that it was ever used of a married woman. Consequently, one is tempted to wish that those who repeat the old assertion that it may be used of a woman, whether married or not, would produce some evidence for their statement.

In the light of this fact that the word is never used of a married woman, and in the light of the Ras Shamra texts, where it is found as a practical synonym of *bethulah* ["virgin"], both words there referring to an unmarried goddess, we believe that the translators of the Septuagint brought out the true force of the passage when they rendered the word by *he parthenos* ["virgin"].[5]

Actually, it does not matter how many authorities one can find who will agree that the Hebrew word means "young woman

---

[4]Robert Dick Wilson, "The Meaning of 'Alma (A.V. "Virgin") in Isaiah VII. 14" in *Princeton Theological Review* XXIV (1926), 316.

[5]E. J. Young, "The Immanuel Prophecy" in *Studies in Isaiah*, 183-84; see also J. Gresham Machen, *The Virgin Birth of Jesus Christ* (New York: Harper and Brothers, 1930), 288.

of marriageable age" whether married or not, or how many authorities one can find who say that the Hebrew word means "virgin." Were it the case that one could find none in the latter category it is still a fact that Matthew, guided by the Holy Spirit, had already placed the validity of the latter conclusion beyond all doubt when he declared (1) that the Lord meant "virgin" (*parthenos*) when he said what he did to Ahaz, and (2) that Jesus' miraculous conception and birth were the fulfillment of Isaiah's prophecy:

> All this took place to fulfill what the Lord had said through the prophet: "The virgin will conceive and give birth to a son, and they will call him Immanuel" – which means, "God [is] with us." (Matt. 1:22-23)

If Matthew is following the LXX here, as many scholars urge, an interesting feature of the LXX translation is that it reflects the *pre-Christian Jewish interpretation* of Isaiah 7:14. It is simply not the case, as some modern Jewish scholars have maintained, that the original reading of the LXX was *hē neanis*, "the young woman") rather than *hē parthenos* ("the virgin") and that early Christians tampered with the text by substituting the latter for the former. The truth of the matter is that Aquila, a second-century convert to Judaism, did an independent Greek translation of the Hebrew Bible and deliberately substituted the former for the latter to avoid the Christian interpretation. But the original LXX translators, doing their work two to three centuries before the birth of Christ and knowing nothing of the fact itself, translated *'almāh* by *parthenos*, because they were attempting to deliver a competent translation. Cyrus H. Gordon, one of the most knowledgeable Jewish scholars in Mediterranean studies in this generation, acknowledged as much:

> The commonly held view that "virgin" is Christian, whereas "young woman" is Jewish is not quite true. The fact is that the Septuagint, which is the Jewish translation made in pre-Christian Alexandria, takes *'almah* to mean "virgin" here.

Accordingly, the New Testament follows Jewish interpretation in Isaiah 7:14.... The aim of this note is...to call attention to a source that has not been brought into the discussion. From Ugarit of around 1400 B.C. comes a text celebrating the marriage of the male and female lunar deities [Nikkal and Yarih]. It is there predicted that the goddess will bear a son.... The terminology is remarkably close to that of Isaiah 7:14. However, the Ugaritic statement that the bride will bear a son is fortunately given in parallelistic form; in 77.7 she is called by the exact etymological counterpart of Hebrew *'almah* "young woman"; in 77.5 she is called by the exact etymological counterpart of Hebrew *betulah* "virgin." Therefore, the New Testament rendering of *'almah* as "virgin" for Isaiah 7:14 rests on the older Jewish interpretation, which in turn is now borne out for *precisely this annunciation formula* by a text that is not only pre-Isaianic but is pre-Mosaic in the form that we now have it on a clay tablet.[6]

Two caveats are necessary here, however. Even though Gordon's remarks support the view that Isaiah 7:14 was regarded by Jewish scholars before the birth of Christ as referring to a *virgin* birth, the reader must be cautioned not to follow Gordon in his implied suggestion that the New Testament *via Isaiah* is simply reflecting an ancient pagan annunciation formula used to announce the birth of gods and kings. It may well have been such originally, but in Isaiah, as Young trenchantly notes,

> ...this formula is lifted from its ancient pagan context and made to introduce the announcement of the birth of one who is truly God and King. No longer must this phrase serve the useless purpose of heralding the birth of beings who had never existed and never would exist. Now, for the first time in its history, it becomes a true "divine-royal *euangelion* formula."[7]

---

[6]Cyrus H. Gordon, "*'Almah* in Isaiah 7:14" in *The Journal of Bible and Religion* XXI, 2 (April 1953), 106.

[7]Young, "The Immanuel Prophecy" in *Studies in Isaiah*, 160; see Luke 1:31 for the *final* occurrence of the formula in Gabriel's "birth annunciation."

Finally, Gordon's last comment implies a post-fifteenth-century date for Moses, when in actuality Moses lived contemporaneously with the Ugaritic corpus from ancient Ras Shamra.

Now there can be no doubt that Matthew, even granting that he followed the LXX (but only because of the propriety of its translation), intended by *parthenos* the meaning of "virgin." This is clear from his statements on both sides of his citation of the Immanuel prophecy, specifically, his statements "before they came together" (1:18), "what is conceived in her is from the Holy Spirit" (1:20), and "[Joseph] had no union with her until she gave birth to a [Luke 2:7 reads "firstborn son"; note: Luke's word is "firstborn" (*prōtotokon*), implying that she had other children after Jesus' birth, *not* "only" (*monogenēs*)] son" (1:25).[8]

---

[8]The natural implication of the phrase "before they came together" and the phrase "had no union with her until" is that Joseph and Mary had normal conjugal relations after the birth of her firstborn. This implication is supported by the fact that the Synoptic Gospels mention his "brothers" James, Joseph, Simon, and Judas and "all his sisters" (Matt. 12:46-50; 13:54-56; Mark 3:20-21, 31-35; Luke 8:19-21). But Roman Catholicism, in order to maintain its dogma of Mary's perpetual virginity, contends that these were sons and daughters of Joseph by a previous marriage and thus were Jesus' legal half-brothers and half-sisters. Beside the fact that it is mere supposition that Joseph had been previously married, such a view would mean that not Jesus but the eldest son of Joseph, whoever he was, would have been the legal heir to the throne of David.

Another suggestion, based on a misinterpretation of John 19:25, is that these four named "brothers" and several unnamed "sisters" were Jesus' cousins, the sons and daughters of "his mother's sister, Mary the wife of Clopas." Since it is unlikely, however, that two sisters would have had the same name, it is best to understand John 19:25 to mean that standing by Jesus' cross were his mother, his mother's unnamed sister (likely Salome [see Mark 15:40] who may have been the wife of Zebedee and thus John's mother [see Matthew 27:56]), with the unrelated Mary, the wife of Clopas, likely being the mother of James the younger and of Joseph mentioned in Mark 15:40. Nevertheless, in spite of their misreading of John 19:25 some who espouse the "cousin theory" further compound the problem that Mary the wife of Clopas was Mary's sister by proposing that Clopas himself was Alphaeus the father of James and that James the son of Alphaeus (Matt. 10:3) was the Lord's cousin and thus one of the Twelve. But why then would John

We conclude, then, at this point in our discussion that God's "sign" to the House of David entailed the announcement that a virgin would conceive *while a virgin* and *while still a virgin* bring forth a son – that is, she would be a virgin throughout the entire baby-producing process – definitely a miracle and answering thereby the demands of the implied meaning in the word "sign" that was God's characterization of the future event. This interpretation necessarily eliminates as referents of the *'almāh*, both Ahaz's wife, whom Vriezen and Kaiser suggest,[9] and Isaiah's own wife (see 7:3, 8:3-4 for the evidence that Isaiah was married), as Archer has urged.

The predicted virginal conception, however, does not exhaust the miraculous features of the sign, for it is apparent, if the mother was to conceive virginally, that the Child, having

---

inform us that his "brothers" did not believe in him (John 7:5) when James, one of these "brothers," had long been among the Twelve? And why would these four young men, if they were sons of Mary the wife of Clopas, be so often mentioned with Jesus' mother when their own mother was still alive?

These features of the biblical material render most likely the natural view that these "brothers" and "sisters" were the biological sons and daughters of Joseph and Mary and were thus Jesus' half-brothers and half-sisters. This view also best honors the institution of marriage.

[9]Th. C. Vriezen, *An Outline of Old Testament Theology* (Newton, Mass.: Charles T. Branford, 1958), 360, fn. 1; Walter C. Kaiser, Jr., *Toward an Old Testament Theology*, 209-10; see also Kaiser's article, "The Promise of Isaiah 7:14 and the Single-Meaning Hermeneutic," in *Evangelical Bulletin* 6 (1988), 55-70. In his treatment of the passage Kaiser urges specifically that the *'almāh* was Abi (a variant form of Abijah), daughter of Zechariah and wife of Ahaz (2 Kings 18:2), and that the Immanuel child was Hezekiah. But this cannot be, since, as Kaiser himself recognizes (but discounts because of dating problems surrounding the latter's reign), "on present chronologies [Hezekiah] must have been nine [*sic*] years old at that time (about 734 B.C.)" (209). Actually, in my opinion, Hezekiah may have been around nineteen years old in 734 B.C., coming to the throne as he apparently did in 728/27 B. C. at the age of twenty-five (see 2 Kings 18:1-2, 9, 10). The reference to his "fourteenth year" in 2 Kings 18:13 may refer to the fourteenth year of the special fifteen-year dispensation of *additional* life that God granted him (see 2 Kings 20:1-11). This would be 701 B.C., the year that Old Testament scholars assert was the year in which Sennacherib invaded Judah.

no biological father, while certainly human would himself necessarily be *unique*. Young aptly comments: "The emphasis which has been placed upon the mother of the child leads one to the conclusion that the child himself is unusual."[10] And the direction in which the text itself prompts one to look for help in apprehending the nature of his uniqueness is toward the name he was to be given – "Immanuel." What does this name tell us about his character?

The Hebrew *'immānu'ēl* (Gr. *Emmanouēl*), meaning "With us [is] God," occurs only three times in the Bible as a proper name (Isa. 7:14; 8:8; Matt. 1:23) and, I would urge, it is the name of the same person.[11] Now it does not do justice to the virginally conceived child's uniqueness among men to argue as some do that the name Immanuel was intended merely to symbolize the fact that God was present with the nation in her coming deliverance and nothing more than this. The name by itself, I grant, *might* symbolize nothing more than this, but a *virginally conceived* child who would bear the name "Immanuel" might well *be* in fact what his name suggests. I say this for the following four reasons:

First, in Scripture the name that was given to one (or that one bore) quite often was *descriptive or declarative of what one was* (see, for example, Gen. 17:5, 15-16; 27:36; Exod. 3:13-14; 6:2-3; 1 Sam. 25:25; 2 Sam. 12:25; Matt. 1:21). Just as in Isaiah 4:3 where those who are "called holy" are not simply *nominally* so but *are in fact* holy (see also Hosea 1:10, Isa. 1:26; Luke 1:31, 35), so also in Isaiah 7:14, to *call* the child "Immanuel" can and, I would submit, did intend to designate what he would in fact be.

---

[10]Young, "The Immanuel Prophecy" in *Studies in Isaiah*, 194.

[11]The occurrence of *'immānu'ēl* in Isaiah 8:10, following as it does the Hebrew particle *kî*, "for"], should be taken as a statement and not as a proper name; that is to say, the clause should be rendered "for God is [shall be] with us" rather than "for – [I am] Immanuel!" Therefore, I will not lay any weight upon it in the present discussion except to say that it is an obvious play on the proper name in 8:8 and gives the reason why Assyria's impending devastation of Judah would not prove to be ultimately fatal for Immanuel's land – "for God [in the person of *'immānu'ēl*] is with us."

Second, the occurrence of the name in Isaiah suggests that the Child of the Immanuel prophecy was divine. From 8:8 we learn that Immanuel was the *Owner* of the land of Israel, and that he would protect the people of God (see 8:10), clearly implying that the Child would possess divine prerogatives and attributes.

Third, the fact that Matthew "by-passed" the name "Jesus" (but see the angel's explanation of "Jesus" which is reminiscent of Ps. 130:8) which was equally "un-Greek" and translated "Immanuel" (the third occurrence of the name) into Greek (1:23) surely suggests, against the background of the angel's earlier statement that "what is conceived in her is from the Holy Spirit" (1:20), that he intended to teach that in the person of the virginally conceived offspring of Mary God himself had come to dwell with his people *en sarki* ("in flesh") (see Jesus' later promises to *be with his people* in Matt. 18:20 and 28:20).

Fourth, the further descriptions of this Child in Isaiah 9:6 – "wonderful Counselor, mighty God, everlasting Father, Prince of peace" (not to mention the numerous New Testament applications to Jesus of other descriptions of the Child found in Isaiah 7-12, the so-called "Volume of Immanuel"[12]) – indicate, as we shall see shortly, that the Child of the Immanuel prophecy was to be, as virginally conceived, the divine Son of God.

---

[12]For example, (1) the "Lord of hosts" of Isaiah 8:13 is the "Lord Christ" according to 1 Peter 3:14-15; (2) this same "Lord of hosts" of Isaiah 8:14 who is "a stone that causes men to stumble and a rock that makes them fall" is the Christ whom the Jews rejected according to Romans 9:33; (3) and yet he is to be distinguished from the Lord in some sense for, according to the Author of Hebrews, it is the Christ who says in Isaiah 8:17: "I will put my trust in him" (Heb. 2:13), and who speaks of having received children from the Lord in Isaiah 8:18 (see "everlasting Father" in Isa. 9:6) (Heb. 2:13); (4) the geographic locale specified in Isaiah 9:1-2 is applied to the locale of Jesus' ministry in Matthew 4:13-16; (5) the nature of the Child's reign described in Isaiah 9:7 is the background to Gabriel's statement in Luke 1:32-33; (6) the statement that only a remnant in Israel relies upon the Lord and returns to the mighty God in Isaiah 10:20-23 (see "mighty God" in Isaiah 9:6) Paul in Romans 9:27-28 applies to the then-current wide-scale rejection of Jesus Christ; and (7) the Root of Jesse to whom the natives will rally in

Only such an understanding of the name as we have suggested here explains the uniqueness of the Child who was to be conceived in the womb of the virgin mother without the benefit of a human biological father. The biblical evidence, in sum, is quite overwhelming in support of this virginally conceived Child being God in the flesh and thus the rightful bearer of the descriptive name "Immanuel" – "With us [is] God!"

The problem of relevance
The major exegetical objection to this understanding of Isaiah 7:14 is that to insist upon its sole fulfillment in Christ scuttles any relevance of the prophecy for Ahaz's day. A "sign" that was not to be fulfilled for seven and a half centuries, it is often urged, could hardly have been of any value to the House of David in the eighth century B.C. This objection is found in both non-evangelical and evangelical studies of the passage. Of course, in the case of the latter, a valiant effort is made so to interpret the passage that it portends a birth in Isaiah's own day *and* the birth of Christ later. For example, William Sanford LaSor has argued that the Hebrew word *'almāh* must be interpreted broadly enough so that, in addition to its ultimate application to the *virgin mother* of Jesus Christ, it may refer penultimately to an earlier *young woman* in Isaiah's day who would conceive and bear a son *by natural means* whose son would bear the name Immanuel and who would thus become a sign of hope to Ahaz of a deliverance which God was to bring to pass within a dozen years.[13]

Isaiah 11:10 is the Christ according to Paul in Romans 15:12. Clearly, the Child of the "Volume of Immanuel" is Deity incarnate and yet is in some sense to be distinguished from Deity. Only the postulation of the correlative doctrines of the Incarnation and the Trinity can resolve this otherwise clear contradiction. More examples could be given: As a further explication of the content of that one "more superior name [than "angel"]" of "Son," the Author of Hebrews declares that when this Child was born, God commanded that all the angels should worship him (Heb. 1:6; see Deut. 32:43 LXX), and that as God's Son he is himself the "God" of Psalm 45:6-7 and the "Lord" of Psalm 102:25-27. Surely he is deity.

[13]William Sanford LaSor, "Isaiah 7:14 – 'Young Woman' or 'Virgin'?" (Pasadena: privately published, 1952), 8-9.

Gleason L. Archer also understands the Immanuel prophecy in 7:14 as having a dual fulfillment, the typical fulfillment being in Maher-Shalal-Hash-Baz (8:1-4), son of Isaiah, with the antitypical fulfillment being, of course, in Jesus, son of Mary.[14] But in order to justify this interpretation, Archer must postulate, first, that Shear-Jashub (7:3) was Isaiah's son by a previous wife who had died leaving Isaiah a widower, and second, that he was engaged to be married to a prophetess who was, at the time of the prophecy and her marriage to Isaiah, a virgin but who, of course, would not have been a virgin at the time of her conception and delivery. But both of these features in his interpretation – Isaiah's widower-hood and his engagement to be married again to the virgin prophetess – are pure assumptions since the Scriptures say nothing about *two* wives. They are simply assumptions that Archer must necessarily make if he is to hold his particular dual-fulfillment view.

A careful reading of both Isaiah 7:14 and Matthew 1:22-25 will disclose, however, that the *'almāh* was to be a virgin not only at the time of her marriage but also *at the time of her conception and her delivery*. Consider the following: The *parthenos*, whom Matthew expressly affirms was a " virgin" (and whom Archer happily acknowledges was a virgin at the time of the prophecy), both Isaiah and Matthew also represent as the *same* subject who both conceived and delivered: "…the *virgin* shall *conceive* and [the virgin shall] *bring forth* a son." There is no hint that the virginal status of the *parthenos* changed between the description of her as such and the two verbs ("conceive" and "bring forth") that follow that description. An analogy would be John 1:14 where we are informed that "the Word *became* flesh and *dwelt* among us." The Word, evangelicals would argue, without changing into something else and ceasing to be all that he is as the Word *became* flesh. And the same Word is the subject of the next verb "dwelt" as well. Similarly, the *parthenos*, without ceasing to be a *parthenos*, both conceived and delivered. This is the reason – what other reason can account for it? – that Matthew underscored

---

[14]Archer, "Isaiah" in *The Wycliffe Bible Commentary*, 618.

the truth that Joseph had no sexual relations with Mary until *after* she had given birth to Jesus (1:25). He clearly understood that Mary's virginity throughout the duration of her pregnancy was vitally necessary as a fulfillment feature of the Isaiah 7:14 statement that he had cited. In my opinion, this fact necessarily eliminates a dual fulfillment for Isaiah 7:14 and requires that the Immanuel prophecy be applied exclusively to Christ. The reader will have to judge whether a woman who would be a virgin at her marriage but a virgin neither at conception nor at delivery (that is, the prophetess) could have possibly served as a type of the future antitypical woman who during the days of her betrothal would be a virgin both at conception and at delivery (that is, Mary), and whether Isaiah 7:14 can be so read that it allows both of these quite dissimilar situations to fall within the parameters of the linguistic tolerances of the verse. In my opinion, this resort to "double fulfillment" or "double meaning," as J. Barton Payne urges, fails to take seriously the fact that "the *'almāh* of Isa 7:14 either was a virgin or was not and cannot simultaneously predict these two opposing meanings."[15] As I have said, it flies in the face of Matthew's assertion that the Immanuel prophecy describes the *'almāh* as a virgin *not only at the moment of conception but also throughout her pregnancy up to and including the event of her delivery.*

The solution to the problem of relevance

What is the solution, then, to the problem of relevance for its contemporaries of a "sign" prophecy that was not to be fulfilled for seven and a half centuries? At least four solutions have been proposed in response to this objection:

1. Joseph Addison Alexander in his great critical commentary on Isaiah argued that the assurance that Christ was to be

---

[15]J. Barton Payne, *Enyclopedia of Biblical Prophecy* (New York: Harper and Row, 1973), 292, fn. 61; see also J. A. Alexander, *Isaiah Translated and Explained* (Philadelphia: Presbyterian Board of Publication, 1851), I, 106-07.

born in Judah, of its royal family, might be a *sign* to Ahaz that the kingdom should not perish in his day; and so far was the remoteness of the sign in this case from making it absurd or inappropriate that the further off it was, the stronger the promise of continuance of Judah which it guaranteed.[16] The problem with this response is that it seems to make the relevance of the prophecy turn on the *awareness* on the part of the original recipients that its fulfillment was to be in the *distant* future.

2. J. Barton Payne, with keener insight, argued that the relevance of the prophecy for the eighth century B.C. was dependent neither upon the immediacy of its fulfillment nor upon Ahaz's awareness of its distant future fulfillment. A prophecy, he writes,

...may serve as a valid force in motivating conduct [and instilling consolation], irrespective of the interval preceding its historical fulfillment, provided only that the contemporary audience *does not know* when this fulfillment is to take place. Even as the Lord's second coming should motivate our faithful conduct, no matter how distant it may be..., so Isaiah 7:14, on His miraculous first coming, was equally valid for motivating Ahaz, 730 years before Jesus' birth.[17]

That is to say, according to Payne, precisely because Ahaz *did not know* when the prophecy would be fulfilled, "the time lapse need not diminish the contemporary relevance of Isaiah's warning" even though Immanuel was not to appear for more than seven centuries.[18] Payne's

---

[16]J. A. Alexander, *The Earlier Prophecies of Isaiah* (New York: Wiley and Putnam, 1846), I, 119; Charles Lee Feinberg, "The Virgin Birth in the Old Testament and Isaiah 7:14" in *Bibliotheca Sacra* 119 (1962), 258, also seems to support this proposal.

[17]Payne, *Enyclopedia of Biblical Prophecy*, 292, emphasis supplied.

[18]Payne, *Enyclopedia of Biblical Prophecy*, 291.

interesting solution is the antithesis to that proposed by Alexander, inasmuch as Alexander's view looks to the recipients' *awareness* of the prophecy's distant fulfillment as the ground of its relevance whereas Payne's view roots the relevance of the prophecy in the recipients' *lack of awareness* of the time of its fulfillment. Payne's view resolves the difficulty implicit in Alexander's proposal. But his view also appears to cut off from 7:14 the following two verses, verses which as a part of the sign statement seem to provide the very measure of time (in relative terms) between that moment and Judah's subsequent deliverance from the threat from the north that Payne seems to suggest is absent from the passage.

3. As did John Calvin, Robert I. Vasholz attempts to show the relevance of the prophecy to Ahaz's day by arguing that, while Isaiah 7:14-15 predicts the virgin birth of Christ, 7:16 does not refer to him.[19] He thinks it "regrettable" that English translations invariably suggest by their translation of *hanna'ar* ("the boy") that 7:16 speaks of the same child that is in 7:14-15. He translates 7:16: "Before a boy knows enough to reject the wrong and choose the right, the land of the two kings you dread will be laid waste." He recognizes that the Hebrew employs the article with the word "boy," but he cites *Gesenius' Hebrew Grammar*, 126q-r, to the effect that the Hebrew article may denote an indefinite person or thing that is present to the mind of the narrator, as grounds for his translation.

I acknowledge the validity of the syntactical rule he cites but question its applicability in this instance since in verse 14 specific reference is made to the virgin's "son" (*bēn*) and in verse 15 *that* son is the antecedent referent of

---

[19]Robert I. Vasholz, "Isaiah and Ahaz: A Brief History of Crisis in Isaiah 7 and 8" in *Presbyterion: Covenant Seminary Review* XIII/2 (Fall 1987), 82-83.

the third masculine singular form of the verb *yō'kēl* ("he will eat") and the third masculine singular suffix attached to the infinitive construct *lᵉdha'tô*) ("when he knows"). It is very unlikely, against this background, that *hanna'ar* in the next verse (vs 16) would then refer to just any boy in general and not to the boy just mentioned. It is also striking, to say the least, that when precisely the same terms (*bēn... hanna'ar*) occur again only a few verses later (8:3-4), Vasholz himself translates: "Before the boy [the "son" referred to in the preceding verse] knows."

4. Therefore, I believe that the solution proposed by J. Gresham Machen, E. J. Young, and R. Laird Harris is the best to date, all three arguing that the "sign" is not to be restricted to the virgin's miraculous conception and to the unique character of her Son (7:14) but must include the words of 7:15-16 as well, and making, accordingly, *the period of the early years of the miraculous child's life the measure of the time of Judah's dread.*[20]

In these two verses we are informed that the child would "eat curds and honey when he knows enough to reject the wrong and choose the right." What does this mean? According to Isaiah 7:21-22, "curds and honey" would be the common fare of the remnant who remained in the land after the king of Assyria had assaulted the nation and deported much of its populace. Because of the diminished number of people in the land, there would be an abundance of milk, with the result that they "will have curds to eat. All who remain in the land will eat curds and honey." In other words, this aspect of God's sign to the House of David warned of a coming period of humiliation that, in light of verse 17, would envelop not only Israel but Judah as well *for a time*. The statement that the marvelous Immanuel Child would eat curds and honey symbolically meant then

---

[20]They differ only on details.

for Judah that the Immanuel child would identify himself
with the remnant people from whom he would eventually
come. But that the nation's then-present distress was to
be a relatively short period of humiliation is evident from
the fact that God declared that "before the child knows
enough to reject the wrong and choose the right, the land
of the two kings you dread will be laid waste." This time
frame may be understood in either of two ways: It may
mean that in the time it would take for the child to come
to years of *moral* discretion, that is, within a period of a
couple of years or so, the threat from the northern alliance
would have been removed. If this is the intent of the
"time phrase," God was saying that the time of dread for
Judah would come to an end with the Assyrian invasion
in 732 B.C. at which time Damascus fell and the northern
kingdom was so despoiled (see 2 Kings 15:29) that for all
intents and purposes it was only a " rump" state during
Hosea's reign. It could also be taken to mean that in the
time it would take for the child to reach the age of *legal*
accountability, that is, within a thirteen-year period (twelve
years plus the original gestation period of the Child), the
time of dread would come to an end. If this is the intent
of the "time phrase," then God was referring to the period
of time (if we commence the period from 734 B.C.) from
734 B.C. to 721 B.C. during which period of time both
Damascus (in 732 B.C.) and Samaria (in 722 B.C.) were
overthrown.

   To sum up, then, it is not the time between the giving
of the sign and its fulfillment that should be made the
basis of relevance for Ahaz's day; rather, it is the time
between the miraculous birth of the child and his coming
to the age of discernment or legal accountability that
makes the prophecy relevant to Ahaz's day.

Taking now the entire sign together, it is as if Isaiah had said,
to employ Machen's paraphrase,

I see a wonderful [virginally-conceived] child...whose birth shall bring salvation to his people; and before such a period of time shall elapse as would lie between the conception of the child in his mother's womb and his coming to years of discretion [or legal accountability], the land of Israel and of Syria shall be forsaken.[21]

This paraphrase, endorsed in principle by both Young[22] and Harris,[23] takes all of the features of the sign into account and demonstrates how the sign, specifically because of the "time" indicator attached to it, although not to be fulfilled for hundreds of years, nevertheless could have had – and did in fact have – relevance for Isaiah's contemporaries in that it provided them a measurable, relatively short time-frame within which Judah's period of humiliation would come to an end.

As a parallel short-term prophetic sign that Judah's period of humiliation would be relatively short, God had Isaiah write on a large scroll the name, Maher-Shalal-Hashbaz, which name – meaning as it does "Quick to the plunder; swift to the spoil" – suggested an imminent assault from the Assyrians. He then had this act witnessed by two reliable witnesses. Then Isaiah "went to the prophetess [doubtless his wife, and most likely at God's command], and she conceived and gave birth to a son." God then commanded that the child should be named Maher-Shalal-Hashbaz, and declared that before the boy would know how to say "my father" or "my mother," Assyria would plunder Judah's two northern enemies (8:1-4). This prophecy was surely fulfilled within the space of a year or so with Tiglath-pileser III's capture of Damascus and the spoliation of Samaria in 732 B.C. And its fulfillment, in accordance with its stated short-term time feature, both confirmed and illustrated the similar

---

[21]J. Gresham Machen, *The Virgin Birth of Christ* (New York: Harper and Brothers, 1930), 293.

[22]Young, "The Immanuel Prophecy" in *Studies in Isaiah*, 190, 195-96.

[23]See R. Laird Harris's comment on Isaiah 7:14 in J. Oliver Buswell, Jr.'s *A Systematic Theology of the Christian Religion*, II, 548.

time feature attached to the previous long-term Immanuel prophecy – enhancing thereby the latter's relevance to Isaiah's contemporaries.[24]

In my opinion, the interpretation of Isaiah 7:14-16 shared by Machen, Young, and Harris is to be preferred above all the others. I believe that they have demonstrated that the prophecy *exclusively* predicted Mary's virginal conception and the supernatural birth of Jesus Christ, and that in doing so it provided at the same time the time measure for the length of duration of Judah's eighth-century B.C. trouble as well. I would suggest also that Jesus' uniqueness as the uniquely conceived son of Mary came to expression precisely in terms of his being God incarnate, "the Word become flesh," as the name "Immanuel" suggests. Moreover, for our present purpose I would contend that in Isaiah's prediction of Christ's virginal conception and the New Testament fulfillment of that prediction in the supernatural birth of Jesus Christ the church has one more argument for the truthfulness of Christian theology as a whole.

The virgin birth of Christ according to the New Testament

At the outset of my comments on "the miracle of Christmas" *per se*, I would observe, using the words of J. Gresham Machen,

---

[24]A variation on this explanation of the Isaiah 8 prophecy is that of J. A. Motyer in "Context and Content in the Interpretation of Isaiah 7:14" in *Tyndale Bulletin* 21 (1970): 118-25, who, with the "Machen-Young-Harris proposal," understands the Immanuel prophecy to have single and direct fulfillment only in Christ, but who also argues that Isaiah knew from the start that Judah and Jerusalem would ultimately fall, necessarily projecting the birth of Immanuel as the nation's ultimate hope into the undated future. Immanuel, in other words, was to inherit a "disestablished" Davidic dynasty. Therefore, Isaiah "introduced the second child into the sequence of prophecies (8:1-4), allowing Maher-Shalal-Hash-Baz *to take over from Immanuel* the task of providing a time-schedule for the immediately coming events" (124; emphasis supplied). But this proposal, it seems to me, "disestablishes" the minority years of Immanuel from being the time indicator of a short period of devastation for Judah, the very thing which God himself declared that it was to be.

that "it is perfectly clear that the New Testament teaches the virgin birth of Christ; about that there can be no manner of doubt. There is no serious question as to the *interpretation* of the Bible at this point."[25] That is to say, there is no room for any other "theory" concerning the event. One either believes it or he does not.

The biblical data

Clear indications that the Bible teaches the doctrine of Jesus' virginal conception are to be found in Isaiah 7:14 ("the virgin will be with child"), Matthew 1:16 ("out of *whom* [fem.] was born Jesus"), 1:18 ("before they came together, she was found to be with child through the Holy Spirit"), 1:20 ("that which has been begotten in her is through the Holy Spirit"), 1:22-23 ("All this happened *in order that* [*hina*] *the utterance* [*to rhēthen*] of the Lord through the prophet might be fulfilled: 'Behold, the virgin will be with child, and shall bear a son, and they shall call his name "Immanuel"' – which means, 'God is with us'"), 1:25 ("…he [Joseph] knew her not until she gave birth to a son"), Luke 1:27 ("to a virgin…and the virgin's name was Mary"), 1:34 ("How shall this be, since I know not a man?"), 1:35 ("The Holy Spirit will come upon you, even the Power of the Most High will overshadow you. Wherefore, the One to be born will be called holy – [after all, he is] the Son of God"), and 3:23 ("being the son, so it was supposed, of Joseph"). The reader is also referred to (1) Mary's musings in Luke 2:19 and 2:51b, (2) the snide intimations that something (illegitimacy?) was unusual about his birth in Mark 6:3 when compared with its parallels in Matthew 13:55 and Luke 4:22, as well as in the similar suggestions in John 8:41 and 9:29, and (3) Paul's "made of a woman" reference in Galatians 4:4. In light of this biblical data, the single most indisputable fact about the tradition respecting Jesus' conception is that his conception occurred out

---

[25]J. Gresham Machen, *The Virgin Birth of Christ* (New York: Harper & Row, 1930), 382.

of wedlock. We have, in other words, to do with either a virginal conception or an illegitimate conception. And the Bible clearly endorses the former as the ground of the rumors of the latter.

We must acknowledge, it is true, that only two New Testament writers – Matthew and Luke – directly mention the virginal conception of Jesus, but then it is equally true that they are the only two to record his birth at all. This may be explained on the assumption that a certain reserve respecting public discussion of this matter was maintained in the first-century church out of respect for Mary's privacy. As to whether other New Testament writers knew of his virginal conception, it certainly seems likely that Paul, working as closely as he did with Luke and being familiar with Luke's Gospel as he was (see 1 Tim. 5:18 and Luke 10:7), would have known about it. Mark's reference to Jesus as "Mary's son" (Mark 6:3), an unusual way to describe parentage in Jewish culture, may indicate some awareness of Jesus' unusual birth. And it is also most likely that John, writing his Gospel after Matthew and Luke, would have known about it as well. He certainly understood that "the Word [who "was God"] became flesh" (1:14) by human birth (19:37) and that he had a human mother (2:1; 19:25). And in light of his recurring statements that Jesus "came from above" (3:31; 8:23), "came down from heaven"(6:38), "came from the Father into the world" (16:27, 28), and "was sent by the Father" (5:36; 6:57; 10:36), John would have had to believe that some form of supernatural intervention intruded itself at the point of Jesus' human conception if all of these features that he reports about Jesus are to be harmonized. This much is clear: *no New Testament writer says anything that would contradict the Matthean and Lukan testimony.*

Testimony from church history
With regard to how the church has understood the Matthean and Lukan birth narratives, there is no doubt that Jesus' literal virginal conception has been uniformly seen in them, as evidenced by the united testimonies of Irenaeus (Asia Minor and Gaul),

Ignatius (Antioch of Syria), Tertullian (North Africa), Justin Martyr (Ephesus and Rome) and the Old Roman Baptismal Symbol in the second century[26] right down through the great creeds of the church to the present day (see the Apostles' Creed, the present Nicene Creed," the Definition of Chalcedon, the so-called "Athanasian Creed" [*homo est ex substantia matris*, that is, "He is man from the substance [nature] of his mother"], the *Augsburg Confession*, Article III, the *Belgic Confession*, Article XVIII, the *Westminster Confession of Faith*, Chapter VIII, and the *Thirty-Nine Articles*, Article II). The current suggestion of some modern scholars that Matthew (in particular) was writing "midrash" (the expansion and embellishment of actual history with the "non-historical") is simply unproven. There is, in fact, a real question whether midrash was a common literary genre at the time when Matthew wrote. It is clear, at any rate, that the early church fathers did not understand Matthew's birth narrative as a midrash. So when men like E. Brunner, W. Pannenberg, and the "Jesus Seminar" scholars,[27] whatever their reasons and

---

[26]For specific references in the writings of these early Fathers, see Machen, *Virgin Birth*, 2-43 (the first chapter, "The Virgin Birth in the Second Century"). There were, of course, some sects that dismissed the story of Christ's virginal conception (the Jewish Ebionites, the heretic Marcion), but they clearly understood what the birth narratives intended to report, namely, history and not myth.

[27]Representing itself as part of the modern "Quest of the Historical Jesus" movement, the Jesus Seminar, founded by Robert W. Funk in 1985 and chaired by Funk, John Dominic Crossan (who believes Jesus' body was never buried but was dumped in a trash heap and eaten by dogs and birds), and Marcus Borg, is a group of American New Testament scholars that meets twice a year to debate technical papers that have been circulated in advance. At the close of each debate on the agenda item the Fellows of the Seminar vote, using colored beads, to indicate the degree of authenticity of Jesus' words and deeds. A *red* bead means Jesus undoubtedly said or did such-and-such or something like it, a *pink* bead means Jesus probably or might have said or done something like such-and-such, a *gray* bead means Jesus did not say or do such-and-such but the idea or deed is close to what he might have said or done, and a *black* bead means Jesus did not say or do such-and-such but is a later tradition. Of 1500 reported sayings of Jesus that the Seminar examined, only 18% received a red or pink vote; of 176

however well-intentioned they might be, deny the fact of the virginal conception of Jesus, it is not only the New Testament witness but also the consistent, universal testimony of the church that they reject – no small departure from Christian doctrine on the part of any man in any age.

Then there are the irresponsible pseudosophs who have suggested that "the virgin birth myth" was able to establish a beachhead in the minds of first-century Christians because they simply did not know "back then" as we know now, so these Bobadils allege, that human births require copulation between the male and the female of the species. I would only say to this ridiculous explanation that it is quite apparent that Joseph certainly knew how babies get here for when he learned that Mary was pregnant he concluded that she had been unfaithful to her marriage vow and "resolved to divorce her quietly" (Matt. 1:19). He went forward with his marriage to Mary only because an angel appeared to him and reassured him that Mary was virtuous and had not betrayed him and that her conception was due to the Holy Spirit's "overshadowing" her (Matt. 1:20; Luke 1:35).

Why I Believe in Christ's Virginal Conception

My reasons for believing in Christ's virginal conception in the womb of the Virgin Mary through the power of the Holy Spirit may be summarized as follows:

- First, of course, is the teaching of Scripture itself about which, as we have already noted, there is no question. This reason is paramount and sufficient as far as I am concerned for believing it, but then I speak as a Christian. But more can be said.

---

reported deeds of Jesus that the Seminar examined, only 16% received red or pink votes. These are *radical* conclusions indeed! The Seminar, it is true, includes along with Jesus' sayings and deeds in the four canonical Gospels his sayings and deeds from the gnostic Gospel of Thomas (which fact in itself says a great deal about the Seminar's commitment to canonical truth), but its conclusions even so are still radical!

- Second is the weight of the church's *historical* testimony that I reviewed in a cursory way above.

- Third is the *Christian theistic* reason: Jesus' virginal conception is simply one aspect of the total supernaturalism of Scripture and of Christian theism in general. If one can believe, for example, Genesis 1:1, or that God speaks to men in Scripture, or in Jesus' miracles, or that he rose from the dead and left this world by ascending to his Father, it is asking very little more of one to believe that Jesus entered this world also miraculously by being virginally conceived.

- Fourth is the *psychological* reason: Only the virginal conception can explain Mary's willingness to be included in the company of those who *worshiped* Jesus as the divine Son of *God* (Acts 1:14). It taxes one's credulity to accept that Mary could have believed that her Son died for her sins and was her *divine* Savior deserving of her worship or that she would have allowed others to believe so if she knew in her heart that his origin was like that of every other man and that he had been conceived out of wedlock.

- Fifth are the *theological* reasons: (1) the virginal conception of Jesus is the Bible's explanation for the "how" of the Incarnation, and (2) while the virginal conception is not necessarily the total explanation for Jesus' sinlessness, it is a fact that if Jesus had been the offspring of the union of a human father and mother, such a natural generation would have entailed depravity (John 3:6) and implicated Jesus in Adam's first sin (Rom. 5:12, 19).

- Sixth and finally are the *apologetic* or *polemical* reasons: (1) If Jesus was not virginally conceived, then Matthew and Luke were in error and cease to be trustworthy, authoritative guides and teachers of doctrine not only here but in other matters of faith as well, such as Christ's resurrection (see Machen, *Virgin Birth*, 382-87). (2) If Jesus was not virginally conceived, serious gaps are left in any effort to understand the person of Christ and the Incarnation (Machen, *Virgin*

Birth, 387-95). (3) If Jesus was conceived like all other men, then he stood under the Adamic curse like the rest of those who descend from Adam by natural generation, as we just noted, and this in turn means that he would not have been an acceptable Savior of men before God. But this would mean in turn the end of Christianity as a redemptive religion for sinful men since there would then be no one who could offer himself up to God as an acceptable, unblemished sacrifice to satisfy divine justice and to reconcile God to man. I fully realize that this last point assumes a particular doctrine of sin ("original and race sin") and a particular view of the atonement ("satisfaction"), but then it is a fact that the Bible teaches this doctrine of sin (Rom. 5:12-19) and this kind of atonement – the kind that Jesus accomplished by his sinless life and substitutionary death on the cross.[28]

The Purpose of Christ's Virginal Conception

Now I want to draw out the implications of Jesus' virginal conception for the nature of his person. Given the fact of his virginal conception, what was its purpose relative to the person of Jesus himself? Perhaps we should begin our discussion here by underscoring two things that we must not say the purpose of Jesus' virginal conception was.

First, we must not understand the birth narratives as teaching that Mary's virginal conception of Jesus through the power of the Holy Spirit was the efficient cause or source of his deity. Geerhardus Vos quite properly declares that while "there is truth in the close connection established between the virgin birth of our Lord and His Deity," it would be "a mistake to suspend the Deity on the virgin birth as its ultimate source or reason." To do so "would lead to a lowering of the idea of Deity itself."[29]

---

[28]The reader is referred to Warfield's brief article, "The Supernatural Birth of Jesus" in *Biblical and Theological Studies* (Philadelphia: Presbyterian and Reformed, 1952), 157-68, for further argument in behalf of the salvific necessity of the virgin birth of Christ.

[29]Geerhardus Vos, *The Self-Disclosure of Jesus* (Phillipsburg, N. J.: Presbyterian and Reformed, 1978 rewritten edition), 191, fn. 15.

What we intend to highlight here is the obvious fact that "neither sinful nor holy human parents could produce an offspring *who is God*. That is beyond their humanity. And neither could a virgin human mother do this!"[30] If our understanding of New Testament Christology is correct, another ground exists for believing that Jesus Christ is God, namely, the fact that as God the Son, he was fully and truly God prior to and apart from his virginal conception. So we say again, his virginal conception in Mary's womb must not be viewed as the ultimate cause or source of his deity. Nor did the virginal conception, we must say in this same connection, produce a hybrid or a sort of demi-god, an offspring of the union between a god (the Holy Spirit) and a human woman, who was neither fully god nor fully man but only half-god and half-man. This is simply mythology for which there is *no* scriptural warrant. Another purpose, as we hope to show, underlay the virginal conception of Jesus.

Second, the virginal conception of Jesus by Mary through the power of the Holy Spirit was probably not the efficient cause of Jesus' sinlessness (see 2 Cor. 5:21; Heb. 4:15). At least, it is most unlikely, for the reason that one occasionally hears espoused, that Jesus' virginal conception was essential to His sinlessness because "original [or race] sin" is transmitted through the *male* line. Women, as well as men, share in the sinfulness of the human race and are corrupted by it, and this pervasive sinfulness encompassed Mary as well, who possessed a sinful nature, committed sins, and confessed her need of a Savior (Luke 1:47). All the biblical, not to mention the biological, evidence suggests that the woman contributes equally to the total physical, spiritual, and psychic make-up of the human offspring who comes from natural generation. It is striking, for example, that in his great penitential Psalm, it is specifically his mother whom David mentioned when he traces his sinful deed back to his sinful nature: "With sin," he declares, "did *my mother* conceive me"(51:5). There is reason

---

[30]Kenneth S. Kantzer, "The Miracle of Christmas," *Christianity Today* 28, 18 (December 14, 1984), 15.

to assume, therefore, that, except for a special divine work of preservation beyond the virginal conception itself, Mary would have transmitted her human bent to sin to her firstborn. John Calvin was even willing to assert as much:

> ...we make Christ free of all stain not just because he was begotten of his mother without copulation with man, but because he was sanctified by the Spirit that the generation might be pure and undefiled as would have been true before Adam's fall.[31]

Luke 1:35 also suggests as much, if we construe *hagion* ("holy") as a predicate and understand it in the moral/ethical sense. John Murray also entertains the same possibility, although with a certain degree of discretionary reserve:

> [Jesus' preservation from defilement] may reside entirely in the supernatural begetting, for it may be that depravity is conveyed in natural generation. [Note that he does not place the transmission of racial sin in the male line *per se* here but rather in the "natural generation" that involves the union of male *and* female.] In any case, natural generation would have entailed depravity (John 3:6). Yet it may not be correct to find the whole explanation of Jesus' sinlessness in the absence of natural begetting. So it may well be that preservation from the stain of sin (cf. Psalm 51:5) required another, supernatural factor, namely, the preservation from conception to birth of the infant Jesus from the contamination that would otherwise have proceeded from his human mother.[32]

Obviously, great care should be expended in any explanation of the ground of Jesus' sinlessness. But until we know a great deal more than we do about natural generation and human

---

[31]John Calvin, *Institutes of the Christian Religion*, translated by Ford Lewis Battles (Philadelphia: Westminster Press, 1960), 2.13.4.

[32]John Murray, "The Person of Christ" in *Collected Writings* (Edinburgh: Banner of Truth, 1977), 2, 135; see also J. Oliver Buswell, Jr., *A Systematic Theology of the Christian Religion* (Grand Rapids: Zondervan, 1962), I, 251; II, 57.

reproduction, we would be wise to refrain from suspending Jesus' sinlessness simply and solely on the obvious fact that in the virginal conception the male factor had been eliminated in his human generation. In any event, it seems quite safe to say, even if Jesus' sinlessness is a secondary effect of the virginal conception, that his sinlessness was not the effect that his virginal conception was primarily intended to bring about.

What then was the primary purpose of Jesus' virginal conception? Before I respond directly to this question, it is appropriate that I point out that Jesus' conception in a *human* mother's womb, although virginal in nature, followed by his normal development in that human mother's womb, and his altogether normal passage from that human womb into the world at birth, as recorded in both Matthew and Luke, are features of his human origination which insure and guarantee to us that Jesus was and is truly and fully human. The Bible is quite adamant that Jesus' full and true humanity was in no way threatened or impaired by the miracle of his virginal conception, but just to the contrary, by being conceived by a human mother he "shared" our humanity (Heb. 2:14), and was "like" us in every way (Heb. 2:17). To the objection of some that a virginal conception precludes at the outset the possibility of our Lord being truly and fully man, I would say that such an objection is simply hypothetical and indemonstrable, for "it is not the method as such by which a human being comes to be such that is decisive but the end product itself, namely a human being" (R. F. Aldwinkle). Furthermore, as A. N. S. Lane writes:

> The role of Christ requires that that there should be both continuity and discontinuity between him and us; that he should be one of us (Heb. 2:10-18) and yet also different from us. Jesus is the second "Adam" – one of the human race, yet inaugurating a new redeemed humanity. The virgin birth points to this combination of continuity and discontinuity.[33]

---

[33]A. N. S. Lane, "Virgin Birth" in *New Dictionary of Theology*, edited by Sinclair B. Ferguson and David F. Wright (Downers Grove, Ill.: Inter-Varsity, 1988), 709-10.

When we then penetrate to the mysterious and marvelous primary purpose of the Christmas miracle, we should understand *before everything else* that, by means of the virginal conception, "the [pre-existent] Word *became flesh*" (John 1:14)! Mary's virginal conception, in other words, was the means whereby *God became man*, whereby he who "was rich for our sakes became poor, that through his poverty, we might become rich" (2 Cor. 8:9). It is the Bible's answer to the question that naturally arises in men's minds as soon as they learn that Jesus Christ is the God-man: "How did this occur?" The virginal conception is the effecting means of the "Immanuel event" (Isa. 7:14; Matt. 1:22-23) that made God man with us without uniting the Son of God to a second (human) person that would have surely been the effect of an incarnation by *natural* generation. By Mary's virginal conception, God the Son, without ceasing to be what he is – the Second Person of the Holy Trinity and the Word of God – took into union with his divine nature in the one divine person our *human nature* (not a *human person*) and so came to be "with us" as "Immanuel." Any other suggested purpose for the virginal conception of Jesus as reported in the Matthean and Lukan birth stories pales into insignificance in the glorious light of this clear reason for it. And when this is clearly perceived, one will acknowledge that the Matthean and Lukan birth narratives take their rightful place along with all the other lines of evidence in the New Testament – grander no doubt than some – for the deity of Jesus Christ and thus for the classical doctrine of an incarnational Christology.

Chapter Six

Faith's Reasons for Believing in Biblical Miracles in General and Jesus' Miracles in Particular

Without a definition of the word "miracle" this discussion will be vitiated *ab initio*. So by the word "miracle" I intend an extraordinary objective occurrence in the external world effected by the immediate power of God, an event that is neither a mental phenomenon nor caused by a natural but rather by a supernatural force injected into nature. It is this understanding of what a "miracle" is that will be before me throughout this chapter.

Biblical Miracles in General

As I begin this defense of biblical miracles in general I must say that I have no sympathy with the contention of many theologians who, in order to satisfy the unbeliever, say that the biblical miracles are simply interventions of God into human affairs in ways that run counter to *known* or *observable* processes but that do not really violate the laws of nature. (By saying this much they are at least acknowledging that some things out of the ordinary happened in biblical history that require an explanation.) But biblical miracles are clearly contrary to the laws of nature such as Jesus' changing water into wine, and it seems to me that it is catering too much to modern man's hostility to the whole idea of the supernatural so to define biblical miracles that they are emptied of their supernatural uniqueness and efficiency. I believe that the *Westminster Confession of Faith* accurately reflects the true situation when it states: "God, in his ordinary providence, makes use of means, yet is free to work without, above, and against them, at his pleasure" (IV.3).

The biblical miracles do not occur willy-nilly, for no rhyme or reason, in salvation history. The Bible suggests to the contrary that they served the *revelatory* process (that in turn served as the interpretation of God's objective central redemptive activity) by authenticating the human organs of special revelation who gave men the propositional truth of God. That is to say, they occurred during great periods of special revelation. This fact Reformed scholars have observed. For example, John Calvin writes:

> [Our adversaries] do not cease to assail our doctrine and to reproach and defame it with names that render it hated or suspect. They call it "new" and "of recent birth." They reproach it as "doubtful and uncertain." They ask what miracles have confirmed it…by calling it "new" they do great wrong to God, whose Sacred Word does not deserve to be accused of novelty. Indeed, I do not at all doubt that it is new to them, since to them both Christ himself and his gospel are new. But he who knows that this preaching of Paul is ancient, that "Jesus Christ died for our sins and rose again for our justification," will find nothing new among us.
>
> That it has been long unknown and buried is the fault of man's impiety. Now, when it is restored to us by God's goodness, its claim to antiquity ought to be admitted just as the returning citizen resumes his rights.
>
> The same ignorance leads them to regard it as doubtful and uncertain. This is precisely what the Lord complains of through his prophet, that "the ox knew its owner, and the ass its master's crib; but his own people did not know him." But however they may jest about its uncertainty, if they had to seal their doctrine in their own blood, and at the expense of their life, one could see how much it meant to them. Quite the opposite is our assurance, which fears neither the terrors of death nor even God's judgment seat.
>
> In demanding miracles of us, they act dishonestly. For *we are not forging some new gospel, but are retaining that very gospel whose truth all the miracles that Jesus Christ and his disciples ever wrought serve to confirm.* But, compared with us,

they have a strange power: even to this day they can confirm their faith by continual miracles! Indeed, they allege miracles that can disturb a mind otherwise at rest – they are so foolish and ridiculous, so vain and false! And yet, even if these were marvelous prodigies, they ought not to be of any moment against God's truth, for God's name ought to be always and everywhere hallowed, whether by miracles or by the natural order of things.

Perhaps this false hue could have been more dazzling if Scripture had not warned us concerning the legitimate purpose and use of miracles. For Mark teaches that those signs that attended the apostles' preaching were set forth to confirm it [Mark 16:20]. In like manner, Luke relates that our "Lord... bore witness to the word of his grace," when these signs and wonders were done by the apostles' hands [Acts 14:3]. Very much like this is that word of the apostle: that the salvation proclaimed by the gospel has been confirmed in the fact that "the Lord has attested it by signs and wonders and various mighty works" [Heb. 2:4]. When we hear that these are the seals of the gospel, shall we turn them to the destruction of faith in the gospel? When we hear that they were appointed only to seal the truth, shall we employ them to confirm falsehoods?...And we may also fitly remember that Satan has his miracles, that, though they are deceitful tricks rather than true powers, are of such sort as to mislead the simple-minded and untutored. Magicians and enchanters have always been noted for miracles. Idolatry has been nourished by wonderful miracles, yet these are not sufficient to sanction for us the superstition either of magicians or of idolaters.

The Donatists of old overwhelmed the simplicity of the multitude with this battering-ram: that they were mighty in miracles. We, therefore, now answer our adversaries as Augustine then answered the Donatists: the Lord made us wary of these miracle workers when he predicted that false prophets with lying signs and divers wonders would come to draw even the elect (if possible) into error. And Paul warned that the reign of Antichrist would be "with all power and signs and lying wonders." But these miracles, they say, are done neither by idols, nor by magicians, nor by false prophets, but by the saints.

As if we did not understand that to "disguise himself as an angel of light" is the craft of Satan!...What shall we say except that it has always been, and ever will be, a very just punishment of God to "send to those" who have not received the love of truth "a strong delusion to make them believe a lie." We, then, have no lack of miracles [he refers to the New Testament miracles], sure miracles, not subject to mockery. On the contrary, those "miracles" that our adversaries point to in their own support are sheer delusions of Satan, for they draw the people away from the true worship of their God to vanity.[1]

In the same way Warfield approaches the purpose of biblical miracles. He speaks of "the inseparable connection of miracles with revelation, as its mark and credential; or more narrowly, of the summing up of all revelation, finally, in Jesus Christ." Miracles, he writes:

...do not appear on the pages of Scripture vagrantly, here, there, and elsewhere indifferently, without assignable reason. They belong to revelation periods, and appear only when God is speaking to His people through accredited messengers, declaring His gracious purposes.[2]

This perception of miracles as the authenticating credentials of bearers of revelation receives striking verification in the Scriptures themselves. For example, in the Old Testament, the great period of special revelation known as Mosaism (Exodus through Deuteronomy) arose in connection with and as a result of the great (typical) redemptive event of the exodus-redemption of the people of God from Egypt that culminated in the miraculous parting of the Sea in Exodus 14:21-29 and later in the parting of the Jordan River in Joshua 3:15-17. Moses – himself the central conduit of that revelation – received attestation to his authenticity as God's spokesman from all the miracles of the

---

[1]John Calvin, "Prefatory Address to King Francis I of France" in *Institutes of the Christian Religion* (emphasis supplied).

[2]Benjamin B. Warfield, *Miracles: Yesterday and Today* (Grand Rapids: Eerdmans, n. d.), 25-6.

exodus itself (see Exod. 4:1-9) and from the miracles recorded in Numbers (see Num. 12:1-11; 17:1-8; 21:5-9). The subsequent body of revelation known as Prophetism, that spanned Israel's history from the conquest under Joshua down to post-exilic times, should not be construed as unrelated or detached from the former body of revelation, inasmuch as Prophetism, dealing as it does by its revelational material both historically and hortatorily with the Mosaic community founded at the exodus, continued to explain and unfold the implications of the earlier Mosaic redemption (see, for example, Josh. 1:5-17; 2:10-11; 4:23; 9:24; Ezek. 23; Mal. 4:4). The miracles of the age of Prophetism in turn served to authenticate the prophets as the revelatory organs of that age. Consider the following examples:

> After Elijah raised the widow's son from the dead, she exclaimed: "Now I know that you are a man of God and that the word of the Lord from your mouth is the truth" (1 Kings 17:17-24).

> In his later conflict with the prophets of Baal on Mount Carmel, Elijah prayed: "O Lord, God of Abraham, Isaac and Israel, let it be known today that you are God in Israel and that I am your servant and have done all these things at your command. Answer me, O Lord, answer me so these people will know that you, O Lord, are God." "Then," we are informed, "the fire of the Lord fell and burned up the sacrifice, the wood, the stones and the soil, and also licked up the water in the trench" (1 Kings 18:36-39).

> "Elijah answered the captain, 'If I am a man of God, may fire come down from heaven and consume you and your fifty men!' Then fire fell from heaven and consumed the captain and his men" (2 Kings 1:10; see also 1:12; 20:8-11; Dan. 2).

Old Testament revelation, when rightly viewed, is then essentially unitary in its concern to explicate Old Testament redemption, both principially and typically, and thereby to prepare the way for its antitypical fulfillment in the New Testament age. And the miracles of the Old Testament age in turn authenticated Moses and the prophets as men of God and organs of revelation.

All of this accords with the New Testament's representation that Old Testament redemption foreshadowed by its revealed principles, and pointed forward to, its grand climactic New Testament antitype – the objectively historical redemption accomplished by Christ in his Incarnation. Then the entire New Testament corpus of revelation, related to the Old Testament corpus as fulfillment is related to promise, provided the climactic special revelatory explanation of the New Testament complex of historical redemptive events. And the miracles of the New Testament age, as we shall see, authenticated in turn Christ and his apostles as the bearers of this new corpus of revelation.

If what we have suggested is correct, it means that the biblical miracles in general served the organs of special revelation by authenticating them as such. It was non-repeatable objective historical events of redemption that called forth their special revelatory explanation, and it was special revelation in turn that called forth "miracles of power" as authenticating signs of the bearers of revelation. Where the first was absent, there was no necessity for the second; where the second was absent, there was no necessity for the third, so all three ceased with the close of the apostolic age.[3] When the first had been sufficiently and

---

[3] Against the prevailing view that the "miracles of power" (*dunameis,* Matt. 11:21) of the New Testament age slowly died out of the life of the church and ceased altogether about the time of Constantine in the fourth century when Christianity was established as a licit religion of the empire (so Middleton, Uhlhorn) or perhaps a little later (so Dodwell, Chapman), Warfield contends in his *Miracles: Yesterday and Today*, 10, just to the contrary, that a careful reading of the church fathers shows that

...there is little or no evidence at all for miracle-working during the first fifty years of the post-Apostolic church; it is slight and unimportant for the next fifty years; it grows more abundant during the next century (the third); and it becomes abundant and precise only in the fourth century, to increase still further in the fifth and beyond.

permanently explicated (in inscripturated form) by the second, and the second sufficiently authenticated by the third, there was no further need for the continuation of either the second or the third, and in fact the revelatory process and the occurrence of authenticating miracles of power ceased (see *Westminster Confession of Faith*, I.1).[4] Accordingly, once the second and the third occurred, the supernatural events of redemption took their place in the world as recorded, explicated, authenticated, incontrovertible facts of world and human history.

Jesus' Miracles in Particular

The biblical data

As we approach the issue of the facticity and historicity of Jesus' miracles we would be well advised before we do anything else to gather the biblical data before us. The following specific healing miracles having to do with the alleviation of human suffering are mentioned in the Gospels:

How does Warfield account for their increase rather than their decrease as the prevailing view maintains? He reminds his readers that the gospel did not advance upon an anti-supernaturalistic world but into a world that was permeated with all kinds of superstition and marvels and with a readiness of mind of believe on the flimsiest of evidence or no evidence at all any and every kind of claim to supernatural occurrences. As the church brought into its membership what were little more than baptized heathen these people brought with them their superstitions, their mysticism, and their belief in the miraculous. Accordingly, they would have, and indeed increasingly, claimed the occurrence of miracles as their numbers increased and brought their "miracles" with them. It is the occurrence of these counterfeit miracles that gullible early church fathers report in their writings. Warfield concludes that in this respect the conquering church was conquered by the very people whom it conquered (*Miracles*, 74)!

See also Richard B. Gaffin, Jr., "A Cessationist View" in *Are Miraculous Gifts for Today?*, edited by Wayne A. Grudem (Grand Rapids: Zondervan, 1996), 25-64.

[4]When we speak of miracles ceasing we intend only the authenticating "miracles of power"; "miracles of grace," of course, such as God's quickening dead spirits by regenerating them and answering the prayers of the saints continue to occur throughout this age.

- the royal official's son (John 4:46-54),
- Peter's mother-in-law (Matt. 8:14-17; Mark 1:29-31; Luke 4:38-40),
- the woman with the hemorrhage of blood (Matt. 9:20-22; Mark 5:25-34; Luke 8:43-48),
- the centurion's servant (Matt. 8:5-13; Luke 7:1-10),
- the man suffering from dropsy (Luke 14:1-6),
- the blind (Matt. 9:27-31; John 9:1-7; Matt. 20:29-34; Mark 10:46-52; Luke 18:35-43),
- the deaf (Mark 7:31-37),
- the paralyzed and lame (Matt. 9:1-8; Mark 2:1-12; Luke 5:17-26; John 5:1-15; Matt. 12:9-13; Mark 3:1-5; Luke 6:6-10; 13:10-17),
- the lepers (Matt. 8:1-4; Mark 1:40-45; Luke 5:12-16; 17:11-19),
- Malchus' ear (Luke 22:49-51).

I must also mention here both Jesus' *exorcisms of demons,* which, in the mastery over the forces of Satan that they demonstrated, signalized in a unique way his divine authority over and messianic assault against the cosmic kingdom of evil (Matt. 8:28-34; Mark 5:1-20; Luke 8:26-39; Mark 1:23-27; Luke 4:33-37; Matt. 15:21-28; Mark 7:24-30; Matt. 17:14-21; Mark 9:14-29; Luke 9:37-43) and his *raising again to life* of Jairus' daughter (Matt. 9:18-19, 23-26; Mark 5:22-24, 35-43; Luke 8:41-42, 49-56), the widow's son (Luke 7:11-16), and Lazarus (John 11:1-54).

In addition to these specific examples of healing – against which much effort has been expended unsuccessfully to rationalize them away, we have those general narrative statements found in all of the Synoptic Gospels that cannot be explained away. In his Gospel Matthew alone gives us six reports of such activity:

- 4:23-24 (take note of the Evangelist's use of "universals" here): "Jesus went throughout Galilee,…healing *every* disease and sickness among the people. News about him spread all over Syria, and people brought to him *all* who were ill with various diseases, those suffering severe pain, the demon-possessed, the epileptics and the paralytics, and he healed them."

- 8:16: "When evening came, many who were demon-possessed were brought to him, and he drove out the spirits with a word and healed *all* the sick."

- 9:35: "Jesus went through all the towns and villages, …healing *every* disease and sickness."

- 14:14: "When Jesus…saw a large crowd, he had compassion on them and healed their sick."

- 14:35-36: "People brought *all* their sick to him and begged him to let the sick just touch the edge of his cloak, and *all* who touched him were healed."

- 15:30-31: "Great crowds came to him, bringing the lame, the blind, the crippled, the dumb and many others, and laid them at his feet; and he healed them. The people were amazed when they saw the dumb speaking, the crippled made well, the lame walking and the blind seeing."

Mark adds the following four narrational accounts of Jesus' healing labors:

- 1:32-34: "…the people brought to Jesus all the sick and demon-possessed. The whole town gathered at the door, and Jesus healed many who had various diseases. He also drove out many demons."

- 1:39: "So he traveled throughout Galilee,…driving out demons."

- 3:10: "He…healed many, so that those with diseases were pushing forward to touch him."

- 6:56: "And everywhere he went – into villages, towns or countryside – they placed the sick in the marketplaces. They begged him to let them touch even the edge of his cloak, and *all* who touched him were healed."

And Luke the physician provides us with three more:

- 4:40: "When the sun was setting, the people brought to Jesus *all* who had various kinds of sickness, and laying his hands on each one, he healed them."

- 6:17-19: "A large crowd of his disciples was there and a great number of people from all over Judea, from Jerusalem, and from the seacoast of Tyre and Sidon, who had come to hear him and to be healed of their diseases. Those troubled by evil spirits were cured, and the people all tried to touch him, because power was coming from him and healing them *all*."

- 9:11: "...the crowds...followed him. He welcomed them and spoke to them about the kingdom of God, and healed those who needed healing."

Matthew and Luke also report Jesus' own description of his ministry in his response to John the Baptist's impatient query, "Are you the one who is to come or shall we look for another?" in these words: "The blind receive sight, the lame walk, those who have leprosy are cured, the deaf hear, and the dead are raised" (Matt. 11:4-5; Luke 7:22).

Jesus furthermore declared that if his "powers" that had been done in Chorazin, Bethsaida, and Capernaum had been done in Tyre, Sidon, and even Sodom, those ancient cities would have repented (Matt. 11:20-24; Luke 10:12-13). Even his enemies at the time acknowledged his authority over demons (Matt. 12:22-32; Mark 3:20-30; Luke 11:14-23).

In addition to his own works of healing, Jesus gave to his twelve disciples the authority to "drive out evil spirits and to cure every kind of disease and sickness" (Matt. 10:1), including even the authority to raise the dead (Matt. 10:8); and Mark informs us that "they went out and...drove out many demons and anointed many sick people with oil and healed them" (Mark 6:13). Then later, he commissioned seventy(-two) other disciples to go and to do the same thing (Luke 10:1, 9, 17, 19).

Peter summed up Jesus' healing activity in a two-fold manner by declaring, first, in his Pentecost sermon to the Jews of Jerusalem that Jesus was "a man attested to you by God with mighty works and wonders and signs that God did through him, *as you yourselves know*" (Acts 2:22), this remark implying that Christ's many miracles were not done in a rural corner of the land but were done everywhere in the full light of day so that even his enemies had to acknowledge them, and second, in his sermon to Cornelius' household that Jesus "went about doing good and healing all who were oppressed" (Acts 10:38).

With pardonable overstatement, if it is overstatement at all, Benjamin Warfield writes: "For a time disease and death must have been almost banished from the land."[5]

To these "signs and wonders" having to do with the alleviation of human suffering, one must add Jesus' so-called "nature miracles" such as

- the changing of water into wine (John 2:1-11),
- the two miraculous catches of fish (Luke 5:1-11; John 21:1-14),
- the stilling of the storm on the Sea of Galilee (Matt. 8:23-27; Mark 4:35-41; Luke 8:22-25),
- the feeding of the five thousand (Matt. 14:15-21; Mark 6:34-44; Luke 9:12-17; John 6:5-14),
- the walking on the sea (Matt. 14:22-27; Mark 6:45-52; John 6:16-21),
- the feeding of the four thousand (Matt. 15:32-39; Mark 8:1-10),
- the four-drachma coin in the fish's mouth (Matt. 17:24-27), and
- the cursing of the fig tree (Matt. 21:18-22; Mark 11:12-14, 20-21).

---

[5]Benjamin B. Warfield, "The Historical Christ" in *The Person and Work of Christ* (Philadelphia: Presbyterian and Reformed, 1950), 31.

If the New Testament record is reliable here, as we believe it is and showed it to be in Chapter Three, never had any other age of the world witnessed such a dazzling display of "wonders," "signs," "powers," and "works" of God – a display that accords with such prophecies as Isaiah 35:5, "Then the eyes of the blind shall be opened and the ears of the deaf unstopped," and is therefore precisely what the elect could and would have expected with the advent of the Messiah and the dawning of the Messianic age. All the more is this shown to be true by the man born blind (who doubtless had made inquiry into the matter) whom Jesus had healed who declared: "Never since the beginning of the world has it been heard that anyone opened the eyes of a man born blind" (John 9:32). Indeed, not only the canonical Gospels but also higher criticism's so-called "earlier sources" underlying the Gospels – *Ur-Markus*, the hypothetical Matthean *Logia*, the Lucan "special sources," indeed, every so-called "earlier source" of the Gospel narratives that has been advanced to date – "give us not only a miracle-working Jesus, but a Jesus whose miracle-working is an essential element of his manifestation."[6] One must conclude that the consistent historical portrait of the four Gospels' representation of Jesus' miracles in its entirety is such that it really cannot be rationally doubted that such extraordinary events occurred. To deny that they occurred is to assert that all four Evangelists (as well as Peter [see Acts 2:22] and Paul [see 1 Cor. 15]) erred in this matter of Jesus' miracles and are not trustworthy guides in matters of faith.

Critical responses

Much effort has been expended nonetheless through the centuries to explain away Jesus' works of power, some explanations more speculative, some more crassly rationalistic than others, but all having as their chief aim the reduction of Jesus to manageable human dimensions.

---

[6]Benjamin B. Warfield, "The Question of Miracles" in *Selected Shorter Writings of Benjamin B. Warfield* (Nutley, N. J.: Presbyterian and Reformed, 1973), II, 187.

Baruch Spinoza (1632–1677), the Dutch rationalist philosopher, for example, argued in his *Tractatus Theologico-politicus* (1670) that God was a God of such unchangeable order that were he to work a miracle, since that miracle would then be as much God's law as the law of nature it violated, he would violate the unchangeable order he had decreed for the laws of nature and thus contradict himself.

David Hume (1711–1776), the Scottish philosopher of the Enlightenment, argued in his "Essay on Miracles," a section of his *Philosophical Essays Concerning Human Understanding* (1748), that the only case in which the evidence for a miracle could prevail over the evidence against it would be that situation in which the falseness or error of the affirming witness would be a greater miracle than the miracle to which he bore witness.

Friedrich Schleiermacher (1768–1834), considered the father of liberal Protestant theology, contended in his *The Christian Faith* (1821) that Christ's miracles were such only for those in respect to whom they were first done but not miracles in themselves, being but the anticipation of the discoveries of the laws that govern in the kingdom of nature. According to Schleiermacher, by the providence of God Christ simply possessed a deeper acquaintance with the laws of nature than any other man before or after him, and was able to evoke from the hidden recesses of nature those laws that were already at work therein and to employ them for others' benefits.

Another German theologian of the same period, Heinrich Paulus (1761–1851), in his *Exegetical Handbook Concerning the First Three Gospels* (1830–1833) argued that the Evangelists did not intend their reports to be understood as miracles but only as ordinary facts of everyday experience. Thus Christ

> ...did not heal an impotent man at Bethesda, but only detected an imposter; He did not change water into wine at Cana, but brought in a new supply of wine when that of the house was exhausted; He did not multiply the loaves, but, distributing his own and his disciples' little store, set an example of liberality, which was quickly followed by others who had like stores,

and thus there was sufficient for all; He did not cure blindness
otherwise than any skilful oculist might do it; – which, indeed,
they [the Evangelists] observe, is clear; for with His own lips He
declared that He needed light for so delicate an operation – 'I
must work the works of Him that sent Me, while it is day; the
night cometh, when no man can work' (John 9:4); He did not
walk on the sea, but on the shore; He did not tell Peter to find a
stator in the fish's mouth but to catch as many fish as would sell
for that money; He did not cleanse a leper, but pronounced him
cleansed; He did not raise Lazarus from the dead, but guessed
from the description of his disease that he was only in a swoon,
and happily found it as He had guessed.[7]

Then there was David Strauss (1808–1874) who under the
influence of Hegelian thought, in his famous *Life Of Jesus,
Critically Examined* (1835–1836), argued that the supernatural
elements in the Gospels, including the miracles of Jesus, were
simply Hellenistic "myth," created between the death of Christ
and the writing of the Gospels in (so he thought) the second
century.

Rudolf Bultmann also espoused a position not too different
in its final conclusion from that of Strauss. And Joachim
Jeremias, in his *New Testament Theology* (I) (Eng. trans., 1971),
after critical literary and linguistic analyses, comparisons with
Rabbinic and Hellenistic miracle stories, and form-critical
analyses of the individual miracle stories, contends that one is
left with only a "historical nucleus" of "psychogenous" healings
(exorcisms) and healings through "overpowering therapy" – in
short, healings produced by psychic powers.

G. Vermes in his *Jesus the Jew* (1973) takes a different
approach, categorizing Jesus as a "charismatic" similar to other
"Galilean charismatics" such as Honi the Circle-Drawer and
Hanina ben Dosa. Morton Smith, the title of whose book, *Jesus
the Magician* (1978), leaves little to guesswork respecting his
estimate of Jesus, makes Jesus out to be simply a magician.

[7]Cited by Richard C. Trench, *Notes on the Parables of Our Lord* (London:
SPCK, 1904), 82-83.

A. E. Harvey's *Jesus and the Constraints of History* (1982) is not as radical in its denials as the former two books, but he reduces the authentic miracles of Jesus to eight in number – those dealing with healings of the deaf, dumb, blind, and lame.

Evangelical responses

A separate and detailed response in support of the historicity and authenticity of each of Jesus' mighty works would require far more time than is possible here. Suffice it to say that this has been done, ably and often when the need has risen, by such men as R. C. Trench in his *Notes on the Miracles of our Lord* (see Chap. V, "The Assaults on the Miracles"), J. B. Mozely in his *Eight Lectures on Miracles,* J. Gresham Machen in his *Christianity and Liberalism* (see Chap. 5, "Christ,"), C. S. Lewis in his *Miracles,* Bernard Ramm in his *Protestant Christian Evidences* (see Chap. 5, "Rebuttal to Those Who Deny Miracles"), H. van der Loos in his *The Miracles of Jesus,* Norman L. Geisler in his *Miracles and Modern Thought, Gospel Perspectives: The Miracles of Jesus,* edited by David Wenham and Craig L. Blomberg, Blomberg's *Gospel Truth: Are the Gospels Reliable History?* (see Chap. 3, "Miracles"), and Robert B. Strimple, *The Modern Search for the Real Jesus.* It has been shown time and again that every assessment of the supernatural Christ and his miracles as being spurious or rationally explicable has been the result of the antagonist making his own *a priori* opinion of the nature of God or of the world, that is, his own worldview, the touchstone of what is and is not possible.

The Christian, of course, places the question of the historicity and authenticity of Jesus' miracles within his worldview as well. But his worldview, divinely given him in grace, includes the total context of Christian theism *per se.* J. Gresham Machen writes:

> Once admit the existence of a personal God, Maker and Ruler of the world, and no limits, temporal or otherwise, can be set to the creative power of such a God. Admit that God once

created the world, and you cannot deny that He might engage in creation again.[8]

Yes, indeed! Admit that God once created the world, and you cannot deny that he might divide the Sea at the time of the exodus (Exod. 14:21-29) and later part the Jordan River to facilitate Israel's conquest of Canaan (Josh. 3:15-17). Admit that God once created the world, and you cannot deny that he might cause the sun to stand still in the days of Joshua (Josh. 10:12-14). Admit that God once created the world, and you cannot deny that he might withhold rain three years from Israel according to Elijah's word (1 Kings 17:1-7). Admit that God once created the world, and you cannot deny that he might cause an iron ax head to float on water (2 Kings 6:5-7). Admit that God once created the world, and you cannot deny that he might cause a great fish to swallow Jonah and regurgitate him on to dry land. Admit that God once created the world, and you cannot deny that he might send his angel to kill 185,000 Assyrians in one night (2 Kings 19:35). Admit that God once created the world, and you cannot deny that he might cause the shadow of the sun to reverse itself ten degrees on the sundial of Ahaz (2 Kings 20:9-11). Admit that God once created the world, and you cannot deny that he might fertilize Mary's ovum without the aid of a human father. Admit that God once created the world and you cannot deny that he might create a moving "star" low in the sky that led the Magi to the very house in which the young Jesus resided (Matt. 2:2, 9-10). Admit that God once created the world, and you cannot deny that he might cause the land to go dark during our Lord's crucifixion at Passover time when the moon was at its full and not between the earth and the sun in order to cause a solar eclipse (Matt. 27:45; Mark 15:33; Luke 23:44).[9] Admit

---

[8]J. Gresham Machen, *Christianity and Liberalism* (Grand Rapids: Eerdmans, 1923), 102.

[9]Nor was the darkness the result of a mid-eastern sirocco, that insufferably hot wind that carries sand that frequently obscures the light, because it would not have resulted in causing complete darkness.

that God once created the world, and you cannot deny that he might raise Jesus from the dead (Rom. 6:4). Admit that God once created the world, and you cannot deny that he might seat Jesus Christ on the throne of the universe "far above all rule and authority and power and dominion, and above every name that is named, not only in this age but also in the one to come" (Eph. 1:20-21). Admit that God once created the world, and you cannot deny that he might again send Jesus Christ from heaven someday to raise all men from death, to transform the living, and to separate his people from evildoers (Matt. 25:31-46; 1 Cor. 15:51-55). Now replace all these recurring "might's" here with the words "did" or "will" (in the case of the last one) and you have the truth of the matter, because the Bible that we have already shown is inspired teaches so. In fact, admit Christian theism and every supernatural act and every recorded miracle of God in Holy Scripture takes its rightful place in the divine purpose. Paul expressed this truth when he asked Agrippa and his court: "Why is it thought incredible by any of you that God raises the dead?" (Acts 26:8).

The Christian also places the question of the historicity and authenticity of Jesus' miracles in the more narrow context of the reality of sin and its effects. He realizes that man's only hope of conquest over it is in the coming to him of supernatural aid from outside the human condition.[10] He believes this exigency is fully met in the supernatural Savior who gave evidence of his supernatural origin and character through, among other means, his working of mighty miracles during his earthly ministry.

Grant, in other words, the fact of the infinite, personal God and the exigencies for mankind caused by human sin and no philosophical or historical barrier stands in the way of the historicity of any of the supernaturalism and miracles of Scripture. The miracles of the Gospels follow as a matter of course as a natural aspect of Christian theism.

---

[10]Machen, *Christianity and Liberalism*, 104-06.

The Significance of Jesus' Miracles

Within the context of biblical theism, the weight of Jesus' miracles (so also all of the New Testament miracles), both separately and collectively, point, according to Jesus' own testimony, to a two-fold conclusion: First, they testified to the dawning of the messianic age in the coming of the Messiah (Matt. 12:28); second, they testified to his own divine character as the Son of God who visited this poor planet on a mission of mercy (Matt. 20:28; Mark 10:45) to seek and to save that which was lost. Consider Jesus' testimony regarding the significance of his miraculous works:

• **John 5:36**
In the John 5 context, where may be found a most amazing series of Jesus' claims to equality with God, in addition, Jesus said, to John the Baptist's witness (5:33-35), the Father's witness (doubtless including but not to be restricted to the confirmation from heaven at the time of his baptismal "commissioning") (5:37), and the witness of the Old Testament Scriptures (5:39, 46): "...the very work that the Father has given me to finish, and that I am doing, testifies that the Father has sent me" (5:36). These unique works – unique because they were "works...that no one else did" (John 15:24), unique too because they "bear upon them the hallmark of their divine origin"[11] – underscored, he said, his uniqueness as one not of human origin but as one whom "the Father sent" from heaven.

• **John 9:1-41**
The man born blind properly concluded from his healing that the one who had healed him was a prophet (9:17) and from God (9:33). That was all he could conclude at that point, knowing no more about Jesus than he did. But when Jesus informed him later, after the man had been expelled from the synagogue, that he

---

[11]Leon Morris, *The Gospel According to John* (Grand Rapids: Eerdmans, 1971), 328.

was the Son of Man he believed on Jesus as such and worshiped him (9:35-38), giving him that reverence that is appropriate to God. This is the only place in John's Gospel where someone is *said* to worship Jesus though others did, of course, such as Thomas (John 20:28).

• John 10:24-25, 37-38

In these verses, in direct response to the demand from the religious leaders, "If you are the Messiah, tell us plainly," Jesus replied: "I did tell you, but you do not believe. The miracles I do in my Father's name speak for me." He then said: "Do not believe me unless I do what my Father does. But if I do it, even though you do not believe me, believe the miracles, that you may learn and understand that the Father is in me and I in the Father." By these remarks, Jesus asserts that his miracles bore testimony both to his messianic investiture and to that intimate union between the Father and himself that he describes in terms that some theologians have urged come nothing short of a mutual indwelling or interpenetration of the persons of the Father and the Son.

• John 14:11

In his Upper Room Discourse, after making the marvelous claims that "anyone who sees me has seen the Father" (14:9) and that he and the Father were in personal union one with the other (14:10-11), Jesus urged his disciples to believe him for his own words' sake, but if they had any hesitancy concerning his words, then "at least," he said, "because of the works themselves believe." Again, his works, he declared, testified to his divine nature.

• Matthew 11:4-5; Luke 7:22

As confirmation to John the Baptist that he was indeed the "one who was to come," that is, the divine Messiah, Jesus said to John's disciples: "Go back and report to John what you hear and see: The blind receive sight, the lame walk, those who have leprosy are cured, the deaf hear, the dead are raised, and the good news is preached to the poor." Clearly, Jesus implied that his miracles validated and authenticated the fact that the messianic age had come in his own person as the divine Messiah.

• Matthew 9:1-8; Mark 2:1-12; Luke 5:17-26

On this occasion Jesus vindicated his right as the Son of Man to forgive sin – a prerogative of God alone – by healing the paralytic.

I must also note the testimony of John and Peter regarding Jesus' miracles. By his first miracle, John informs us in John 2:11, Jesus "revealed his glory." And what glory was that? His was just "the glory of the one and only [Son] who came from the side of his Father" (John 1:14). What is it then that John says Jesus' first miracle, as a "sign," signified but just his glory as the divine Son of God!

Then Peter's opening remark (Acts 2:22) in his sermon on the Day of Pentecost is also quite revealing: "Jesus of Nazareth [was] a man attested to you by God with miracles and wonders and signs that God performed through him in your midst, as you yourselves know" (see also Acts 10:38-39). Here Peter attests to the authenticating value of Jesus' miracles – they testified to God's approval of the "man" Jesus. And his statement, "as you yourselves know," makes the point that Jesus' miracles were not done in a rural corner of the land but were done everywhere and so publicly that they could not be denied. He challenged his audience by implication to deny them if they dared. Jesus' miracles meant then that God approved of his teaching. And in that teaching he claimed to be the Son of God, one with the Father, and in possession of the rights and privileges of deity. Finally, the author of Hebrews writes that God bore witness to the "great salvation" in Christ by "signs and wonders and various miracles and gifts of the Holy Spirit distributed according to his will" (Heb. 2:3-4).

We must conclude that Jesus' miraculous works, when viewed as Jesus and the New Testament writers doubtless intended that they should be viewed, namely, as supernatural events in space-time history, both authenticated his teachings and were themselves direct and immediate indications of the presence of the messianic age and his divine character as the messianic King.

Jesus' Transfiguration

Another of Jesus' miracles, one of a most unusual kind, must now be addressed for the sake of completeness. I refer to his transfiguration in which the glory of his deity "metamorphasized" his humanity.

Its background

Peter's great confession at Caesarea Philippi that Jesus was "the Christ, the Son of the living God" (Matt. 16:16; see Mark 8:29; Luke 9:20) marked the beginning of a new emphasis in Jesus' instruction of his disciples. Now that they were fully convinced that he was the Messiah, Jesus began to emphasize the necessity of his death and resurrection[12] (which latter event, as the instrumental means to his enthronement at the Father's right hand, he apparently thought of in "shorthand" fashion for both his resurrection *and* ascension since he says nothing about the latter event but rather assumes it when later he speaks about his Parousia or coming – Matt. 16:21; Mark 8:31; Luke 9:22). Assured by Peter's confession, it was now both possible and needful for him to infuse the messianic concept with the content of the Servant Song of Isaiah 52:13–53:2 and to correct the purely nationalistic associations that still lingered in the

---

[12]This incident at Caesarea Philippi should not be regarded as marking the point of the emergence of a totally new *doctrine* in Jesus' teaching, as dispensationalists suggest. Rather, it pinpoints only the beginning of a new *emphasis* upon a doctrine that can be found in his earliest teaching (see John 2:19-22; 3:14; by implication also in Matt. 9:15; Mark 2:20; Luke 5:35).

disciples' minds (see Matt. 16:22-23; Mark 9:32-33; 10:35-37; Luke 9:46: Acts 1:6). So from that moment to the end of his ministry, even though his disciples did not understand him (Mark 9:32; Luke 18:34), Jesus kept constantly and prominently before them the fact of his "departure that he was about to accomplish at Jerusalem" (see Matt. 17:22-23; 20:17-19, 22, 28; 21:39; 26:2, 11-12, 24, 28; Mark 9:31; 10:32-34, 38, 45; 12:8; 14:8, 21, 24; Luke 9:51, 53; 13:33; 17:11; 18:31-33; 22:20).

But he not only began to speak more often than he had done before about *his* suffering and death but in this context he also informed them that they as his disciples must be prepared to die as well and must never be ashamed of him, else "the Son of Man will be ashamed of [them] when he comes in his glory and in the glory of his Father and of the holy angels" (Luke 9:23-26; see Matt. 16:24-27; Mark 8:34-37). Solemn words these – both those concerning his own passion and those concerning his demand from his disciples for unflagging loyalty to him. The Synoptic Evangelists all report that following immediately upon this reference to his return in glory (that is in itself an implicit claim to the messianic investiture), our Lord then cryptically declared: "Some who are standing here shall not taste death before they see the Son of Man coming in his kingdom" (Matt. 16:28),[13] words doubtless intended to be words of encouragement to counterbalance the apprehension that his previous words concerning martyrdom must have invoked in the minds of those present with him on that occasion. This

---

[13]The other Synoptists report this "Son of Man" saying in essentially the same way. Luke's account reads simply: "...until they see the kingdom of God" (9:27), that I take to mean, because in all the Gospels the Kingdom of God and the person of Jesus as the Messiah are integrally and inseparably bound together, "until they see the kingdom of the divine Messiah"; Mark's account reads: "until they see the kingdom of God having come in power" (9:1), that adds the idea that the Messiah's kingdom will have come with accompanying manifestations indicative of the presence of divine omnipotence. See Gruenler, "Son of Man," *Evangelical Dictionary of Theology,* 1036, for the view that Jesus employs the title in a *corporate* sense both here and in Matthew 10:23.

cryptic saying implicitly enjoined them to view his passion and their own persecution against the background of his and (by extension) their own ultimate and eternal glory.

C. E. B. Cranfield neatly summarizes seven suggestions that have been proposed for the fulfilling referent of this saying,[14] any one of which, I would submit, is infinitely to be preferred to the widely-held view that Jesus mistakenly expected his Parousia to take place within the lifetime of that generation of disciples. For myself, with Cranfield,[15] William L. Lane,[16] and (I would suspect) most evangelicals, I believe that Jesus was referring to his transfiguration that took place a week later, which event all three Synoptic Gospels place immediately after this saying. Such a fulfillment meets all the requirements of the saying:

- The phrase, "*some* who are standing here," would refer to his "inner circle" of disciples, Peter, James, and John, who alone were present at the transfiguration.

- The phrase, "shall not taste of death," that is, "shall not die," finds explanation for its presence in the reference that our Lord had just made to the need for the disciple to "take up his cross" and "lose his life for me." The argument of some that if Jesus' transfiguration is made the fulfilling referent of Jesus' remark, then the "some" in the first phrase would imply

---

[14]C. E. B. Cranfield, *The Gospel According to Saint Mark* (Cambridge: University Press, 1966), 285-88. The seven, briefly, are as follows: (1) Dodd's use of it in support of his view of "realized eschatology"; (2) the view that "shall not taste of death" refers to spiritual death, from which faithful disciples will be exempted; (3) Michaelis' view that the meaning is that there will be some at least who will have the privilege of not dying before the Parousia, but that it is not said when these will live and not implied that they must belong to Jesus' contemporaries; (4) the destruction of Jerusalem in A.D. 70; (5) Pentecost; (6) Vincent Taylor's view that Jesus was referring to a visible manifestation of the Rule of God displayed for men to see in the life of the Elect Community; and (7) the transfiguration.

[15]Cranfield, *The Gospel According to Saint Mark*, 287-88.

[16]William L. Lane, *The Gospel of Mark* (Grand Rapids: Eerdmans, 1974), 313-14.

that at least some if not all of the others there present *would* die in the next few days, is a *non sequitur*. For while Jesus' remark implies that the majority of those present would not see this thing themselves in their lifetime, it does not mean that they must necessarily die before *some* did see it.

- The phrase, "before they *see*," fits well with the sustained emphasis in the transfiguration narrative on this inner circle of disciples *seeing* him in his "unearthly" radiance (see the phrases "transfigured *before* them" and "what you have *seen*" in Matt. 17:2, 9; the phrases "transfigured *before* them," "there *appeared* before them," and "what they had *seen*" in Mark 9:2, 4, 9; and the phrases "they *saw* his glory" and "what they had *seen*" in Luke 9:32, 36).

- The phrase, "the Son of Man coming in his kingdom" (Mark: "with power") "is a not unfair description of what the three saw on the mount of Transfiguration,"[17] for Jesus' transfiguration was, although momentary, nonetheless a real and witnessed manifestation of his sovereign power and glory that pointed forward, as an anticipatory foretaste, to his Parousia when his kingdom would come "with power and glory" after he had put all his enemies under his feet (Mark 13:26).

Its historicity

Before we comment further on the significance of the transfiguration, I need to address the issue of its historicity in view of the modern assaults upon it. Regarding the view of Bultmann that continues to find steady support to this day that the transfiguration account "is an Easter-story [that is, a resurrection appearance] projected backward into Jesus' lifetime,"[18] that is, a legendary resurrection appearance mistakenly displaced backward in time into the pre-resurrection material, it

---

[17]Cranfield, *The Gospel According to Saint Mark*, 288.
[18]Bultmann, *Theology of the New Testament*, translated by Kendrick Grobel (London: SCM, 1952), I, 26, 27, 30, 45, 50.

need only be said that G. H. Boobyer[19] and C. H. Dodd[20] have convincingly demonstrated that nothing about it resembles Jesus' later resurrection appearances. For example, all of the accounts of the resurrection appearances in the Gospels begin with Jesus being absent while here he is present from the beginning. Again, in all of the accounts of Jesus' resurrection appearances, Jesus' spoken word is prominent where here he is silent as far as any encouragement or instruction to his disciples is concerned. He speaks, but to Moses and Elijah about *his* future death (Luke 9:31). Then again, the presence of Moses and Elijah here is strange if this is a resurrection appearance, since no figure from beyond the grave ever appears at the same time with him in the resurrection appearances. Finally, this account contains none of the features that one might have expected if it is an appearance in the context of which Peter is present as a guilt-ridden disciple (see John 21). Consequently, Dodd concludes:

> To set over against these points of difference I cannot find a single point of resemblance. If the theory of a displaced post-resurrection appearance is to be evoked for the understanding of this difficult *pericope*, it must be without any support from form-criticism, and indeed in the teeth of the presumption which formal analysis establishes.[21]

Against the view of E. Lohmeyer[22] and others that it is a non-historical, symbolical expression of a "theological conviction" concerning Jesus derived (By whom? They do not say) from

---

[19]G. H. Boobyer, *St. Mark and the Transfiguration Story* (Edinburgh: T. & T. Clark, 1942), 11-16.

[20]C. H. Dodd, "The Appearances of the Risen Christ: An Essay in Form Criticism of the Gospels" in *Studies in the Gospels*, edited by D. E. Nineham (Oxford: Basil Blackwell, 1955), 9-35. See also J. Schiewind, *Das Evangelium Nach Markus* (Göttingen: Vandenhoeck & Ruprecht, 1949), 123.

[21]C. H. Dodd, "The Appearances of the Risen Christ," 25.

[22]E. Lohmeyer, *Das Evangelium des Markus* (Göttingen: Vanderhoeck & Ruprecht, 1937), 173-81.

imagery drawn from the Old Testament Feast of Tabernacles (see Peter's reference to "booths"), Cranfield marshals details in the account that are very strange if the pericope was only a theological statement created by the early church, such as Mark's "after six days" and Peter's use of "Rabbi" and his absurd statement about the booths. This title of Jesus as "Rabbi" and Peter's thoughtless statement are hardly likely to have been put in the mouth of a chief apostle if the post-Easter church was creating a symbolic narrative with a lofty theological statement about Jesus as its purpose.[23] A fairer analysis will conclude that Mark was intending to relate something that really happened.

Finally, Matthew's *to horama* ("the vision") (17:9), that I would translate by "that which you have seen," need not mean that what is reported here occurred merely in a vision that the disciples had. Three facts register tellingly against the view that Jesus' transfiguration was simply a visionary experience shared by the three disciples: First, a single vision is not shared, at least normally, by a plurality of persons at the same time; second, *horama* may be used of what is seen in the ordinary way (see Deut. 28:34); third, Luke expressly declares that the disciples "had been very sleepy," but it was when "they became fully awake" that "they saw his glory and the two men standing with him" (9:32). So much then for this event being simply a vision that the disciples shared.

Everything about the Gospel accounts suggests that the Evangelists intended to report an event that actually happened, an event that could have been seen by others had they been present; and no argument has been advanced by solid scholarship to date that overthrows the traditional view of the church that represents the transfiguration as an actual occurrence in the life of Jesus and the lives of the three disciples. Therefore, I will presume the historicity of the event and proceed to an exposition of its meaning.

---

[23]Cranfield, *The Gospel According to Saint Mark*, 293-94.

Its meaning

The "metamorphosis" itself

The accounts all begin by informing the reader that a week after Jesus' cryptic prophecy,[24] Jesus took Peter, James, and John up into a mountain.[25] Luke alone adds, "to pray." And while he was praying, we are told, Jesus was "transfigured" (*metemorphōthē*) before them. We are not left to wonder about the nature of this "metamorphosis." Two aspects of his physical appearance in particular are singled out for comment: His face (but this probably included his entire body as well because of the reference to his garments) and his clothing. While Luke simply states that "the appearance of his face was changed" (9:29), Matthew writes: "His face shone like the sun" (17:2). And while Matthew simply states that "his clothes became as brilliant as the light" (17:2), Mark adds that they became "dazzling white, whiter than any cleaner on earth could bleach them" (9:3), and Luke writes that they were "gleaming as lightning" (9:29). If this transformation took place at night, as some details in the Lukan account suggest (see 9:32, 37), the scene unfolding before the disciples must have been all the more fearsomely awesome (Mark 9:6), beyond the capacity of any words fully to describe.

This "transfiguration" of Jesus' appearance Luke characterized in two words: It was a revelation of "his glory" (9:32)

---

[24]Matthew's and Mark's "after six days" could place this event on the seventh day, especially if it occurred at night after the close of the sixth day, whereas Luke's "some eight days after," by inclusive reckoning, as in John 20:26, also means "on the seventh day." In any event, Luke's *hōsei* ("about") suggests that he was conscious that his number of days was an approximation to the figure given in the other Gospels.

[25]See Walter L. Liefeld, "Theological Motifs in the Transfiguration Narratives" in *New Dimensions in New Testament Study*, edited by R. N. Longenecker and M. C. Tenney (Grand Rapids: Zondervan, 1974), 167, fn. 27, for an interesting defense of Mt. Meron rather than the more traditional Mt. Tabor or Mt. Hermon as the most likely site of the transfiguration. I mention this fact that a scholar could debate on which mountain the event occurred to underscore the space/time historical character of the transfiguration.

– a momentary substantiation of the essence of his prophecy in Luke 9:26 where he makes mention of "his glory." Because Luke declares that Moses and Elijah, whose appearances are mentioned by all three Synoptics, also appeared in "glorious splendor" (9:31), one might at first be disinclined to make too much of Jesus' transfiguration insofar as that feature in the accounts indicating anything unique about him is concerned, and conclude that the combined glory of all three is simply indicative of the "supernaturalism" of the occasion. But Peter would declare later that, in seeing what they saw, the disciples were made "eyewitnesses of [*Jesus'*] *megaleiotēs*" (2 Pet. 1:16), that is, *his* "grandeur," "sublimity," or "majesty." He says nothing about Moses and Elijah. This word is used on only two other occasions in the New Testament – as an attribute of God in Luke 9:43 and as an attribute of the goddess Diana of Ephesus in Acts 19:27, clearly indicating that it is a word that designates the glory of deity. For Peter the word took up into itself the idea also of divine power (see *dunamis*, 2 Pet. 1:16). So Jesus' "metamorphosis" was a visible manifestation, we may safely conclude, of his divine "glory" (Luke 9:32) and "majesty" (2 Pet. 1:16), revealed in "power" (2 Pet. 1:16).

The voice from the cloud
In response to Peter's thoughtless statement invoked by this awesome sight: "Rabbi, it is good for us to be here. Let us put up three shelters – one for you, one for Moses and one for Elijah" (Mark 9:5), in order to remove even the remotest notion that these three "glorious" figures should be regarded in any sense as "equal in power and glory," God appeared theophanically in the form of a bright cloud that enveloped them, and a voice from the cloud said: "This is my beloved Son, in whom I am well pleased. Listen to him!" (Matt. 17:5-6). Whereas the Father's voice from heaven at his baptism *confirmed to Jesus* his rightful claim to Sonship, here it *attests to his disciples* his unique station as the Son of God. Here, as there, these words signalized Jesus' personal and essential divine Sonship as the antecedent ground

and presupposition of his messianic investiture that is alluded to in the final words, "Listen to him," words reminiscent of Deuteronomy 18:15, "The Lord your God will raise up for you a prophet like me [that is, Moses; recall his presence here on this occasion] from among your brothers. *You must listen to him.*" Peter was later to confirm that the voice was that of God the Father and that the Father's attestation "honored" and "glorified" the Lord Jesus Christ (2 Pet. 1:17). Here, then, in the Father's attestation to his Son, in addition to the feature of the transfiguration itself, do we find the second indication in the transfiguration accounts of Jesus' essential deity.

The disciples' question
Coming down from the mountain the next day (Luke 9:27), the disciples asked Jesus: "Why, therefore, do the teachers of the law say that Elijah must come first?" (Matt. 17:10; Mark 9:11). Their mention of Elijah, of course, was prompted by the fact that they had just seen him. But what lay behind their question about him? There can be no doubt that it was something in Malachi's prophecy that now was perplexing them. Malachi had said that Elijah would come *before* the Lord came (3:1), *before* the great and terrible day of the Lord (4:5) that they had just seen "in miniature." The implications of their question for the identity of Jesus must not be overlooked. The only conclusion that one can fairly draw is that for them Jesus – just attested as such by the glory of his deity shining through his humanity and by the heavenly Voice – was Malachi's "Lord who was to come," the Yahweh of the Old Testament, but the order of their historical appearances – Jesus had first appeared then Elijah came – seemed to them to be the reverse of what Malachi had predicted. This seeming inversion of the prophet's order was what was creating for them the quandary that provoked their question. Jesus solved their problem for them by informing them that "Elijah" (in the person of John the Baptist) had indeed come first, whom Jesus had then followed as that "Elijah's" Lord. By his exposition of Malachi's prophecy here, Jesus laid

unmistakable claim to being the Lord of Hosts, the Messenger of the Covenant, who had promised he would come *after* "Elijah," his messenger, had come.

The entire account of the transfiguration is replete – resplendent might be the more appropriate word – with indications of Jesus' essential divine Sonship. It is not surprising that those who deny his deity are so willing to reduce this miraculous event, together with the rest of his and his apostles' miracles, to legend or myth. But the Gospel accounts of Jesus' transfiguration stand, unfazed by the attempts of critical scholarship to make them into something that they are not, and thus they lend their combined voice to the larger consentient witness of Scripture to the biblical miracles in general and to Jesus' miracles in particular that testify to his essential divine Sonship in the Godhead and to his being the sole Savior of the world.

Chapter Seven

Faith's Reasons for Believing in Paul's Supernatural Conversion on the Damascus Road

F. F. Bruce has observed: "...no single event, apart from the Christ-event itself, has proved so determinant for the course of Christian history as the conversion and commissioning of Paul. For any one who accepts Paul's own explanation of his Damascus-road experience, it would be difficult to disagree with the observation of an eighteenth-century writer[1] that the 'conversion and apostleship of St. Paul alone, duly considered, was of itself a demonstration sufficient to prove Christianity to be a divine revelation.'"[2] What this writer meant by his remark

---

[1] That eighteenth-century writer was Lord George Lyttleton. Lyttleton, a brilliant English barrister, set out in his research into Saul's conversion to disprove it and to show that Christianity was a fraud. But his research compelled him to conclude otherwise, which conclusion may be found in his *Observations on the Conversion and Apostleship of St. Paul* (London: R. Dodsley, 1747), paragraph 1. Lyttleton's work, later published as "The Conversion of St. Paul" in *Infidelity* (New York: American Tract Society, n. d.), argued that Paul's conversion could be explained in only one of four ways: Either he was (1) an imposter who reported what he knew was false, or (2) an enthusiast driven by an overheated imagination and was therefore self-deceived, or (3) deceived by the fraud of others; or (4) telling the truth about his conversion and therefore the Christian religion is a divine revelation. If any one of the first three is the truth then it follows as certainly as night follows day that Christianity is a false faith for it would mean that the Bible erred in reporting his conversion the way it did, and it would mean that Protestantism in particular is in serous error because it has primarily followed Paul's lead in its theological formulations. Lyttleton, of course, endorsed the fourth explanation.

[2] F. F. Bruce, *Paul: Apostle of the Heart Set Free* (Reprint; Grand Rapids: Eerdmans, 1996), 75.

is that the entire "Paul phenomenon" – that is, the man together with his literary corpus – is inexplicable apart from the bodily resurrection of Jesus Christ. The conversion of Saul of Tarsus, if it could be shown to be true, would become a fourth great strand of biblical evidence – joining the facts of the empty tomb, Jesus' post-crucifixion appearances to his disciples, and their sudden transformation from fear to faith – for the reality of Christ's resurrection and the supernatural origin and character of Christianity. What is the evidence for this event?

The biblical material
The Acts accounts of Saul's conversion on his way to Damascus are recorded in Acts 9:1-9 (Luke's historical account in the third person), 22:3-16 and 16:2-18 (Luke's reports of Paul's personal accounts in the first person). Paul's own references to his conversion may be found in Galatians 1:15-16, 1 Corinthians 9:1, 15:8-10, Philippians 3:4-11, and 1 Timothy 1:12-16. In a sentence these passages make it clear that Saul's conversion was effected *objectively* by the glorified Christ's sudden appearance to him on the Damascus Road. Romans 7:7-25 is the only passage in Paul's writings that addresses his spiritual turmoil at the time. It suggests that God had prepared him *subjectively* for this encounter by bringing him under deep conviction of his sin and convincing him of his impotence regarding true and full obedience to the law of God. I think Robert Gundry is correct when he writes: "…we may call [Romans 7:7-25] the biography of Everyman if we like, but here Everyman's biography is the autobiography of Paul."[3]

Harvard theologian Krister Stendahl has argued that Saul's experience of meeting the glorified Christ, since it involved no change of religion or change of Gods but only a change of assignments, should be seen as a call and not a conversion.

---

[3]Robert H. Gundry, "The Moral Frustration of Paul Before His Conversion: Sexual Lust in Romans 7:7-25" in *Pauline Studies: Essays Presented to F. F. Bruce on His 70th Birthday*, edited by Donald A. Hagner and Murray J. Harris (Grand Rapids: Eerdmans, 1980), 229.

Saul, however, would later describe his experience much more radically than simply the receiving of a new assignment. In 1 Corinthians 15:8 he speaks of it as an "irregular birth." In Philippians 3:12 he speaks of it as an "arrest" – he was "apprehended by Christ Jesus." In Galatians 1:13 he speaks of his "previous life in Judaism,"[4] setting his former religious experience within Judaism off over against "the church of God," implying by the contrast that the one living and true God was in the church of Jesus Christ and not in Judaism.[5] In Philippians 3:4-8 he declares that he had come to regard his prior "Judaic" reasons for confidence in the flesh as "rubbish," which suggests a radical and complete break with his "Judaic" past. And in transferring his confidence as he did in his search for personal righteousness before God away from personal obedience to the Mosaic Law and the temple ritual to the cross work of Jesus Christ, who was the fulfillment and embodiment of these two central features of the Old Testament, Paul created a new religious pattern for others to follow. For while it is true that Paul continued to think of himself as a Jew, his radical reinterpretation of the Mosaic covenant and its law as a glorious anachronism (2 Cor. 3) and his rejection of the Gentile's need of circumcision for salvation did in fact constitute for him a religious conversion – a conversion away from the Judaism of the Second Temple period, the man-made deconstruction of Old Testament Yahwism (see Mark 7:6-8), to New Testament Yahwism, the fulfillment of Old Testament religion, which fulfillment would later come to be known under Paul's own influence as "Christianity."

Rationalizing explanations of the event

Extreme rationalizations of the event include the view that Saul either suffered a physical seizure of some kind or a sun

---

[4]The term "Judaism" occurs only twice in the New Testament – both times in Galatians 1:13-14. It denotes the national Jewish religion and way of life.

[5]One must remember that Judaism's God is an undifferentiated Monad while the triune God of Christianity is much more interesting.

stroke or, seeing a flash of lighting that blinded him and being thrown from his horse when it became startled and bolted under him (Luke's account says nothing about Saul being on a horse though he may well have been), struck his head on the ground and in the daze that followed imagined that he had seen Jesus Christ. But these explanations have not generally commended themselves even to the critical mind.

More popular is the view that, under the stress of his persecution of the church, Saul suffered a mental breakdown on the road to Damascus, and in his broken mental state imagined that the Lord of the very ones he was persecuting had called upon him to desist in his persecution and instead to serve him.

Probably the most popular naturalistic explanation is that Saul was subconsciously being conditioned by the logic of the Christian position and by his observance of the dynamic and gentle quality of Christians' lives and their patient fortitude under oppression. Then, it is said, when he underwent that "mood-changing" crisis experience, the precise nature and cause of which no one has been able to recover, he became convinced because of this prior pre-conditioning of mind that he should become a follower of Christ rather than his persecutor. In support of this explanation it is urged that the risen Christ's alleged statement to Paul, "It is hard for you to kick against the goads" (Acts 26:14), may mean that "Paul had been resisting a better conviction, gradually forming in his mind, that the disciples might be right about Jesus and he might be wrong."[6] In other words, for some time he had been stifling serious doubts of conscience about the propriety of his attitude about Christ by engaging himself in ever more feverish activity in persecution but his resistance to these doubts had brought him no peace of mind and the "goads" of conscience continued to afflict him. But near Damascus the subconscious conviction that had been afflicting him was at last allowed to

---

[6]See Janet Meyer Everts, "Conversion and Call of Paul" in *Dictionary of Paul and His Letters*, edited by Gerald F. Hawthorne, Ralph P. Martin, and Daniel G. Reid (Downers Grove, Illinois: Inter-Varsity, 1993), 156-63.

come to the surface, to overcome his resistance to Christ, and to begin to rule his life.

With Machen I would urge, since Paul would later say in 1 Timothy 1:13 that he had persecuted the church "in ignorance and unbelief," that Paul was "not conscious of any goad that before his conversion was forcing him into the new faith.... The meaning [of Jesus' statement] may be simply that the will of Christ is resistless, all opposition is in vain, the appointed hour of Christ has arrived,...all resistance...all hesitation, is as hopeless as for the ox to kick the goad; instant obedience alone is in place."[7]

It should be apparent that all psychologico-psychoanalytical explanations of Saul's Damascus Road experience leave too many questions unanswered. In addition to the impossibility of psychoanalyzing a person who lived almost two thousand years ago with any degree of clinical accuracy, what real evidence is there that Saul suffered a mental breakdown or that his conscience had been troubling him? (While we have already suggested, on the basis of Romans 7:7-25, that he was deeply troubled by the knowledge of his innate sinfulness, it is equally certain that he was not laboring under any guilt springing from his activities of persecution, for he knew he was acting under the auspices of the Sanhedrin, and he believed, with a zealot's passion, that he was serving God.) And what was the nature of the crisis experience that triggered his conversion? Such questions as these, and many more besides, must be answered satisfactorily before any credence can be given to these theories.

Then there is the view of Rudolf Bultmann who believed that all such depictions of "biblical supernaturalism" are actually reflections of either Gnostic mythology or Jewish Apocalyptic. But his own explanation of Saul's conversion is wholly unsatisfactory in that it fails to come to terms to any degree with the historical character of the Acts narrative itself: "Not having

---

[7]J. Gresham Machen, *The Origin of Paul's Religion* (Reprint; Grand Rapids: Eerdmans, 1965), 61-62.

been a personal disciple of Jesus, *he was won to the Christian faith by the kērygma of the Hellenistic church.*"[8] But neither is James D. G. Dunn's view any better when he concludes that it is impossible to know for sure whether Jesus was "'out there,' alive and making himself known to Paul." All that one can say with any certainty, Dunn continues, is that "Paul himself was convinced that what he saw was external to him" but it may well have been, "after all, all 'in the mind.'"[9]

Such conclusions frankly fail to come to terms with or to do justice to Luke's historical narration regarding Paul's conversion in Acts 9 or with Paul's later accounts in Acts 22 and 26 that he gave on the solemn occasions of defending his office and actions under the auspices of the Roman commander and before high governmental dignitaries respectively. The pertinent data indicate that his conversion was not subjectively induced. We are expressly informed that, while Saul alone saw the glorified Christ, the men who were traveling with him both heard a voice (Acts 9:7), though they did not understand its words (Acts 22:9), and saw a brilliant light (Acts 22:9; 26:13-14). And while it is true that Paul would later call the event a "vision from heaven" (Acts 26:19), which description by the way imputes an *ab extra* character to it, the accounts make it clear that his conversion was not subjectively self-induced in the sub-conscious but rather that it resulted from an initiating action external to him (Acts 9:3-4; 22:6-7; 26:13-14). Indeed, the ascended Christ represents *himself* as the initiator of the event in Acts 26:16: "I have appeared to you." And Ananias will say later that God had chosen Saul "to see the Righteous One and to hear words from his mouth" (Acts 22:14).

When all the facts in Acts 9, 22, and 26 and in Galatians 1:15-17, 1 Corinthians 9:1, and 15:8-10 are considered Richard Longenecker's judgment seems clearly justified:

---

[8] Rudolf Bultmann, *Theology of the New Testament*, translated by Kendrick Grobel (London: SCM, 1971), 1:187, emphasis original.

[9] James D. G. Dunn, *Jesus and the Spirit* (Philadelphia: Westminster, 1975), 107-08.

Only the Damascus encounter with Christ was powerful enough to cause the young Jewish rabbi to reconsider the death of Jesus; only his meeting with the risen Christ was sufficient to demonstrate that God had vindicated the claims and work of the One he was opposing. Humanly speaking, Paul was immune to the Gospel. Although he was ready to follow evidence to its conclusion, he was sure that no evidence could overturn the verdict of the cross, that is, that Christ died the death of a criminal. But…the eternal God "was pleased," as Paul says by way of reminiscence, "to reveal his Son to me" (Gal. 1:16). Thus Paul was arrested by Christ, and made his own (Phil. 3:12).[10]

Paul's Argument in Galatians for the Validity of his Apostleship Based upon His Own Life History and Religious Experience

In support of the facticity and historicity of Paul's conversion, the validity of his apostleship, and the "revealedness" of the gospel he proclaimed, one can produce no better argument than the one that he himself adduced under inspiration in Galatians 1:13–2:21 where he defends his apostolic authority and message against the Judaizers who had come to his churches in South Galatia, denied his apostolic authority, and proclaimed "another gospel" to his converts. The issue we are now facing is, in one sentence: What was the ultimate origin of Paul's apostolic commission and the gospel he proclaimed as an expression of that commission? A little reflection will show that he could have obtained his gospel and the authority to preach it from only one of three possible sources: Either from his Judaistic training, from the first apostles, or from Christ himself. I will explain:

From his Judaistic training?
Did Paul obtain his apostolic authority and the law-free gospel[11] he was preaching prior to his conversion from his *previous* life in

---

[10]Richard N. Longenecker, *The Ministry and Message of Paul* (Grand Rapids: Zondervan, 1971), 34-35.

[11]By "law-free gospel" I do not intend what flies under the flag of anti-nomianism, namely, that the gospel delivers the Christian from his or her

Judaism? To ask the question is to answer it. Certainly not! Paul describes his life experience in Judaism for us five times:

- Galatians 1:12-14 (the passage under discussion): "For you have heard of my previous way of life in Judaism, how intensely I persecuted the church of God and tried to destroy it. I was advancing in Judaism beyond many Jews of my own age and was extremely zealous for the traditions of my fathers."

- Acts 22:3: "I am a Jew, born in Tarsus of Cilicia, brought up in this city af the feet of Gamaliel, thoroughly trained in the law of our fathers, being zealouos for God...."

- Acts 26:4-5: "The Jews all know the way I lived ever since I was a child, from the beginning of my life in my own country, and also in Jerusalem. They have known me for a long time and can testify, if they are willing, that according to the strictest sect of our religion, I lived as a Pharisee."

- Philippians 3:4-6: "If anyone else thinks he has reasons to put confidence in the flesh, I have more: Circumcised on the eighth day, of the people of Israel, of the tribe of Benjamin, a Hebrew of the Hebrews; in regard to the law, a Pharisee, as for zeal, persecuting the church; as for legalistic righteousness, faultless."

- 1 Timothy 1:13: "...I was once a blasphemer and a persecutor and a violent man...."

It should be evident from these autobiographical descriptions that Paul was not proclaiming as the Christian apostle and

---

obligation to obey God's moral law as that law comes to expression in the ten commandments, in the two great love commandments, and in Christ's pattern of life. Obviously, the Christian should live under the law as the covenant rule of life. Rather, I intend what Paul intended when again and again he stated that "a man is not justified by works of law, but by faith in Jesus Christ" (Gal. 2:16) and that "a man is justified by faith apart from works of law" (Rom. 3:28). In this sense the gospel is "law-free."

missionary theologian what he had learned from his life in Judaism. To the contrary, as the Christian apostle and missionary theologian he directed men's trust away from Torah and Temple and personal law-keeping as means of salvation where his confidence as a Pharisee had resided and toward Jesus Christ for salvation.

From apostolic tutoring and authorization?

Did Paul obtain the gospel he was preaching and the authority to preach it *after* his conversion, if not at the feet of Gamaliel, at the feet of the original apostles? Luke informs us that immediately after his conversion on the Damascus Road he "proclaimed Jesus in the synagogues, saying, "He is the Son of God," and "confounded the Jews who lived in Damascus by proving that Jesus was the Christ" (Acts 9:20, 22). And Barnabas declared that at Damascus Paul "preached boldly in the name of Jesus" (Acts 9:27). So we know that Paul was preaching before he ever met any of the original Twelve. Listen now to Paul himself:

> "…when God…was pleased to reveal his Son to me…, I did not consult any man nor did I go up to Jerusalem to see those who were apostles before I was, but I went immediately into Arabia and later returned to Damascus." (Gal. 1:15-17)

In Arabia Paul did not devote himself to a life of quiet contemplation and reflection but in fact began to missionarize the populace there. There is separate corroborating evidence for his missionary labor there if Paul intended by his reference to "Arabia" the Nabataean Kingdom, for he informs us in 2 Corinthians 11:32-33 that "the governor under King Aretus [IV (9 B.C–40 A.D.), of the kingdom of the Nabataeans] guarded the city of Damascus in order to seize me." But why would the governor do this? One does not stir up the kind of trouble with civil authorities that he alludes to in the passage merely by quiet meditation. He was doubtless preaching to the populace. This data shows that long before Paul made any contact with the Jerusalem apostles he had already engaged himself in Gentile evangelization.

Then Paul informs us under a self-imposed oath (see Galatians 1:20: "I assure you before God that what I am writing to you is no lie") that three years elapsed after his conversion before he finally met any of the apostles. Even then, he informs us, it was only Peter and James he met and only for the space of fifteen days (Gal. 1:18-19). This was doubtless the visit Luke records in Acts 9:26-28, and while it is likely that it was at this time that Paul "received" the precise details of the "tradition" about Jesus' post-resurrection appearances, particularly those to Peter and to James, that he later "delivered" to the Corinthians in 1 Corinthians 15:5-7, it is evident, since the apostles had no opportunity to do so, that they conferred no authority upon him at that time. Acceding to the Jerusalem church's desire to get him out of town Paul then went into the regions of Syria and Cilicia and eleven years transpired during which time there was no contact between the Jerusalem apostolate and Paul. Paul informed his Galatian readers: "I was personally unknown to the churches of Judea that are in Christ. They only were hearing it said: 'He who used to persecute us is now preaching the faith he once tried to destroy'" (Gal. 1:22-23). Then Paul informs us that at the end of that eleven-year period (I am assuming here the correctness of the South Galatia view with respect to Paul's first missionary journey), that is, fourteen years after his conversion, he saw the apostles for only the second time, this time on the occasion of his so-called "famine relief" visit to Jerusalem recorded in Acts 11:27-30. So during these fourteen years he had contact with only two of the Jerusalem church leaders and that for only a two-week period. But he was preaching the gospel continually and throughout this entire period of time.

On the occasion of his famine-relief visit Paul informs us: "I set before [the apostles] the gospel that I preached among the Gentiles" (Gal. 2:2). The outcome of this meeting, Paul writes, was that the apostles "added nothing to my message" (Gal. 2:6) but to the contrary saw that "I had been entrusted with the gospel" (Gal. 2:7), that "God who was at work in Peter as an apostle to the circumcision was also at work in me [as an apostle] to the Gentiles" (Gal. 2:8), and accordingly, he says, they "gave me the right hand of fellowship" (Gal. 2:10). Their approval of his gospel indicates that Paul had not simply created out of whole cloth the content of his gospel. Again, they conferred no authority on him but rather acknowledged the authority from God that was already his, by virtue of which he had been engaged in his apostolic ministry among the Gentiles for fourteen years.

We may justly conclude, then, that throughout this entire period of time and beginning immediately after his conversion Paul apart from any human authorization was proclaiming with God's approval the true gospel, a fact that the Jerusalem apostles officially acknowledged.

From Christ's divine call and authorization?

If Paul was not preaching what he had learned during his life in Judaism *antecedent* to his conversion, it is equally clear from his review of the first fourteen years of his apostolic ministry that he was not preaching what he had learned from the original apostles *subsequent* to his conversion. Nor had they conferred the authority on him to engage in his ministry as an apostle. In fact, if any instruction passed between them, we may affirm from Galatians 2:11-14, it was he during an incident that arose later in Antioch who had to correct Peter publicly for the latter's actions that would have compromised the truth of the law-free gospel and that would have led to the permanent division of the church.

All of this means that the gospel Paul was proclaiming and the authority with which he was proclaiming it, he received neither from his Judaistic training before his conversion nor from the apostles after his conversion. Rather, he received them from the only remaining source, namely, *from his conversion experience itself* – "by revelation from Jesus Christ" (Gal. 1:12)! I do not mean to suggest that Saul had known nothing before his conversion about Jesus Christ or about the church's doctrinal teaching about him. He knew some things well enough, which was the reason he had persecuted the church, and as the church's persecutor he had confronted them often enough. What I mean is that Jesus' post-ascension appearance to Paul on the Damascus Road forced upon Paul the need to filter his knowledge about Jesus through an entirely new "hermeneutical grid." In sum, for Paul his encounter with Jesus Christ meant a new hermeneutical paradigm shift.

Nor do I mean to suggest by my remarks that Paul did not grow in his understanding of Christ during those fourteen years, for indeed, he continued to grow in his knowledge of Christ to the very end of his life (Eph. 4:11-13; Phil. 3:10-14). What I mean is that in all his "growing up" in his understanding of Christ he never "grew away" from that first clear "vision from heaven." It was *then* and it was *there* that his understanding of free grace and the gospel of justification by faith alone apart from works of law were made his apostolic possession.

Arguments Showing the Improbability of Another Explanation for His Radical Transformation Being Better than the Explanation Luke and Paul Himself Offer

Was Saul's conversion due to a sunstroke, hallucination, or some form of psychological seizure? We have already observed that some have proposed such as possible causes behind the transformation of the Jewish zealot into the great Christian apostle that he became. None of these is a likely cause for his change, however, since his travel companions, as we have already noted, also saw the blazing light and with him fell to the ground (Acts 22:9; 26:13-14). They also heard the sound of a voice though they did not understand what the voice was saying to Saul (Acts 9:7; 22:9).

Was Saul's conversion simply the expression of the wild and extravagant fanaticism of one who was given to serious psychological mood swings? Some have proposed this as the explanation for his conversion. But completely apart from the difficulty (really, the impossibility) of psychoanalyzing someone's mental state two thousand years after his death with any degree of clinical accuracy, anyone who considers the wisdom, the prudence, the calmness, and the serenity that Paul evidenced under extremely difficult circumstances, and above all, his humility (which characteristic is inconsistent with fanaticism) that he displayed in his letters, will find it very difficult to believe that his transformation was due simply to a major bipolar mood swing.

Was Saul simply a religious charlatan who changed his religious allegiance purely for purposes of self-aggrandizement? Some have proposed this but they must be able satisfactorily to answer the following four questions:

1. Is it likely that the prospect or the ostentation of some new learning produced his transformation? It is extremely difficult, if not impossible, to believe that Saul, zealot that he was for the "traditions of the fathers," would have cast aside all that he had been taught by Gamaliel and what he had learned through long years of study in favor of the opinion of fishermen of Galilee whom he had probably scarcely seen and who had never been educated in the approved schools of Jewish learning.

2. Is it likely that the love of authority prompted his change? It is extremely difficult, if not impossible, to believe that he who was already at the center of Jewish political and religious power – precisely where he wanted to be – abdicated in a moment the authority that he already possessed for authority within a "little flock" whose "Shepherd" had been executed and who themselves were being led as lambs to the slaughter and which "new authority" could only promise him that he too would be marked out for the same knife that he himself had drawn against them.

3. Is it likely that the love of material wealth provoked his conversion? It is extremely difficult, if not impossible,

to believe, whatever may have been the level of his own worldly possessions at the time, that the prospect of wealth would have been a factor in his conversion, for it is apparent that he was uniting himself to those who at the time were certainly poor, and the prospect before him was that which he actually came to know, namely, never having much and having to minister to his own necessities with the labor of his hands as a tentmaker.

4. Is it likely that the prospect of fame and worldwide prestige led him to become a follower of Jesus Christ? It is extremely difficult, if not impossible, to believe that his prophetic intuition at the time was so great that he could look beyond the shame and scorn that then rested on the servants of the crucified Christ and see that earthly glory that Christendom now heaps upon his memory.

What may we conclude from all this for apologetic and evangelistic purposes? In light of Paul's argument drawn from Galatians 1–2 and the improbability, if not the impossibility, of the contrary alternatives, I would urge, *first*, that the facticity and historicity of his conversion just as Luke's Acts reports are placed beyond all reasonable doubt. Accordingly, I would urge, *second*, that the conversion of Saul of Tarsus on the Road to Damascus in the manner that Luke records is in fact the fourth great strand of biblical evidence – joining the fact of the empty tomb, Jesus' numerous post-crucifixion appearances to his disciples, and their sudden transformation from fearful friends to fearless "kērygmatics" – for the supernatural origin and character of Christianity. *Third*, because the glorified Christ accompanied Saul's conversion with the following revelation: "…I have appeared to you for this purpose, to appoint you as a servant and witness to the things in which you have seen me and to those in which I will appear to you, delivering you from your people and from the Gentiles – to whom I am sending you to open their eyes, so that they may turn from darkness to light and from the power of Satan to God, that they may receive forgiveness of sins and a place among those who are sanctified by faith in me" (Acts 26:16-18), then to Ananias: "Go [to him], for he is a chosen instrument of mine to carry my name before the Gentiles and kings and the children of Israel" (Acts 9:15), then later again to Paul during his first post-conversion visit to Jerusalem: "Go, for I will send you far away to the Gentiles" (Acts 22:21) – because of these words from the glorified Christ himself, I say, that Saul was to be his apostle to the Gentiles, and accompanied as Paul's apostolic ministry was with the "signs of the apostle," namely, "signs and wonders and mighty works" (2 Cor. 12:12; see also Acts 9:12), the church can be certain that what Paul preached (1 Cor. 2:6-13) and what he wrote in his letters is inspired, inerrant special revelation (2 Tim. 3:16; 2 Pet. 3:16). So for apologetic purposes we may say that Saul's supernatural conversion guaranteed that his letters to the churches are "God-breathed" Scripture.

* * * * *

We have now defended the historicity of Christian theology as an intellectual discipline as a whole, Christ's virginal conception in the womb of the Virgin Mary, his mighty miracles during his earthly ministry, his bodily resurrection from the dead and ascension to heaven, and Saul's conversion on the Damascus Road, any one of which would prove that the Christian faith is historically true and supernatural and with their combined weight places the truthfulness of the Christian faith beyond all legitimate controversy. We have seen in each case that those who reject them as unhistorical or mythological do so on highly questionable critical and philosophical grounds with which they, with their world and life views as "biblical fools," are simply more comfortable psychologically and religiously. All of us are now responsible to bear witness courageously to Christ's gospel. We should do it with no fear that we will or can be refuted! But we should remember Paul's admonition as we do so:

The servant of the Lord must not quarrel, but be gentle to all, patient, teaching the ones who oppose him, that God may grant them repentance unto a knowledge of the truth, and that they may regain their senses and escape from the snare of the devil, having been taken captive by him to do his will. (2 Tim. 2:23-26)

Chapter Eight

Faith's Reasons for Rejecting Evidentialism: A Case Study in Apologetic Methodology

In the first chapter I observed that such responses as I have given in the preceding chapters to specific objections and difficulties raised against the Christian faith are usually possible only at the beginning of the apologetic "conversation." I said there that sooner or later apologetics will shift to the ultimate question of "first principles" and/or of one's "presuppositions." At this deeper level apologetics as a philosophical or epistemological discipline comes into its own. At this level of ultimate premises or of foundational issues the Christian apologist will deal with the question of apologetic methodology, the Bible as man's only *pou stō* for the justification of knowledge and personal significance, and the nature of truth. Once it is seen that these questions fall specifically and properly within the domain of Christian apologetics it will become clear that Christian apologetics as a discipline often entails an exercise in philosophical theology and takes us into the sphere of epistemology. These matters I will now begin to address.

Where should the Christian apologist begin methodologically in his argumentation for the truthfulness of Christianity and why? Should he in his effort to defend the faith and to persuade the unbeliever of Christianity's truth claims stand within the circle of special revelation and argue from there for its truthfulness as I have been doing in the foregoing chapters? Or should he begin his defense of the faith standing with the unbeliever outside the circle of special revelation and, putting his deeply held religious beliefs "on the shelf," so to speak, and assuming nothing ahead of time about the teaching of the Bible, argue for the truthfulness of the Christian Faith by employing the tests of truth endorsed by the unbeliever? For our answer to these questions we will consider the "Old Princeton [that is, before 1929] apologetic" as it came to expression in the so-called "Warfield apologetic."

Benjamin B. Warfield, born in 1851, was for almost thirty-four years from 1887 until his death in 1921 professor of didactic and polemic theology at Princeton Theological Seminary. He was a voluminous writer, penning an *Introduction to the Textual Criticism of the New Testament* (1886) that went through nine editions; *The Gospel of the Incarnation* (1893); *Two Studies in the History of Doctrine* (1893); *The Right of Systematic Theology* (1897); *The Significance of the Westminster Standards* (1898); *Acts and the Pastoral Epistles* (1902); *The Power of God Unto Salvation* (1903); *The Lord of Glory* (1907); *Calvin as a Theologian and Calvinism Today* (1909); *Hymns and Religious Verse* (1910); *The Saviour of the World* (1915); *The Plan of Salvation* (1915); *Faith and Life* (1916); and *Counterfeit Miracles* (1918).

In addition to his books, published sermons, and numerous popular articles,[1] Warfield wrote many lengthy essays over his professorial career that now appear in the ten-volume set, *The Works of Benjamin B. Warfield* (Reprint; Grand Rapids, Baker, 1991), on

- diverse biblical and theological topics such as Christian supernaturalism, the deity, virgin birth, sinlessness, mighty miracles, atoning death, and bodily resurrection of Christ, the biblical doctrine of the Trinity, predestination, modern theories of the

---

[1]See, for example, the one hundred and nineteen articles in the two-volume work, *Selected Shorter Writings of Benjamin B. Warfield*, edited by John E. Meeter (Nutley, N. J., Presbyterian and Reformed, 1970). There are others also, including two volumes of handwritten scrapbooks and fifteen volumes of *Opuscula (1880–1918)* (minor essays), collected and bound by Warfield himself.

atonement, Jonathan Edwards and the New England theology, and mysticism;
- the theological thought of Tertullian and Augustine;
- Calvin, both the man and his work, and Calvinism;
- the Westminster Assembly and its work of writing the *Westminster Confession of Faith* and *Catechisms*;
- twelve huge articles on perfectionism, totaling one thousand and ten pages, that provide entry into his understanding of the Christian life; and finally,
- forty-six critical reviews totaling 483 pages.

Although he wrote no book on the subject of apologetics, virtually all of his writings had a strong apologetic flair to them. Arguably the primary purpose of Warfield's apologetic was to uphold and defend the supernatural character of Christianity. For him Christianity could not be affirmed or accepted without the supernatural. He lamented the fact that many people were rejecting Christianity's supernaturalism while clinging to it in name. That people do this is testimony to the significance of Christianity in the world, he argued, but it is still wrongheaded and misleading. A naturalistic Christianity was for him a mere moralism, a theologically liberal philosophy of human self-improvement inspired by the idea of the divine that rests on "assumptions devoid of argumentative value because it lack[s] any genuine connection with Christianity's origin in the Bible."[2] True Christianity is a religion of redemption, a revelation of the one true and living God's grace that transforms human beings through faith in Jesus Christ.

While Warfield lectured, preached, and wrote as a staunch Calvinist, the general tenor and focus of his writing tended to support the foundational elements of orthodox Christianity and it is specifically his defense of the inspiration, inerrant truthfulness, and authority of the Bible that is his most enduring legacy and for which he is best remembered today. He wrote

---

[2]W. Andrew Hoffecker, "Guardian of the Word" in *Tabletalk* (April 2005), 12.

no fewer than forty-one major articles, essays, pamphlets, and reviews espousing the church's historic view of an inspired, inerrant Bible with respect to its autographs.

He was a leading representative throughout his professorial tenure of "the Old Princeton apologetic." This apologetic method, influenced by Thomas Reid's Scottish Common-Sense Realism,[3] sought to build upon the base of adequate evidence grounds for the Christian's personal faith and the validity of the Christian

---

[3]Mark Noll, "Princeton Theology, Old" in *Evangelical Dictionary of Theology*, edited by Walter A. Elwell (Grand Rapids: Baker, 1984), states that the main emphases of Archibald Alexander, the first professor at Princeton Seminary, were "the reliability of Scripture and the ability of human reason to understand Christian truth. His intellectual sources [included] the Scottish philosophy of common sense" (877). Douglas F. Kelly, "Scottish Realism" in *Evangelical Dictionary of Theology*, writes: "…it has long been recognized that the conservative Calvinistic theologians of Princeton adopted Scottish Realist epistemology wholesale" (990). David B. Calhoun, *Princeton Seminary: The Majestic Testimony 1869-1929* (Edinburgh: Banner of Truth, 1996), writes: "At Princeton…Scottish Sense Philosophy reigned" (2:413). Thomas Reid (1710-96), the founder of Scottish realism, argued that

> the human mind…perceives external objects directly through intuitive knowledge. We know reality, not by a "conjunction" of separated sense experiences, but by immediate "judgements of nature," which we make because our mind is constituted by God to know reality directly. These "original and natural judgements…make up what is called the *common sense of mankind*; and what is manifestly contrary to any of those first principles is what we call *absurd*" (*An Inquiry into the Human Mind on the Principles of Common Sense*, VII, 4). These first principles [of common sense]…cannot and need not be proved: they are self-evident to the common experience of mankind. Among these principles are the experience of external objects, cause and effect, and the obligations of morality. Any philosophy that denies these commonly accepted principles on which all men must base their lives is of necessity defective. (Kelly, "Scottish Realism," 990-91)

The major problem with this naïve epistemology is that it ignores the facts of the noetic effects of sin and that now there are, by redemptive grace, two kinds of people in this world – covenant breakers and covenant keepers – with fundamentally different world and life views who do not share the same "natural judgements" of common sense (I will discuss this further in Chapter Ten).

faith as a whole prior to personal commitment, making its appeal on terms that would be acceptable to the reasonable non-believer. Warfield, reflecting his allegiance as a modified empiricist[4] to Scottish Common Sense Realism, specifically wanted to show that Christianity's belief in the supernatural was not an irrational or blind faith but one that was grounded in evidence. He was, writes Samuel Craig, "about the last man to be found anywhere that could rightly be called a Christian 'fideist.'"[5]

In 1893 Warfield wrote an article for *The Presbyterian and Reformed Review* entitled "The Real Problem of Inspiration."[6] This article will afford us a "doorway" into his apologetic as a whole. Since inspiration was not a problem for him, what did he mean by his title? At that particular time many theologians and ministers were being so impressed by the "assured results" of biblical criticism that they were relinquishing or, what amounted to the same thing, reinterpreting the church doctrine of inspiration. Warfield, convinced that every word of the Bible was divinely given, felt it necessary to react in writing to this movement within the church away from the church's earlier doctrine. He felt it necessary to point up all that was involved in such a departure. He thought it imperative to emphasize what the "real problem" was when the church surrendered its once lofty view of the Bible.

As he viewed "the exact state of the case" as it stood then in his day Warfield saw "a special school of Old Testament criticism, which has for some years, been gaining somewhat widespread acceptance of its results, [which] has begun to

---

[4]Even though there is a large strain of empiricism in Warfield, I call him a "modified empiricist" because Warfield also argues his case for Christianity, as any Reformed theologian will, from Scripture.

[5]Samuel Craig, "Benjamin B. Warfield" in *Biblical and Theological Studies* (Philadelphia: Presbyterian and Reformed, 1952), xliv.

[6]The Presbyterian and Reformed Publication Company reprinted Warfield's article in 1948 in *The Inspiration and Authority of the Bible*, a collection of eight articles by Warfield on the Bible's special place in and value for Christian theology. All quotations and pagination are from this volume.

proclaim that these results having been accepted, a 'changed view of the Bible' follows which implies a reconstructed doctrine of inspiration, and, indeed, also a whole new theology" (170). While not averse to "all legitimate criticism" of the church's doctrine of inspiration, Warfield remained unconvinced by the "ever-enlarging mass of evidence" that one should abandon the church's doctrine. He saw implications in such a rejection of the church's doctrine that were far-reaching and dangerous in the extreme. In his article Warfield endeavors to articulate those implications in relinquishing the doctrine of inspiration as the church had historically conceived it.

Warfield's Argument for Inspiration

Warfield begins this article by stating precisely what the church's doctrine of inspiration is:

> The Church…has held from the beginning that the Bible is the Word of God in such a sense that its words, though written by men and bearing indelibly impressed upon them the marks of their human origin, were written, nevertheless, under such an influence of the Holy Spirit as to be also the words of God, the adequate expression of His mind and will…the Spirit's superintendence extends to the choice of the words by the human authors (verbal inspiration), and preserves its product from everything inconsistent with a divine authorship – thus securing, among other things, that entire truthfulness which is everywhere presupposed in and asserted for Scripture by the Biblical writers (inerrancy) (173).

Along with other means of commending this position Warfield writes: "The primary ground on which it has been held by the church as the true doctrine is that it is the doctrine of the Biblical writers themselves, and has therefore the whole mass of evidence for it which goes to show that the Biblical writers were trustworthy as doctrinal guides" (173; note in this statement the word "primary"). Warfield saw the evidence upon which the church's doctrine is based as twofold:

First, there is the exegetical evidence that the doctrine held and taught by the Church is the doctrine held and taught by the Biblical writers themselves. And secondly, there is the whole mass of evidence – internal and external, objective and subjective, historical and philosophical, human and divine – which goes to show that the Biblical writers are trustworthy as doctrinal guides. If they are *trustworthy* teachers of doctrine and if they held and taught this doctrine, then this doctrine is *true* and is to be accepted and acted upon as *true* by us all. (174, emphasis supplied).

If criticism is to overthrow the church doctrine, Warfield continues: "It must either show that this doctrine is not the doctrine of the Biblical writers, or else it must show that the Biblical writers are not trustworthy as doctrinal guides." (174)

From these statements it is clear that Warfield is thinking deductively here. The logic of his argument may be constructed syllogistically as follows:

- **Major premise:** "The doctrinal teaching of the Bible writers is trustworthy (based on a great mass of evidence)."
- **Minor premise**: "The doctrinal teaching of the church on inspiration is the doctrinal teaching of the Bible writers (based on exegetical evidence)."
- **Conclusion**: Therefore, the doctrinal teaching of the church on inspiration is true.

If this syllogistic construction is a fair and accurate portrayal of Warfield's position it would seem that his argument is built up inductively from exegetical and other kinds of evidence to the deduction that the church doctrine that the Bible is an inspired body of literature is true.[7] That it is a fair and accurate construction would appear to be verified by the fact that again and again (I count some 26 times in the article) Warfield affirms

---

[7]Warfield's syllogistic deduction is actually invalid because of its "four-term error" in logic. The only way he can avoid this four-term error is to maintain that "trustworthy" necessarily means "true." But this is a *non sequitur* since many "true" positions have later turned out to be untrustworthy,

in almost identical words to the words already quoted that the truth of the church's doctrine is based upon the evidence for the trustworthiness of the biblical writers as teachers of doctrine. The following citations are but a few from this lengthy article:

- "The doctrine of verbal inspiration is based on the broad foundation of the carefully ascertained doctrine of the Scripture writers on the subject." (179)

- "If criticism has made such discoveries as to necessitate the abandonment of the doctrine of plenary inspiration, it is not enough to say that we are compelled to abandon only a "particular theory of inspiration," though that is true enough. We must go on to say that that "particular theory of inspiration" is the theory of the apostles and of the Lord and in abandoning *it* we are abandoning them as our doctrinal teachers and guides.... This real issue is to be kept clearly before us, and faced courageously. Nothing is gained by closing our eyes to the seriousness of the problem which we are confronting. Stated plainly it is just this: Are the New Testament writers trustworthy guides in doctrine? Or are we at liberty to reject their authority and frame contrary doctrines for ourselves?" (180)

And how may we be sure that they are trustworthy guides in doctrine?

- "...the evidence for the truth of the doctrine of the plenary inspiration of Scripture is just the whole body of evidence which goes to show that the apostles are trustworthy teachers of doctrine." (208)

---

and a trustworthy person may not always be true in all that he says but still be regarded as trustworthy. Of course, if Warfield intended "trustworthy" to be a synonym for "true" then he needed to go no further than the major premise as stated and simply argue for the truthfulness of all of Christianity on the basis of the great "mass of evidence" supporting it. He does appear to mean this. Hence, his argument may be regarded as a form of methodological natural theology as we shall demonstrate.

- "Language is sometimes made use of which would seem to imply that the amount or weight of the evidence offered for the truth of the doctrine that the Scriptures are the Word of God in such a sense that their words deliver the truth of God without error, is small. It is on the contrary just the whole body of evidence which goes to prove the writers of the New Testament to be trustworthy as deliverers of doctrine. It is just the same evidence in amount and weight which is adduced in favor of any other Biblical doctrine. It is the same weight and amount of evidence precisely which is adducible for the truth of the doctrines of the Incarnation, of the Trinity, of the Divinity of Christ, of Justification by Faith, of Regeneration by the Holy Spirit, of the Resurrection of the Body, of Life Everlasting…however explicitly or incidentally, however frequently or rarely, however emphatically or allusively, they may be taught, when exegesis has once done its work and shown that they are taught by the Biblical writers, all these doctrines stand as supported by the same weight and amount of evidence – the evidence of the trustworthiness of the Biblical writers as teachers of doctrine." (208-9)

- "The question is not how they teach a doctrine, but do they teach it, and when that question is once settled affirmatively, the weight of evidence that commends this doctrine to us as true is the same in every case; and that is the whole body of evidence which goes to show that the Biblical writers are trustworthy as teachers of doctrine." (209)

- "The Biblical doctrine of inspiration…has in its favor just this whole weight and amount of evidence…it cannot rationally be rejected save on the ground of evidence which will outweigh the whole body of evidence which goes to authenticate the Biblical writers as trustworthy witnesses to and teachers of doctrine." (209-10)

- "Let it not be said…[that] we found the whole Christian system upon the doctrine of plenary inspiration. We found the whole Christian system on the doctrine of plenary inspiration as little as we found it upon the doctrine of angelic existences.

Were there no such thing as inspiration, Christianity would be true, and all its essential doctrines would be credibly witnessed to us in the generally trustworthy reports of the teaching of our Lord and of His authoritative agents in founding the Church, preserved in the writings of the apostles and their first followers, and in the historical witness of the living Church. Inspiration is not the most fundamental of the Church doctrines, nor even the first thing we prove about the Scriptures. It is the last and crowning fact as to the Scriptures. These we first prove authentic, historically credible, generally trustworthy, before we prove them inspired." (210)

• "We are in entire sympathy in this matter...with the protest which Dr. Marcus Dods raised in his famous address at the meeting of the Alliance of the Reformed Churches at London, against representing that 'the infallibility of the Bible is the ground of the whole Christian faith.' We judge with him that it is very important indeed that such a misapprehension, if it is anywhere current, should be corrected.... We do not think that the doctrine of plenary inspiration is the ground of the Christian faith, but if it was held and taught by the New Testament writers, we think it an element in the Christian faith...that appeals to our acceptance on precisely the same ground as every other element of the faith, viz., on the ground of our recognition of the writers of the New Testament as trustworthy witnesses to doctrine...." (211-12)

• "...on the emergence of the exegetical fact that the Scriptures of the New Testament teach this doctrine [inspiration], the amount and weight of evidence for its truth must be allowed to be the whole amount and weight of the evidence that the writers of the New Testament are trustworthy as teachers of doctrine. It is not on some shadowy and doubtful evidence that the doctrine is based – ...but first on the confidence which we have in the writers of the New Testament as doctrinal guides, and *ultimately on whatever evidence of whatever kind and force exists to justify that confidence.*" (214, emphasis supplied)

It is transparent from these citations that Warfield is fervently working to avoid building up a view of inspiration that is open to the charge of committing the logical fallacy of "begging the question." It is equally transparent that Warfield is willing to build up his support for the doctrine of inspiration inductively. It is also equally transparent that his faith in the truthfulness not only of inspiration but also of all of the doctrines of the Christian faith is grounded in the evidence for the trustworthiness of the biblical writers as authoritative teachers of doctrine. Warfield's view may be illustrated by the following diagram:

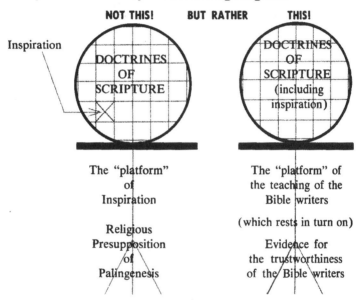

Warfield's Larger View of Apologetics

Nowhere in this particular article does Warfield go into the specifics of the evidence for the trustworthiness of the biblical writers as authoritative teachers of doctrine. In fact, he states: "…our present purpose is not to draw out the full value of the testimony" (214). But taking a cue from his reference to "the whole mass of evidence – internal and external, objective and subjective, historical and philosophical, human and divine – which goes to show that the Biblical writers are trustworthy as doctrinal guides" (174), we may safely conclude that it includes all the results of the sciences involved, as Warfield comprehends them, in the five subdivisions of apologetics set forth in his article, "Apologetics," in *The New Schaff-Herzog Encyclopedia of Religious Knowledge*.[8] It will be helpful to note Warfield's remarks on these subdivisions:

> When apologetics has placed these great facts in our hands – God, religion, revelation, Christianity, the Bible – and *not till then* are we prepared to go on and explicate the knowledge of God thus brought to us [this is the department of exegetical theology], trace the history of its workings in the world [this is the department of historical theology], systematize it [this is the department of systematic theology], and propagate it in the world [this is the department of practical theology].
>
> The primary subdivisions of apologetics are therefore five, unless for convenience of treatment it is preferred to sink the third into its most closely related fellow. 1. The first, which may perhaps be called philosophical apologetics, undertakes the establishment of the being of God, as a personal Spirit, the Creator, preserver, and governor of all things. To it belongs the great problem of theism, with the involved discussions of the antitheistic theories. 2. The second, which may perhaps be called psychological apologetics, undertakes the establishment of the religious nature of man and the validity of his religious sense. It involves the discussion alike of the psychology, the philosophy, and the phenomenology of religion, and therefore includes what is loosely called "comparative religion" or the "history of religions." 3. To the third [Warfield does not give a title to this subdivision; I suggest from his description of it "theistic apologetics"] falls the establishment of the reality of the supernatural factor in history, with the involved determination of the actual relations in which God stands to his world, and the method of his government of his rational creatures, and especially his mode of making himself known to them. It issues in the establishment of the fact of revelation as the condition of all knowledge of God, who as a personal Spirit can be known only so far as he expresses himself; so

---

[8]This article is reprinted in *The Works of Benjamin B. Warfield* (Reprint; Grand Rapids: Baker, 1991), IX, 3-21.

that theology differs from all other sciences in that it the object is not at the disposal of the subject, but vice versa. 4. The fourth, which may be called historical apologetics, undertakes to establish the divine origin of Christianity as the religion of revelation in the special sense of that word. It discusses all the topics which naturally fall under the popular caption of "the evidences for Christianity." 5. The fifth, which may be called bibliographical apologetics, undertakes to establish the trustworthiness of the Christian Scriptures as the documentation of the revelation of God for the redemption of sinners. It is engaged especially with such topics as the divine origin of the Scriptures; the methods of the divine operation in their origination; their place in the series of redemptive acts of God, and in the process of revelation; the nature, mode, and effect of inspiration, and the like. (I, 236, emphasis supplied)

It might appear at first that only the fifth (perhaps too the fourth) subdivision relates to the specific question that we have before us, namely, the evidence for the trustworthiness of the New Testament (or biblical) writers as teachers of doctrine. But when one recalls that the biblical writers teach at least something about each of these five broad subdivisions, it is clear that evidence from each of these areas could call into question their authority as writers of true doctrine. Consequently, I submit that the evidence from all these areas must be brought to bear on the question of the biblical writers' trustworthiness as teachers of doctrine if one determines to follow Warfield in the method he outlined in the original article under discussion. Warfield himself appears to affirm this when in his "Introductory Note" to Francis Beattie's *Apologetics*,[9] in opposition to Abraham Kuyper's apologetic method, he writes:

[Kuyper] has written an *Encyclopaedia of Sacred Theology*, and in it he gives a place to Apologetics among the other disciplines.

[9]This "Introductory Note" is reprinted in *Selected Shorter Writings of Benjamin B. Warfield* (Reprint; Nutley, N. J.: Presbyterian and Reformed, 1973), II, 93-105.

But how subordinate a place! And in what a curtailed form! Hidden away as a subdivision of a subdivision of what Dr. Kuyper calls the "Dogmatological Group" of disciplines (which corresponds roughly to what most encyclopaedists call "Systematic Theology"), one has to search for it before he finds it, and when he finds it, he discovers that its function is confined closely, we might almost say jealously, to the narrow task of defending developed Christianity against philosophy, falsely so called. After the contents of Christianity have been set forth thetically in Dogmatics and Ethics, it finds itself, it seems, in a three-fold conflict. This is waged with a pseudo-Christianity, a pseudo-religion, and a pseudo-philosophy. Three antithetic dogmatological disciplines are therefore requisite – Polemics, Elenchtics, and Apologetics, corresponding, respectively, to heterodoxy, paganism, philosophy. The least of these is Apologetics, which concerns itself only with the distinctively philosophical assault on Christianity. Meanwhile, as for Christianity itself, it has remained up to this point – let us say it frankly – the great Assumption. The work of the exegete, the historian, the systematist, has all hung, so to speak, in the air; not until all their labor is accomplished do they pause to wipe their streaming brows and ask whether they have been dealing with realities, or perchance with fancies only.

Naturally it is not thus that Kuyper represents it to himself. He supposes that all these workers have throughout wrought in faith. But he seems not quite able to conceal from himself that they have not justified that faith, and that some may think their procedure itself, therefore unjustified, if not unjustifiable. He distributes the departments of theological science into four groups, corresponding roughly with the Exegetical, Historical, Systematic, and Practical disciplines which the majority of encyclopaedists erect, although for reasons of his own, very interestingly set forth, he prefers to call them, respectively, the Bibliological, Ecclesiological, Dogmatological, and Diaconiological groups of disciplines. Now, when he comes to discuss the contents of these groups of discipline in detail, he betrays a feeling that something is lacking at the beginning. "Before dealing separately with the four groups of departments of study into which theology is divided," he says [Vol. III,

4f.], "we must give a brief resumé from the second part of this *Encyclopaedia*, of how the subject arrives at the first group. Logical order demands that the first group bring you to the point where the second begins, that the second open the way for the third, and that the third introduce you to the fourth. But no other precedes the first group and it is accordingly in place here to indicate how we arrive at the first group." Just so, surely!

Dr. Kuyper proceeds to point out that the subject of theology is the human consciousness; that in this consciousness there is implanted a *sensus divinitatis*, a *semen religionis*, which impels it to seek after the knowledge of God; that in the sinner this action is renewed and quickened by the palingenesis [new birth], through which the subject is opened for the reception of the special revelation of God made first by deed, culminating in the Incarnation, and then by word, centering in the Scriptures. Thus, by the *testimonium Spiritus Sancti*, the subject is put in possession of the revelation of God embodied in the Scriptures, and is able to proceed to explicate its content through the several disciplines of theological science. Now, what is it that Mr. Kuyper has done here except to outline a very considerable – though certainly not a complete – Apologetics, which must precede and prepare the way for the "Bibliological Group" [that is, the first] of theological departments? We must, it seems, vindicate the existence of a *sensus divinitatis* in man capable of producing a natural theology independently of special revelation; and then the reality of a special revelation in deed and word, and as well, the reality of a supernatural preparation of the heart of man to receive it; before we can proceed to the study of theology at all, as Dr. Kuyper has outlined it. With these things at least we must, then, confessedly, reckon at the outset; and to reckon with these things is to enter deeply into Apologetics.

As the case really stands, we must say even more. Despite the attractiveness of Dr. Kuyper's distribution of the departments of theological science, we cannot think it an improvement upon the ordinary *schema*. It appears to us a mistake to derive, as he does, the *principium divisionis* from the Holy Scriptures. The Scriptures, after all, are not the object of theology, but only its source; and the *principium divisionis* in this science, too, must be taken, as Dr. Kuyper himself argues, from the object. Now the object of theology, as Dr. Kuyper has often justly insisted, is the ectypal knowledge of God. This knowledge of God is deposited for us in the Scriptures, and must needs be drawn out of them – hence "Exegetical Theology." It has been derived from the Scriptures…for the life of the Church through the ages, and its gradual assimilation must needs be traced in its effects on the life of the Christian world – hence "Historical Theology." It is capable of statement in a systematized thetical form – hence "Systematic Theology." And, so drawn our from Scripture, so assimilated in the Church's growth, so organized into a system, it is to be made available for life – hence "Practical Theology." But certainly, *before we draw it from the Scriptures*, we must assure ourselves that there is a knowledge of God in the Scriptures. And, *before we do that*, we must assure ourselves that there is knowledge of God in the world. And, *before we do that*, we must assure ourselves that a knowledge of God is possible for man. And, *before we do that*, we must assure ourselves that there is a God to know. Thus, we inevitably work back to first principles. And, in working thus back to first principles, we exhibit the indispensability of an "Apologetic Theology," which of necessity holds the place of the first among the five essential theological disciplines. (21-24, last four emphases supplied)

This long quotation from Warfield bristles with interesting items for discussion. For instance, it would be very interesting to ask Warfield how he intends, without assuming the truthfulness of anything that the Scriptures affirm about the nature of God, the nature of man, and the relationship that exists between them, to prove the Christian God's existence, to prove that man can know the Christian God, to prove that the Christian God has revealed himself in the world, and to prove that the Christian God has revealed himself in the world at the point of the Hebrew-Christian Scriptures, and to do all this "before we draw it from the Scriptures." Van Til certainly appears to be correct when he observes that the traditional method of apologetics as reflected here by Warfield has

explicitly built into it the right and ability of the natural man, apart from the work of the Spirit of God, to be the judge of the claim of the authoritative Word of God. It is man who, by means of his self-established intellectual tools, puts his "stamp of approval" on the Word of God and then, only after that grand act, does he listen to it. God's Word must first pass man's tests of good and evil, truth and falsity. But once you tell a non-Christian this, why should he be worried by anything else that you say? You have already told him he is quite all right just the way he is! Then the Scripture is not correct when it talks of "darkened minds," "willful ignorance," "dead men," and "blind people"![10]

In sum, if men could do all that Warfield describes *before they draw any of it from Scripture*, it may be legitimately asked, would they need revelation at all? Logical consistency requires from Warfield a negative response, but then, is such a response really biblical and thus Christian? And how does a logically necessary negative response comport with his view, noted earlier, that revelation is "the condition of all knowledge of God, who as a personal Spirit can be known only so far as he expresses himself?" ("Apologetics," I, 236). There certainly appear to be irreconcilable contradictions in Warfield's thought on this matter. But our purpose is not at this point to ask Warfield questions. It is to indicate (1) the first place Warfield feels apologetics must occupy relative to the traditional "theological groups" of theological encyclopedia before they have validity, (2) the immense amount of data that one would have to sift through before one can be assured that the New Testament writers are trustworthy teachers of doctrine, and (3) his insistence that all this must be done *before* we can begin to propagate our knowledge of God in the world.

The Nature and Degree of Christian Certainty in Warfield's Apologetic

Warfield holds that part of the data that validates the trustworthiness of the biblical writers as teachers of doctrine is the teaching of Jesus Christ:

---

[10]Cornelius Van Til, "My Credo" in *Jerusalem and Athens*, edited by E. R. Geehan (Nutley, N. J.: Presbyterian and Reformed, 1971), 11.

...to say that the amount and weight of the evidence of the truth of the Biblical doctrine of inspiration is measured by amount and weight of the evidence for the general credibility and trustworthiness of the New Testament writers as witnesses to doctrine, is an understatement rather than an overstatement of the matter. For if we trust them at all we will trust them in the account they give of the person and in the report they give of the teaching of Christ; whereupon, as they report Him as teaching the same doctrine of Scripture that they teach, we are brought face to face with divine testimony to this doctrine of inspiration. (212-13)

But how do we know that we meet with divine testimony when we are confronted with Christ's teaching? Certainly, as Warfield affirms, "in the account [the New Testament writers] give of the person and in the report they give of the teaching of Christ." But the trustworthiness of their testimony concerning Christ, according to Warfield, must be established on other grounds than the mere fact that they report his teachings on Scripture if one is to avoid the charge of reasoning in a circle. Such evidential verification Warfield desperately wants to establish on the basis of a whole mass of evidence – internal and external, objective and subjective, historical and philosophical, human and divine – which shows to the secularist that the biblical writers are trustworthy as doctrinal guides. But this he can never do since the secularist's assumptions forbid him to take anything on faith; everything must be proven independent of faith.

But suppose Warfield was able to establish on these "other grounds" that the testimony of the biblical writers is reliable with respect to the person and the words of Christ and thus it cannot be denied that Christ is divine and that as a divine person he authenticated the Scriptures as God's Word. Why, then, does Warfield, indeed, how can Warfield speak of the evidence, when finally all in and catalogued (and remember, this includes the testimony of the divine Son of God) as only "probable" evidence:

We do not adopt the doctrine of the plenary inspiration of Scripture on sentimental grounds, nor even, as we have already had occasion to remark, on *a priori* or general grounds of whatever kind. We adopt it specifically because it is taught us as truth by Christ and His apostles, in the Scriptural record of their teaching, and the evidence for its truth is, therefore, as we have already pointed out, precisely that evidence in weight and amount which vindicates for us the trustworthiness of Christ and His apostles as teachers of doctrine. Of course, *this evidence is not in the strict logical sense "demonstrative"; it is "probable" evidence. It therefore leaves open the metaphysical possibility of its being mistaken...we have not attained through "probable" evidence apodeictic certainty of the Bible's infallibility.* But neither is the reality of the alleged phenomena inconsistent with the Bible's doctrine, to be allowed without sufficient evidence. (218-19, emphasis supplied)

Two points are in order here: First, in this quotation Warfield is discussing primarily the evidence for the doctrine of inspiration. He affirms that though "it is about as great in amount and weight as 'probable' evidence can be made" (and recall that he includes in the whole mass of evidence that points to and validates inspiration the *divine* testimony of Christ), it is nonetheless "probable evidence," yielding no apodeictic, incontestable demonstrability or certainty. Should one not wonder about an apologetic methodology that reduces divine testimony to probable evidence at best? He admits that the evidence for inspiration is not absolutely demonstrable. But has not Warfield already declared (208-09) that all of the doctrines of Scripture (this would include Christ's deity) are supported by the same evidence as that which supports the doctrine of inspiration? Does it not follow then that none of the doctrines of Scripture are demonstrable or apodeictically certain, at least absolutely, that at best the evidence for their truthfulness is only probable? And should Warfield, following Kuyper and the *Westminster Confession of Faith* (I.5), appeal at this point to "the inward work of the Holy Spirit bearing witness by and with the Word in our hearts" for the final and full persuasion and assurance of the infallible truth and divine authority of the Scriptures, I would have to point out to him that according to his methodology the doctrine of the *testimonium Spiritus Sancti* is, like all the other doctrines of Scripture, on the basis of the "evidence" only probable and not demonstrable evidence!

Of course, in reality it is not "probable" evidence, for by "probability" is meant the degree of verifiability that may be attributed to a belief. But for any belief there is an indefinite number of test consequences. This means that it is mathematically impossible to declare that a belief is even probable, much less "highly probable." To illustrate, suppose a certain belief has a given number of confirming test instances, say ten. What is its degree of verifiability, that is, the probability that it is true? To discover this, one would have to divide the number of confirming test instances (ten in this case) by the number of possible test consequences. But the latter number is precisely what one does not know when testing a belief. That number is indefinite if not infinite. Therefore, the probability of that belief is, at best, unknown, and if the number of possible test consequences is infinite, can never rise above zero. It is really meaningless, therefore, to speak of a given belief, on the basis of empirical testing, as probable, or highly probable.

Second, what does Warfield do with the "alleged phenomena" inconsistent with the Bible's doctrine of inspiration? As one reads Warfield one cannot help but feel that he is operating, although inconsistently, with an unflinching conviction that the Bible is self-attestingly divine or at least divinely attested to on some ground not open to doubt, and therefore, that it is infallible, for he will not admit that any single fact has ever been advanced that contradicts the biblical doctrine of inspiration in spite of the fact that many scholars in his time were affirming otherwise:

> If then we ask what are we to do with the numerous phenomena of Scripture inconsistent with verbal inspiration, which, so it is alleged, "criticism" has brought to light, we must reply: Challenge them in the name of the New Testament doctrine [Which is what? Is that not what his entire effort intended to

show?], and ask for their credentials. They have no credentials that can stand before that challenge. No single error has as yet been demonstrated to occur in the Scriptures as given by God to His church. (225)

What then precisely is the nature of these allegedly contradictory phenomena? Warfield views them simply as "difficulties":

> ...any objections brought against the doctrine of inspiration from other spheres of inquiry are inoperative; it being a settled proposition that so long as the proper evidence [What criterion determines what is proper and what is improper evidence?] by which a proposition is established remains unrefuted, all so-called objections brought against it pass out of the category of objections to its truth into the category of difficulties to be adjusted to it. (174)

But why are they, for Warfield, only "difficulties" and not refuting objections? A moment ago I suggested that Warfield was operating with an unspoken presupposition throughout his article. Warfield unwittingly suggests as much, for try as he might to ground his view of Scripture in the "evidences," try as he might to disguise or escape it, his insistence that no phenomenon can negate his view is due, because he is a Christian, to his commitment to the "first principle" of our faith, namely, that God is there and has spoken inerrantly in Scripture. Apart from such a presupposed "first principle" Warfield is in no better position to distinguish between difficulties and proved errors than is the critic. He will not admit the presence of any proved errors and, of course, as a Christian illumined by the Holy Spirit he is correct in doing so. But apart from such a religious commitment, which Warfield does not want to acknowledge is operative in his argument, referring to the biblical doctrine as simply a "clue" (225), on the grounds that he has assumed throughout his article he is, I say, unable to distinguish between difficulties and actual errors. For since he has provided us with no doctrine of inspiration that carries with it apodeictic certainty, on what ground can he confidently affirm *a priori* that no phenomena are able to stand against his theory of inspiration? His critic, it seems to me, may justifiably ask: "How, Dr. Warfield, can you so confidently distinguish between 'difficulties' and 'proven errors' when I can't?"

Our review of Warfield's apologetic is completed. We have seen that he sought to build upon the base of adequate evidence grounds for the validity of the Christian faith prior to personal commitment, making its appeal on terms that would be acceptable to the non-believer. Before Warfield, Charles Hodge, whose three-volume *Systematic Theology* remains a monument to American theological genius, espoused the same basic methodology: "Reason must judge," he wrote, "of the credibility of a revelation" (I, 50); "Christians concede to reason the *judicium contradictionis*, that is, the prerogative of deciding whether a thing is possible or impossible" (I, 51); "Reason must judge of the evidence of a revelation" as preparation for faith that he defined as "an intelligent reception of the truth on adequate grounds" (I, 53); and finally, "…the Scriptures recognize…the right of those to whom a revelation is addressed to judge [the] evidence" for it (I, 54). I will now summarize my difficulties with the Warfield (or "the Old Princeton") apologetic by the following eight points:

1. His method by Warfield's own admission is a possibility (he says "probability") construct that reduces even revelational material, including Christ's witness, to brute facts that have no meaning until meaning is placed upon them in the argument by human ratiocination. Therefore, it does not confront the "biblical fool" with truth statements.

2. His method is not actually a probability argument. Because its argument entails supernatural conclusions, its mathematical probability cannot be calculated. At best, it is a possibility argument.

3. His method forces saving faith to rest in doctrines that are certified by the declared "probability" of massed evidence and ultimately in the skill, craft, and art of the apologist and not on the truth of God's Word and the work of God's Spirit.

4. His method cannot give subjective certitude. If it is reached at all it is attained by a leap of faith that goes beyond the data since the data of the argument, not entailing objective certitude, do not and cannot carry one to certainty.

5. His method maintains that conflicting data are simply "difficulties" to be adjusted to its supernatural conclusion and not nullifying contradictions, but it provides no clarifying criterion for distinguishing between "difficulties" and "nullifying contradictions."

6. His method suggests that the "biblical fool" can do what the Bible says he cannot do. It allows him to believe that he has ready at hand the tests for truth to be the judge of spiritual truth. Therefore, it does not challenge his unbelief at its depth at the outset.

7. His method places the task of theological encyclopaedia as well as evangelism beyond the realm of doing since the apologetic task itself is never completed.

8. His method is a form of methodological natural theology that necessarily entails all of the compromises that Cornelius Van Til spells out as follows in his "My Credo":

   • His method compromises God himself by maintaining at the outset of its investigation that his existence is only "possible" albeit "highly probable," rather than ontologically and "rationally" necessary.

- His method compromises the counsel of God by not understanding it as the only all-inclusive, ultimate "cause" of whatever comes to pass.
- His method compromises the special revelation of God by

  a. compromising its *necessity*: natural revelation can be understood "on its own" apart from special revelation;
  b. compromising its *clarity*: both general and special revelation by implication are so unclear that man may say at the outset of his investigation that God's existence is at best "probable";
  c. compromising its *sufficiency*: "facts," uninterpreted and unexplainable in terms of God's general or special revelation and that are therefore wholly new for God and for man, may come from an ultimate realm of "chance";
  d. compromising its *authority*: the self-attesting character of Scripture is secondary to the authority of man's reason and experience that must authenticate the Scripture.

- His method compromises man's creation as the image of God by implying that man need not "think God's thoughts after him" in his acquisition of knowledge.
- His method compromises mankind's covenantal relationship with God by not understanding Adam's representative action as absolutely determinative of the future.
- His method compromises the sinfulness of man by not understanding man's ethical depravity as extending to the whole of life, even to his thoughts and attitudes.
- His method compromises the grace of God by not understanding it as the necessary prerequisite for "renewal of knowledge."[11]

---

[11]Cornelius Van Til, "My Credo" in *Jerusalem in Athens: Critical Discussions on the Philosophy and Apologetics of Cornelius Van Til*, edited by E. R. Geehan (Nutley, N. J.: Presbyterian and Reformed, 1971), 18-19.

Should anyone conclude from all this that I do not revere Warfield and hold him in the highest regard I would only note that I cite him in the second edition of my *Systematic Theology* more than any other theologian with the exception of John Murray, some ninety-seven times to be exact, most by far of these citations being favorable and used to support my own theological assertions. In my opinion, as a Reformed theologian he had no equal in his time, whose knowledge of the entire range of theological encyclopedia other theologians can only dream of attaining. It is only in the area of apologetics that I am convinced mine is the more scriptural method.

The Evidentialist School of Apologetics

The Princeton apologetic is representative of the larger traditional evidentialist school of apologetics that stands in the tradition historically on its Protestant side with Butler's *Analogy of Religion*. This method, as we have seen, in seeking to build upon the basis of whatever kind of grounds for the unbeliever's faith response, makes its appeal to the autonomous man as "capable man." This is a major error. Man in his natural state is *not* capable of assessing aright truly spiritual issues. Paul declares in Romans 8:7-8 that mankind is not only noetically hostile toward God, for their thoughts refuse to be subject to God's laws (this is depravity), but also they are not able to subject their thoughts to God (this is inability). In Ephesians 4:17-19 Paul states that the nations walk

> in the futility of their minds. They are darkened in their understanding, alienated from the life of God because of the ignorance that is in them, due to their hardness of heart. They have become callous and have given themselves up to sensuality, greedy to practice every kind of impurity.

If it should appear too sweeping a judgment to assert that the unregenerate man, because of his darkened understanding, is incapable, left to himself, of believing or savingly understanding even the smallest modicum of divine truth, Paul's statements in

1 Corinthians 1:21 to the effect that "the world did not know God through [its] wisdom" and in 1 Corinthians 2:14, "The natural [unregenerate] person does not accept the things of the Spirit of God, for they are folly to him [due to his depravity], and he is not able to understand them [due to his inability] because they are spiritually discerned," justify just such a judgment. (See here also Romans 1:18-32; 3:10-18.)

This is not to say that the unregenerate person cannot, by reading the Bible, *rationally* understand what it teaches about God, himself, Christ, and salvation, for he can. But because one's understanding of the *meaning* of "facts" is always controlled by one's religiously governed *philosophy* of "facts," the unregenerate man will not believe or accept biblical supernaturalism as true, nor will he believe the Bible's message until he is enlightened by the Holy Spirit by regeneration. Until the Holy Spirit regenerates him he *will not* and *cannot* recognize Christ and the Scriptures for what they are. He *will not* and *cannot* hear his "Master's voice" speaking to him in Scripture. And he has not the capability, even if he were of a mind to do so, to seek the true God. Any and every truth about God, coming to him by whatever means, apart from the Spirit's convicting, saving, and illuminating work, he immediately suppresses in the form in which it comes. And when his darkened understanding has restructured it, the original truth emerges in his consciousness dressed in the covenant breaker's manufactured clothing of falsehood that points in turn to an idol that he then worships and that in turn leads him to run to all kinds of immoral excesses, spiritual pride, and sinful self-righteousness. Therefore, because they ought to acknowledge the true God and worship him as their Creator but do not, "they are without excuse [*anapologētous*]" (Rom. 1:20).

Nevertheless, one adherent of this methodology, with Warfield, may compile a mass of evidence for the trustworthiness of the biblical writers and apply their teachings to the unbeliever. Another may compile evidence for Christ's bodily resurrection from the dead, using such things as the Shroud of Turin. But evidence, apart from scriptural presuppositionalism, that is, apart from the meaning that the Bible places on it, is at best only probable (if it could even be calculated) and at worst meaningless in the natural man's world where Chance is ultimate. Furthermore, the evidentialist method concedes to the natural man by implication the autonomous right to judge the value of the evidence. Hence when the unbeliever concludes that the evidence is uncertain, and if he is not stupid he must do so, his response cannot be refuted on evidentialist grounds, nor can he be charged with dishonesty on such grounds when he refuses to respond positively to the evidence. The evidentialist himself admits his case is at best a probable one, carrying with it no demonstrable certainty. This approach leaves the man who refuses to regard the evidence as compelling with the delusion that the best basis the Christian can claim for his faith is a possibility construct. How tragic, as if every fact in the universe did not scream out its testimony to the truthfulness of the Christian faith! Yet the "evidentialist" approach, operating in isolation from Scriptural commitment, has no available means of preventing the unbeliever from pushing the data aside, actually believing as he does so that there could be some facts somewhere that would show the Christian faith to be untrue.[12]

This is the outcome of the evidentialist method: There is never anything more than probability, at best, which "probability" is only one kind of possibility. But is this an adequate ground for faith? I think not. Faith, when properly conceived, is Spirit-wrought, whole-souled assent to Spirit-taught knowledge data (John 6:45) gained from self-attesting divine revelation. There is nothing "fideistic" about it; biblical faith eschews a "leap" of any kind. J. I. Packer has correctly stated that the nature of faith is to be certain; any degree of doubt or uncertainty is not a degree of faith but is an assault upon it. Faith must "rest on something more sure than an inference of probability."[13] Clark Pinnock may retort that "a probable argument

---

[12]For further discussion of evidentialist apologetics see my *The Justification of Knowledge*, Chapter Five on "Empirical Apologetics," 117-59.

[13]J. I. Packer, *'Fundamentalism' and the Word of God*, 117.

is better than an improbable one,"[14] but as Van Til has shown, apart from the truth of Christian theism, the world is a world in which Chance is ultimate, which means in turn that the very concept of probability is meaningless:

> Clearly any view of probability which is based on the ultimacy of Chance cannot possibly contact reality in any way. For it can say nothing about the probability of any particular event, for all events proceed equally from the belly of Chance. Therefore, a "probable" argument for any particular event [or phenomenon] is of no more value than an improbable one, for both arguments are meaningless in terms of that one "event." A probable argument is not better than an improbable one if the very idea of probability is without meaning.[15]

Let no one conclude that I am not appreciative of Warfield's unparalleled efforts to call men to commitment to the full inspiration and authority of the Bible. And in the sense that his was a faith that was not a blind faith but a faith that sought to elucidate its ground, a faith that militated against mysticism, all believers stand in his debt. Moreover, I appreciate his powerful logic in demonstrating the rank inconsistency in those theologians and pastors in his time who were speaking glowingly of Jesus as their "Master" and the "great Teacher" but who at the same time were picking and choosing among his teachings and rejecting among other things his testimony to the inspiration, authority, historical integrity, and revelatory nature of the Old and New Testaments. Nevertheless, I feel no good is done – indeed, only positive harm results – by developing a method of vindicating the doctrine of inspiration that, when done, has reduced all of the evidence, including Christ's testimony, to probable evidence at best, and that, by implication, denies the depravity of the natural man by granting him the right to judge whether a given revelation from God is in fact from God or not.

---

[14]Clark H. Pinnock, "The Philosophy of Christian Evidences" in *Jerusalem and Athens*, 423.

[15]Cornelius Van Til, *Jerusalem and Athens*, 426-27.

What I would advocate is an apologetic approach to the unbeliever that presents all of its evidence for the Christian faith consciously and unashamedly from within the framework of a scriptural commitment as Proverbs 26:4 requires, an approach that takes seriously the "first principle" of the Christian faith, namely, that God is there and that he has revealed himself self-attestingly to humankind in and by the creation of the universe through the agencies of his Son and Spirit, providentially in world history through deed and word, and most magnificently, through his incarnate Son (Heb. 1:1-3).

Evidences of any and all kinds could then be presented to the unbeliever by the believer, but for the unbeliever under these circumstances to thrust aside the biblically informed evidence presented to him would constitute not just an "honest blunder" on his part but intellectual immorality and rebellion, the sinful refusal of the covenant breaker to acknowledge the only possible interpretation of the data. The data, since within the Christian-theistic framework it carries apodeictic certainty, would bear now, in addition to its value as evidence, also a kērygmatic and condemning value. Only when unbelievers are confronted with evidences interpreted by the Christian frame of reference can we escape the tragic results that ensue from building the Christian message upon possibility arguments. Only then can the apologist really challenge the unbeliever to forsake his unbelief.

What about the charge of circular reasoning? Is not such an apologetic method as I have outlined here, when it begins its assault against unbelief by appealing to the self-attesting Scripture as its authority, vulnerable at this point? John Murray acknowledges that to affirm the fact of a self-attesting revelation *might* seem to be arguing in a circle, but in this one case, he insists, it is not. Rather, in the case of the reception by men of the Word of God, it is the one situation that requires the rational creature to bow before divine authority coming "linearly" to him and unquestioningly to acknowledge God's Word as the standard by which he is to live. Murray writes:

It might seem to be analogous to the case of a judge who accepts the witness of the accused in his own defense, rather than the evidence derived from all the relevant facts in the case. We should, however, be little disturbed by this type of criticism. It contains an inherent fallacy. It is fully admitted that normally it would be absurd and a miscarriage of justice for a judge to accept the testimony of the accused, rather than the verdict required by all the relevant evidence. But the two cases are not analogous. There is one sphere where self-testimony must be accepted as absolute and final. This is the sphere of our relation to God. God alone is adequate witness to himself.[16]

In sum, the presuppositional or scripturalist method recognizes that in the case of God's revelation of himself, from the very nature of the case, his revelation must be self-authenticating, addressing itself *linearly* to mankind. All that the creature can do by way of proper response to it is to receive this revelation with thanksgiving. This is hardly reasoning in a circle. It is simply recognizing that God alone can properly bear witness to his Word, that man is a creature before him, and that salvation is by grace. The Christian is what he is by the grace of God. His faith is not the result of a fideistic "leap of faith" but rather the inevitable response to the sovereign regenerating work of the Holy Spirit who works by and with the self-authenticating truths of God revealed in Holy Scripture. As a Christian he will begin to think within and ever speak from the circle of revelation. He can avoid doing so only by being untrue to Christ and by rejecting some part of the gift that God has given him. Let it be clearly understood that a scripturalist apologetic does not mean mysticism; it does not mean that the Christian will make no effort to set forth his reasons for placing Scripture at the base of his thinking as his first principle. But it does mean that he "believes in order that he may understand" (see Heb. 11:3: "by faith we understand..."). And this means that he has a real base for justifying his knowledge claims.

---

[16]John Murray, "The Attestation of Scripture" in *The Infallible Word*, edited by N. B. Stonehouse and Paul Wooley (Philadelphia: Presbyterian Guardian, 1946), 9-10.

The "Apologetic" of the *Westminster Confession of Faith*

The ironic thing in all this is that Warfield's own church confession, the *Westminster Confession of Faith*, flies in the face of his methodological natural theology. It declares that the Bible's authority,

> ...for which it ought to be believed and obeyed, dependeth not upon the testimony of any man or church, but *wholly upon God* (who is truth itself), the author thereof; and therefore *it is to be believed, because it is the word of God. (WCF,* I.4, emphasis supplied)

This article, explicating the ground of the Bible's authority "for which it ought to be believed and obeyed," first states the ground upon which the Bible's authority does *not* depend: It does not depend upon the testimony of any man or church. For any man or church to insist that people should believe and obey the Bible because he or it has demonstrated from a great amount of evidence that they should believe and obey it is to ground the Bible's authority in the amassed evidence and ultimately in the skill, craft, and art of the apologist – shaky ground indeed!

Then the article states the sole reason why the Bible ought to be believed and obeyed: God, who is truth itself,[17] is in a unique sense its author, and therefore it is the very Word of the one living and true God. In sum, it receives its authority from heaven; it requires no earthly advocacy in regard to the issue of its authority. Its authority is intrinsic, immediate and inherent, that is, it is self-validatingly authoritative because God is its author. In no sense does the Bible derive its authority from human testimony.[18]

---

[17]We must not forget that the authority of Scripture is inevitably bound up with the issue of its *inerrant* truthfulness. As J. I. Packer observes: "Statements that are not absolutely true and reliable could not be absolutely authoritative" (*'Fundamentalism' and the Word of God,* 96).

[18]Warfield argues in "The Westminster Doctrine of Scripture" in *Selected Shorter Writings of Benjamin B. Warfield* (Nutley, N. J.: Presbyterian and Reformed, 1973), II, 560-87, that because the *Confession of Faith* lists the

This article was intended originally to inveigh against the Roman Catholic dogma that maintains that the authority of the Bible depends upon the authority of the church for its credibility. Rome teaches, wrongly I showed in Chapter Three: "Since it was the church that determined the Scripture canon in the first place,[19] the Scriptures are obviously reliant upon the church for its authority." Rome often cites here Augustine's unfortunate comment to bolster its point: "I would not believe in the Gospel, had not the authority of the Catholic Church already moved me."[20] Rome's position, of course, is based upon the erroneous notion that the church "canonized" the Scriptures when in fact the church, founded as it is on the prophets and apostles (Eph. 2:20), was divinely led providentially to collect and preserve the already inspired (and thus canonical) Scriptures as they were written.

---

sixty-six books of the Bible in I.ii a and declares in I.ii b: "All which are given by inspiration of God," that the evidentiary issues of canonics and inspiration were being presupposesd when it stated what it did in I.iv about the Bible's authority. In other words, asserts Warfield, the *Confession of Faith* is teaching that "the authority of a book of Scripture rests on its being of divine inspiration and part of the canon as previously settled facts" (565), and that "the order of procedure in ascertaining Scripture is to settle first the canon, then its inspiration, and then, as a corollary, its authority" (565).

This procedure accords with his apologetic method but it is a stretch to derive an apologetic method from the order in which the *Confession* logically presents its confessional data. What Warfield says about the authoritative character of Holy Scripture as a whole is just as true with respect to the several books of the Bible viewed individually. Each was intrinsically authoritative the moment it existed at all. And before the issue of canonics was ever addressed in the early church the Old Testament and the individual books of the New, being immediately inspired by God, were already at work in the church, growing and nurturing the church. They were both recognized as inspired Scripture and authoritative and received the church's submission to them long before the issue of canonics was addressed in any formal sense.

[19]The *Baltimore Catechism* (Question 1327) declares: "…it is only from Tradition (preserved in the Catholic Church) that we can know which of the writings of ancient times are inspired and which are not inspired."

[20]Augustine, *Contra epistolam Manichaei*, 5, 6. See *Catechism of the Catholic Church* (1994), para. 119, 34.

This article also flies in the face of much contemporary evangelical thinking. So-called classical apologetics, represented by Ligonier apologist R. C. Sproul, argues for the infallible authority of the Bible as the Word of God on the basis of a progression from a "neutral" premise respecting the Bible's general reliability or trustworthiness to the conclusion of its infallibility and hence of its divine authoritativeness. This reasoning proceeds as follows:

Neutral (?) Premise A – The Bible is a basically reliable and trustworthy document.

Premise B – On the basis of this (basically) reliable document we have sufficient evidence to believe confidently that Jesus Christ is the Son of God.

Premise C – Jesus Christ, being the Son of God [conclusion of premise B], is an infallible authority.

Premise D – Jesus Christ teaches that the Bible is more than generally trustworthy: it is the very Word of God.

Premise E – The Word, in that it comes from God, is utterly trustworthy because God is utterly trustworthy.

Conclusion – On the basis of the infallible authority of Jesus Christ, the church believes the Bible to be utterly trustworthy, i.e., infallible (and therefore divinely authoritative).[21]

These five premises are stated in a manner, however, that is self-serving to the Christian apologist who already believes in the infallibility of Scripture. I do not believe the progression is valid as written in that the conclusion declares more than the original premise will allow. If one approaches the issues raised in these premises apart from the full range of Christian presuppositions, I do not see how one can conclude to anything more, at best,

---

[21]R. C. Sproul, *Reason to Believe* (Grand Rapids: Zondervan, 1982), 30-31. One could ask Sproul at this point why, if this line of reasoning is sound, should he or anyone else use any other line of argument for the Christian faith. Why not just make the case with the unbeliever for the infallible authority of Scripture and argue everything else from this "presupposition"?

than a high degree of probability and, at worst, mere possibility that the Bible is God's Word. I will explain.

With regard to Premise A, can we simply assert that the Bible is generally trustworthy or must we demonstrate it? Surely the latter is the chosen path within the classical argument. But how does one do this? The Bible is a big book, claiming to record accurately the occurrence of hundreds, indeed, thousands of supernatural events (most of them, indeed, purporting to be divinely planned and induced), any one claim of which, if untrue, would nullify the indefectibility and infallibility of Scripture. Consider for a moment the intriguing biblical event of Jesus' transfiguration that we discussed in Chapter Six. How is one to go about proving it happened and happened the way the Evangelists report it? By citing archaeological evidence? I think we would all admit that we can cite no archaeological evidence for its occurrence. By citing then perhaps what purports to be eyewitness testimony? Just so, surely! But Peter's is the only testimony we have that purports to be such. We have nothing from the other two reported eyewitnesses – James and John. And Matthew, Mark, and Luke who report the event in their respective Gospels were not eyewitnesses but rather second-hand (or even further removed) reporters. So let us say that one cites Peter's purported eyewitness testimony in 2 Peter 1:16-18 as his primary proof for the event's occurrence. Will such a simple appeal to one eyewitness *per se* satisfy the skepticism of the secular historian? I do not think so. So now the apologist must begin to amass the requisite evidence showing, first, that it was Peter who in fact wrote these words (the reader should recall here that most critical New Testament scholarship [I think wrongly] denies the Petrine authorship of 2 Peter), and second, that when he wrote them he wrote the truth. Note in the first case that the evidence would have to establish both a first-century date for 2 Peter and an apostolic, indeed, Petrine authorship of the letter. Note too in the second case, since secular assumptions forbid taking the veracity of apostles on faith and because Peter's testimony includes a reference to a voice from heaven, that one would have to establish beyond reasonable doubt the possibility, indeed, the probability of the existence of such a voice and the probability that the voice said what Peter reports that it said. This would take one presumably into the matter of justifying the validity of and then the utilizing of at least one of the so-called arguments for the existence of God, namely, an argument that would proceed from the "effect" of our capacity as persons to speak to the same capacity to speak in a personal God as the "cause" of our speech capacity – no mean task! And it would require one to demonstrate that a favorable relationship existed between Christ and that voice on the basis of which the voice said what it did. This in turn would necessitate that one enter deeply into the highly charged theological areas of Christology and Trinitarianism where much that is concluded flows out of an even larger theological vision, namely theism *per se*. This theological vision in turn would need to be justified. One might also be challenged to demonstrate that the voice from heaven was God's voice and not the voice of a demon who was seeking to mislead Peter. Note as well that the demonstration would not only have to vindicate the veracity of what these particular verses say but also would have to mount independent proofs for at least the general trustworthiness of the teaching of every other verse of the letter. Then one would have to do the same with the secondary sources in the New Testament who report its occurrence – no small task, to say the least.

But let us assume that one accomplished this work to his satisfaction. Now the general trustworthiness of the rest of the Bible writers would have to be demonstrated in the same way with regard to everything else that they report in the Bible, and they report thousands of supernatural events. Of course, there simply is no available evidence beyond the reports themselves for the occurrence of the supernatural events recorded in the Bible such as the Spirit of God hovering over the waters in Genesis 1:2 or God's hardening of Pharaoh's heart during the Exodus deliverance. I suppose that such *theological* statements would have to be accepted on the basis of the generally reliable *historical* record corroborated elsewhere. If so, *we would be asking the secularist to accept the reliability of the Bible's explicit and replete supernaturalism on the basis of the Bible's generally reliable naturalism.* Even so, a great number of "natural" events would still remain to be investigated and generally corroborated. Many would turn out to be maddeningly resistant to corroboration. Could one be pardoned were he to suggest that this would be a mammoth undertaking, to say the least? I think so. Might it not even involve a lifetime of research? Again, I think so. But, for the sake of argument, let us say that one completes this task in due course and is now satisfied that the Bible is a basically or generally trustworthy book, at least in those areas where it can be corroborated (which areas are relatively few in number in comparison to the whole). Now he proceeds to draw the stated inferences.

But Premise B, based as it is on Premise A ("The Bible is a basically or generally reliable and trustworthy document"), should really state: "On the basis of this basically or generally reliable and trustworthy document, shown to be so at least in those relatively few areas where we could conduct an investigation, we may conclude that *possibly* we have evidence that Jesus Christ is the Son of God."

But then this means in turn that Premise C should read: "Jesus Christ, *possibly* being the Son of God, is *possibly* therefore an infallible authority." But this means that his testimony, being only possibly infallible, does not really finally settle this or any other issue. His testimony is just one more part of the total evidence in a possibility construct for some desired conclusion.

Premise D should then read: "Jesus Christ, *possibly* being accurately portrayed by the Scriptures as the Son of God (Premise B) and therefore *possibly* being infallible (Premise C), *possibly* taught infallibly (Premise C) that the Bible is more than generally trustworthy, that is, that it is the very Word of God." We can say no more than this about Jesus' testimony about the Bible on the basis of a report about him that is represented as only generally reliable.

Premise E should then read: "The Bible, *possibly* the very Word of God (Premise D), is therefore *possibly* utterly trustworthy, in that the God about whom it speaks is represented as utterly trustworthy in his utterances."

The conclusion should then read: "On the basis of the *possibly* infallible authority of Jesus Christ, the church believes the Bible to be *possibly* utterly trustworthy, i.e., possibly infallible and therefore authoritative."

It seems to me that this is the only way the argument's progression could be rewritten to win the approval of an intelligent non-believer schooled in logic. But God is neither honored nor flattered when men draw such conclusions about his Son and his Word from data, all of which are really revelational in nature and are thus self-authenticating.

The Ligonier apologists (Sproul, Gerstner, and Lindsley) also offer a variation of this argument in their *Classical Apologetics*: Premise A – It is virtually granted [they do not say by whom] that the Bible (not assumed to be inspired) contains generally reliable history.

Premise B – The Bible records miracles as part of its generally reliable history.

Premise C – These miracles authenticate the Bible's messengers and their message.

Conclusion #1 – Therefore, the Bible message ought to be received as divine.

Premise D – The Bible message includes the doctrine of its own inspiration.

Conclusion #2 – Therefore, the Bible is more than a generally reliable record. It is a divinely inspired record.[22]

I will not repeat those aspects of the argument given above which register equally here against what I regard as a rather naive line

---

[22]R. C. Sproul, John Gerstner, and Arthur Lindsley, *Classical Apologetics* (Grand Rapids: Zondervan, 1984), 141. One could ask again, if this line of reasoning is sound, why should they not argue everything else with the unbeliever on the basis of this "established" fact of the Bible's divine authority?

of reasoning except to say that once again the skeptic is being asked by Premise B to accept the Bible's supernaturalism on the basis of the Bible's "generally reliable history." But as John Frame declares:

> The authors overestimate, I think, the current scholarly consensus on the reliability of the Gospels. They assume that almost every NT scholar will concede that the Gospels are "generally reliable." I doubt it.[23]

I doubt it too! Consider just one example – admittedly a radical one – namely, the work of the infamous Jesus Seminar which casts doubt on 82% of Jesus' sayings![24] As for their Premise C that the Gospel miracles authenticate Jesus' message as from God, Frame remarks:

> Even if we grant that some very unusual events took place in the ministry of Jesus [in a footnote Frame states: "And of course the question must be raised as to *how* unusual an event must be before we call it a miracle."], how can we be sure that these can be explained *only* as a divine attestation to Jesus' authority? It is extremely difficult to prove (apart from Christian presuppositions) the negative proposition that no other cause could have produced these events. The authors need to prove this proposition in order to make their case, but nothing in the book amounts to such a proof.[25]

What Frame is highlighting by his second comment is the problem that always arises when one attempts to prove a universal negative proposition. Such propositions are always extremely difficult, if not impossible, to prove. So much for this kind of proof for the Bible's authority.

Another equally unsalutary argument for the Bible's truthfulness Edward John Carnell advances in his prizewinning

---

[23]John M. Frame, "Van Til and the Ligonier Apologetic," *WTJ* 47 (1985), 297.

[24]See Robert Funk, Roy Hoover, and The Jesus Seminar, *The Search for the Authentic Words of Jesus* (New York: Macmillan, 1993).

[25]Frame, "Van Til and the Ligonier Apologetic," 297.

An Introduction to Christian Apologetics. He affirms there that the "logical starting point" of his apologetic, that is, the highest principle that one introduces to give unity and order to his view of reality, is the triune God. But he then states that "all logical ultimates must be tested…, and the only way to do this is to work out a still more primitive procedure" that he calls the "synoptic starting point."[26] This "starting point," he says, is "systematic consistency" that alone can judge truth.[27] That is to say, the Bible's claim to truthfulness must pass a rigid application of the law of contradiction, that is, its teachings must be internally self-consistent (the "horizontal" test), and must be consistent with all the data of history, archaeology, sociology, scientific cosmogony and human antiquity, as well as the nature of man (the "vertical" test). Only by the test of systematic consistency can one select one claim to revelation from among the many claims to revelation in addition to the Bible such as the Vedas, the Shastras, the writings of Confucius, the Koran, the Book of Mormon, the works of Mary Baker Eddy, and the *ex cathedra* pronouncements of the popes. Carnell writes:

> Accept that revelation which, when examined, yields a system of thought which is horizontally self-consistent and which vertically fits the facts of history…Bring on your revelations! Let them make peace with the law of contradiction and the facts of history, and they will deserve a rational man's assent. A careful examination of the Bible reveals that it passes these stringent examinations *summa cum laude*.[28]

Systematic consistency as the test for truth, however, is the very test devised by the apostate autonomous man (the "biblical fool") to determine what can and cannot be possible and what is and is not true, the very test that has for its theory of fact pure contingency and which has for its goal, at best, only probability!

---

[26]Edward John Carnell, *An Introduction to Christian Apologetics* (Grand Rapids: Eerdmans, 1948), 124.

[27]Carnell, *An Introduction to Christian Apologetics*, 106-13.

[28]Carnell, *An Introduction to Christian Apologetics*, 178.

How a man will apply the law of contradiction to Scripture and how he will judge whether or not the Bible "fits all the facts" will depend upon his prior *religious* commitment. The unbeliever, starting from his unbelieving *pou stō* and using the test for truth that Carnell grants him, will declare that he finds many contradictions in the Bible that conflict with the "facts." The Bible's view of history, sociology, cosmogony, human antiquity and the nature of man is the last interpretation the unbeliever will adopt. Using this method the autonomous man, putting *his* meaning on the facts, will not be able finally to conclude that the Bible is true in the whole and in the part.

Let me make it crystal clear that I believe in the validity of the law of contradiction. By it I reject as false all of the other claims to revelation such as the Vedas, the Shastras, the writings of Confucius, the Koran, the Book of Mormon, the works of Mary Baker Eddy, and the *ex cathedra* pronouncements of the popes because they disagree with the truth of the self-attesting Christ of Holy Scripture and are therefore false. Let me also make it crystal clear that I believe the biblical revelation is true to the cosmogony and nature of the material universe, to history, and to the nature of man. I believe these things, not because I tested the entire Bible first for its systematic consistency in these matters (neither did Carnell or the apostle Paul or any other Christian) but because I am a Christian. But I will resist any effort to invite the unsaved "rational man" to judge the Scriptures by his understanding of what can and cannot be, not because his logic is different in kind from mine or because I fear he might find an error in the Bible, but because the religious *pou stō* from which he conducts his test is not Christian. When he judges Holy Scripture in a way consistent with his autonomous *pou stō* he will and must conclude that the Bible cannot be true. The Bible contains matters that not even the Christian can fully comprehend (Rom. 11:33-34). How much less can the autonomous man who cannot know the things of the Spirit of God comprehend and judge the Bible (1 Cor. 2:14)? I will invite him, however, to read the Bible with the hope and prayer that the

Spirit of God will enable him to hear therein the self-attesting voice of the Son of God calling him from the tomb of spiritual death. And I will do all I can to answer his questions concerning the biblical cosmogony, biblical history, archeology, and any and all alleged contradictions, praying that the Holy Spirit will give him ears to hear and eyes to see. I will even assume his position with him to help him see that until he makes the self-attesting Word of Holy Scripture his *pou stō* his "whole effort [as the "biblical fool"] at asking and answering questions ceases to have significance, and worse than that, he himself remains under the wrath of the Lamb."[29]

Carnell wrote other highly engaging books, searching for a point of contact between Christianity and culture. He writes in his *The Kingdom of Love and the Pride of Life*:

> I have consistently tried to build on some useful point of contact between the gospel and culture. In *An Introduction to Christian Apologetics* the appeal was to the law of contradiction; in *A Philosophy of the Christian Religion* it was to values; and in *Christian Commitment* it was to the judicial sentiment. In this book I am appealing to the law of love.[30]

In these later works Carnell fails to distinguish clearly between the Christian's values, judicial sentiment, and understanding of the law of love and the unbeliever's values, judicial sentiment, and understanding of the law of love. He continues to make his appeal to the "rational man," only now he speaks of him as "moral man" and asks him to choose from among the religious options the one that "leaves the whole individual with the least cause for regret."[31] But in doing so Carnell once again appeals to man *as he is*, granting him the liberty to choose his life commitment on the basis of what he concludes most adequately

---

[29]Cornelius Van Til, *Jerusalem and Athens*, 366.

[30]Edward John Carnell, *The Kingdom of Love and the Pride of Life* (Grand Rapids: Eerdmans, 1960), 6.

[31]Carnell, *A Philosophy of the Christian Religion* (Grand Rapids: Eerdmans, 1952), 229.

fulfills the "whole individual." And once again he grants the natural man the right to determine the criteria for testing the truth claims of Christianity, failing to insist that he must forsake his autonomy and confess the apostasy inherent in his claimed "neutrality."

Francis A. Schaeffer also states that systematic consistency is the test of truth in his *The God Who is There*. In response to the question, How do we know the Bible is true? he writes:

> ...scientific proof, philosophical proof and religious proof *follow the same rules*. We may have any problem before us which we wish to solve; it may concern a chemical reaction or the meaning of man. After the question has been defined, in each case proof consists of two steps:
>
> A. The theory must be non-contradictory and must give an answer to the phenomenon in question.
>
> B. We must be able to live consistently with our theory. For example, the answer given to the chemical reaction must conform to what we observe in the test tube. With regard to man and his "mannishness", the answer given *must conform to what we observe* in a wide consideration of man and how he behaves.[32]

Note Schaeffer's expression "what we observe." Surely Schaeffer is aware that what a man observes is governed by his religious *pou stō*. What Schaeffer observes is not at all what the natural man observes. Still, with Carnell, Schaeffer allows the unbeliever to judge Christianity with his apostate epistemology. Schaeffer employs an interesting illustration at this point. He asks us to imagine a book that has had all of its pages torn out, leaving only an inch of print on each page that remains in the binding. When the torn-out pages are finally located, the test that they belong to this particular book is the inch of print that remains in the binding. The inch of printed matter, Schaeffer states, corresponds to the universe and the "mannishness of

---

[32]Francis A. Schaeffer, *The God Who Is There* (Downers Grove, Ill.: Inter-Varsity, 1968), 109, emphasis supplied.

man," the torn-out pages to the Bible.[33] Hence, the test or proof that the Bible is true is whether it conforms to what we observe in a wide consideration of the nature of the universe and how man behaves. But we cannot permit the unbeliever to judge whether the Bible is true on the basis of whether, in his opinion, it explains the universe and the nature of man. From his religious perspective it would be the last view he would accept because he does not agree with the Christian, to continue Schaeffer's illustration, concerning what the "inch of print" says, that is, what the universe and man's behavior in it mean. Consequently, Schaeffer, when he invites the unbeliever to test the truth of Scripture by its conformity to the observable universe and the nature of man and to do so *prior* to faith, allows the unbeliever to conclude that the Bible is untrue.

The same verdict must be handed down with respect to Clark H. Pinnock's apologetic methodology. In his *Biblical Revelation – the Foundation of Christian Theology* Pinnock judges John Calvin, Abraham Kuyper, Herman Bavinck, Edward J. Young, John Murray, Cornelius Van Til, and Gordon H. Clark to be "fideists" because of their common affirmation that "the self-testimony of Scripture itself is sufficient to establish its inspiration."[34] Such a ground for inspiration he regards as a "flimsy base" for the case for inspiration. (Imagine calling what the Bible teaches a "flimsy base" for believing it!) He insists that the gospel must be sustained by historical data; otherwise, "it cannot be sustained at all." "The validity of Christian theism," he writes, "rests on its historical credentials."[35] Pinnock admits that in his method the historical evidence for Christian theism does not prove with certainty that Christianity is true, but he maintains that "when we enter the realm of fact, we deal in probabilities"; in fact, probability, he says, is the "guide to

---

[33]Schaeffer, *The God Who is There*, 108.

[34]Clark H. Pinnock, *Biblical Revelation – the Foundation of Christian Theology* (Chicago: Moody, 1971), 40.

[35]Pinnock, *Biblical Revelation*, 45.

religious truth."[36] But it reflects unfavorably on the living God to suggest that his revelation of himself in nature and in Scripture so lacks in clarity that men do justice to it if they conclude that the biblical God *may* exist. Where is there in such an approach any challenge to the apostate motive that is at work in the unbeliever's thinking? Once again, apostate man is allowed to judge the claims of Christian theism by his apostate test of truth with the end result being that the absolute truthfulness of Christian theism is compromised at its heart.

As I said earlier, I, of course, believe that the Bible is internally self-consistent and that it does indeed "fit the facts" of history and archaeology. But this is because I am a Christian, having been persuaded as a result of the Holy Spirit's regenerating work that the Bible is in fact the authoritative Word of God, is intrinsically authoritative, and *is to be believed because it is the Word of God.*[37]

Warfield's own church confession also affirms the self-attesting character of Holy Scripture and man's need of the Holy Spirit's work to believe it savingly:

> We [Christians] may be moved and induced by the testimony of the church to an high and reverent esteem for the Holy Scripture. And *the heavenliness of the matter, the efficacy of the doctrine, the majesty of the style, the consent of all the parts, the scope [purpose] of the whole (which is to give all glory to God), the full discovery [disclosure] it makes of the only way of man's salvation, the many other incomparable excellencies, and the entire perfection thereof, are arguments whereby it doth abundantly evidence itself to be the word of God*; yet, notwithstanding, our full persuasion and assurance of the infallible truth and divine authority thereof, is from the inward work of the Holy Spirit, bearing witness by and with the word in our hearts. (*WCF*, I.5, emphasis supplied)

---

[36]Pinnock, *Biblical Revelation,* 46.

[37]See my *The Justification of Knowledge*, 130-48, for a more extensive rebuttal of systematic consistency as man's test of religious truth.

This article of the *Confession* asserts both the Bible's *self-authenticating, self-evidencing, self-attesting, self-validating* character as the Word of God and the necessity of the Holy Spirit's saving work if one is to believe it savingly. It recognizes that the Word of God would, of necessity, have to be self-authenticating, self-attesting and self-validating, for if it needed anyone or anything else to authenticate and validate its divine character – based on the principle that the validating source is always the higher and final authority (see Heb. 6:13) – it would not be the Word of God because the validating source would be the higher authority.[38] And while this article recognizes that the testimony of the church to the Bible's divine character, as a motivating appeal for the Bible's claims (a *motivum credibilitatis*), *may* move Christians (see the "we") to a "high and reverent esteem for the Holy Scripture" (Packer declares, "The church bears witness, but the Spirit produces conviction"), it also recognizes that the Bible's ultimate attestation as God's Word does not derive from human or church testimony. Rather, the Bible carries within its bosom, so to speak, its own *divine indicia*.[39] The article generalizes eight such self-evidencing

---

[38]When Christ as the incarnate Son of God authenticated the Scriptures, he was authenticating his own Word, and he was doing it according to his own declared authority in keeping with the principle he enunciated in John 8:14: "…if I testify on my own behalf, my testimony is valid, for I know where I came from and where I am going." The point to note here is that Jesus validated his claims by appealing to his knowledge of himself, unintimidated by the charge of *petitio principii* or "begging the question" (Jesus' appeal to self-knowledge here accords with the divine procedure stipulated in Hebrews 6:13: "When God made his promise to Abraham, since there is no one greater for him to swear by, he swore by himself"). Since then the words of Scripture are the words of Christ, one must never separate the words of Scriptures from the Christ of Scripture. It is the same self-attesting Word speaking in and through both. To doubt the truthfulness of Scripture is to doubt the Christ of Scripture, and to doubt the Christ of Scripture is both immoral and to operate with a false ideal and test of truth.

[39]John Calvin in the Latin version of his *Institutes* states that Scripture is *autopiston*, that is, "self-authenticating" (1.7.5). In his French translation of the same work he affirms that the Scripture "carries with[in] itself its [own] credentials" (*porte avec soi sa crevance*).

features: (1) the heavenliness of its subject matter, (2) the efficacy of its doctrine, (3) the majesty of its style, (4) the consent of all its parts, (5) the purpose of the whole, namely, to give all glory to God, (6) the full disclosure it makes of the only way of man's salvation, (7) its many other incomparable excellencies, and (8) its entire perfection. These, the article states, "are arguments whereby it *doth abundantly evidence itself* to be the word of God."[40]

But if the Bible, as the *Confession* declares, is self-evidencingly the Word of God, why do not all men acknowledge it to be such? The answer is because something more is needed for such acknowledgment due to the human situation. What is this missing component? The *Confession* would not for a moment place this inadequacy in the Bible. Rather, taking seriously what the Bible teaches about the darkness of the human heart (see *WCF*, VI.4; *Larger Catechism*, Question 25), it presupposes here the spiritual blindness of man. If we may employ the analogy of a radio station and the home radio, the *Confession* would say that there is nothing wrong with the "radio station's," that is, the Bible's, transmission. It is "transmitting" precisely as it should. If its transmission is not received, the problem lies at the reception end, with the "home radio," the human heart. Therefore, the *Confession* declares, something more is needed if people are to become fully persuaded and assured of the infallible truth and divine authority of the Holy Scriptures – namely, people need a "major repair job" done in their lives by an "expert Technician." Indeed, "repair" does not go far enough. They need, to cite Warfield, "in ordinary language, a new heart, or in the *Confession's* language, 'the inward work of the Holy

---

[40]*Westminster Larger Catechism*, Question 4, says the same only in somewhat different words: "The Scriptures *manifest themselves* to be the word of God, by their majesty and purity, by the consent of all the parts, and the scope of the whole, which is to give all glory to God; by their light and power to convince and convert sinners, to comfort and build up believers unto salvation."

Spirit, bearing witness [to these things] by and with the word in our hearts.'"[41]

The reference here in the *Confession* to "the inward work of the Holy Spirit" is often called the "internal testimony of the Holy Spirit."[42] What precisely is this work? Louis Berkhof replies:

> What is the ground on which our faith in the Word of God rests? Or, perhaps better still, By what means is the conviction respecting the truth of the special revelation of God wrought in our hearts? In answer to these questions Reformed theologians point to the testimony of the Holy Spirit.... The Reformers...derived their certainty respecting the truth of the divine revelation from the work of the Spirit of God in the hearts of believers....
>
> We should bear in mind that the particular work of the Holy Spirit described by [this] name does not stand by itself, but is connected with the whole work of the Holy Spirit in the application of the redemption wrought in Christ. The Spirit renews the spiritual darkness of the understanding and illumines the heart, so that the glory of God in Christ is clearly seen.... The work of the Holy Spirit enables [people] to accept the revelation of God in Christ, to appropriate the blessings of salvation, and to attain to the assurance of faith. And the testimony of the Holy Spirit is merely a special aspect of His more general work in the sphere of redemption....

After underscoring the two facts that this special testimony of the Spirit neither brings a new revelation for then this new revelation would call for further attestation *ad infinitum* nor is it identical with the faith experience *per se* inasmuch as the Spirit's testimony is the efficient cause (*causa efficiens*) of faith, Berkhof continues:

---

[41]Warfield, "The Westminster Doctrine of Holy Scripture" in *Selected Shorter Writings of Benjamin B. Warfield*, edited by John E. Meeter (Nutley, N. J., Presbyterian and Reformed, 1973), II, 567.

[42]Paul teaches in 1 Corinthians 2:14-15 that only those who receive the Spirit's saving enlightenment can savingly accept and understand the truths that come from the Spirit of God. Such truths must be "spiritually discerned" (*pneumatikōs anakrinetai*), that is, by the Spirit's aid.

The Testimony of the Holy Spirit is simply the work of the Holy Spirit in the heart of the sinner by which he removes the blindness of sin, so that the erstwhile blind man, who had no eyes for the sublime character of the Word of God, now clearly sees and appreciates the marks of its divine nature, and receives immediate certainty respecting the divine origin of Scripture.... The Christian believes the Bible to be the Word of God in the last analysis on the testimony which God Himself gives respecting this matter in His Word, and recognizes that Word as divine by means of the testimony of God in his heart. The testimony of the Holy Spirit is therefore, strictly speaking, not so much the final ground of faith, but rather the means of faith. The final ground of faith is Scripture only, or better still, the authority of God which is impressed upon the believer in the testimony of Scripture. The ground of faith is identical with its contents, and cannot be separated from it. But the testimony of the Holy Spirit is the moving cause of faith. We believe Scripture, not because of, but through the testimony of the Holy Spirit.[43]

Edward J. Young likewise responds:

...of one point we may be sure. [The testimony of the Holy Spirit] is not the communication to us of information beyond what is contained in the Bible. It is not the impartation of new knowledge. It is not a new revelation from God to man. It is rather that aspect of the supernatural work of the new birth in which the eyes of our understanding have been opened so that we, who once were in darkness and bondage of sin, now see that to which formerly we had been blind. The new birth is the work of the Spirit of God alone, and one of the blessed consequences of this new birth is that the eyes of the blind are opened. As a result, the mind has understanding; it sees clearly, whereas formerly it had been in the darkness of spiritual blindness. Now, at last, the sinner is convinced that this Book is different from all other books. He beholds that it is from God in a sense that is true of no other writing. The divinity of the Scriptures is for

---

[43]L. Berkhof, *Introductory Volume to Systematic Theology* (Grand Rapids: Eerdmans, 1932), 182-85.

the first time clearly perceived, and the voice of the heavenly Father distinctly heard.

It is then from God Himself that we learn the true character of the Scriptures. In the very nature of the case, it must be so. Only God can identify what He Himself has spoken. If man, unaided, could identify God's Word, man would have powers which are God's alone. And if man really has these powers, God, whatever else He might be, would not be the One of whom the Bible speaks. We are in reality face to face with the question of theism. Unless we first think rightly of God, we shall be in error about everything else. Unless we first think rightly of God, we shall indeed be in error when we come to consider His Word. We Christians need not be ashamed to proclaim boldly that our final persuasion of the Divinity of the Bible is from God Himself. God, in His gentle grace, has identified His Word for us; He has told us that the Bible is from Himself. Those who know Him may not depreciate this doctrine of the internal testimony of the Spirit; those who are His know that God has truly brought them out of darkness into light.[44]

* * * * *

I must bring this chapter to a close. It should now be apparent from the concessions to unbelief and from the weakened portrayal of biblical authority within the evidentialist's apologetic methodology that only an apologetic that takes

---

[44]Edward J. Young, *Thy Word Is Truth* (Grand Rapids: Eerdmans, 1957), 34-35. See also J. I. Packer, *'Fundamentalism' and the Word of God*, 119:

...this part of the Spirit's ministry as His witness to divine truth...is a healing of spiritual faculties, a restoring to man of a permanent receptiveness towards divine things, a giving and sustaining of power to recognize and receive divine utterances for what they are. It is given in conjunction with the hearing or reading of such utterances, and the immediate fruit of it is an inescapable awareness of their divine origin and authority.

And when this starts to happen, faith is being born. Faith begins with the according of credence to revealed truths, not as popular, or probable, human opinions, but as words uttered by the Creator, and uttered, not only to mankind in general, but to the individual soul in particular.

with utter seriousness the authority of Christ is consistent with the Christian faith. Only such an apologetic will challenge the autonomy of the fallen man at the root of his apostasy. Only such an apologetic can ground human predication.

The church cannot expect to know the fullest blessing of God upon its evangelistic endeavors until it sets aside all accommodation to the autonomous unbeliever and insists, in conjunction with its proclamation of the true gospel, that the authority of the Word of the self-attesting Christ and his self-attesting Scripture is the only ground capable of justifying human truth claims (see Col. 2:3) and the only ground from which it should launch its apologetic for the Christian faith. Moreover, until Christ's authoritative, self-authenticating Word is placed at the base of human knowledge systems these systems will remain unjustified and no truth assertion by them can be shown to have any significant meaning at all.

Packer again writes in *Jerusalem and Athens*, 143:

> ...the Scriptures *authenticate themselves* to Christian believers through the convincing work of the Holy Spirit, who enables us to recognize, and bow before, divine realities. It is he who enlightens us to receive the man Jesus as God's incarnate Son, and our Saviour; similarly, it is he who enlightens us to receive sixty-six pieces of human writing as God's inscripturated Word, given to make us "wise unto salvation through faith which is in Christ Jesus" (2 Tim. 3:15). In both cases, this enlightening is not a private revelation of something that has not been made public, but the opening of minds sinfully closed so that they receive evidence to which they were previously impervious. The evidence of divinity is there before us, in the words and works of Jesus in the one case and the words and qualities of Scripture in the other. It consists not of clues offered as a basis for discursive inference to those who are clever enough, as in a detective story, but in the unique force which, through the Spirit, the story of Jesus, and the knowledge of Scripture, always carry with them to strike everyone to whom they come. In neither case, however, do our sinful minds receive this evidence apart from the illumination of the Spirit. The church bears witness, but the Spirit produces conviction, and so, as against Rome, evangelicals insist that it is the witness of the Spirit, not that of the church, which authenticates the canon to us.

Chapter Nine

Faith's Reasons for Believing
in the God of Christian Theism

No philosophical defense of Christianity would be complete without an explanation of why Christians believe in the Christian God. This I will now give, beginning with a description of the God about whom we are speaking.

Responding to its fifth question, "Are there more Gods than one?" the *Westminster Shorter Catechism* declares: "There is but one only, the living and true God." The *Catechism* derives its description of God here from Jeremiah 10:10: "But the Lord is the true God; he is the living God, the everlasting King." Its monotheistic assertion is expressly supported and everywhere assumed by both the Old and New Testaments:

Deuteronomy 6:4: "Hear, O Israel, The Lord our God, *the Lord is one.*"

Isaiah 45:5-6: "I am the Lord, and *there is no other; apart from me there is no God*...I am the Lord, and *there is no other.*"

Zechariah 14:9b: "In that day *the Lord will be one*, and his name one."

Mark 12:29: "Hear, O Israel, The Lord our God, *the Lord is one.*"

Romans 3:30: "*...there is only one God*, who will justify the circumcised by faith and the uncircumcised through that same faith."

1 Corinthians 8:4: "We know that an idol is nothing at all in the world and that *there is no God but one.*"

1 Timothy 2:5: "*For there is one God*, and one mediator between God and men, the man Christ Jesus."

James 2:19: "You believe that *there is one God.* Good! Even the demons believe that – and shudder."

His perfections

This one living and true God is "spirit, infinite, eternal, and unchangeable in his being, wisdom, power, holiness, justice, goodness, and truth" (*Westminster Shorter Catechism*, Question 4).[1] When the *Shorter Catechism* speaks as it does here of God, it is speaking of his perfections that comprise what the Scriptures sum up by the one word "glory." That is to say, *God's glory is the sum total of all of his perfections or attributes*, which is to say that the glory of God is just *the inescapable weight of the sheer intrinsic "Godness" of God.* And for the creature, whether angel or man, to seek to arrogate to himself any one of God's attributes and thereby to attempt to become "like God" as did Adam (see Genesis 3:5, 22) is to attack the very glory of God by attempting to make himself equal with God. Or for the creature to seek to deny to him any one of his attributes is also to attack the glory of God for it would deny to him that without which he would no longer be God. Or for the creature to ascribe to him any attribute that he himself does not expressly declare he possesses is equally to attack his glory for such an attribution will very likely be erroneous and implies that the creature knows God as well as God knows himself and knows him apart from revelation, which is an idolatrous absurdity and impossibility. Therefore, it is absolutely essential – indeed, it is a vital imperative for our spiritual health – that we creatures should always listen carefully to God's description of himself in Holy Scripture alone, submit our hearts to that description without murmuring against it, endeavor to live our lives in accordance with it, and worship him in a way that befits his revealed perfections, that is, with reverence and awe (Heb. 12:28). Speaking of worship, the intrusion into the contemporary church of the superficial worship styles that

---

[1]See my book on the divine perfections entitled *What Is God?* (Ross-shire, Scotland: Mentor, 2007).

abound everywhere today with their applause for the church's "performers" and their sappy contemporary music is not and should never have been regarded as simply a matter of "cultural preference." Rather, as an infusion of the popular culture into the church it is a symptom of what A. W. Tozer describes in his book, *The Knowledge of the Holy*, as

> the loss of the concept of [the] majesty [of God] from the popular religious mind. The Church has surrendered her once lofty concept of God and has substituted for it one so low, so ignoble, as to be unworthy of thinking, worshiping men....
>
> The low view of God entertained almost universally among Christians [today] is the cause of a hundred lesser evils everywhere among us. A whole new philosophy of the Christian life has resulted from this one basic error in our religious thinking.
>
> With our loss of the sense of majesty has come the further loss of religious awe and consciousness of the divine Presence. We have lost our spirit of worship and our ability...to meet God in adoring silence. Modern Christianity is simply not producing the kind of Christian who can appreciate or experience...life in the Spirit. The words, "Be still, and know that I am God," mean next to nothing to the self-confident, bustling worshiper in this...century.[2]

This is a dreadfully serious situation due to the fact that idolatry does not consist merely in bowing in adoration before man-made images. The essence of idolatry, as Tozer reminds us, is "the entertainment of [any] thoughts about God [as true] that are not worthy of him."[3] As we do our apologetic labors we must constantly bear this in mind. We should not think we do God service by attempting to prove to the unbeliever that just any God exists. The unbeliever does not need this proven to him anyway; he already knows this. What is far more important, as

---

[2]A. W. Tozer, *The Knowledge of the Holy* (New York: Harper & Row, 1961), 5.

[3]Tozer, *The Knowledge of the Holy*, 10.

we shall see, and what the unbeliever needs is that we tell him *what* God is.

His triunity

Not only is the Christian God the one living and true God of infinite, eternal, and unchangeable perfections but he is also triune. Why does the church believe in God's triunity? The simplest answer is because the Bible teaches it. As part of the biblical warrant for believing in the Trinity we have, for instance, the following twenty biblical texts in which the three Persons of the Godhead are expressly mentioned together in one way or other:

Isaiah 48:16: "...at the time it happens I [a divine speaker] am there. And now the sovereign Lord has sent me, with his Spirit."

Isaiah 61:1: "The Spirit of the Lord is on me [a divine speaker], because the Lord has anointed me." (see Luke 4:16-21)

Isaiah 63:9-10: "...the Angel of [God's] presence saved them. In his love and mercy he redeemed them; he lifted them up and carried them all the days of old. Yet they rebelled and grieved his Holy Spirit."

Zechariah 2:1-10: "'I am coming, and I will dwell among you,' declares the Lord. 'Many nations...will become my people. I will live among you and you will know that the Lord Almighty has sent me.'"

Matthew 28:19: "...in the name of the Father and of the Son and of the Holy Spirit."

Mark 1:10-11 (and the synoptic parallels): "...the Spirit descended on Jesus like a dove. And a voice came from heaven: 'You are my Son, whom I love; with you I am well pleased.'"

John 14:16-26: "I will ask the Father, and he will give you another Counselor to be with you forever – the Spirit of truth...if anyone loves me,...my Father will love him, and *we will come...and we will make* our home with him...the Counselor, the Holy Spirit, whom the Father will send in my name, will teach you all things...."

John 15:26: "When the Counselor comes, whom I will send to you from the Father, the Spirit of truth who *comes forth from* [*ekporeuetai*] the Father, he will testify of me."

John 16:7-15: "Unless I go away, the Counselor will not come to you; but if I go, I will send him to you...when he, the Spirit of truth, comes, he will guide you into all truth...All that belongs to the Father is mine. That is why I said the Spirit will take from what is mine and make it known to you."

Romans 8:1-11: "You...are controlled not by the sinful nature but by the Spirit, if the Spirit of God lives in you. And if anyone does not have the Spirit of Christ, he does not belong to Christ...And if the Spirit of him who raised Jesus from the dead is living in you, he who raised Christ from the dead will also give life to your mortal bodies through the Spirit, who lives in you."

1 Corinthians 12:3-6: "There are different kinds of gifts, but the same Spirit. There are different kinds of service, but the same Lord. There are different kinds of working, but the same God works all of them in all men."

2 Corinthians 13:14: "May the grace of the Lord Jesus Christ, and the love of God, and the fellowship of the Holy Spirit be with you all."

Galatians 4:4-6: "...when the time had fully come, God sent his Son...to redeem those under the law that we might receive the full rights of sons. Because you are sons, God sent the Spirit of the Son into our hearts, the Spirit who calls out, 'Abba, Father.'"

Ephesians 1:3, 14: "Praise be to the God and Father of our Lord Jesus Christ, who has blessed us...having believed, you were marked in [the Lord] with a seal, the promised Holy Spirit."

Ephesians 2:18: "...through [Christ] we...have access to the Father by one Spirit."

Ephesians 4:4-6: "...there is...one Spirit...one Lord...one God and Father of all...."

2 Thessalonians 2:13-14: "...from the beginning God chose you to be saved through the sanctifying work of the Spirit and belief of the truth. He called you...that you might share in the glory of our Lord Jesus Christ."

Titus 3:4-6: "But when the kindness and love of God our Savior appeared, he saved us...because of his mercy. He saved us through the washing of rebirth and renewal by the Holy Spirit, whom he poured out on us generously through Jesus Christ our Savior."

1 Peter 1:2: "[You] have been chosen according to the foreknowledge of God the Father, through the sanctifying work of the Spirit, for obedience to Jesus Christ and sprinkling by his blood." And

Jude 20-21: "...dear friends,...pray in the Holy Spirit. Keep yourselves in God's love as you wait for the mercy of our Lord Jesus Christ to bring you to eternal life."[4]

However, we are not restricted for our evidence for the Trinity just to the biblical affirmations in which all three persons are mentioned in a given context. Since the deity and personal subsistence of the Father may be viewed as a given, the evidence for the Trinity is also discoverable in the totality of biblical data that teaches the deity of Jesus Christ and the distinct personhood of God the Holy Spirit. Said another way, whatever biblical evidence of whatever kind, wherever expressed in Scripture, that can be adduced in support of the deity of Christ and the distinct personhood of the Holy Spirit is also evidence for the doctrine of the Trinity. And the biblical evidence supporting these two doctrines is manifest and massive. The evidence for Christ's deity includes the Old Testament's adumbrations and predictions of a divine Messiah, Jesus' own self-testimony in word and deed, his resurrection from the dead, and the New Testament writers' united witness to his deity, specifically their employment of *theos* ("God") as a christological title in Acts 20:28, Romans 9:5, Titus 2:13, Hebrews 1:8, 2 Peter 1:1, John 1:1, 1:18, 20:28, and 1 John 5:20. And the evidence for

---

[4]But not the Hebrew title *ĕlōhim*, or 1 John 5:7-8 of the Received Text! See my *A New Systematic Theology of the Christian Faith* (Second edition; Nashville, Tenn.: Thomas Nelson, 2002), 154, and Bruce M. Metzger, *A Textual Commentary on the Greek New Testament* (New York: United Bible Societies, 1971), 716-18, respectively for the reasons for excluding these as evidences for the Trinity.

the Spirit's distinct personhood includes the *personal* pronouns that the Scriptures use of him in John 15:26, John 16:13-14, Acts 10:19-20, and Acts 13:2, the *personal* attributes such as wisdom (Isa. 11:2, 1 Cor. 2:10-11), will (John 3:8, 1 Cor. 12:11), and power (Isa. 11:2, Micah 3:8, Acts 10:38, Rom. 15:13, and Eph. 3:16) that the Scripture ascribe to him, and the many *personal* activities (Mark 13:11b, Acts 13:2, 21:11, Luke 12:12, Rom. 15:30) that the Scriptures attribute to him. Beyond controversy, if the biblical witness is given its just due the God depicted therein is, while one God, also three distinct Persons at the same time.

Christians of the first five centuries – as monotheistic in their outlook as the ancient Israelites and who in fact believed that they were worshiping the God of Israel when they worshiped God the Father, God the Son, and God the Holy Spirit – began to formulate their doctrine of God in Trinitarian terms. That is to say, the early church's creedalized Trinitarianism was a deduction from its conviction that Jesus Christ and the Holy Spirit were both distinct divine persons. The formulating process itself, precipitated in the first three centuries particularly by the emergence of second century Gnosticism and the Logos Christologies, by third century Monarchianism, and by early fourth century Arianism, brought the church to a basic but real crystallization of the doctrine of the Trinity in the Nicene Creed of 325, a crystallization that it continued to refine, especially with regard to the person of God the Son, in the Nicaeno-Constantinopolitan Creed of 381, the fifth century anti-Nestorian statement of the Council of Ephesus in 431, and the Definition of Chalcedon in 451.

The efforts of these ancient Fathers who formulated these creedal statements are to be revered. Their creedal statements make it clear that three doctrines are absolutely essential to the biblical God's triunity:

- First, there is but one living and true God who is eternally and immutabably *indivisible*. This is the Bible's doctrine of monotheism, and to deny this doctrine is to fall into the error of tritheism.

- Second, the Father, the Son, and the Holy Spirit are each *distinct* Persons (Please note: *distinct* but not separate since comprising as they do the one *indivisible* God they mutually indwell each other[5]). This is the Bible's doctrine of the three Persons' distinct personal properties, namely, the Father's ingeneration, the Father's eternal generation of the Son, the meaning of which it is quite impossible to explicate safely beyond the idea of internal order within the Godhead, and the

---

[5]This aspect of orthodox Trinitarianism – the doctrine of the *perichōrēsis* that is largely the teaching of the Cappadocian theologians and John of Damascus in his *Exposition of the Orthodox Faith*, Book IV, Chapter XVIII – is vital to the divine unity. I believe it is necessarily true given the two facts that the triune God is one indivisible divine being and that each person has the entire fullness, that is, the entire undivided being, of God in himself (see Col. 2:9). But I do not think it is true for the reason that is usually given for it, namely, Jesus' statement in John 10:38: "The Father is in me, and I [am] in the Father" (see also 14:10, 11; 17:21, 22). How could Jesus' hostile contemporaries, simply by observing his works, have deduced the doctrine of the ontological coinherence or interpenetration of the Persons of the Godhead? They could, however, have deduced from an observation of Jesus' miraculous works that his ministry was in accord with God's will, that it enjoyed God's blessing, and that God was in some sense *in union with* him and that he was in some sense *in union with* God.

An analogy here would be Reformed theology's interpretation of the preposition *en* in Paul's εν Χριστω phrase and his *Christos en humin*, phrase (Col. 1:27), the same preposition found in John 10:38. Does any Reformed theologian contend that Paul's phrases speak of a mutual ontological coinherence or interpenetration of persons? Is it not consistently asserted that these phrases speak of the Christian's vital spiritual union with Jesus Christ? When Jesus prayed that all of his people "may be one, Father, *just as [kathōs]* you are in me and I am in you. May they also be *in us*" (John 17:21), has any Reformed theologian ever contended that he was praying that Christians would experience a mutual ontological coinherence or interpenetration of persons with themselves and with the Godhead? When Jesus stated that the glory the Father had given him he had in turn given to his people "that they may be one *just as [kathōs]* we are one" (John 17:22), has any Reformed theologian ever contended that he was teaching that Christians would experience a mutual ontological coinherence or interpenetration of persons? Has not Reformed theology consistently taught that Jesus was praying for the church's *observable* spiritual oneness in purpose, in love, in action in this world?

Spirit's eternal procession from the Father and the Son, again about the meaning of which it is safe to say that we know virtually nothing beyond the idea of internal order within the Godhead[6]; and to deny this doctrine and these distinguishing properties is to embrace some form of modalism.

• Third, the Father, the Son, and the Holy Spirit are each *fully and equally* God. This is the Bible's doctrine of the three Persons' *homoousian* "identity in divine essence," and to deny this doctrine is to embrace some form of essential subordinationism within the Godhead.

All this means, first, since each Person of the Godhead is fully God, that each Person has the entire fullness of God's being in himself (see Col. 2:9). We must not think of the three Persons as each occupying a third of God's being. Being God as each is, each Person possesses the whole being of God. This means that the three Persons taken together are not to be regarded as a greater divine being than any one of the Persons viewed singly and also that any one of the Persons viewed singly is not to be regarded as a lesser divine being than when the three are viewed together. This means also that each Person possesses all of the attributes of the one God, or to say this differently, each Person possesses the entire undivided being of God.

All this means, second, because the three Persons are as real and eternal as the one divine being that each possesses is real and eternal, that we must conceive of the Persons as distinct (not separate) "egos," with each possessing his own distinguishing property that differentiates him from the other two. It is commonly said that the Father's distinguishing property is his paternity or fatherhood, the Son's distinguishing property is his filiation or sonship, and the Spirit's distinguishing property is his spiration or procession.

---

[6]Morton H. Smith, *Systematic Theology* (Greenville, S. C.: Seminary Press, 1994), I, 152, affirms that the exact nature of the Son's eternal generation and the Spirit's eternal procession "is a mystery to us." So also a host of other writers.

All this means, third, that while we must affirm, if we would be faithful to Scripture, that each Person is a distinct Person, nevertheless, because of the reality of their divine sameness in the one undivided divine essence (the famous Nicene *homoousia*), we can never properly think of the three Persons as existing independently of each other. God the Father is eternally "the Father of the Son" and God the Son is eternally "the Son of the Father" while God the Holy Spirit is eternally "the Spirit of God [the Father]" and "the Spirit of Christ [the Son]."

All this means, fourth, that not only is the doctrine of the Trinity a vital tenet of the true faith but also, as Calvin observed, the one living and true God who revealed himself in Holy Scripture

> ...so proclaims himself the *sole* God as to offer himself [at the same time] to be contemplated in three persons. Unless we grasp these, *only the bare and empty name of God flits about in our brain to the exclusion of the true God* [*nudum et inane duntaxat Dei nomen sine vero Deo in cerebro nostro volitat*].[7]

Note Calvin's words: "to the exclusion of the true God [*sine vero Deo*]." Calvin apprehended that the tripersonality of God is not an idea that is to be *added* to one's already complete idea of God but is a truth that enters into the *very idea* of the one living and true God without which he cannot be conceived in the truth of his Being. In other words, since the only God who is there, is, in point of fact, a Trinity, if we think and talk about God and his attributes as if he were simply an undifferentiated divine Monad we are, as a matter of fact, thinking of a god that has no existence. We are thinking of – how does Calvin put it? – "the bare and empty name of God" that is *not the true God* at all. What this father of the Magisterial Reformation of the sixteenth century is saying is this: If we do not give due regard to God's triunity as we reflect upon him, we have created for ourselves and are talking about a non-existent idol. Only faith in the one living and true God as

---

[7]Calvin, *Institutes*, 1.13.2, emphasis supplied.

trinity in unity and unity in trinity keeps one from idolatry. The unitarian theist who rejects the doctrine of the Trinity has only "the bare and empty name of God flitting about in his mind," or as Herman Witsius says, "an empty phantom and an idol."[8] I would urge, therefore, that we must never think or talk about God to the unbeliever as if he were simply an undifferentiated divine Monad but always remember that the biblical God's *special* mark of distinction, in addition to his perfections, is his triunity that is a major aspect of his "whatness."

The implications of God's triunity for apologetics

If it is true, as Calvin says, that to think of God apart from the special mark of his triunity is idolatry, then one must not try to prove that *any* god exists and later attempt to prove that he is triune. Even if one could prove that *a* god exists, all he will have done is to prove that a god *is*. But the copula "is" says nothing about this god that distinguishes him in any way from anything and everything else. For anything and everything that has any faint meaning at all *is*. So does God exist? Of course, he exists! But it makes a great deal of difference whether God is a dream, a mirage, the square root of minus one, or the infinite personal triune God of Holy Scripture. Which is just to say that at the same time one talks about the "thatness" of God one must be concerned with his "whatness." Van Til writes:

> To talk about the existence of God, the *fact* of God's existence, without bringing the whole of what God in Christ through the Holy Spirit has done and is doing for man…is not only an abstraction, but complete distortion. To tell someone *that* God exists means nothing unless you tell him who God is and what he does.[9]

---

[8]Herman Witsius, *The Economy of the Covenants Between God and Man*, translated by William Crookshank (Reprint; den Dulk Foundation, 1990; distributed by Presbyterian and Reformed), I:52.

[9]Cornelius Van Til, "Response" to Clark H. Pinnock in *Jerusalem and Athens*, edited by E. R. Geehan (Nutley, N. J.: Presbyterian and Reformed, 1971), 427.

And for his "whatness" one must consult God's revelation of himself in Holy Scripture. The many attempts to discover parallels and analogies to the nature of the Trinity in heathen religious thought, physical nature, the spheres of logic and grammar, the processes of the mind, and philosophical reconstructions,[10] in my opinion, are invalid, first, because in none of them does one find tripersonality in unity of substance, and second, because we do not know for certain what it is exactly for which we are attempting to find an analogy since there is not yet total unanimity of opinion even to this day among Christian theologians about the meaning and nature of the Father's generation of the Son and the meaning and nature of the Spirit's procession from the Father and the Son. Nathan R. Wood suggests in *The Secret of the Universe*[11] that the universe's three-dimensional space, three aspects of time, the alleged (but erroneous) tripartite nature of man, a person's intellect, emotion, and will, and solid, liquid, and gas as forms of matter reflect the triune nature of the Creator, but the concept of personality is wanting in all but one of these analogies and none has anything that resembles the "generation" and "procession" of the scriptural Godhead, whatever these terms may mean; therefore they break down as legitimate parallels. I agree with Herman Bavinck that none of the proffered parallels and analogies "can prove the divine trinity; for that doctrine we are dependent wholly on Scripture."[12]

In sum, the only God who exists is the triune God and to think of him apart from his triunity is to hold an idol in the mind. So

---

[10]See Herman Bavinck, *The Doctrine of God* (Reprint: Grand Rapids: Baker, 1977), 321-30.

[11]Nathan R. Wood, *The Secret of the Universe* (New York: Revell, 1932).

[12]Bavinck, *The Doctrine of God*, 322. Benjamin B. Warfield expresses the same opinion in "The Biblical Doctrine of the Trinity" in *Biblical and Theological Studies*, edited by Samuel G. Craig (Philadelphia: Presbyterian and Reformed, 1952), 22-27: "...the doctrine of the Trinity is purely a revealed doctrine....There are no analogies to it in Nature, not even in the spiritual nature of man, who is made in the image of God." In this article Warfield also discusses B. Keckermann's argument for the Trinity from God's

when we talk to the unbeliever about God's existence we must make it clear that we are talking about the God of Holy Scripture who is not only infinite, eternal, and unchangeable in his being, wisdom, power, holiness, justice, goodness, and truth but also triune in his essence.

His creatorship

Holy Scripture teaches that this one living and true triune God created the universe *ex nihilo* (Gen. 1–2; Heb. 1:2; 11:3), not because of an ontological need to complement himself (Isa. 40:12-31; Acts 17:25) for he was ontologically exactly the same after his creative activity as before (Ps. 90:2), but solely because he willed to do so (Rev. 4:11) and for the purpose of glorifying himself (Isa. 43:6-7). He needs nothing outside of himself in order to be fully God. In sum, the God of Scripture is *self-contained* and *self-sufficient*, in no way ontologically correlative to his creation.[13]

After creating the universe, unlike the god of Deism, the infinite personal God of Scripture continues to preserve and govern all his creatures and all their actions (Ps. 103:19; 104:24; 145:17; Matt. 10:29-30; Heb. 1:3). All that he does and all that occurs in heaven and on earth are determined by his eternal decree (Ps. 115:3; Dan. 4:17, 25, 35; Acts 2:23; 4:27-28; Rom. 9:11-23; Eph. 1:3-14; 1. Pet 1:20).

In this discussion of God's being, it goes without saying that I intend by the word "God" the one living and true triune Creator God of Holy Scripture who revealed himself in Jesus Christ. It is the existence of this God alone that I confess. With reference to the claimed existence of any other god as the true God, I am

self-consciousness, Richard of St. Victor's argument for it from the nature of love, and Jonathan Edwards' ontological argument for it, and demonstrates the flaws and inconclusive nature of each of these arguments.

[13]Not only is God himself self-contained and self-sufficient but his special revelation is also *self-validating* and *self-authenticating* for if the latter needed anyone or anything else to authenticate its divine character – based on the principle that the authenticating source is always the higher and final authority (see Heb. 6:13) – it would not be the Word of God.

not simply agnostic, I am a convinced atheist. I deny that any other gods exist save as idolatrous creations in the minds of sinful men who have "exchanged the truth of God for a lie, and worship and serve the creature rather than the Creator – who is forever praised. Amen" (Rom. 1:25).

Why Christians Believe in the Triune God of Christian Theism

Students who have taken my seminary course on the doctrine of God have occasionally asked me why I do not begin with a lecture on the value of the traditional "proofs" or arguments for God's existence as many published "systematic theologies" do (see, for example, Francis Turretin's *Institutes of Elenctic Theology*, Charles Hodge's *Systematic Theology*, Robert Lewis Dabney's *Lectures in Systematic Theology* and Louis Berkhof's *Systematic Theology*). My answer to them has been and is simply this: I do not commend these arguments, as I have stated in my *The Justification of Knowledge*,[14] because, as empirical arguments, they are not sound and there is no way to make them so, and because Christians should neither use unsound arguments nor urge unbelievers to place their confidence in the conclusions of unsound arguments when propagating the truth of their faith. Of course, I believe God is "really there" because he has revealed himself to all men *generally* by creation and providence, that is to say, all men already have an awareness of God (*sensus deitatis*) by virtue of his divine image within them and his revelation of himself both in nature without and his providential dealings with his world, *propositionally* in the Scriptures of the Old and New Testaments, *personally* in his Son, the Lord Jesus Christ, and *savingly* through the work of his Word and Spirit.[15] And I believe he is "really there" because,

---

[14]Robert L. Reymond, *The Justification of Knowledge* (Phillipsburg, N. J.: Presbyterian and Reformed, 1984).

[15]I should make one thing clear at this point. While I believe with all my heart that God has revealed himself to me in these four ways, I do not believe that I came to know him savingly by means of these four modes of revelation

without him as the universe's final reality, there is no ultimate intelligibility anywhere. But I do *not* confess his existence on the basis of the traditional theistic arguments. I will give you my reasons.

The ontological argument

The ontological argument, written by Anselm (1033–1109) in the form of a prayer in his *Proslogion* (1078), contends that the very concept of God in the understanding as "the being than which no greater can be thought" (*aliquid quo nihil maius cogitari possit*) necessitates his existence because such a concept conceives of the most perfect being that can be imagined as existing, but, he continues,

> …suppose it exists in the understanding alone: then it can be conceived to exist in reality, which is greater.
>
> Therefore, if that than which nothing greater can be conceived exists in the understanding alone, the very being than which nothing greater can be conceived is one than which a greater can be conceived. But obviously this is impossible. Hence there is no doubt that there exists a being than which

in the order in which I just presented them. Before my conversion, while I "knew" God and his righteous ordinances (Acts 17:23; Rom. 1:20, 21, 32; 2:14-15), I suppressed this knowledge in my unrighteousness (Rom. 1:18) and worshiped and served the creature rather than the Creator. I came to know him first and savingly only when the Holy Spirit, working by and with his propositional revelation, regenerated me and revealed Christ to me. Only then, and not before then, did I understand aright the revelational evidence for him (that was there all the time) in creation and providence. I totally agree with Calvin's comment: "Just as old or bleary-eyed men and those with weak vision, if you thrust before them a most beautiful volume, even if they recognize it to be some sort of writing, yet can scarcely construe two words, but with the aid of spectacles will begin to read distinctly; so Scripture, gathering up the otherwise confused knowledge of God in our minds, having dispersed our dullness, clearly shows us the true God" (*Institutes*, 1.6.1). He says the same thing later when he writes: "…just as eyes, when dimmed with age or weakness or by some other defect, unless aided by spectacles, discern nothing distinctly; so, such is our feebleness, unless Scripture guides us in seeking God, we are immediately confused" (1.14.1).

nothing greater can be conceived, and it exists both in the understanding and in reality.

And it assuredly exists so truly that it cannot be conceived not to exist. For it is possible to conceive of a being that cannot be conceived not to exist; and this is greater than one that can be conceived not to exist. Hence if that than which nothing greater can be conceived, can be conceived not to exist, it is not that than which nothing greater can be conceived. But this is an irreconcilable contradiction. There is then so truly a being than which nothing greater can be conceived to exist, that it cannot even be conceived not to exist; and this being Thou art, O Lord, our God.[16]

… Why then has the fool said in his heart, there is no God, since it is so evident, to a rational mind, that Thou dost exist in the highest degree of all? Why? except that he is dull and a fool!

As has been often noted, this argument at best only proves that people are incapable of holding the concept of a perfect God in the mind that does not include its existence in reality. But their *concept* of God existing in reality and the *actual* existence of such a God are not the same; the former no more establishes the objective reality of its corresponding entity than a merchant's writing zeroes in his ledger increases his actual wealth (so Kant). Gaunilo, a French monk of Marmoutier and Anselm's contemporary, in his rejoinder, *On Behalf of the Fool*, said in effect: "I have an idea of an island than which no more perfect can be conceived, an idea which therefore includes the island's existence, but my idea of such an island

---

[16]Of course, for some Eastern religions the ascription to God of existence would not be an ascription of perfection but of imperfection. For instance, in Hinayana Buddhism *nirvana*, the "enlightened" state of the extinction of desire, suffering, and self-consciousness and the goal sought by all *arhats*, that is, by those who have reached this stage of "enlightenment," is non-being, while in Mahayana Buddhism *nirvana* is neither existent nor non-existent, neither non-existent nor existent. It is simply thusness or void. These facts show that Anselm's ontological argument is presupposing the Western, that is, the Christian, concept of perfection.

does not mean the island really exists for such an island really does not exist."

Not without some justification has this argument been described as the attempt to define God into existence. It is essentially a tautology that merely defines God as a necessarily existing perfect being without supplying any reasons beyond the definition itself for thinking that such a being actually exists. But human thought *per se* imposes no necessity on things.

J. Oliver Buswell, Jr., attempts to validate the ontological argument in an inductive form (that he says he found in Descartes) by supplying some reasons beyond the definition itself. He writes: "Of course we do not hold that every idea corresponds to an ontological existent. What we do hold is that every idea in human culture has some cause." He offers an illustration of what he means:

> If we should discover a tropical island, apparently flat, and if we should find that the people on such an island had a language quite distinct from any other known to us, and if we should discover that these people on this apparently flat tropical island had a word for a snow-capped mountain, we should find it necessary to make inquiries as to the source of their idea. We should conclude that either there was a snow-capped mountain far in the interior of their island, or that they had migrated from some region containing high mountains, or that some traveler had told them of snow-capped mountains. From the data of a flat tropical island natives could not build up the idea of a snow-capped mountain.[17]

His point here, of course, is that our idea that a perfect being, namely God, exists is the effect of a cause. This cause (and here is the induction) is the data of the universe from which men infer their idea that a perfect being exists who is the ultimate cause of the universe.

Buswell's island illustration, however, ignores the fact that not every idea men may have can or must be traceable to an

---

[17]Buswell, *Systematic Theology*, I, 99-100.

empirical datum. Men have very active imaginations (recall our modern "sci-fi" novels and horror movies), even delusions, and every culture has developed its own mythology. Any one of these non-empirical causes could be the original source of the word for a snow-capped mountain for these flatlanders. Similarly, an active imagination or a cultural mythology could account for the idea of a perfect being that exists. Buswell's attempt to validate the ontological argument does not persuade me.

The Ligonier apologists (R. C. Sproul, John Gerstner, and Arthur Lindsley) advance an ontological argument in their *Classical Apologetics*[18] that is worth mentioning. They assert, following Jonathan Edwards:

---

[18]By their volume's title, *Classical Apologetics* (Grand Rapids: Zondervan, 1984), the Ligonier apologists intend to suggest that their apologetic method by which the effort is made to erect a methodological natural theology prior to and apart from any appeal to special revelation is the method, over against the more recent "fideistic" or "leap of faith" presuppositionalists, that the thinking side of the church has always employed. These "classical apologists," however, are the ones who are "fideistic" and the so-called presuppositionalists are not, as I will show in this chapter.

Their volume's *chief* flaw is its fideism that is expressed in its blind incorrigible faith in the powers of mere human reason to erect a methodological natural theology in the face of truly formidable objections to such a scheme from logic, epistemology, and Scripture. The book devotes nearly half of its pages attempting to refute presuppositionalism, branding it as a species of circular reasoning, but it then goes on to plead its own set of axioms or presuppositions, namely, the validity of the law of causality, the validity of the law of noncontradiction, and the basic reliability of sense perception (72), and as a subset of its third presupposition, the proposition that "induction can yield absolute truth" (89). The authors, acknowledging that "naked empiricism" is impotent to avoid skepticism, write: "Without a priori equipment such as Kant's pure intuitions of space and time, or Locke's abilities of combining, relating, and abstracting, or Aristotle's categories, sensation cannot give rise to perceptions" (85-86) – a strange epistemological soup these three, Kant, Locke, and Aristotle! But they go on and insist that man possesses such equipment. But were Karl Popper, Max Black, and Bertrand Russell, not to mention David Hume, all mistaken when they argued that induction is a deductive fallacy? Where is the authors' demonstration of their mistake? Bertrand Russell, for example, put the inductivists' problem this way:

…we have an idea of being and we cannot have even an idea of nonbeing. That there should be nothing at all is utterly impossible….

All inductive arguments in the last resort reduce themselves to the following form: "If this is true, that is true: Now that is true, therefore this is true." This argument is, of course, formally fallacious [its fallacy is its asserting the consequent]. Suppose I were to say: "If bread is a stone and stones are nourishing, then this bread will nourish me; now this bread does nourish me; therefore it is a stone and stones are nourishing." If I were to advance such an argument, I should certainly be thought foolish, yet it would not be fundamentally different from the argument upon which all scientific laws are based.

Karl Popper, one of the leading philosophers of science in the last century, affirmed that science, based as it is on empiricist epistemology, is nothing but "conjectures and refutations" (the title of his book) of conjectures:

…although in science we do our best to find the truth, we are conscious of the fact that we can *never* be sure whether we have got it…we know that our scientific theories always remain hypotheses…in science there is no "knowledge" in the sense in which Plato or Aristotle understood the word, in the sense which implies finality; in science, we *never* have sufficient reason for the belief that we have attained the truth…. Our attempts to see and to find the truth are not final, but open to improvement;…our knowledge, our doctrine is conjectural;…it consists of guesses, of hypotheses, rather than of final and certain truths.

The Ligonier apologetic method, relying as it does on sense perception as one of its starting premises, destroys every prospect of syllogistic reasoning, one of their chief boasts. Sense perception by finite individuals, even were it infallible (which it is not), must partake of all the limitations that naturally attend such individuals and cannot yield universal propositions. But without universal propositions syllogistic reasoning is impossible since it is a rule in syllogistic logic that unless the middle term of the syllogism is distributed across both premises no conclusion is implied or validly possible. In sum, it is universally acknowledged that every attempt to derive knowledge from a combination of *apriori* intuitions and categories plus sensory data is doomed to share the same fate that attended Kant's system, namely, total unrelenting skepticism.

The Ligonier apologists simply have not and cannot make good on their boast that they "can move from the phenomenal to the noumenal by the application of the law of non-contradiction, the law of causality, and the basic reliability of sense perception" (89)!

> Therefore, we cannot think of being not being ever or anywhere.... Consequently, this eternal, infinite being must necessarily exist because we cannot think of it not existing; and the only ultimate proof of the existence of anything is that we cannot think of it not existing, ever.[19]

This necessary being, they conclude, is God. This is the sum and substance of their argument.

I suppose the first and simplest thing to say regarding their argument, apart from the fact that such a god would be an idol since nothing is said concerning his triunity, is that it is naive, for unless I have missed something, I for one, and I suspect I speak for a good many others as well, can do precisely what they insist cannot be done, namely, "have an idea of [in the sense of "imagine"] nonbeing." I for one can "think of [in the sense of "imagine"] being not being ever or anywhere." And apparently the Ligonier apologists themselves also have some idea of what nonbeing is; otherwise, the word as they use it is a meaningless term and their sentence is saying nothing meaningful. John Frame also raises another objection against this argument:

> There is an obvious objection to this, however, which the book doesn't even mention. However infinite being may be, our idea of being extends to finite being as well. Therefore, if "being" is divine, then finite beings are part of that divine being. In other words, without some modifications, the argument proves pantheism. And the argument fails to draw any distinction between the kind of "infinity," "eternity," "omnipresence," etc. attributable to a pantheistic god, and the very different (but similar-sounding) attributes revealed concerning the God of Scripture.[20]

---

[19]R. C. Sproul, John Gerstner, and Arthur Lindsley, *Classical Apologetics*, 106.

[20]John M. Frame, *Van Til and the Ligonier Apologetic*, WTJ 47 (1985), 296.

The empirical arguments

Neither do I confess God's existence on the basis of the empirical or inductive arguments of methodological natural theology.[21]

---

[21]By "methodological natural theology" I intend that theological method – espoused, for example, by Thomas Aquinas who tried to combine two axioms, the secular axiom of sense perception that he obtained from Aristotle and the Christian axiom of revelation that he got from the Bible (see his famous "Five Ways" in his *Summa Theologica*, I, 2, 3, and *Summa Contra Gentiles*, I, XIII) – whereby a "first floor" philosophical prolegomenon is first built by natural reason working independently from sense data that is said to "prove" the bare existence of God upon which a "second floor" set of beliefs derived from special revelation is later placed. In this kind of "natural theology," the Christian revelation, not intended to displace or to function as the ground of the philosophical prolegomenon, is said to presuppose the philosophical prolegomenon and presumably confirms and supplements it. I argued against this methodological synthesis in my *The Justification of Knowledge*, Chapter Five, showing that Thomas' synthesis failed. Here is that argument again: For the following reasons Thomas' arguments are invalid:

1. One simply cannot begin with the existence of sensory data and proceed by formal laws of logic to the existence of a non-sensory conclusion.

2. Thomas believed that the mind, prior to sense impressions, is a *tabula rasa*. But a *tabula rasa* epistemology is freighted with insurmountable obstacles to the build-up of knowledge, for if all the mind has to work with are sense perceptions as reports of what is going on in the external world, knowledge can never rise to the universal and the necessary since from flux only flux can come. In other words, Thomas' denial to the mind of an innate idea of God or of innate ideas in general makes the build-up of knowledge impossible.

3. In order to arrive at a first unmoved mover, Thomas argues that the series of things moved by other things in motion cannot regress to infinity since such a regress would rule out a first mover. Of course an infinite series of moving causes is inconsistent with a first unmoved mover, but if the argument is designed to demonstrate the existence of the latter, the latter's existence cannot be used ahead of time as one of the premises in the argument. This is a blatant "assertion of the consequence."

4. Thomas' arguments require that the universe as a whole be an effect. But to be quite blunt about it, no one, certainly not the empiricist, has ever observed the universe as a whole, and no observation of the observed parts of the universe gives this necessary assumption. There is no demonstrable reason why the universe as a whole might not be made up of inter-dependent contingencies that, operating together, sustain and support each other (see Buswell, *Systematic Theology*, I, 80).

All of the empirical arguments of natural theology (construed methodologically[22]) for a god's existence attempt simply to

---

5. Because Thomas was convinced that nothing can be predicated of creation in the same sense that it is predicated of God, when he argues from the "existence" of the world to the "existence" of God, he intends the word "existence" in two different senses and thereby commits the logical fallacy of equivocation.

6. Granting, for the sake of argument, the validity of the cause and effect relationship, if it is valid to conclude from observed effects the existence of their cause(s), it is not valid to ascribe to their cause(s) any properties beyond those necessary to produce them. All the existence of a finite world would demand is the existence of a cause (or causes) sufficiently powerful to cause it, a far cry from the omnipotent Creator of the Bible. Moreover, since much of what one observes in the world is what Christians call moral evils, a strict application of the cause and effect relation would require the conclusion that the ultimate cause of these effects is not completely morally good.

7. Granting, again for the sake of argument, that Thomas demonstrated from motion the existence of an unmoved mover, yet when he adds, "And everyone understands this to be God," we may demur. The argument taken at face value would prove the existence merely of an unmoved cause of physical motion. But such a mover has no qualities of transcendent personality. I think it is highly significant that the terms Aquinas employs to denote the God he believes he arrives at by this method are all neuter: *ens perfectissimum, primum movens*, etc. In other words, if his arguments were valid, since there is nothing transcendent or supernatural about Thomas' first cause, they would be destructive of Christianity with its infinite, personal God.

See Carl F. H. Henry's rejection of methodological natural theology in favor of a "revelational alternative" on similar grounds in his *God Who Speaks and Shows*, Vol. II of *God, Revelation and Authority* (Waco, Texas: Word: 1976), 104-23. See also Karl Barth's opposition to the theistic arguments in his *Church Dogmatics*, edited and translated by G. W. Bromiley (Edinburgh: T. & T. Clark, 1957), II/1, 79ff.

Apparently Protestant apologists in general today, for whom the dominant form of epistemology is empiricism, and the Ligonier apologists in particular have learned little from Thomas's failure. If Thomas' efforts failed, one may question, as I do in footnotes 18 and 40, whether the Ligonier apologists have succeeded.

[22]There is a legitimate sense in which the awareness of God which all men have by virtue of their being created in his image and by virtue of his inescapable revelation of himself to them in nature (Rom. 1:20) may be called "natural theology." (Of course, this "natural theology" humankind seeks to suppress.) With this use of the term I have no problem; indeed, I wholeheartedly endorse such a usage.

prove its "is-ness" that says nothing about its "what-ness," and all may be reduced to the cosmological argument or variations of it.[23] This argument, ignoring God's triunity which must never be done, assumes at least five things that should not and cannot be assumed but rather must be demonstrated if the argument is to be accepted:

1. the validity of the epistemological theory of empiricism itself,

2. an empirical criterion to screen out unwanted sense data;

3. the "effect" character of the universe;

4. the validity of the cause and effect relationship; and

5. the impossibility of an infinite causal regress.

To validate and demonstrate these matters (and there are many other issues that would have to be addressed along the way) will require the Christian's engagement in endless and intricate argumentation that, if wrong at any single point in his chain of reasoning, would nullify his entire intellectual enterprise. I will elaborate with the following ten points:

First, the validation of the epistemological theory of empiricism, it seems to me, would require that it be done *empirically*. Empiricists, believing that a world of real "brute facts" are "really there" to be studied, comprehended and "rationalized" for the first time, urge that knowledge is to be gained through the inductive method of the scientist – observing, forming hypotheses, experimenting, and inferring conclusions from that experimentation. They are satisfied that such a procedure provides mankind with a program for the acquisition of the universal truths that are necessary for the achieving of knowledge. But

---

[23]See my *The Justification of Knowledge*, 118-30.

aside from the fact of myriad *a priori* assumptions (may I say axioms or presuppostions?) that are implicit in the inductive method, one who would consistently follow the empirical approach to knowledge must either surrender many claims to knowledge that he would otherwise make without hesitation or find some way to overcome the objections posed by John M. Frame and many others that

> ...empiricism cannot justify a general proposition, such as "all men are mortal,"...cannot justify any statements about the future,...cannot justify any statements about ethical values [for one can never move from "is-ness" to "ought-ness" – RLR].... Therefore empiricism cannot justify empiricism. For empiricism is a view of how one *ought* (an ethical "ought") to justify his beliefs, and on an empiricist basis, we cannot justify from sense-experience the proposition that we *ought* to justify our beliefs in that way.[24]

Thus those who begin with sense-experience, having traded the infallible biblical axiom of revelation for the fallible secular axiom of sensation, fail to realize that such a beginning can provide us with no knowledge at all. Furthermore, if God's being is resistant to empirical checking procedures as he, being pure spirit, most assuredly is according to Christian teaching since he cannot be seen, touched, tasted, smelled, heard, or measured in any way, the Christian evidentialist, since he is an empiricist, must demonstrate how his empiricism does not rule out arriving at any and all claims to a knowledge of the triune Christian God at the outset.

Second, the Christian evidentialist must also face the fact, once he makes his initial appeal to raw sense data as evidence for God's existence, that no sense datum can be excluded from consideration unless he can provide an empirical criterion to screen out the sense data he does not want to consider. I have never seen such a criterion offered. Sense data *per se* include

---

[24]John M. Frame, *The Doctrine of the Knowledge of God* (Phillipsburg, N. J.: Presbyterian and Reformed, 1987), 117-18.

a Nature that is not only seemingly at war with mankind in the latter's survival efforts but also "red in tooth and claw" relative to itself. Sense data also include the evils of history. Hitler gassed several million Jews and Christians, Stalin murdered a larger number of Ukrainians. Mao slaughtered thirty or possibly fifty million Chinese and virtually annihilated the Tibetans. And, of course, there were Genghis Khan, Ivan the Terrible, and Attila the Hun, not to mention the world's recurring natural disasters such as floods and droughts, hurricanes and fires, not to mention the births of congenitally deformed and diseased infants. In other words, sense data intrude the problem of evil into the discussion. But add *these* sense experiences to the experienced "effect" of Thomas' motion of a marble (see his "first way") and see what happens to the argument that attempts to prove the one true God's existence on the basis of empirical data alone.

The great Puritan pastor/theologian, Jonathan Edwards, who is something of a "patron saint" to the Ligonier apologists in their effort to resurrect the evidentialist apologetic in our time, clearly saw the futility of human reason, working independently from special revelation, trying to prove by sense data alone the existence of God precisely because of this fact of the presence of evil in the universe:

> I cannot tell whether any man would have considered the works of creation as effects, if he had never been *told* they had a cause...But, allowing that every man is able to demonstrate to himself, that the world, and all things contained therein, are effects, and had a beginning, *which I take to be a most absurd supposition*, and look upon it to be almost[25] impossible for unassisted reason to go so far; yet, *if effects are to be ascribed to similar causes, and a good and wise effect must suppose a good and wise cause, by the same way of reasoning, all the evil and irregularity in the world must be attributed to an evil and unwise cause.* So that either the first cause must be both good

---

[25]President Edwards could have spared his reader this "almost" since no man has ever observed the "all things" that the world contains in order to demonstrate their "effect" character.

and evil, wise and foolish, or else there must be two first causes, an evil and irrational, as well as a good and wise principle. Thus man, *left to himself*, would be apt to reason, "If the cause and the effects are similar and conformable, matter must have a material cause; there being nothing more impossible for us to conceive, than how matter should be produced by spirit, or anything else but matter." The best reasoner in the world, endeavoring to find out the causes of things, *by the things themselves*, might be led into the grossest errors and contradictions, and find himself, at the end, in extreme want of an instructor.[26]

Third, the "effect" character of the universe must be demonstrated without first assuming that it is an effect since this feature of the universe is a major part of the issue under debate. That is to say, the Christian evidentialist must first prove empirically, that is, from raw sense data, that the universe as a whole had a first moment before he can begin to inquire about its cause. But, to be quite frank about it, no empiricist has ever observed the universe *as a whole* and observation of only parts of the universe cannot provide him this necessary datum since the universe as a whole could be essentially different from the sum of its constituent parts.

Fourth, the cosmological argument, it seems to me, commits the logical fallacy of *petitio principii* ("begging the question"), first, by simply ruling out at the outset infinite causal regress as an impossibility since this would leave no room for a first cause, and second, by "affirming the consequence," namely, by asserting or positing – not demonstrating – the existence of God as the first cause to account for every later cause. It commits another logical fallacy when it insists that the essence of this first cause is altogether different (infinite, supernatural, uncaused, non-empirical) from the essence of all of the second causes upon which its existence is made to rest (finite, natural,

---

[26]Jonathan Edwards, "Observations on the Scriptures; – their authority – and necessity," in *Miscellaneous Observations* from *The Works of Jonathan Edwards* (Edinburgh: Banner of Truth, 1974 edition), 2, 476, emphasis supplied.

caused, empirical) since it is a violation of logic to ascribe to a cause any properties beyond those necessary to account for the effects.

Fifth, the cosmological argument, as traditionally framed, is in form an inductive argument and as such claims to be a probability argument.[27] Of course, apart from Christian theism the world is a world in which Chance is ultimate, rendering the very concept of probability meaningless. In actuality, it is only a *possibility* argument that falls short of apodictic proof or certainty, and in doing so hardly does justice to the evidential data that the Christian knows to be theistic, revelational data pointing *incontrovertibly* to God. In the inductive argument these theistic, revelational data are employed in a way that at best suggests a possibility conclusion. But an argument that reduces revelational data to "brute data" that at best point to the possibility of God's existence is an apostate argument that Christians should not use or endorse.

As with the ontological argument, the Ligonier apologists offer their own version of the cosmological argument that, they claim, overcomes this possibility (or probability) problem. They begin by asserting that every effect, by definition, has an antecedent cause. The world is neither an illusion nor is it self-created. If it is self-existent, that is, non-contingent, then *it* is in effect transcendent and we have found "God." If the world, however, is contingent, since an infinite regress of contingent prior causes (they aver) is inconceivable, it must be the effect of a self-existent, that is, non-contingent being, and once again

---

[27]See, for example, the "probability" character of Warfield's apologetic method in his article, "The Real Problem of Inspiration," in *The Inspiration and Authority of the Bible* (Phillipsburg, N. J.: Presbyterian and Reformed, 1948), 218-19, that I argued in Chapter Eight is not really a probability argument because it cannot calculate the mathematical probability of its truthfulness. It is meaningless, therefore, to speak of a given religious belief, on the basis of empirical testing, as "probable" or "highly probable." In fact, apart from the truth of Christian theism this world is a world produced and governed by chance in which the very concept of probability is meaningless.

we have proven the existence of God, actually, at best a god.[28] As with the ontological argument, John Frame has something to say about this argument as well:

> What is most notable to me is that…the authors fail clearly to rule out the pantheistic alternative, namely that the universe is its own god. About all I can find in the book responding to this objection is one sentence: "(God) is personal because He is the pervasive cause of all things including the purpose and the personal" [123]. But it is by no means obvious that a being must itself be personal in order to be the cause of personality.[29]

Moreover, it is simply not the case that an infinite chain of contingent prior causes is inconceivable. There is nothing illogical about such a conception. J. Oliver Buswell, Jr. who places great value on the theistic arguments in his *Systematic Theology*, rightly acknowledges as much:

> We must reject the notion that an infinite regress of causes is impossible to conceive. Rather, it is the case that it is difficult to conceive of the opposite. To argue that since every event has a cause, therefore there must be some event at the beginning that has no cause, is clearly a fallacy.
> …There is no ground for saying that an infinite chain of contingent beings could not have existed.…
> That the conditional demands that which is absolute and unconditioned is…a fallacy…. There is no logical reason why the entire universe might not be made up of inter-dependent contingencies.[30]

Consequently, I am not persuaded that the Ligonier apologists have made their case.

Furthermore, while these apologists insist that they eschew a Christianity that is only probably true fully as much as

---

[28]R. C. Sproul, John Gerstner, Arthur Lindsley, *Classical Apologetics*, 111, 116-23.

[29]John M. Frame, "Van Til and the Ligonier Apologetic," 296.

[30]Buswell, *Systematic Theology*, I, 79-80.

presuppositional apologists do (for them as well Christianity must be *certainly* true; otherwise, men have an excuse for unbelief), since, however, they do not want to be "presuppositional" and appeal to special revelation for this desired certainty, they appeal, as the ground for their natural theology, to certain "universal and necessary assumptions," namely, the law of noncontradiction, the law of causality, and the basic reliability of sense perception that, they contend, cannot be regularly and consistently denied and that, for them apparently, are more non-negotiably certain at the beginning of their quest for God and truth than God himself is. These assumptions, along with any and all of their implications (one of which, they go on to attempt to show, is the existence of the Christian God), must be regarded as certain.

But by grounding Christian certainty in assumptions that, reasoning "neutrally" as these apologists think they are doing, are not distinctively Christian apart from the Christian world-view and that, in the case of sense perception, can be and often is very unreliable, how, it may be asked, can such assumptions logically imply and compel universals, much less the Christian world-view? Could it be that some intellectual "cheating" (by this I mean an unwitting presupposing of the Christian world-view) is occurring along the way? While these scholars claim that their argument for God here is, in a sense, "transcendental," that is to say, they are positing assumptions that they claim are necessary for life and knowledge to be possible,[31] and whose ultimate implication, they say, is God, I believe that their conclusions are freighted with the problem of uncertainty that empirical apologetical systems have never been able to overcome because of the limitations of empirical epistemology that we have already surveyed and because sense perception in particular is not dependable, indeed, is often unreliable.

---

[31]In private correspondence to me dated April 3, 1996 John Frame described the Ligonier transcendentalism as "at best" an *ad hominem*: "They hope the unbeliever will concede these assumptions. Perhaps most unbelievers will. Then the Ligoniers get busy drawing implications. But you do run into some skeptics who won't grant any initial assumptions."

Sixth, the entire approach of methodological natural theology treats men (some, at least) as though they are "neutral" about the fact of God's existence, "simply operat[ing] according to human nature,"[32] and as though they are open to having – indeed, need (at least some of them) to have – the existence of God proven to them. But Holy Scripture teaches otherwise – that men do not need to have their Creator's existence proven to them, that they already know at some level of consciousness or unconsciousness that God exists but they neither glorify him as God nor are they thankful to him, and are therefore without excuse before him (Rom. 1:20-25, 32; 2:14-15),[33] and that they, far from being neutral, are now doing everything they can, because it is now

---

[32]So the Ligonier apologists, *Classical Apologetics*, 233. Frame rightly asks: "Seriously now: is this a doctrine of depravity worthy of Calvinists?" ("Van Til and the Ligonier Apologetic," 292).

[33]Some theologians have argued on the basis of the aorist (punctiliar) tense of the participle *gnontes* ("knowing") in Romans 1:21 that, while the entire race may have known God at some point in the past, that knowledge has not continued into the present and therefore the aorist participle does not describe everyone today. John Frame has responded to this argument in his *Apologetics to the Glory of God* (Phillipsburg, N. J.: Presbyterian and Reformed, 1994), 8, fn. 12, as follows:

Paul's purpose in this passage…is part of his larger purpose in 1:1–3:21, which is to show that all have sinned and therefore that none can be justified through the works of the law (3:19-21). In chap. 1 he shows us that even without access to the written law, Gentiles are guilty of sin before God (chap. 2 deals with the Jews). How can they be held responsible without access to the written law? Because of the knowledge of God that they have gained from creation. If that knowledge were relegated to the past, we would have to conclude that the Gentiles in the present are not responsible for their actions, contrary to 3:9. The past form is used (participially) because the past tense is dominant in the context. That is appropriate, because Paul intends to embark on a "history of suppressing the truth" in vv. 21-32. But he clearly does not regard the events of vv. 21-32 merely as past history. He clearly is using this history to describe the present condition of Gentiles before God. Therefore, the aorist *gnontes* should not be pressed to indicate past time exclusively. As the suppression continues, so does the knowledge that renders the suppression culpable.

their nature to do so, to suppress that knowledge, bringing God's wrath down upon them as the result (Rom. 1:18).

Seventh, the God of Scripture calls upon men to "presuppose" him in all of their thinking (Exod. 20:3;[34] Prov. 1:7). But beginning as the Christian evidentialist does in his quest for knowledge, not with God as his ultimate standard and basic reference point for all human predication (in order to avoid circular reasoning at all costs), but either with no criteria at all or with the "provisional" criteria of the non-Christian and with "facts" viewed simply as "brute, uninterpreted facts," he

> posits an exception to 1 Cor. 10:31: that when you are just beginning your quest for knowledge, you do not need to think "to the glory of God"; you can justifiably think to the glory of something/someone else.[35]

But such a beginning is out of the question for the Reformed believer for whom "the fear of the Lord is the beginning of knowledge."

Benjamin B. Warfield is a leading exemplar of those who are guilty of beginning their apologetic for Christianity at the wrong place when, in his "Introductory Note" to Francis R. Beattie's *Apologetics*, he writes:

> ...*before we draw it from Scripture*, we must assure ourselves that there is a knowledge of God in the Scriptures. And, *before we do that*, we must assure ourselves that there is a knowledge of God in the world, And, *before we do that*, we must assure ourselves that a knowledge of God is possible for man. And, *before we do that*, we must assure ourselves that there is a God to know.[36]

---

[34]The Westminster Assembly's *Larger Catechism*, Question 106, informs us that the words "before me" in the first commandment is intended, among other things, "to persuade us to do as in His sight whatever we do in His service."

[35]John M. Frame, "Van Til and the Ligonier Apologetic," 287.

[36]Benjamin B. Warfield, "Introductory Note" to Francis Beattie's *Apologetics* (Richmond, Va.: Presbyterian Committee of Publication, 1903), 24, emphasis supplied.

Here Warfield calls for a very complete natural theology to be erected by (sinful) human reason. But if men could assure themselves of all this on their own – that the one living and true God exists, that men can know him, that he has revealed himself in the world, and that he has done so propositionally at the point of the Hebrew-Christian Scriptures – and assure themselves of all this before they draw any of this from Scripture, it may be legitimately asked, would they need Scripture revelation at all? And would not their "religion" be grounded in their labors, a monument to their own intelligence? With greater insight into mankind's need to reason theistically (that is, "presuppositionally") President Edwards writes:

> Ratiocination, *without...spiritual light*, never will give one such an advantage to see things in their true relations and respects to other things, and to things in general.... A man that sets himself to reason *without divine light* is like a man that goes in the dark into a garden full of the most beautiful plants, and most artfully ordered, and compares things together by going from one thing to another to feel of them all, to perceive their beauty.[37]

For Christian evidentialists such reasoning smacks of circularity, of course, and circular reasoning is the big "bugbear" for them – to be avoided at all costs. It is also their major criticism of what is known today as "presuppositional apologetics" (though I prefer to describe this view simply as "scripturalism"). Presuppositionalists, they declare, "presuppose" rather than prove the conclusions that they hold and insist also that the unbeliever should presuppose them as well. Thus, according to evidentialists, the church is left with no defense of its beliefs.

The evidentialist concern not to leave the church defenseless is certainly legitimate and commendable. But presuppositionalists do not believe that they leave the church in that state, as evidentialists charge. To the contrary, they believe, first, that it

---

[37]Jonathan Edwards, "Miscellanies #408," *The Philosophy of Jonathan Edwards*, ed. by H. G. Townsend (Westport, Conn.: Greenwood, 1972 reprint of the 1955 edition), 249, emphasis supplied.

is the evidentialist who leaves the church in that state in that the church is left on evidentialist grounds with no absolutely certain authority, and second, that it is the presuppositional apologetic alone that offers a sound defense of the Christian faith that does not at the same time compromise the "Godness" of the one living and true God and his triunity and the self-authenticating character of Scripture. A word of explanation about this apologetic approach is in order. It is, at bottom, really quite simple.

Recognizing that no one comes to any question neutrally, presuppositionalists employ the word, "presupposition" both objectively and subjectively. Employed objectively, it refers to the *actual* transcendental foundation of universal meaning and intelligibility, namely, the triune God. Used subjectively, it refers to a person's most basic personal heart commitment, this commitment having (1) the greatest authority in one's thinking, being the least negotiable belief in one's network of beliefs, and (2) the highest immunity to revision. In matters of ultimate commitment then, if one is consistent, the intended *conclusion* of one's line of argument will also be the *standard* or presupposition that governs one's manner of argumentation for that conclusion – or else the intended conclusion is not one's ultimate commitment at all. Something else is. For the Christian presuppositionalist, "the two concepts coincide, for his basic commitment is allegiance to the One who really is the foundation of all universal intelligibility."[38]

The presuppositional apologist, believing that "the fear of the Lord is the beginning of knowledge" (Prov. 1:7), and that "all the treasures of wisdom and knowledge are hidden in Christ" (Col. 2:3), and *therefore* that the triune God (and/or the self-attesting Christ) is the *transcendental* ground of all meaning, intelligibility and predication, maintains that the truth of God's self-authenticating Word as well as the impossibility of the contrary[39]

---

[38]From private correspondence to me from John M. Frame, dated May 6, 1996.

[39]By the "impossibility of the contrary" I have in mind the inability of non-Christian systems of thought to account for rationality and morality, these systems ultimately sliding into skepticism and irrationalism.

should be presupposed from start to finish throughout one's apologetic witness. Convinced that Holy Scripture is the certain revelation of God he refuses to approach any question related to the Scriptures and the gospel as if they were in doubt. After all, it is not God who is the felon on trial; men are the felons. It is not God's character and word that are questionable; men's are (Job 40:1, 8; Rom. 3:4; 9:20). And "this is *his* Father's world." It is not then the Christian who must justify his presence in the world but the non-Christian who must be made to feel the burden of justifying his non-Christian views in this Christian theistic world.

The presuppositional apologist believes that his propagation and defense of the faith should be worked out then in a manner that is consistent with his fundamental commitment to Scripture lest it become ineffective and incoherent. Accordingly, he does not believe that he can improve upon the total message that God has commanded him to give to fallen men. Taking very seriously all that the Scriptures say about the inability of fallen people to understand the things of the Spirit (1 Cor. 2:14; see also Rom. 8:7-9; Eph. 4:17-18[40]), he speaks (and argues for)

---

[40]Richard B. Gaffin, Jr., points out in his article, "Some Epistemological Reflections on 1 Cor. 2:6-16," *WTJ* 57 (1995), 122-23: "...where we might most expect [1 Cor. 2:6-16] to be treated [in *Classical Apologetics*, such as in chapters 4, 'The Biblical Evidence Confirming Natural Theology,' 13, 'The Noetic Influence of Sin,' 16, 'The Self-Attesting God,' or 17, 'The Internal Testimony of the Holy Spirit'] there is nothing, not even a parenthetical reference [neither do they cite Ephesians 4:17-18]. Most remarkably, v. 14 (the inability of the unbeliever to understand) and the antithesis in vv. 14-15 are not even mentioned, much less addressed." Gaffin, in my opinion, is justified when he goes on to demand:

> ...it will hardly do, in trying to make a case for natural theology, simply to bypass 1 Cor. 2:6-16. Apparently the authors of *Classical Apologetics* consider the passage irrelevant. Then they at least need to show us how that is so: for example, ...how the cognitive inability of unbelievers in v. 14 does not exclude the rational competence to arrive at a sound natural theology, or how the "all things" of v. 15 must be circumscribed and does not include the truths of such a theology. (123)

God's message, not with the so-called "rational, neutral person" who claims to be standing before him (this is the fallen person's erroneous presupposition about himself), but with the spiritually blind, spiritually hostile, and spiritually dead person whom God says is standing before him. And he does this with the confidence that God's Spirit, working by and with God's Word, will regenerate those who are elect and call them to himself. When the evidentialist, objecting that the presuppositionalist is only "throwing gospel rocks at the unbeliever's head" when he insists that the unbeliever must accept his biblical criteria for truth verification, declares that the burden is on the Christian to prove rationally and empirically the existence of God by the classical proofs, the presuppositionalist, undaunted, will respond that he must continue to employ this approach just as the psychiatrist must continue to reason with a mental patient even though the latter lives in his own chaotic world and believes that it is the therapist who is out of his mind. And he reminds the evidentialist that Holy Scripture never attempts to prove the existence of God but always assumes its doctrine of God, man, sin, and redemption. In presupposing then the Bible's theism the presuppositionalist is simply following the example of Scripture itself, which means that if presuppositionalists are "fideistic" in the sense that they presuppose the truth of the Bible, so Scripture is "fideistic" as well.

In his argumentation with the unbeliever the presuppositionalist is happy, of course, to employ all the biblical data and all their implications for nature and history as (divinely-pre-interpreted) *evidence* for the truthfulness of the Christian position (and it is powerful evidence indeed as we have shown in the first half of this book).[41] But he will not grant a prereligious

---

[41] See John Calvin, *Institutes*, 1.8. A careful reading of this much-discussed chapter that, in my opinion, would be better titled, "Evidences from Scripture for the Credibility of Scripture," will show, I think, that Calvin is in the main presenting biblical data in favor of the Bible's truthfulness. Virtually all of his argumentation for the credibility of Scripture ("the heavenly character of its doctrine," its "very heavenly majesty," "the beautiful agreement of all

neutrality to the investigation of evidence and view the evidence as brute or uninterpreted data. He is unwilling, as we argued in our second chapter, to answer the "biblical fool" (that is, the unbeliever) according to his folly, that is, he will not argue the case for Christian theism utilizing the tests for truth of the unbeliever's "world-and-life-view" lest "he become like the fool" (Prov. 26:4). When he does "answer the fool according to his folly," he does so only in an *ad hominem* fashion, to show him the unintelligibility of this world without God and the dire results of living consistently with his godless world-view (for no unbeliever, as Francis Schaeffer consistently argued through the years, is living or can live consistently with his anti-theistic world-view); this the presuppositionalist does in order to keep the unbeliever from "becoming wise in his own eyes" (Prov. 26:5).

Presuppositional apologists wish the evidentialist would recognize that he too has his presuppositions as do all other men, and that he too reasons circularly.[42] For instance, though the evidentialist will not permit the Bible to be self-authenticating, he presupposes (wrongly) that sensory data (cosmic, historical, archaeological, etc.) are self-authenticating,[43] and thus he is as much a "dogmatist" for

---

the parts," its "incontestable miracles" and "confirmed prophecy") is drawn from the Bible. What little evidence he advances that is not drawn directly from Scripture (the indestructibility of Scripture through the ages, its wide acceptance by the nations, martyrs willing to die for it) (1.8.12, 13) is not the main thrust of his chapter by any means and, in my opinion, just because it is not drawn from Scripture, is not compelling since the same could be said of other books such as the Koran. To the degree that he used them, he compromised his own *sola Scriptura* principle.

[42]See John Frame, *The Doctrine of the Knowledge of God*, 130-33.

[43]The following admission, however, by Warfield the evidentialist virtually overthrows his evidentialist apologetic:

...if doctrines which stand out of relation to facts are myths, lies [and they would be – RLR], [then] facts which have no connection with what we call doctrine could have no meaning for us whatsoever. It is what we call doctrine which gives all their significance to facts. A fact without

sensory experience as the presuppositionalist is for revelation. Hence the objection of circularity that the evidentialist levels against the presuppositionalist actually applies to him. But his method, starting where it does, namely, with "uninterpreted" brute sensory data, is rendered logically invalid for the reasons already stated and thus can never arrive at the one living and true God or get the facts either.

Eighth, the Bible declares in no uncertain terms that men (and this includes Aristotle and Thomas Aquinas after him who sought to demonstrate from cosmic data the existence of the unmoved Mover) have never been able, beginning with themselves, to reason themselves to God (1 Cor. 1:21).[44] And their very attempt to do so, though not self-consciously intended to be such, is an expression of apostate thinking. Moreover, it is simply bad history to insist that it has ever been done. President Edwards writes in this connection:

> ...he that thinks to prove that the world ever did, in fact, by wisdom know God, that any nation upon earth or any set of men ever did, *from the principles of reason only without assistance from revelation*, find out the true nature and true worship of the deity, must find out some history of the world entirely different

doctrine is simply a fact not understood. That intellectual element brought by the mind to the contemplation of facts, which we call "doctrine"...is the condition of any proper comprehension of facts.... So closely welded are those intellectual elements – those elements of previous knowledge, or of knowledge derived from other sources – to facts as taken up into our minds in the complex act of apperception, that possibly we have ordinarily failed to separate them, and consequently, in our worship of what we call so fluently "the naked facts," have very little considered what a bare fact is and what little meaning it could have for us. ("The Right of Systematic Theology," *Shorter Selected Writings* [Nutley, N. J.: Presbyterian and Reformed, 1973], 2, 235-36)

[44]If men can do and have done so, then Paul is wrong when he declares: "...in the wisdom of God the world through its wisdom did not know him." But if Paul is right, then we must conclude that all of the theistic arguments launched from earth toward heaven, even if we are not able to pinpoint their fallacies, fail to accomplish what their advocates claim for them.

from all the accounts which the present sacred and profane writers do give us, or his opinion must appear to be a mere guess and conjecture of what is barely possible, but what all history assures us never was really done in the world.[45]

Ninth, by the evidentialist method the base of Christian belief is shifted and faith is made to rest in doctrines that are certified by the acknowledged "probability" of massed evidence, and more ultimately in the skill, craft, and art of the human amasser of the evidence and not on the truth of God's Word. That is, the ultimate ground of faith becomes the work of man and not the Word of God.[46] But Paul expressly rejects such a ground when he writes:

> My message and my preaching were not with wise and persuasive words, but with a demonstration of the Spirit' power, so that your faith might not rest on men's wisdom, but on God's power. (1 Cor. 2:4-5)

Tenth, and finally, methodological natural theology does not square with the actual apologetic activity of the early church as we find it depicted in the book of Acts. Only a cursory reading of Acts will disclose that Peter, Stephen, Philip, and Paul, in their missionary sermons to the nations never urged lost men to do anything other than to repent of sin and to bow in faith before the God who revealed himself in Jesus Christ. They never implied in their argumentation that their hearers could legitimately question the existence of the Christian God, the truth of Scripture, or the historicity of the death and bodily resurrection of Jesus Christ *prior* to personal commitment. Never did they by their appeal to the "evidences" – for example, the healed lame man (4:9-10), the rain and fruitful seasons (14:17), the altar to the unknown god

---

[45]Jonathan Edwards, "Miscellanies #986," *The Philosophy of Jonathan Edwards*, 213, emphasis supplied.

[46]A classic example of this shift may be seen in Warfield's defense of inspiration in his "The Real Problem of Inspiration," in *The Inspiration and Authority of the Bible* (Phillipsburg, N. J.: Presbyterian and Reformed, 1948), 169-226. See my critique of Warfield's apologetic in Chapter Eight.

(17:23, 28) – imply that such evidence "probably" vindicated their message. They regarded the "evidence" as incontrovertible and their message as an unassailable witness to truth, the inherent authority of which rendered the unbeliever and the skeptic culpable of "making God a liar" (1 John 5:10) when they refused to believe, and they went forth, not as philosophers, but as *kērygmatics*, that is, proclaimers of divine truth.

The methodological natural theologian does not think that it is right, so far removed in time and distance from the historical center of God's redemptive activity as we are, to ask people today to believe in Christ on the basis of apostolic authority before they have had a chance to consider for themselves all the evidence, pro and con, supportive of the Christian claims. While I take no umbrage at unbelievers considering the proper evidence for Christianity, indeed, I encourage them to do so, this notion is wrong. *Does the modern unbeliever possess some independent criterion of verification that can and should determine the truth of Christian revelation in advance of faith?* I think not. Furthermore, is the modern unbeliever on any continent of the world in any different situation today from Dionysius the Areopagite in Athens around A.D. 50? Dionysius was in no position to check out the truthfulness of Paul's *Areopagitica.* If anything, it is easier today to check out the truthfulness of Christianity, for the simple reason that we have in the Bible the testimonies of several apostles, not just one. All are commanded to repent and to believe on the authority of apostolic testimony, the only difference between Dionysius and the modern unbeliever is that the former *heard* Paul in person while Paul has *written* some letters to his churches that the modern unbeliever may read as well. But all are obligated to believe the apostle's message by virtue of the fact that he was commissioned to preach by the self-attesting divine Christ. If this is not so, then we must conclude that Dionysius the Areopagite, who believed in Christ simply on the basis of Paul's testimony prior to any direct historical investigation into what Paul proclaimed, was the biggest fool on Mars' Hill that day in A.D. 50 (Acts 17:22-34), and that the most intelligent men there were those who determined to hear Paul again on some subsequent occasion! No, the missionary sermons of Peter, Stephen, Philip and Paul never urge lost men to do anything other than to repent and trust. When they debated they drew their arguments *from the Scriptures* (Acts 17:2; 18:28). They went forth into the world not as professional logicians and philosophical theologians but as preachers and witnesses, confident that their message, as to its truthfulness, was incontrovertible and unassailable. They insisted that repentance toward God and faith in Jesus Christ are the sinner's only proper responses to the apostolic witness. J. I. Packer has written concerning all non-Christian arguments for Christianity's truth claims:

> ...all arguments for God's existence, all expositions of the analogy of being, of proportionality and of attribution, as means of intelligibly conceptualizing God, and all attempts to show the naturalness of theism, are logically loose. They state no more than possibilities (for probabilities are only one kind of possibility) and can all be argued against indefinitely. They cannot be made watertight, and if offered as such they can be shown not to be watertight by anyone who knows any logic. This will damage the credit of any theology that appears to be building and relying on these arguments.[47]

I concur wholeheartedly with Packer and affirm once again as I bring this chapter to a close what I affirmed at its beginning, namely, that I believe in the triune God because I am a Christian who has believed by the grace of God the mass of incontrovertible evidence for the self-attesting truthfulness of Jesus Christ and his Lordship that the Christian Scriptures provide. In sum, mine is a Christian commitment attempting to be based upon the Bible alone. And let no one – certainly no Christian, especially no Reformed Christian committed to the Westminster standards – brand such a faith commitment as simply "fideism," that is,

---

[47]J. I. Packer, "Theism for Our Time" in *God Who is Rich in Mercy* (Grand Rapids: Baker, 1986), 13.

a faith commitment founded on nothing, a leap of faith in the dark, for my faith in the triune God and the self-attesting Christ of the New Testament is the result of the regenerating work of the Spirit of God that he wrought in my heart by and with the objective, revealed truth of the self-evidencing, self-validating Word of God (with this all Reformed thinkers should concur).[48] And the charge that such a commitment is grounded in wishful thinking, though not intended to be so perhaps, is still itself essentially apostate in nature and will someday fall before the judgment of God.

Now how would I respond if someone should say that any Muslim could say the same thing about why he believes in Islam and the Koran? I would reply that I would be happy to take the Muslim carefully and gently through the entire argument of this book with its massive collection of *biblical* evidences for the truthfulness of Christianity and show him that I have the true Jesus while his is a false one and that I have the true verbal revelation of God while his is false and filled with errors and I would urge him to turn from Islam and to believe in my Jesus. I would do this because the proclamation to him of the truth of Holy Scripture has the advantage over false non-Christian arguments of providing the propositions that the Holy Spirit will use to bring the Muslim to faith. Saving faith, we must not forget, comes from God as the Holy Spirit, working by and with God's Word in the sinner's heart, regenerates the soul.

---

[48]Christians committed to the theology of the Westminster standards believe that "the authority of the Holy Scriptures, for which it ought to be believed, and obeyed, dependeth not upon the testimony of any man, or church; but wholly upon God (who is truth itself) the author thereof: and therefore it is to be received, because it is the Word of God" (I.4). They also believe that the Holy Scripture "doth abundantly *evidence itself* to be the Word of God" (I.5) by clear incontrovertible "arguments" such as "the heavenliness of the matter, the efficacy of the doctrine, the majesty of the style, the consent of all the parts, the scope of the whole (which is to give all glory to God), the full discovery [disclosure] it makes of the only way of man's salvation, the many other incomparable excellencies, and the entire perfection thereof" (I.5).

Psalm 65:4 declares that God chooses a man and causes him to accept Christian truth. So Gordon H. Clark is right when he declares:

> In evangelistic work there can be no appeal to secular, non-christian material. There is an appeal – it is the appeal of prayer to the Holy Spirit to cause the sinner to accept the truths of the gospel. Any other appeal is useless.
>
> If now a person wants the basic answer to the question, Why does one man have faith and another not, or, Why does one man accept the Koran and another the Bible, this is it. God causes the one to believe. But if a person asks some other question or raises an objection, he will have to read the argument [of my book] over again.[49]

An *Ad Hominem* Addendum for the Benefit of the Atheistic "Biblical Fool"

Astute Christians do not ask the question "Does God exist?" – the question of God's "is-ness" – apart from a consideration of his "what-ness." Of course, God exists. As I said earlier, anything that has any faint meaning at all *is*. But when we take into account God's "what-ness" we must say that the only true God is the infinite, personal triune God of Christian theism. No one needs to have this God's existence proven to him. Every human being already has a God-created innate knowledge of the living and true God (Rom. 1:21) – John Calvin called this knowledge man's *sensus deitatis, sensus divinitatis,* and *semen religiosus*[50] – by virtue of the light of nature within him and general revelation outside of him, and he knows in his heart, because of the requirements of the law that God has written on his heart (Rom. 2:15), that someday God will judge him for his transgressions of that law (Rom. 1:32). Really, then, no atheists exist anywhere among mankind; only theists exist, a very small

---

[49]Gordon H. Clark, *Three Types of Religious Philosophy* (Nutley, N. J.: Craig, 1973), 123.

[50]"Sense [or perception] of deity" (*Institutes*, 1.3.1), "sense [or perception] of divinity" (1.3.3), and "seed of religion" (1.3.1; 1.4.1; 1.4.4).

percentage of whom *claim* to be atheists.[51] To them I offer the following *ad hominen* argument.

Today many of these "practicing atheists" believe with the greatest leap of the imagination – against both the *sine qua non* ("without which nothing") of all scientific inquiry that "out of nothing, nothing comes" and its corollary that if something now exists then something (and the biblical God is certainly something!) has always existed – that the entire material universe of which they themselves are a part accidentally "decayed" (MIT's Alan Guth's term) into being *out of nothing* according to established laws of physics and that this universe is therefore the product of an *impersonal* beginning plus time plus chance and is thus the *sole* and *final* reality; intelligence does not stand behind this universe. Sir James Jeans believed he could assert without fear of refutation that "into [the] universe [the human race has] stumbled, if not exactly by mistake, at least as the result of what may properly be described as an accident."[52] Sir Arthur Eddington declared that the human race is "one of the gruesome results of [Nature's] occasional failure [to take] antiseptic precautions."[53] The National Association of Biology Teachers here in the United States has explicitly declared that all life is the outcome of "an unsupervised, impersonal, unpredictable, and natural process," that is to say, all life originated by chance. Atheist Quentin Smith asserts: "...the most reasonable belief is that we came from nothing, by nothing, and for nothing."[54] And Oxford biologist Richard Dawkins states that Darwin's theory of natural selection "makes it possible to be an intellectually fulfilled atheist."[55] But does

---

[51]This means incidentally that it is not atheists who go to hell; only unbelieving theists go to hell.

[52]James Jeans, *The Mysterious Universe* (New York: Macmillan, 1930), 4.

[53]Arthur E. Eddington, *New Pathways in Science* (New York: Macmillan, 1935), 310.

[54]William Lane Craig and Quentin Smith, *Theism, Atheism, and Big Bang Cosmology* (Oxford: Clarendon, 1993), 135.

[55]Richard Dawkins, *The Blind Watchmaker* (New York: Norton, 1986), 6.

it? In my opinion, these assertions are laughable, for Darwinian scientists have to believe, at bottom, that

- Nothing produced everything,
- Random chance produced this finely tuned universe,
- Non-life produced life,
- Chaos produced cosmos,
- Mindless matter produced the conscious mind,
- Non-reason produced reason, and
- Non-purpose produced humans who are obsessed with purpose.[56]

Furthermore, does Darwinism make an unbiased atheist? Darwinian scientists presume at the outset of their research a *naturalistic* view of reality that is profoundly atheistic.[57] They presuppose as a matter of first principle that purposeless *material* processes do all the work of biological evolution because, according to their philosophy, *nothing else is available*. They have *pre-defined* their task as biologists to be the discovery of the most plausible – or the least implausible – *naturalistic* or *materialistic* explanation of how biological evolution occurs. This approach, of course, rules out an intelligent Creator, requiring adherence at the outset to the Darwinian worldview that assumes that the material universe is all that exists. This is hardly doing "unbiased science" as it should be done. Rather,

---

[56]A variation on Lee Strobel, *The Case for a Creator* (Grand Rapids: Zondervan, 2004), 277.

[57]This presumption is the "Achilles' heel" of the entire evolutionary enterprise. Evolutionary scientists, acknowledging as they must that they are working with a *naturalistic* philosophy of science, make an admission fatal to scientific objectivity here. Their acknowledgement patently reveals that the theory of Darwinian evolution does not present to the public value-free data. Philip E. Johnson, in "Shouting 'Heresy' in the Temple of Darwin," *Christianity Today*, 26, rightly observes: "Biologists have authority to tell us facts that they know from the study of biology, but they have no intellectual or moral authority to order us to adopt a particular philosophy that they prefer." And once these biologists admit that behind their "biological facts" lies their naturalistic philosophy of science, the rest of us as nonbiologists should understand that we may decide whether we want to believe what the biological evolutionists are saying about life origins.

this is a prejudicial *naturalistic philosophy of science* that is biased to the core and that dictates the materialistic outcome of all scientific pronouncements before the facts are even known and considered![58]

The findings of molecular biochemistry, however, not to mention the recent findings of cosmology, physics, astronomy, and biology, fly in the face of the evolutionary assumption. Darwin wrote in his *The Origin of Species*:

> If it could be demonstrated that any complex organ existed which could not possibly have been formed by numerous, successive, slight modifications, my theory would completely break down.[59]

Michael J. Behe, a molecular biologist at Lehigh University in Bethlehem, Pennsylvania, in his *Darwin's Black Box*[60] has taken Darwin at his word and has advanced the sustained argument that the countless molecular systems in the typical living cell – itself built by ten million million atoms – are *irreducibly complex* chemical "machines" made up of finely calibrated interdependent parts.[61] This means they cannot have originated by a gradual step-by-step process. All these parts had to be there in the cell from the start – each doing its specific thing – or *life never would have begun*. Franklin M. Harold describes the single-cell organism as a "high-tech factory" complete with

> ...artificial languages and their decoding systems, memory banks for information storage and retrieval, elegant control systems regulating the automated assembly of parts and

---

[58]For more on this, see Gene Edward Veith, "Science's new heresy trial," *World* (February 19, 2005), 26.

[59]Charles Darwin, *The Origin of Species* (Sixth edition; New York: University Press, 1998), 154.

[60]"Black box" is a term that scientists use to describe a system or a machine that they find interesting but they do not know how it works. The cell was Darwin's "black box."

[61]Michael J. Behe, *Darwin's Black Box: The Biochemical Challenge to Evolution* (New York: Free Press, 1996).

components, error fail-safe and proof-reading devices utilized for quality control, assembly processes involving the principle of prefabrication and modular construction...[and] a capacity not equaled in any of our own most advanced machines, for it would be capable of replicating its entire structure within a matter of hours.[62]

Permit me to elaborate a bit on this comment. According to Behe, the living cell has

...molecular machines [that] haul cargo from one place in the cell to another; they turn cellular switches on and off; they acts as pulleys and cables; electrical machines let current flow through nerves; manufacturing machines build other machines; solar-powered machines capture the energy from light and store it in chemicals. Molecular machinery lets cells move, reproduce, and process food. In fact, every part of the cell's function is controlled by complex, highly calibrated machines.[63]

With reference to Behe's comment on cells moving, the bacterial cell, for example, is propelled by its *flagellum* consisting of both a rotary paddle and its motor that is about 1/100,000ths of an inch in length that can spin at 10,000 revolutions per minute (the state-of-the-art engine of the highly touted Honda S2000 has a redline of only 9,000 rpm) and stop spinning within a quarter turn and instantly start spinning in the other direction at 10,000 rpm – the most efficient motor in the universe, says Harvard University's Howard Berg.[64] And how is the cell steered? It is guided by sensory systems that tell the *flagellum* when to turn on and off in order to guide the cell to food and light. Moreover, if one of the thirty to thirty-five proteins that are

---

[62]Franklin M. Harold, *The Way of the Cell* (Oxford: University Press, 2001), 329.

[63]Behe, cited by Lee Strobel, "The Evidence of Biochemistry: The Complexity of Molecular Machines," *The Case for a Creator*, 198-99.

[64]Behe, cited by Lee Strobel, "The Evidence of Biochemistry: The Complexity of Molecular Machines," *The Case for a Creator*, 205.

needed to create a functional *flagellum* is eliminated the result is not a *flagellum* that spins at only five or two thousand rpm; the result is that it does not spin at all! Hence, the *flagellum* is *irreducibly* complex.

All this only scratches the surface of the complexity of the living cell, what with its more than twenty compartments along with the nucleus where the DNA molecule resides,[65] its mitochondria that produce energy, its endoplasmic reticulum that processes protein, its secretory vesicles that store cargo, its peroxisome that helps metabolize fats, its lysosome that disposes of garbage, its "room" of ribosomes that make new components to replace old ones, and so on. Consider the last mentioned, the "factory room" of ribosomes, for example. Centrally located in the cell, each ribosome – a collection of some fifty large molecules containing more than one million atoms – is an automated factory that can synthesize any protein that the DNA instructs it to make including another ribosome, and it can do so in a matter of minutes. Motorized molecular machines (Behe calls them "trucks") traveling on tiny highways within the cell then collect and deposit these new proteins in their right compartments. This in turn requires other components that signal where the truck is to go and where it is to unload its cargo and that physically open up the right compartment and allow the material to go inside.[66] In order to drive all this home for the reader, I want to cite the PBS documentary *Unlocking the Mystery of Life*[67] that describes in the following way this

---

[65]The six-feet long, tightly coiled double helix of deoxyribonucleic acid (DNA for short) inside the nucleus of every one of the human body's one hundred trillion cells with its four-letter chemical alphabet is the information storehouse where the genetic instructions for building proteins are encoded.

[66]Behe, cited by Lee Strobel, "The Evidence of Biochemistry: The Complexity of Molecular Machines," *The Case for a Creator*, 208-09. Behe muses: "Does this microscopic transportation system sound like something that self-assembled by gradual modification over the years? I don't see how it could have been. To me, it has all the earmarks of being designed" (209).

[67]The documentary was produced by Illustra Media and is available at *www.illustramedia.com*.

elaborate manufacturing process in which the right amino acids are linked together with the right bonds in the right sequence to produce the right kind of proteins that fold in the right way to build biological systems in the cell:

> In a process known as transcription, a molecular machine first unwinds a section of the DNA helix to expose the genetic instructions needed to assemble a specific protein molecule. Another machine then copies these instructions to form a molecule known as messenger RNA. When transcription is complete, the slender RNA strand carries the genetic information...out of the cell nucleus. The messenger RNA strand is directed to a two-part molecular factory called a ribosome.... Inside the ribosome, a molecular assembly builds a specifically sequenced chain of amino acids. These amino acids are transported from other parts of the cell and then linked into chains often hundreds of units long. Their sequential arrangement determines the type of protein manufactured. When the chain is finished, it is moved from the ribosome to a barrel-shaped machine that helps fold it into the precise shape critical to its function. After the chain is folded into a protein, it is then released and shepherded by another molecular machine to the exact location where it is needed.[68]

Clearly, this absolutely mind-boggling, *irreducibly complex* process must have originated already complete in order to function. While Intelligent Design scientists know that ID does not prove the existence of any one specific God, the living cell does demonstrate that things did not simply evolve to the state that they are in today. Rather, it suggests that a highly intelligent designer possessing both elegant ingenuity and the astonishing capability to create life was the cell's originator. The force of this argument has not been lost on octogenarian Antony Flew – for decades the icon and champion of atheism for unbelievers – who recently declared that the intelligent design argument

---

[68]Cited by Lee Strobel, "The Evidence of Biological Information: the Challenge of DNA and the Origin of Life," *The Case for a Creator*, 220.

for God's existence convinced him that he had to abandon his avowed atheism (he is now a deist, which admittedly is as far as the argument will carry one, but not a Christian)![69]

It should also be noted that random chance cannot be a cause of anything because chance is not a material thing. It is not being, not energy, not mass, not power, not intelligence. It is only a mathematical concept we employ to calculate possibilities, and in the present instance the mathematical odds that this universe with its complexity created itself is one over infinity or zero. To prefer, then, the notion that by chance "nothing"[70] created this universe over the opening words of Genesis, "In the beginning God created the universe," represents the nadir of theoretical thought and leaps over reason into the sea of absurdity. For it is nothing short of absurdity to personalize nature as does Peter Atkins, a secular physicist, for example, when he says: "Once molecules have learned to compete and to create other molecules in their own image, elephants and things resembling elephants will in due course be found roaming through the countryside."[71]

Nevertheless, these "practicing atheists" insist that the burden of proof lies with acknowledged theists to prove God's existence to them. But wait; as I have said: "This is *my* Father's world"; I am not the trespasser here. In reality, it is they who should justify their atheism in this theistic world. The burden of proof is actually theirs to prove that this physical world is the sole and

---

[69]Antony Flew and Gary R. Habermas, "My Pilgrimage from Atheism to Theism: An Exclusive Interview with Former British Atheist Professor Antony Flew," in *Philosophia Christi* (Winter 2005), the journal of the Evangelical Philosophical Society, edited by Craig J. Hazen.

[70]These theoretical physicists, to hedge their bets here, now propose around fourteen different kinds of "nothing," which would be laughable if it were not so tragic.

[71]Cited by Colin E. Gunton, in *The Triune Creator. A Historical and Systematic Study* (Grand Rapids: Eerdmans, 1998), 38. An alleged example of these "educated molecules" doing their "creative activity" is the so-called "Cambrian explosion" – that point in the so-called evolving fossil record when dozens of distinct animal body forms allegedly suddenly sprang into existence.

final reality and that *no* supernatural *spiritual* being anywhere exists. Though they strive mightily to do so, this they cannot do since one cannot prove a universal negative. Thus their "atheism" is *their* unproven "grand assumption" – a faith by the way with which they cannot live consistently,[72] for it often takes, as the English poet Robert Browning says in his poem, "Bishop Blougram's Apology" (lines 182-87), little more than "a sunset touch, a fancy from a flower-bell, someone's death, a chorus-ending from Euripides, – and that's enough for fifty hopes and fears...to rap and knock and enter in [their] soul," and thus to disquiet their avowed atheism. And before Browning John Calvin correctly insisted that their knowledge of God is ineradicable so that "willy-nilly they from time to time feel an inkling of what they desire not to believe."[73]

For myself, I happily affirm here that I believe that the triune Creator God of the Bible is the God who created the living cell because he has revealed himself to all mankind, first, *generally* by his marvelous works of creation – which creation reflects *cosmos* (order) rather than *chaos* (disorder) (Rom. 1:18-23) – and providence (Acts 17:25b-28), second, *propositionally* in the divinely inspired Scriptures of the Old and New Testaments (2 Tim. 3:15-17; 2 Pet. 1:20-21), third, *personally* in his incarnate divine Son, the Lord Jesus Christ, who died, rose from death on the third day after he was crucified, and showed himself alive by "many convincing proofs" (*pollois tekmēriois*) (Acts 1:3), and fourth, *savingly in the case of his elect by his Word and animating Spirit.*

---

[72]Francis Schaeffer, as much as any man of his time, made this point again and again in his trilogy, *The God Who Is There, He Is There and He Is Not Silent,* and *Escape from Reason.*

[73]John Calvin, *Institutes,* 1.3.2.

Chapter Ten

Faith's Reasons for Believing the Bible Is Man's Only *Pou Stō* for Knowledge and Personal Significance

When God gave his children his Word and Spirit, he gave them much more than simply basic information about himself, about them, and about the relationship between them. The Christian faith is more than salvation from sin, more than adherence to a few fundamentals, more than a creed recited on the Lord's Day, more than a code of morality. It is actually a distinct world and life view. And although Christians may not realize it, and regrettably many of them do not, God has given them by virtue of his Word and their regeneration a view both of being (ontology) and of knowing (epistemology) that differs radically from that of the unregenerate. This means that there are two kinds of people in this world, who have everything in common metaphysically but *in principle* nothing in common epistemologically and who therefore seek to do two kinds of science[1] – covenant keepers who seek to think in accordance with the revealed Word of God and covenant breakers who continue to think as independent, autonomous unbelievers. (Of course, neither thinks absolutely consistently with his world and life view but a fundamental difference still exists between them.) The covenant keeper becomes *in principle* "receptively reconstructive" in heart commitment, desiring to think God's thoughts after him; the covenant breaker remains "creatively constructive" in heart commitment, making himself the "measure of all things."

---

[1]See Abraham Kuyper, *Principles of Sacred Theology*, translated by Hendrik De Vries (Reprint: Grand Rapids, Eerdmans, 1968), 150-76.

Therefore, if the Christian and the non-Christian were both totally self-conscious, epistemologically speaking, and did their sciences with total consistency from their respective *pou stōs*, the Christian's sciences would be performed for the glory of God, with meaning and purpose everywhere evident to him on the level of finite comprehension, and the non-Christian's sciences would destroy meaning and purpose, with absolute contingency prevailing everywhere in a universe where pure Chance is ultimate. In fact, there could be and would be no *uni*verse at all! All this means that the Christian apologist must not assume that there is a human consciousness in general or, in Thomas Reid's words, a "common sense of mankind." He will take with utter seriousness the biblical description of unregenerate man as one so controlled by a *pou stō* hostile to God that, if invited to examine the special grace principle from his perspective, he will explain it away because it is a threat to his autonomy. He cannot do otherwise (Rom. 2:14; 8:7).

Of course, because of the effects of sin still with him the Christian scientist will not totally achieve the end he desires for his sciences, namely, that his sciences give all glory to God, and because of God's common grace the non-Christian is spared the nihilistic end of his sciences. Consequently, the Christian and the non-Christian will often even cooperate in subduing nature by means of their respective sciences that outwardly in method will resemble each other. But when the revelational pressure of God upon them forces them to ask ultimate questions such as "What is the ultimate origin of...?" and "Why are things the way they are?" and "How can we be sure we know that...?" then their sciences diverge and appear in their true nature as mutually exclusive systems.

By way of illustration take the Christian's view of being or ontology. Ontology is concerned with the nature of being or reality. "Being" is commonly defined in philosophy as that which has actuality, either materially or ideally. A materialist then is one who regards matter (and its motions) as constituting the universe and all phenomena, including those of the mind, as due to material agencies. Lucretius (96–55 B.C.) and Thomas Hobbes (1588–1679) would be examples here. An idealist is one who views all reality as of the essence of idea or spirit. Hegel (1770–1831) perhaps best mirrors pure idealism, maintaining that "thought and being are one." Now it may not seem at first glance that the materialist and the idealist have anything metaphysically in common but by their reductionism they are both *monists*, that is, they both have concluded that there is only *one* kind of reality. The Christian, however, will not talk about being in general, as if somehow all reality is on the same scale of being, and only afterwards make a distinction between God and the universe. The Christian denies ontological correlativity between the Creator and creation at the outset. This is because fundamental to the Christian view of being is the Creator-creature distinction. God is Spirit, infinite, eternal, and unchangeable. His name is "I am that I am." He is in no sense dependent upon his universe for anything (Ps. 50:10-12; Acts 17:25). The universe, however, is created, finite, and continually dependent upon God's upholding powers (Heb. 1:3). Therefore, properly to conceive of reality the Christian thinks in terms of God's *uncreated* being and then the *created* being of everything else. As Van Til writes:

> Such then...is the Christian conception of being.... We may speak of it as a two-layer theory of reality. When men ask us, What is, according to your notion, the nature of reality or being?, we shall have to say that we cannot give an answer unless we are permitted to split the question. For us God's being is ultimate, while created being is, in the nature of the case, derivative.[2]

A Christian View of Knowing

Just as there are two levels of being in the Christian view of being – God's being as ultimate and absolute and created being

---

[2]Cornelius Van Til, *The Defense of the Faith* (Third edition; Nutley, N. J., Presbyterian and Reformed, 1967), 46.

as derivative and dependent – so also there are two levels (or subjects) of knowing in the Christian view of knowing – God's knowledge that is again ultimate and absolute and man's knowledge that is again derivative and dependent.

God's knowledge

God's knowledge – intuited in the sense that he never had to learn anything through the learning process – encompasses all possible and actual knowable data. He knows to perfection and without qualification all things – all things visible and invisible in heaven and on earth; all spirits, thrones, and dominions in heaven and in hell; all matters past, present, and future; all the thoughts of every mind, all the words of every tongue, and all the activities of every creature living and dead; all their purposes, all their plans, all their relationships, all their complicities, and all their conspiracies; all physical and spiritual causes, all natural and supernatural forces, and all real and contingent motions; all mysteries and all unuttered secrets; all true propositions as true and all false propositions as false, all valid conclusions as valid and all invalid conclusions as invalid – and always has known them and always will know them. And his knowledge is related to his wisdom so that God judiciously employs his knowledge to accomplish perfectly his holy and just ends.

This means that God has never learned anything simply because he has always known everything there is to know. God has never investigated any datum to learn about it simply because there is no datum in the universe independent of him. God has never learned anything through the discursive process or through research. God has never had to recall anything to mind simply because he has never forgotten anything.

This means too that God's knowledge is coextensive with all that is. All created things fall within the compass of his knowledge because nothing in this universe is outside of his plan and will. It is God's plan and God's will that executes the plan that makes all things what they are. This means, as we have already affirmed, that God knew all created things in all possible actual relationships even prior to their creation, and it is because of his plan that all things are finally and actually what they are. This has an important implication for apologetics and it is this: It is an epistemological axiom that unless there is comprehensive knowledge of all things somewhere there can be no knowledge anywhere. This is because all knowledge data is inextricably interrelated. For the finite knower to begin from himself alone with any datum, whether that datum be subjective or objective, ideal or material, mental or non-mental, and to seek to understand it comprehensively and exhaustively must inevitably lead him to other data, but being finite he cannot examine any datum or all possible relationships of that one datum comprehensively or exhaustively, not to mention examining all the other data in the universe. Furthermore, there is no way he can be assured, given his finiteness, that the next datum he might have examined at the point at which he concluded his research, due either to weariness, old age, or death, would have accorded with all that he had concluded to that point or would have required him to reevaluate his entire enterprise to that point. *The only way men can escape the force of this fact of the interrelatedness of all knowledge data is simply to avoid the entire question of epistemology.*

The Christian, however, understands that because there is absolutely comprehensive knowledge with God real and true knowledge is possible for man (of course, never exhaustively) since God who does know all data in all their relationships and therefore possesses true knowledge of all things is in a position to impart any portion of that knowledge he so desires univocally to man, and in fact he did impart a portion of his knowledge in Holy Scripture. Of course, the finite knower must be humble enough to receive such assistance from God, which necessitates his willingness to admit his own creatureliness and finiteness, and which necessitates the fallen creature to set new goals for himself, namely, living for the glory of the Creator rather than for the creature. Of course, fallen people, apart from the gracious work of God's Spirit within their hearts, are unable and unwilling to do this. They prefer their ignorance and their inability to justify their knowledge claims that they ground in their own research.

Man's knowledge

God's prior comprehensive knowledge of all things means that there are no such things as "brute," that is, "uninterpreted" data anywhere in the universe. No fact exists independently of God; every datum that is enjoys its existence by virtue of God's prior knowledge and some activity of God and thus carries with it a divine "interpretation" placed upon it by God by virtue of its place in his creative activity, his providential care, and subsequent special revelation, this interpretation screaming out its testimony to its Creator. *There is not one single non-theistic datum anywhere in the universe; even the most insignificant single datum reveals God as its Creator as surely as the most obvious one does.* Man himself, physically, rationally, reveals God. If one wonders how it is that the God of Christian theism has interpreted data in the universe, that is, how he has placed meaning on them, I would reply, first, by his eternal plan, second, by his creative activity by which he interpreted this fact a star and that fact a bird, and third by subsequent special revelation by which he called the light he created "day," the expanse he created "heaven," the tree in the midst of the garden "the tree of knowledge of good and evil." It would follow then that if a man learns any fact to any degree his knowledge of that fact, to the degree he learns it, would have to agree with God's prior interpretation of it that he has given in Holy Scripture. If his interpretation of that fact in no away agrees with God's prior interpretation then his "knowledge" would be false. God's knowledge then is prior and necessary as comprehensive knowledge to man's knowledge that is secondary and derivative knowledge. This means, as Van Til notes, that man's knowledge, if it is true knowledge, would of necessity have to be "receptively reconstructive" and never "creatively constructive," that is, as man as a knowing subject learns, he is, to the degree he truly learns, simply thinking God's thoughts after him; he never places for the first time by his sciences a meaning on some "brute" fact of the universe.

Though I have only sketched here in outline form the Christian view of knowing, its implications for all human sciences are truly revolutionary, even "Copernican." In his search for knowledge in his universe the scientist – physical, behavioral, or otherwise – can only claim to know a fact if his understanding of that fact agrees with God's prior knowledge of that fact. And among other things God knows the facts with which the human sciences work to be *created* facts that in turn are part of his larger plan. No fact, then, is truly known unless the scientist affirms its createdness. But this means, of course, that the scientist would have to consult Holy Scripture to learn what the limitations of possibility are before he makes a final pronouncement in the area of his philosophy of science. He would assume no position that would rule out the occurrence of miracle, for example. In other words, as a true scientist he will worship and serve the Creator rather than the creature with his science and his arts.

In sum, the Word of God, that is, the Holy Scripture, must be viewed as the final and ultimate "court of appeal" in every area of human existence – epistemologically, metaphysically, axiologically, ethically. God's knowledge would then be the *pou stō* or base necessary to man's justification of all his knowledge claims and to his claim to personal significance here in this life. Let me develop the notion of the justification of knowledge a little more.

The justification of knowledge

The student of philosophy knows that the entire history of philosophy up to more recent times may be summarized as man's rational effort,[3] beginning with himself and accepting no outside help, to examine enough of certain chosen particularities

---

[3]From Hegel's time to the present many philosophers have given up trying to find purpose and meaning in the universe by thinking rationally. They have rejected the notion of any real antithesis in logic and opted for epistemological irrationalism or relativism.

of the universe – these particularities may be both subjective and objective, ideal and material, mental and non-mental – to find the universals that give to these particularities their meaning. To be more specific, men have attempted to come to knowledge and then to the justification of their claims to knowledge via the epistemological methods of rationalism or empiricism.

Rationalists (Descarte, Leibniz, Spinoza), believing that all knowledge begins with innate criterial *a priori* truths from which further truths are derived by the deductive process, urge that by this method one will arrive at knowledge that is certain. But even if these criterial *a priori* ideas were to include the laws of logic, our own mental states, and the existence of objective truth, we can, as Frame has urged,

> deduce very little from such a priori ideas. Certainly, we cannot deduce the whole fabric of human knowledge from them or even enough knowledge to constitute a meaningful philosophy. Nothing follows from the laws of logic, taken alone, except possibly more laws of logic. From propositions about our own mental states, nothing follows except further propositions about our own mental states. From the statement "there are objective truths," nothing specific follows, and a statement that tell us nothing specific…is not a meaningful statement.… Thus if knowledge is limited to the sorts of propositions we have just examined, we will know only about our own minds and not about the real world because our mental states often deceive us. Thus rationalism leaves us not with the body of certainties that Plato and Descartes dreamed of but with no knowledge at all of the real world. [4]

Empiricists (Locke, Berkeley), believing that a world of "real facts" is "out there" to be studied and comprehended, urge that knowledge is to be gained through the inductive method of the scientist – observing, forming hypotheses, experimenting, and inferring conclusions from that experimentation. They are

---

[4]John Frame, *The Doctrine of the Knowledge of God* (Phillipsburg, N. J.: Presbyterian and Reformed, 1987), 113.

satisfied that such a procedure provides man with a program for the achieving of knowledge. But aside from the fact of myriad *a priori* assumptions that are implicit in the inductive method,[5] one who would consistently follow the empirical approach to knowledge must surrender many claims to knowledge that he would otherwise make without hesitation. For example, to cite Frame again:

(i) Empiricism cannot justify a general proposition, such as "all men are mortal.... Similarly, the propositions of logic and mathematics, propositions that claim to be universally true, cannot be established on an empirical basis. (ii) Empiricism cannot justify any statement about the future.... (iii) Empiricism cannot justify any statements about ethical values. Statements about sensible facts do not imply anything about ethical goodness or badness, right or wrong, or obligation or prohibition.... (iv) [But if empiricism cannot justify the language about ethical values, then it cannot justify any claim

---

[5]Uncharacteristically, even Benjamin Warfield, whose entire academic life was dedicated to an evidentialist apologetic that prizes the "facts" and seeks to authenticate the Christian faith as a reasonable faith based on good and sufficient evidence, argues in one place that "if doctrines which stand out of relation to facts are myths, lies [and they would be – RLR], [then] facts which have no connection with what we call doctrine could have no meaning for us whatsoever. It is what we call doctrine which gives all their significance to facts. A fact without doctrine is simply a fact not understood. That intellectual element brought by the mind to the contemplation of facts, which we call 'doctrine'...is the condition of any proper comprehension of facts.... So closely welded are those intellectual elements – those elements of previous knowledge, or of knowledge derived from other sources – to facts as taken up into our minds in the complex act of apperception, that possibly we have ordinarily failed to separate them, and consequently, in our worship of what we call so fluently 'the naked facts,' have very little considered what a bare fact is and what little meaning it could have for us" ("The Right of Systematic Theology" in *Shorter Selected Writings* (Nutley, N. J.: Presbyterian and Reformed, 1973), 2, 235-36.

No Van Tilian presuppositionalist could have made a better case for the meaninglessness of "brute facts" and for Van Til's insistence that all apologetic argumentation assumes some basic *a priori* heart commitment and is thus circular reasoning.

to knowledge, for] empiricism cannot justify empiricism. For empiricism is a view of how one ought (an ethical "ought") to justify his beliefs, and on an empiricist basis, we cannot justify from sense-experience the proposition that we ought to justify our beliefs in that way.

[And, of course,] empiricism rules out claims to know God, if God is thought to be invisible or otherwise resistant to empirical "checking procedures."[6]

Immanuel Kant attempted to avoid the pitfalls of pure rationalism and pure empiricism, neither of which, he averred, can justify its knowledge claims in isolation from the other, by formally arguing in his monumental *Critique of Pure Reason* that the knowing subject, while he possesses the innate ideas of space and time as well as twelve specific categories of thought (unity, plurality, totality, reality, negation, limitation, substantiality, causality, reciprocity, possibility and impossibility, existence and non-existence, and necessity and contingency), also needs the objective facts of what he called the "noumenal world" – the world as it really is apart from our experience – that are brought to him by sensory experience. Otherwise, these "thoughts without percepts" would be "blank" or "empty." On the other hand, if the knowing subject has only the data of the noumenal world streaming via the senses into a mind that is a blank tablet, these "percepts without concepts" would be "blind" or "chaotic." So he argued for the necessary combining of some elements of both rationalism (which provides the "form") and empiricism (that provides the "matter") in the acquisition and build-up of knowledge.[7]

---

[6]Frame, *The Doctrine of the Knowledge of God*, 117-18.

[7]Kant's epistemological theory that all knowledge is a combination of the *a priori* forms and categories of the mind and the flux of sensory experience has grave implications for theology. According to Kant knowledge of God can only be claimed if either God himself were immediately accessible to our awareness or if "God" were one of the mental categories demonstrably necessary to the ordering and shaping of our understanding. But since God is supposedly pure spirit and thus not directly accessible to us via the senses and since the *a priori* categories that make thinking possible are inapplicable

However, precisely because the mind's innate ideas and categories of thought impose a structure on the sensory data brought to it, one can never know, says Kant, the objective facts of the world as they really are but only as the mind itself has "created" them.[8] Standing always between the knowing subject and the thing to be known is just the knower's creative knowing process itself. But if one can never know "the thing in itself" (*das Ding-an-sich*) but only "the thing as it has been created by the mind," we are left again with skepticism if not total ignorance. Also, Kant's epistemology, as later thinkers noted, raises the prospect of the non-existence of even his objective noumenal world for since it is unknowable it cannot be shown to be objective. Furthermore, although he posited a "pre-established harmony" as the basis of his categories in human minds (having rejected the Christian view of man as a knower created in the divine image for the purpose of cognitive relations with God, the external world, and other selves as the ground for knowledge), Kant could provide no valid reasons why such a pre-established harmony exists. For if, as he contends, knowledge is exclusively a *joint* product of forms and perceptions, he cannot explain how it is possible to acquire valid information about the categories that for him are purely mental.[9]

---

beyond the sphere of sensation, the human mind cannot legitimately think of God as one, as a cause, as necessary, etc. Nor can his existence be proved, for all assertions of existence depend upon sensory verification. He urged, therefore, that the noumenal realm of God, freedom and immortality – concepts he needed in order to ground the "categorical imperative" of his ethic – was knowable by "practical reason," that is, by faith. But this faith of course is devoid of concrete data knowable by pure reason.

[8]John Frame rightly states in his *Cornelius Van Til: An Analysis of His Thought* (Phillipsburg, N. J.: Presbyterian and Reformed, 1995): "Thus, the mind of man not only is its own ultimate authority, but also replaces God as the intelligent planner and creator of the experienced universe" (45). Accordingly, in his *Religion Within the Limits of Reason Alone* Kant argued that "the human mind can never and must never subject itself to any authority beyond itself" (Frame, 45).

[9]See Carl F. H. Henry's critique of Kant's epistemology in *God Who Speaks and Shows*, Vol. I of *God, Revelation and Authority* (Waco, Texas: Word, 1976), 387-92.

It should be apparent that all of these philosophical efforts have ended with dismal results. In more recent times, from Hegel and Kierkegaard to the present, many philosophers, recognizing the failure of this human effort to arrive at the certain knowledge of anything, have concluded that this failure was due to these earlier thinkers thinking rationally. Accordingly, they have abandoned rationality for irrationality and are now urging that meaning has nothing to do with thinking rationally. Truth is relative and life's meaning is to be achieved by a "leap of faith" to anything that gives even a momentary *raison d'etre*.[10]

All this the Christian man eschews in favor of the epistemology graciously given him in the fact and propositional content of Holy Scripture. The intelligent Christian recognizes that in the fact of Scripture itself he has a truly profound solution for man's need for an infinite reference point if knowledge is to become a reality. He understands that because there is comprehensive knowledge with God, real and true knowledge is possible for man since God who knows all the data exhaustively in all their infinite relationships and who possesses therefore true knowledge is in the position to impart some portion of that true knowledge to man. The Christian believes that this is precisely what God did when he revealed himself to man propositionally. And he rests in the confidence that it is precisely in and by the Scriptures – coming to him *ab extra* (from "outside the cosmos") – that he has the requisite "Archimedean *pou stō*" or point of reference that he needs for the build-up of knowledge and the justification of his knowledge claims. Taking all his directions from the transcendent *pou stō* of the divine mind revealed in Holy Scripture, the Christian affirms, first, the created actuality of a real world of knowing persons and knowable objects external to these knowing persons. Second, he affirms the legitimate necessity of both sensory experience and the reasoning process in the activity of learning, for the Scriptures

---

[10]See Francis A. Schaeffer, *Escape from Reason* (Downers Grove, Illinois: Inter-Varsity, 1968), 40-45.

themselves authenticate the legitimacy of these tools of learning. Finally, he happily acknowledges that the divine mind that has revealed something of its knowledge in Scripture is his *pou stō* for universals in order to justify his truth claims. In short, he makes the Word of the self-attesting Christ of Scripture the epistemic basis for all reasoning and knowledge, even when reasoning about reason or about God's revelation.

The Justification of Man's Personal Significance

Not only is the Bible man's *pou stō* for the justification of knowledge, it is also his *pou stō*, via its doctrine of creation and God's interpretation of his created state, for human personal significance. It is the biblical doctrine of creation in a unique and profound way that defines who we are – personal, significant, covenant-creatures – unlike God, true enough, in that we are created but like him in that we are created in his image. The Bible neither knows nor allows another explanation for our existence as a race.

Modern cosmologists who insist that the human race is the product of an *impersonal* beginning plus time plus chance are really saying that there is no intelligible ground for asserting personal significance for the human race. But then this means that there is no intelligible base for human morals either. For these theorists to continue to insist on their personal worth and the necessity of morals under such a condition is simply sheer mysticism – an existential leap to an unfounded dogmatic assertion, for if we are only products of chance, why should not the laws of the jungle – only the fit survive and might makes right – prevail?

Modern secular thought, nevertheless, regards the early chapters of Genesis as at best religious *Saga*, that is, as mythological stories that, while not actually historical, nevertheless intend to convey religious truth. Therefore, before we go any farther, it is appropriate that we say something about the integrity of the Genesis account of creation as reliable, trustworthy history.

Simply put, the problem in these chapters for modern men, influenced as they are by modern scientism's unfounded dogmatic dictum of cosmic and biological evolution, is the distinctly *supernatural* character of the events that they report, namely, the creation of the universe *ex nihilo* and the creation of man by the direct act of God. Because of the supposed "pre-scientific" nature of the events that these chapters record, the trend in modern secularist intellectual life is to regard the so-called "two accounts of creation" in Genesis 1 and 2 as ancient Hebrew cosmogonies comparable to the *Enuma Elish* of ancient Babylon, that is, as religious mythology.

For the following exegetical reasons, however, I believe that the church must resist this secularistic trend and continue to hold, as the church has historically done, to the historical integrity of the early chapters of Genesis:

- The character of the Hebrew itself, employing as it does the *waw* consecutive to describe sequential events, the frequent use of the sign of the accusative and the relative pronoun, as well as the stylistic and syntactical rules of Hebrew narrative rather than Hebrew poetry, gives every indication that the author (Moses) intended these chapters to be taken as straightforward historical narration of early earth history. (If one want a sample in this section of Scripture of what the author's poetry with its parallelism of thought and fixed pairs would look like, he can consider Genesis 4:23-24.)

- In Genesis 12–50 the author uses the phrase "These are the generations of…" four times to introduce a new patriarch's history, the general history of which is not doubted by contemporary scholarship (see 25:12, 19; 36:1; 37:2). But he also employs the same phrase six times in Genesis 1–11 to introduce new blocks of historical material (see 2:4; 5:1; 6:9; 10:1; 11:10, 27), the last one of which (11:27) containing the story of Abraham whose historicity is no longer questioned by most Old Testament scholars. Does this not suggest that he intended the first five occurrences of the phrase also to introduce blocks of historical record? And does this not suggest that he intended the entirety of Genesis to be viewed under the rubric of the literary genre of history?

- In Genesis 1–11 there are 64 geographical terms, 88 personal names, 48 generic names, and at least 21 identifiable cultural terms (gold, bdellium, onyx, brass, bitumen, mortar, brick, stone, harp, pipe, cities, towers), all suggesting that the author was describing the world that we know and not a world belonging to another level of reality or mental conception.

- It should be noted that each divine judgment in Genesis 1–11 is followed by an exhibition of divine grace: God's covering of our first parents after he had pronounced judgment upon them; his protection for Cain after he had judged him; and his establishing his covenant with Noah after the judgment of the Flood. But where is God's exhibition of grace after his dispersing of the race into nations in Genesis 11? Does not God's call of Abraham in Genesis 12, in whom all the dispersed nations of the earth would be blessed, answer to the character of the Babel judgment and thus complete the judgment/grace pattern? It would seem so. Apparently, the author was not aware of the break between Genesis 11 and Genesis 12 brought about by the shift in literary genre between the two sections (1–11, myth; 12–50, history) that many Old Testament scholars want to make and confidently affirm.

- Scripture in its entirety regards the Genesis account of man's early beginnings and doings as reliable history. The Genesis account of creation is referred to many times elsewhere in the Old Testament and New Testament Scriptures. We could with little trouble cite two-dozen passages that do so. For example, direct references and allusions to the Genesis creation may be found in Exodus 20:11, 31:17, Deuteronomy 4:32, Psalms 33:6, 90:2, 136:5-9, 148:2-5, Isaiah 40:25-26, 42:5, 44:24, 45:12, 48:13, 51:13, Amos 4:13, Jeremiah 10:12, Zechariah 12:1; Matthew 19:4-5, John 1:2-3, Ephesians 3:9, Colossians 1:16, 1 Timothy 2:13, Hebrews 1:2, 11:3, and Revelation 4:11, 10:6-7. And this is only a partial list. In every instance the Genesis account of creation lies behind these later references and is assumed by them to be a reliable record of what God did "in the beginning." To call into question the historical reliability of Genesis 1 and 2 is to call into question the trustworthiness of the entirety of Scripture testimony on the issue of origins. The fall of Adam is referred to in Job 31:33, Isaiah 43:27 (?), Hosea 6:7, Romans 5:12-19, 2 Corinthians 11:3, and 1 Timothy 2:14. Cain's murder of Abel is referred to in Matthew 23:35, Luke 11:51, Hebrews 11:4, 1 John 3:12, and Jude 11. Finally, the Genesis flood is referred to in Isaiah 54:9, Matthew 24:37-39, Luke 17:26-27, Hebrews 11:7, 1 Peter 3:20, and 2 Peter 2:5, 3:6. To call into question the historicity of Genesis 3–11, then, is to call into question the trustworthiness of a great deal of later Scripture testimony.

• The genealogies in 1 Chronicles 1 and Luke 3 regard Adam as the divinely created, first human being. Neither genealogy gives the slightest impression that one should realize that he is on generally reliable historical ground back to the time of Abraham but that the names of Abraham's ancestors, given in Genesis 5 and 11, are historically shaky and untrustworthy. These early genealogies, in fact, are treated by the Chronicler and by Luke as being as reliable as the later Genesis genealogy in Genesis 12 through 50 of Abraham, Isaac, and Jacob, or the genealogy of David in Ruth 4:18-20.

• Finally, the integrity of our Lord's own teaching is at stake, for in Matthew 19:4-5 and Mark 10:6-8 he refers to the creation of man in such a way that it is beyond question (1) that he had Genesis 1:27 and 2:24 in mind, and (2) that he viewed these so-called "two diverse accounts of creation" as a trustworthy record of what took place at the beginning of human history. He also refers to the "blood of Abel" (Matt. 23:35) and to the Genesis flood (Matt. 24:37-39). To question the basic historical authenticity and integrity of Genesis 1–11 is to assault the integrity of Christ's own teaching.

For these seven reasons I submit that the church not only may but also must regard the Genesis account of creation as a reliable record of the origin of the universe, a record preserved from error by the superintending oversight of the Holy Spirit (2 Pet. 1:20-21; 2 Tim. 3:15-17). We may encounter difficulties in interpreting some of the details of Genesis 1 and 2 simply because we are working exegetically and hermeneutically with highly circumscribed, greatly compressed, non-technical narrative accounts of the beginning of the universe, but these interpretive difficulties are infinitely to be preferred to the scientific and philosophical difficulties which confront those modern interpreters who propound non-theistic solutions to the question of the origin of the universe.

Modern man has found basically only two ways to live without the one living and true God as the base for his science and morals:

By ignoring the implications of his practical atheism
While still insisting for no justifiable reason on the sanctity of his personal significance and rights, he often refuses to face the implications of his practical atheism and becomes thereby a mere "technician" in his daily labors, leaping then – however irrational such a leap may be (and it is irrational; see the "meaninglessness" theme of the Teacher of Ecclesiastes) and even though his leap may actually finally destroy him physically – to anything that will even temporarily make him feel significant, such as the acquisition of material things, love of the arts or technology, sexual promiscuity, drugs, and therapy, these things having now become his "gods."

By justifying his declared atheism by his sciences
Modern man makes a studied effort to argue by means of his physical and biological sciences that no personal God created the universe out of nothing. Rather, he claims that the universe spontaneously "created" (and is continuing to "create") itself and everything in it. In fact, he regularly argues that there is no infinite, personal Creator. That is, capitalizing the "c" of the word "cosmos," he makes it the cause and end both of itself and

of all things in it, including himself, and without acknowledging that he is doing so offers up to the now-"deified" cosmos the worship and service he as "religious man" (*homo religiosus*) should reserve for his Creator. Tragically, in both cases modern man, in his flight from God and right reason, destroys himself as a person who makes truly significant and meaningful decisions, for he abandons the only base for justifying, first, what he believes in his heart of hearts is true about himself, namely, that he is individually and personally significant, and, second, his conclusions in science and morals.

I must say more about this second path that modern man follows since it gives the appearance of being the more "learned" and therefore the more "respectable" of the two, since more and more men of science are giving it credence by calling it "scientific fact," and since what is the scientist's "scientific fact" today becomes mankind's "religion" tomorrow. I will begin by reminding you that there has always been one non-negotiable, absolutely necessary idea for science. It is the *sine qua non* – the "without which nothing" – of all scientific inquiry. This controlling idea is expressed by the Latin dictum *ex nihilo nihil fit* – "out of nothing, nothing comes." This axiom is universally accepted and everywhere assumed. What is it that Maria sang in *The Sound of Music* upon learning that Captain von Trapp loved her: "Nothing comes from nothing, nothing ever could; so somewhere in my youth or childhood, I must have done something good"? Well, her *non sequitur* theology here is wretched, but her science and logic are impeccable – "Nothing comes from nothing, nothing ever could." Science is hemophiliac at this point. Simply scratch this absolute axiom and modern science will bleed to death since all experimental science will then have to reckon with the real possibility, regardless of the controls erected around its experiments, that at any moment a totally "new beginning" may spontaneously intrude itself into the control area. Indeed, it can never be sure in any experiment that a totally "new beginning" has not already spontaneously intruded itself undetected into its results and skewed its conclusions. Nevertheless, to avoid what they refer to as the "God-hypothesis," modern cosmologists are increasingly willing to ignore this self-evident truth and to espouse some form of spontaneous generation out of nothing as the explanation for the universe.

The June 13, 1988 issue of *Newsweek* magazine, for example, documented this ever-widening trend. Reflect upon the following quotations from its article entitled "Where the Wild Things Are": "Cosmologists are no longer content to invoke the deity" as the ultimate explanation behind the universe."[11] To what do they now look? "For better or worse [they] have cast their lot with the laws of physics and not with Einstein's friend, the Old One, the Creator."[12] "...In the greatest leap of imagination, most [!] cosmologists now believe that the universe arose from nothing, and that nothing is as certain to give rise to something as the night is to sire the dawn."[13] Alan Guth, a brilliant MIT cosmologist, flying in the face of the popular adage, declares that the universe is a "free lunch," that is, that it came from nothing – that there was nothing, not God, not energy, not matter, simply nothing (But wait, he says; there was "possibility"!) – and then suddenly and spontaneously the void of nothing "gave rise to"?, no, "decayed" into all the matter and energy the universe now has. He contends that the universe, "not with a bang so much as with a *pfft*,...ballooned accidentally out of the endless void of eternity, from a stillness so deep that there was no 'there' or 'then,' only possibility." Guth, of course, is fudging here; there could not even be possibility, a mathematical concept, if there was nothing.[14] More technically, he has proposed (with refinements from others) that an infinitely dense, infinitely (note the use of a term traditionally reserved as a description of the infinite, personal God) hot point called a "singularity"

---

[11]"Where the Wild Things Are," *Newsweek* (June 13, 1988), 60.

[12]"Wild Things," 65.

[13]"Wild Things," 60, emphasis supplied.

[14]Dennis Overbye, "The Universe According to Guth," *Discover* (June 1983), 93, emphasis supplied.

(he does not explain why or how this infinite singularity got "there"; apparently it spontaneously "decayed" from nothing) spontaneously exploded, that within a ten-millionth of a quadrillionth of a sextillionth (that is a 1 preceded by "point 42 zeros") of a second later the universe was about the size of a grain of dust, that one-hundred thousandth of a quadrillionth of a quadrillionth (that is a 1 preceded by "point 34 zeros") of a second later it had doubled in size, that – well, you get the point – it has been expanding and forming quarks and leptons (the building blocks of matter), then (possibly) cosmic "strings" (the seeds for galaxies), then protons and neutrons (the building blocks of atomic nuclei), then atoms and galaxies (in that order) ever since. All this supposedly began about fifteen billion years ago, with our own sun and solar system emerging from all this about five billion years ago.

Edward P. Tryon, professor of physics at the City University of New York, proposes that the universe created itself "spontaneously from nothing (*ex nihilo*) as a result of established principles of physics."[15] Alex Vilenkin, a Tufts University cosmologist, explains all this with the following words: "The universe as a young bubble had tunneled like a metaphysical mole from somewhere else to arrive in space and time. That someplace else was 'nothing.'"[16] Edward Kolb of the Fermi National Accelerator Laboratory near Chicago, explains this by informing us that "even when you have nothing, there's something going on"![17] These descriptive explanations of the universe's origin, I think one must agree, sound like something written, if not by college freshmen who flunked their introductory course in logic, at best by romantic poets, rather than deliverances issued by straight-faced, deadly serious scientists.

Carl Sagan, David Duncan professor of astronomy and space sciences and director of the Laboratory for Planetary Studies

---

[15]Edward P. Tryon, "What Made the World?" *New Scientist* 101 (March 8, 1984), 14.

[16] Overbye, *Discover*, 99.

[17]"Wild Things," 62.

at Cornell University, uses different words, but his view is no more scientifically demonstrable or logically respectable. "The cosmos," he dogmatizes "prophet-like" in his best seller, *Cosmos*, "is all that is or ever was or ever will be" – an assertion on the face of it that goes far beyond scientific statement and that enters deeply into metaphysics, speculative philosophy, religion, even eschatology. Apparently, he believes that the material cosmos, if it has not existed forever in some form (a credo, by the way, that is not without its own philosophical difficulties and ambiguities), "created" and is continuing to "create" itself. He explains what he calls the "beauty and diversity of the biological world," the "music of life" – that is poetic, and he is including the human race in that music – by the concept of evolution brought about through "natural [that is, impersonal nature's] selection." For Sagan, this conception, over against the so-called "personal God-hypothesis," is "equally appealing, equally human, and far more compelling."[18] But is it? How can one speak meaningfully or intelligently of impersonal matter "selecting" anything? "Selection" suggests the intelligent choice of one end or course of action rather than a less intelligent end or course of action. But what makes Sagan's "natural selection" work? Said another way, what are the "causal powers" within the evolutionary process upon which he suspends the origin of all things? Does Sagan believe that intelligence governs the powers of nature? No, he does not. So I ask again, what then are the "causal powers" within the evolutionary process? Sagan's response? Accident, randomness, fate, chance! But what are these? All are synonyms for the last word – chance. And what is chance? Chance is a word we use to describe mathematical possibilities, but chance cannot be a cause of anything because chance is not a thing – not being, not energy, not mass, not power, not intelligence, not an entity. It is only a mathematical concept. Once we see this, it is clear that Sagan is asking us once again to believe that "nothing" selected something – including you and me – to be, that out of non-intelligence we have

---

[18]Carl Sagan, *Cosmos*, 15-19.

appeared, that out of impersonal being we have emerged! But how can we, on these grounds, continue to think of ourselves as significant persons? Why is it not now, on these grounds, just as appropriate to think of ourselves as a mere "accident of nature" (as did Sir James Jeans in his *The Mysterious Universe*) or as "the gruesome result of nature's failure to take antiseptic precautions" (as did Sir Arthur Eddington in his *New Pathways in Science*)? And why is it not just as appropriate to regard the elephant as a more advanced stage of the evolutionary process since it has a thicker skin than man? Or the dog since it has a keener sense of smell? Or the horse since it can run at greater speeds? And why is it not also appropriate to conclude, since man seeks to prey upon, tame, imprison, and put to his own use all of the other creatures on this planet, that he among all the living species is the greatest predator of them all and therefore the lowest stage of evolutionary development to date?

These views of the new cosmologists, I insist, are not "equally appealing, equally human, and far more compelling" than the "personal God view." To prefer the frivolous notion that "an impersonal nothing" is the final reality to the majestic concept of the opening words of Genesis, "In the beginning God created," represents the nadir of theoretical thought. This preference reflects the depth to which men are willing to descend into the abyss of the rationally absurd to avoid the religiously obvious. As statements of science, the science these views represent can sink no lower, since these views leap over reason into the sea of absurdity. To paraphrase the Apostle Paul:

> Although [such men] claim to be wise, they [have] become fools and [have] exchanged the glory of the immortal God for the unfathomable mysteries of the created material universe.... They [have] exchanged the truth of God for a lie, and worship and serve created things rather than the Creator – who is forever praised. Amen. (Rom. 1:21-23, 25).

They do this, of course, as Paul also says, in their ungodliness and unrighteousness in order to suppress their innate awareness of the Creator. For to become truly God-conscious is to become truly covenant-conscious, and to become truly covenant-conscious is to become sin-conscious. And this situation they want to avoid at all costs, even to their own hurt. For in their denial of God, they also destroy their own significance as persons who make really significant decisions.

What is ironic, of course, in all this is that the creationist view of origins cannot be taught in the public school systems of America and elsewhere and is not tolerated in the physics, geology, and biology departments of great universities because it is judged to be a purely religious concept even though it best conforms to the *ex nihilo nihil fit* foundation principle of science and answers the two ultimate philosophical questions of being: Why is there something instead of nothing? and, Why is there cosmos (order) instead of chaos (disorder)? R. C. Sproul quite correctly observes in this connection:

> Reason demands that…if something now exists, then something has always existed. To postulate that something comes from nothing is to substitute mythology for science.
> Classical Christianity asserts the doctrine of creation *ex nihilo*. That means creation out of nothing. This, however, does not mean that once there was nothing and now there is something. *Ex nihilo* creation means that the eternal self-existent God (who is something) brought the universe into existence by the power of creation.[19]

Thinking people will judge the views of these new cosmologists for what they are – rank mysticism and sheer intellectual madness. For this reason we trust that judicious scientists such as those advocating "intelligent design" (ID) – not just theologians and philosophers – will continue to step forward and correct them. And they do need correcting, for when educated men make absurd statements they are no less absurd than when uneducated people make them.

---

[19]R. C. Sproul, "Cosmos or Chaos," *Table Talk* (August 25, 1988), 7.

What then is the theological significance of biblical creationism? Not only does it address and satisfy the screaming intellectual need that we all have as thinking persons for a rational explanation of the universe and ourselves, but it also defines who we are as men and women and leaves us, so defined, with great worth and dignity. It also provides the theistic context necessary for moral absolutes and grounds our moral decisions as responsible decisions before God. Without the doctrine of creation we are left with non-answers in these areas.

I would like to call your attention as we conclude this chapter to two men named Francis who saw quite clearly the futility of the world's non-answers and the vacuity and meaninglessness of a universe without God at its base and who accordingly described the threat to human personal significance intrinsic to the two basic paths that modern man takes to avoid God. The first, an English poet of the Victorian Age, is Francis Thompson (1859–1907), who immortalized the futility of life without God in his stirring poem, *The Hound of Heaven*. Poetically cataloging his own flight from God and his search for an alternative refuge in human love, in a careless life of indolent leisure, even in the innocent smiles of children, at line 61 he begins to elaborate what he discovered from his attempt to find lasting fulfillment in the study and mastery of the mysteries of the material universe:

> "Come then, ye other children, Nature's – share
> With me" (said I) "your delicate fellowship;
> > Let me greet you lip to lip,
> > Let me twine with you caresses,
> > Wantoning
> > With our Lady-Mother's vagrant tresses,
> > Banqueting
> > With her in her wind-walled palace,
> > Underneath her azured daïs,
> > Quaffing, as your taintless way is,
> > From a chalice
> Lucent-weeping out of the dayspring."
> > So it was done:
> I in their delicate fellowship was one –

Drew the bolt of Nature's secrecies,
I knew all the swift importings
    On the wilful face of skies;
    I knew how the clouds arise
    Spuméd of the wild sea-snortings;
    All that's born or dies
    Rose and drooped with – made them shapers
Of mine own moods, or wailful or divine –
    With them joyed and was bereaven.
    I was heavy with the even,
    When she lit her glimmering tapers
    Round the day's dead sanctities.
    I laughed in the morning's eyes.
I triumphed and I saddened with all weather,
    Heaven and I wept together,
And its sweet tears were salt with mortal mine;
Against the red throb of its sunset-heart
    I laid my own to beat,
    And share commingling heat;
[Now note carefully! – RLR]
But not by that, by that, was eased my human smart.
In vain my tears were wet on Heaven's grey cheek.
For ah! we know not what each other says,
    These things and I; in sound I speak –
Their sound is but their stir, they speak by silences.
Nature, poor stepdame, cannot slake my drouth;
    Let her, if she would owe me,
Drop yon blue bosom-veil of sky, and show me
    The breasts o' her tenderness:
Never did any milk of hers once bless
    My thirsting mouth.

To live life and to try to understand oneself and the material universe without the God who made all things, Francis Thompson learned, is indeed to live in futility. As Solomon wrote in Ecclesiastes, all becomes vanity!

The second Francis is Francis Schaeffer of recent and revered memory. No man has proven to be more perceptive and expressed himself more profoundly than Schaeffer himself about these matters. The entire ministry of L'Abri Fellowship that he founded was committed to exposing the hollowness of modern man's atheistic world and life view. The following words he dictated to his wife, Edith, from his hospital bed a few days before his death on May 15, 1984. She tells us that they were to become his "last written page, ending the books he had written, set[ting] forth once again the basic foundation he felt so important as a base for life, a world view."[20] We would be well advised to listen to his last dictated words.

> For a long time now, it has been held, and universally accepted, that the final reality is energy that has existed forever in some form and energy that has its form by pure chance. In other words, intelligence has no basic place in the structure of the universe from the Enlightenment onward. Therefore, we are to accept totally the basic structure of the universe as impersonal.
>
> This means, therefore, that neither religion nor intelligence is in the universe. The personality issue does not enter into what the universe is, nor into who people are in this theory. Under this theory, there is no place for morals, nor for there being any meaning to the universe. And the problem here is that [this description of things] is simply not what we observe about the universe – or especially about man himself. In spite of this, modern man continues to press on, saying that this is what the universe is, and especially what the individual is. In other words, we have been told that in faith we must insist blindly on what the universe is and what man is. In other words, man is simply a mathematical thing – or formula – even though it brings him sorrow.
>
> This is simply mysticism in its worst form, and the final denial of rationality. With understanding, one sees the proud egotism of holding this basic philosophic concept against what comes to man from every side.
>
> What would we do with any other theory that postulated such a theorem? Certainly it would be put aside. Why do we

---

[20]Edith Schaeffer, *Forever Music* (Nashville: Thomas Nelson, 1986), 62.

continue to hold this theorem as to what reality is, when in any other area we would simply throw it out?

The answer is clear that it is simply a mystical acceptance. In other words, man is so proud that he goes on blindly accepting that which is not only intellectually unviable but also that which no one can live with in government or personal life, and in which civic life cannot live.

To go back and accept that which is the completely opposite – that the final reality is an Infinite Personal God who created the world – is rational, and returns us to intelligent answers and suddenly opens the door. It not only gives answers but also puts us once more in a cosmos in which people can live, breathe, and rejoice.

If modern man would only be honest, he would say that it is his theory that is in collapse.[21]

Surely Schaeffer is correct. The Bible and right reason roundly condemn as willful moral perversity both the practical atheism of modern men and women and the affirmations of the modern cosmologists, the Bible insisting to the contrary that the one living and true God alone has eternally existed and that the universe began as the result of his creative activity.

Only the biblical response to the question of human origin makes sense, and only the theistic context behind it (1) defines humankind in such a way that they possess genuine worth and dignity, (2) provides the human sciences with an intelligent base for predication and gives to human morality systems the necessary base for just moral decisions, and (3) saves men from becoming caught up in the surd of "chaos and eternal night" (Milton), a meaningless cipher drowning in a meaningless sea of ciphers.

Genesis 1 and 2 are the bedrock of this teaching. The church has traditionally understood Genesis as teaching a divine creation *ex nihilo*, and more particularly, the creation of man in his own image by a direct act of God. In this doctrine is the ground for personal significance and the justification of knowledge and an

---

[21]Schaeffer, *Forever Music*, 61-62.

370 *Faith's Reasons for Believing*

ethic men can live with. The church cannot afford to abandon this absolutely fundamental teaching of Scripture, for it is indeed the only *pou stō* for man's personal significance, his knowledge claims and a universal ethic. And the church will do so only at great cost to itself and to the people it seeks to win to faith and to a home in heaven because only as human beings are his creatures do they have personal significance, and only as they are his creatures are they capable of justifying their truth claims and able to see themselves as responsible moral beings who make significant moral decisions.

Chapter Eleven

Faith's Reasons for Believing
in the Nature of Biblical Truth

A while back I sat by a woman on a flight from Fort Lauderdale to Boston and when she found out that I was a preacher of the gospel, her first question to me after I had disclosed that fact was surprisingly this: "Tell me, are things really as bad as I am told they are?" Talk about a conversation opener! I immediately replied: "Things are much worse than that!"

When she asked me to explain what I meant, I replied: "I believe that conditions in America are much worse that either of us can even begin to imagine, not because I think that abortion, although it has been legalized as a constitutional right, is still murder of the unborn, or because I think that homosexuality, although it has been legalized as a civil right, is still a deviant and sinful and not simply a variant lifestyle, or because I think that child pornography, although its right to exist on the internet has also been legalized as a First-Amendment right, not only undermines this nation's morals but also places every child in America in danger of predatory pedophiles – so much for the secularized wisdom of this nation's highest court! These are symptoms of a far more dangerous condition. Such moral drift in our nation simply reflects the fact that large segments of both the church and our nation's judiciaries, no longer subscribing to the teaching of the Holy Scripture upon which America was founded, believe that no final or absolute truth exists; rather, they believe that truth is relative. But relative truth is no truth at all. Ed Kingsbury, a friend of mine living in Marco Island, Florida has captured the problem with relative truth in simple verse:

> If relative truth is really true,
> Then I am right but so are you;
> Dogs can be cats, and green can be blue,
> And I can be God, and so can you."

She simply looked at me in silence, obviously not comprehending fully what I meant.

The same answer I gave that woman I would give to you my readers, and I trust that you *do* understand that without absolute truth *all* moral absolutes go by the board and as a result anything may be legalized under the citizenry's current clamor for their civil rights. And I would contend, if we are ever going to reclaim this nation and to evangelize our world to any significant degree for Christ, that we must instill once again in the minds of the general population the fact that truth is antithetical and absolute and that believing that truth is relative has dire consequences. To believe that truth is relative is to commit not only national, societal, and religious but also epistemological suicide for it is to hold to a "truth system" that is self-defeating. So I want you to think seriously with me about the God of the Bible as being infinite, eternal, and unchangeable in his truth, and the implications of this fact.

Francis Bacon begins his essay on Truth by declaring that too many people, like jesting Pilate, ask: "What is truth?" and then do not wait for an answer before they act. Since I trust that none of you here is of that ilk, I will begin this chapter on God's infinite, eternal, and unchangeable truthfulness by directing your attention to the following biblical verses:

Biblical Texts on God as Truth

Psalm 31:5: "Yahweh is [the] *true God*."

> Jeremiah 10:10: "…the Lord is the *true God*; he is the living God, the eternal king."
> John 1:17: "…grace and *truth* came through Jesus Christ."
> John 14:6: "I am…*the truth*."
> John 17:3: "Now this is eternal life: that they may know you,

the only true God,[1] and Jesus Christ, who you have sent."
John 18:37: "…for this reason I came into the world, to testify to the truth. Everyone on the side of truth listens to me."
1 John 5:6: "…the Spirit is *the truth.*"
1 John 5:20: "…we are in him *who is true* – even in his Son Jesus Christ. He [Jesus Christ] is *the true God* and eternal life."

The God of the Bible is the one living and *true* God, that is, the only God who is "really there," the only God whose opinion about anything truly counts. When the Bible speaks of God, as in Jeremiah 10:10, as "the true God; …the living God, the eternal King" it intends that we understand that God, as the *true* God, stands off over against all the false gods and idols of this world, all of whom the Scriptures appropriately describe by the word "lies" (Ps. 96:5; 97:7; 115:4-8; Isa. 44:9-10, 20; Jer. 10:2-16; Amos 2:4; Jonah 2:9). Here the words "truth" and "lies" are depicted in their ultimate and final metaphysical or theological sense: The biblical God is the *true* God; by contrast, all the other gods of this world are "lies" or false gods conjured up by godless and immoral persons of darkened understanding reacting to the true God's revelation of himself in nature. The biblical God alone has perfect knowledge of what true "Godness" entails. Job 37:16 tells us that God is "perfect in knowledge" – and thus *his* true and perfect knowledge is, as such, *the standard of truth* for mankind. We do indeed hold to a "correspondence view of truth" but *not* the classic correspondence view of truth, most famously linked with John Locke, that naturalistic philosophers espouse. They state that truth is what corresponds to reality. But the question then arises: "Reality as perceived and determined by whom?" And these naturalistic philosophers answer: "Reality as perceived and determined by man and his sciences! You see, what man can't catch in his net isn't fish, that is to say, it doesn't exist until he catches it." Thus man becomes the standard of

---

[1]John 17:3 refers to the Father and 1 John 5:20 refers to the Son as the "true God."

truth and the measure of all things. But we say that truth is that which corresponds to reality as *God* defines it, for just as God is love so also is he truth in the sense that truth is what God thinks. His truth is firmly rooted and grounded in his immutable nature. It is not a construction of men; it is not variable, not relative, and not dependent upon social or cultural conditions. Thus that which God knows and tells us in his Word is the perfect standard of absolute truth. For example, God's ordinance concerning the institution of marriage as the lifelong union between one man and one woman is unalterably binding upon all human societies at all times. It cannot be altered by human legislative, judicial, or cultural action without doing irreparable harm to human society, and God will hold those whom he has placed in positions of authority accountable if they try to do so.

Moreover, God's truth came incarnationally with Jesus Christ (John 1:17) who claimed to be the living Truth (John 14:6). Indeed, as we just read, Jesus declared: "…for this reason I came into the world, to testify to the truth." We seldom think about this reason for Christ's coming. We are more inclined to say, when asked for a reason for his Advent, that he came to die on the cross, that he came to save sinners, that he came to pay the penalty for sin, that he came to forgive us, and so on and so forth, and *we forget that before every other purpose he came to bear witness to God's truth* and that his entire ministry did so. Jesus, the divine Son of the God of truth, had a passion for God's truth; and he was prepared to die for God's truth (Matt. 26:53-54). Therefore, because he said, "Everyone who is on the side of truth *listens to my voice*" (John 18:37),[2] no Christian should ever assume a cavalier attitude toward God's truth as revealed in Holy Scripture. For as Jesus had a passion for God's truth, so we his disciples should also have a passion for God's truth revealed in Holy Scripture; it should become our passion to know it, our passion to obey it, our passion to propagate it.

---

[2]Jesus' statement suggests that only a minority portion of mankind is on the side of truth today since only a relatively small minority of mankind "listens to his voice."

Truth Univocal for God and Man

Now some evangelical theologians in our time who ought to know better have contended that, while God knows all truth and his Word is certainly true, we can never possess more than an *analogical* comprehension of his truth because we are finite in knowledge and therefore there will always be a *qualitative* difference between the truth content of God's mind and the truth content of our minds. That is to say, not only is God's knowledge prior to and necessary to man's knowledge that is always secondary and derivative, not only is God's knowledge self-validating whereas man's knowledge is dependent upon God's prior self-validating knowledge for its validation, not only is God's knowledge infinite whereas man's knowledge is finite (with these I concur), but also, these theologians contend, God's and man's knowledge of truth is such that man's knowledge of truth will never be more than an analogy of God's knowledge of truth, indeed, they say, man will never univocally know anything as God knows a thing (What about "Two plus two are four?").[3]

---

[3]Even John Calvin errs here. While he does not go as far as these theologians do, he does move perilously close to this position with respect to human knowledge of God when explaining the Bible's anthropomorphic descriptions of God. Calvin contends that not only does God speak "sparingly" of his essence but also even when he does do so his "forms of speaking *do not so much express clearly what God is like* as accommodate the knowledge of him to our slight capacity" (*Institutes*, 1.13.1). In a similar vein he contends in *Institutes*, 1.17.13, that

> ...because our weakness does not attain to his exalted state, *the description of him that is given to us must be accommodated to our capacity so that we may understand it. Now the mode of accommodation is for him to represent himself to us not as he is in himself, but as he seems to us.* Although he is beyond all disturbance of mind [Calvin is expressing his understanding of God's impassibility here which expression I happen to think is erroneous], yet he testifies that he is angry toward sinners. Therefore whenever we hear that God is angered, we ought not to imagine any emotion in him, but rather to consider that *this expression has been taken from our own human experience*; because God, whenever he is

With this I strongly disagree, for what these theologians of analogy fail to realize is that the success of any analogy turns on the strength of the univocal element in it. That is to say, the basis for any analogy is non-analogical, that is, univocal. An "analogy" that has no univocal element in it is really not an analogy at all but an equivocism. Cornelius Van Til, one such theologian of analogy, writes:

> All human predication is analogical re-interpretation of God's pre-interpretation. Thus the incomprehensibility of God must be taught with respect to any revelational proposition.[4]

What does this mean? In his "Introduction" to Warfield's *The Inspiration and Authority of the Bible* Van Til explains

> When the Christian restates the content of Scriptural revelation in the form of a "system," such a system is based upon and therefore analogous to the "existential system" that God himself possesses. Being based upon God's revelation it is, on the one

---

exercising judgment, exhibits the *appearance* of one kindled and angered. (emphasis supplied)

Calvin appears to mean by these comments that because of our finitude God could not have given to us a univocal verbal depiction of himself as he is in himself. Rather, what we possess in the main, if not exclusively, is at best only a finite (analogical?) representation of God and thus ours is an understanding of him "as he seems to us" and not as he is in himself. We should be hesitant about following Calvin here. Indeed, if I have understood him properly I would urge that we should *not* follow him since we *can* know on the basis of God's verbal self-revelation many things about him in the *same* sense that he knows them.

Where Calvin made his mistake is in his explaining the Bible's anthropomorphisms by resorting to linguistic accommodation. It were better had he construed them simply as figures of speech – metaphors designed, in light of God's spiritual essence, to drive home the truth that God is indeed personal.

[4]Cornelius Van Til, *In Defense of the Faith*, volume 5 in *An Introduction to Systematic Theology* (Nutley, New Jersey: Presbyterian and Reformed, 1976), 171.

hand, fully true and, on the other hand, *at no point identical* with the content of the divine mind.[5]

He says virtually the same things in his *An Introduction to Systematic Theology*:

> [The task of human knowledge] is to order as far as possible the facts of God's revelation. The "system" thus produced as, e.g., it finds expression in the Reformed confessions of faith, pretends to be an analogical system. *At no point* does such a system pretend to state, point for point, the identical content of the original system of the mind of God.... To claim for the Christian system identity with the divine system *at any point* is to break the relationship of dependence of human knowledge on the divine will.[6]

How univocality at any single point between "the original system of the mind of God" and the human theological system that finds expression in the Reformed confessions "breaks the relationship of dependence of human knowledge on the divine will," it seems to me, is a *non-sequitur*. In fact, *not* to have univocality between them is what breaks the dependence of human knowledge on the divine will!

In a Complaint filed against the presbytery that voted to sustain Gordon H. Clark's ordination examination, to which Van Til affixed his name as a signatory, which complaint was not upheld by the presbytery, it was declared a "tragic fact" that Clark's epistemology "has led him to obliterate the qualitative distinction between the contents of the divine mind and the knowledge which is possible to the creature."[7] The Complaint

---

[5]Cornelius Van Til, "Introduction" to *The Inspiration and Authority of the Bible* by Benjamin B. Warfield (Philadelphia: Presbyterian and Reformed, 1948), 33 (emphasis original).

[6]Cornelius Van Til, *An Introduction to Systematic Theology* (unpublished classroom syllabus, 1961), 18-19 (emphasis supplied).

[7]*Minutes* of the Twelfth General Assembly of the Orthodox Presbyterian Church, 1945, 15.

affirmed: "We dare not maintain that [God's] knowledge and our knowledge coincide *at any single point*."[8] Then, in an interview that appeared in *Christianity Today* (Dec 30, 1972), 22, Van Til stated:

> My concern is that the demand for non-contradiction when carried to its logical conclusion reduces God's truth to man's truth. It is unscriptural to think of man as autonomous. The *common ground we have with the unbeliever* is our knowledge of God, and I refer repeatedly to Romans 1:19. All people unavoidably know God by hating God. After that they need to have true knowledge restored to them in the second Adam. *I deny common ground with the natural man*, dead in trespasses and sins, who follows the god of this world." (emphasis supplied)

But how, I ask, does my demanding that truth be inherently non-contradictory make man autonomous? And how can Van Til both assert and deny that the believer has common ground with the unbeliever? This is very confusing. My aim here is not to beat up on Van Til but to defend a proper biblical epistemology from one that is unbiblical but very popular in Reformed circles today. It seems to me that Van Til's epistemology is fundamentally anti-biblical because it is anti-logical while Scripture is inherently logical.

Against these strange notions we can and must pit Jesus' teaching that contradicts it. In John 12:49-50 Jesus declared:

> I did not speak of my own accord, but the Father who sent me commanded me *what to say and how to say it....* So whatever I say, *just as* the Father told me, *so* I say.

And in John 17:6-17 Jesus prayed:

> I have manifested your name to those whom you gave me out of the world.... Now they know that all things that you have given me are from you, for *I have given to them the words [teaching]*

---

[8]*Minutes*, 14, emphasis original.

> *that you have given me*, and they have received them...*I have given them your word....*Your word is truth.

Jesus asserts in these passages that he gave to us the Father's word of truth that he received from his Father *just as* his Father had given it to him.

Not only is Van Til's position anti-scriptural but also Gordon H. Clark contended that Van Til's position leads to total human ignorance. He writes:

> If God knows all truths and knows the correct meaning of every proposition, and if no proposition means to man what it means to God, so that God's knowledge and man's knowledge do not coincide at any single point, it follows by rigorous necessity that man can have no truth.[9]

Clark further argued:

> If God and man know, there must with the differences be at least one point of similarity; for if there were no point of similarity it would be inappropriate to use the one term knowledge in both cases.... If God has the truth and if man has only an analogy [of this truth that contains no univocal element], it follows that he (man) does not have the truth.[10]

Clark illustrated his point this way:

> If...we think that David was king of Israel, and God's thoughts are not ours, then it follows that God does not think David was king of Israel. David in God's mind was perchance prime minister of Babylon.
>
> To avoid this irrationality,...we must insist that truth is the same for God and man. Naturally, we may not know about some matters. But if we know anything at all, what we know must

---

[9]Gordon H. Clark, "Apologetics," in *Contemporary Evangelical Thought*, edited by Carl F. H. Henry (New York: Harper Channel, 1957), 159.

[10]Gordon H. Clark, "The Bible as Truth" in *Bibliotheca Sacra* (April 1957), 163.

be identical with what God knows. God knows the truth, and unless we know something God knows, our ideas are untrue. It is absolutely essential therefore to insist that there is an area of coincidence between God's mind and our mind. One example, as good as any, is the one already used, viz., David was king of Israel.[11]

Clark concluded:

> If God is omnipotent, he can tell men the plain, unvarnished, literal truth. He can tell them David was King of Israel, he can tell them he is omnipotent, he can tell them he created the world, and…he can tell them all this in positive, literal, non-analogical [that is, univocal], non-symbolic terms.[12]

I believe Clark is correct. And we Christians should be overwhelmed by the magnitude of this simple fact that we take so much for granted – *that the infinite personal God has deigned to share with us in a univocal way some of the truths that are on his mind. He has condescended to elevate us poor undeserving sinners to the status of "truth-knowers" by actually sharing univocally with us a portion of the truth that he knows.*

But, someone asks, does not Isaiah 55:8-9 teach that an unbridgeable gulf exists between the content of God's knowledge and the content of our knowledge? No, far from it! These verses actually hold out the real possibility that people may know God's thoughts, and they urge the wicked to turn from their thoughts that are fickle and wicked and to learn God's thoughts from him. In Isaiah 55:7 God calls upon the wicked man to forsake his ways and thoughts. Why? "Because," says the Lord, "my thoughts are not your thoughts, neither are your ways my ways" (55:8). The entire context, far from affirming that God's thoughts are beyond the capacity of human beings to

---

[11]Gordon H. Clark, "The Axiom of Revelation" in *The Philosophy of Gordon H. Clark*, edited by Ronald H. Nash (Philadelphia: Presbyterian and Reformed, 1968), 76-77.

[12]Clark, "The Axiom of Revelation," 78.

know, expressly calls on the wicked man to turn, in repentance and humility, from his thoughts and to seek and to think God's thoughts after him.

Accordingly, Holy Scripture declares that saving faith must be grounded upon true knowledge: "[Evil men] perish," Paul writes, "because they refuse to love the truth and so be saved. For this reason God sends them a powerful delusion so that they will believe *the lie* and so that all will be condemned who have not believed *the truth* but have delighted in wickedness" (2 Thess. 2:10-12). Therefore, the church must vigorously oppose any view of truth, however well-intentioned, that would strip from mankind the only ground for a true knowledge of God and accordingly mankind's only hope of salvation. Against the view of human knowledge that would deny to its truth content univocal correspondence at any point with God's knowledge of truth, it is vitally important that pastors and aspiring pastors come down on the side of Christian reason and work with an epistemology that insists upon at least some identity between the content of God's knowledge and the content of man's knowledge. Otherwise, man has no truth. And when truth goes, the Scriptures go; and when the Scriptures go, the church's sermons as wellsprings of blessing and benefit to the church and the world also go as surely as night follows day, with the result that the world is left in spiritual darkness. For make no mistake about it: the Christian church is "the light of the world" only because it possesses God's Word that is, as we shall now see, logically rational, ethically steadfast, and non-contradictory.

God's Truth Logically Rational, Ethically Steadfast, and Covenantally Faithful

God's Word, because it is the exact univocal expression of God's thought, is, first, logically rational, second, ethically steadfast, third, covenantally faithful, and fourth, has always been so and always will be unchangeably so. I will now develop these ideas.

1. *In regard to God's Word as logically rational*, I want to call attention to two verses:

> John 1:1: "In the beginning was the Logos [that is, "the personal, filial Reason of God"], and the [filial] Logos was *"face to face" with [pros]* God [the Father; see 1 John 1:2], and the [personal, filial] Logos was God [the Son]...."

> John 1:9: "[The personal, filial Reason of God was] the true light who enlightens [with his rationality] every man coming into the world."

These verses affirm that God is not *above* logic as one often hears some people piously say (which affirmation is not really pious but misguided piosity) but that logic is intrinsic to God's nature. If these people doubt this, let them ask and answer whether it is true for God that if all dogs have teeth, then some dogs – Welsh terriers, for example – have teeth. Or do they mean that for God, according to his logic, all dogs have teeth while Welsh terriers do not? I ask again: Is this what they mean? I hope not. For as the knowing, speaking, eternal God of truth the laws of thought (which are the laws of truth) are *intrinsic* to his thought and reason. As I said earlier, truth is God thinking. And because the laws of thought are intrinsic to and original with him it follows that they are true. Hence, he is innately rational in all that he thinks and says – another of his attributes.

What are these laws of thought or laws of truth to which I refer? The most basic laws of thought are (1) the *law of identity*, that is, "whatever is, is," symbolically represented by "A is A"; (2) the *law of contradiction*, that is, "a thing cannot both be and not be so and so," and/or "contradictory propositions cannot both be true," symbolically represented by "A cannot be both A and non-A"; (3) the *law of excluded middle*, that is, "a thing either is or is not so and so," symbolically represented by "A is either A or non-A"; and (4) the laws of the valid syllogism. And I should note in passing, because the God of truth created all things, that these laws of thought are true with regard to all created things as well, for unless these laws of thought are also the laws of things we would be unable to apprehend the nature of things since a thing could then have and not have the same character. The Bible justifies the legitimacy of these laws for us in three ways: first, by the very fact that the God of truth employed languages (Hebrew, Aramaic, Greek), the very use of which presupposes the laws of reason, in order to communicate his truth to the human mind; second, by his many uses of various kinds of logical arguments and logical inferences in his inspired Scripture – Gordon Clark calls our attention, for example, to an enthymematic hypothetical destructive syllogism in Romans 4:2, to a hypothetical constructive syllogism in Romans 5:13, and to the sorites in 1 Corinthians 15:15-18; and third, by John's assertion that every person, because he is the image of God, innately possesses them by virtue of the bestowment of the divine Logos himself. And it is because the Logos of God has enlightened them with rationality (John 1:9) that every rational man in this world thinks and speaks according to the *same* laws of reason, for these laws of logic are actually divine laws of truth. Even the attempt to deny them must presuppose and employ them.

Moreover, because our God is logically *rational*, neither in his understanding nor in what he says is there the slightest contradiction. As the God of truth, for him the laws of logic – *his* innate laws of truth and rationality – are intrinsically and inherently valid because they are intrinsic and inherent to his nature. I would even suggest that we should think of logic, if not as a distinct attribute of God and one more of God's "countless attributes" (E. Lange), as the *epistemological* aspect of God's infinite attribute of wisdom and knowledge.

Now there was a time when it was our Lutheran/Arminian opponents who castigated us Calvinists for being "too logical," and we Calvinists bore this witless insult as a compliment. But in our time some neo-Calvinists are using this same absurd accusation against those of us who maintain that God is rational and his Word, the Bible, is non-contradictory. They tell us that faith must curb logic. Even though they ought to know better these theologians compromise God's rationality, telling us that, even after we have understood the Spirit-inspired Bible correctly, it will often represent its inspired truths to the human existent, even the *believing* human existent, in *paradoxical* terms as defined by R. B. Kuiper, professor of practical theology at Westminster Theological Seminary in Philadelphia and president of Calvin Seminary who is one such theologian:

> A paradox is not, as Barth thinks, two truths that are actually contradictory. Truth is not irrational. [Amen to that!] Nor is a paradox two truths which are difficult to reconcile but can be reconciled before the bar of human reason. That is a seeming paradox. [Amen to that as well!] But when two truths, both taught unmistakably in the infallible Word of God, cannot possibly be reconciled before the bar of human reason, then you have a paradox.[13]

"What should one do…with [such an irreconcilable paradox or antinomy]?" asks J. I. Packer, another such Calvinistic theologian. "Accept it for what it is, and learn to live with it. Refuse to regard the apparent contradiction as real."[14] George Marston, a third such Calvinistic theologian, informs us that such doctrines as the Trinity, the hypostatic union of the divine and human natures in the one person of Christ, God's sovereignty and human responsibility, unconditional election and the sincere preaching of the gospel to all, and particular redemption and the universal offer of the gospel – all cardinal doctrines of the Reformed Faith – are all biblical "paradoxes," each respectively advancing antithetical truths unmistakably taught in the Bible that cannot possibly be reconciled by human reason. Right here I will mention another alleged paradox making its rounds today, namely, the contention that the Bible teaches not only

---

[13]R. B. Kuiper, cited by George W. Marston, *The Voice of Authority* (Philadelphia: Presbyterian and Reformed, 1960), 16.

[14]James I. Packer, *Evangelism and the Sovereignty of God* (Chicago: Inter-Varsity, 1961), 18-25.

that justification is by faith alone but also that justification is by faith and works. Cornelius Van Til, yet a fourth such theologian, because he believed that human knowledge is "only analogical" to God's knowledge, even declared that *all* Christian truth will ultimately appear to be contradictory to the human existent.[15] He also writes:

> It is precisely because [the complainants against Clark's epistemology] are concerned to defend the Christian doctrine of revelation as basic to all intelligible human predication that they refuse to make any attempt at "stating clearly" any Christian doctrine, or the relation of any one Christian doctrine to any other Christian doctrine. They will not attempt to "solve" the "paradoxes" involved in the relationship of the self-contained God to his dependent creatures.[16]

What must we say about this notion that the Bible will often, if not always (Van Til), set forth its truths in irreconcilably contradictory terms with which we must simply learn to live and not let them bother us? This sentiment – that God calls upon Christians to believe irreconcilable contradictions and expects them to learn to live with them – reminds me of the conversation between Alice and the Queen in Lewis Carroll's[17] *Alice in Wonderland*: "There is no use trying," said Alice [who is sane!]; "one can't believe impossible things." "I dare say you haven't had much practice," said the Queen [representing the inhabitants of Wonderland who were, to put it bluntly, "nuts"]. "When I was your age I always did it for half an hour a day. Why, sometimes I've believed as many as six impossible things before breakfast." To say the least, if this sentiment

---

[15]Cornelius Van Til, *The Defense of the Faith* (Philadelphia: Presbyterian and Reformed, 1955), 61; see also his *Common Grace and the Gospel* (Philadelphia: Presbyterian and Reformed, 1973), 9, 142.

[16]Cornelius Van Til, *An Introduction to Systematic Theology* (classroom syllabus, 1961), 172.

[17]Carroll, Charles Lutwidge Dodgson's pseudonym, taught logic as a profession!

were true, then every attempt to arrange the Bible's theology systematically is "dead in the water" before it begins since it is impossible to reduce to a system irreconcilable contradictories that steadfastly resist all attempts at harmonization. One must abandon the effort to systematize the propositions of Scripture and be content simply to live with a veritable nest of theological "discontinuities."

Of course, these theologians who believe this are quick to remind us that these paradoxes are not real contradictions but are only *apparently* so to us human existents, for God knows how to and is able to "unpack" them. But does this proposed adjustment help us? These people seem to be oblivious to the following problems inherent in their paradigm:

First, Kuiper's definition of paradox is problematical in that it makes an assertion that no one can know. How does he know that such paradoxes even exist in Scripture, that is, that in the Bible contradictory truths exist that no one can reconcile? Has he polled every biblical scholar who has ever lived, is living now, and will live in the future and has he discovered that not one of them *has been* able, *is* able now, or *ever will be* able to reconcile the alleged contradictions? To ask the question is to answer it. The very assertion that Scripture contains such paradoxes is seriously flawed by the terms of the definition itself. There is simply no way to know that such phenomena are present in Scripture. And to claim that there are is to assert for oneself the attribute of omniscience. And just because a large number of scholars have failed to reconcile to their satisfaction two given truths of Scripture is no proof that the truths cannot be harmonized. And if one scholar claims to have reconciled these alleged paradoxes to his satisfaction, though his efforts may satisfy no one else, this renders the definition both gratuitous and suspect.

Second is the intrinsic problem of *meaning* in paradoxes so defined. What can two true biblical statements that constitute an *unresolvable* contradiction mean? I will explain my point this way: Let us assume that God told us in Scripture that he had created square circles. The fundamental problem for us would be to understand what he *meant* by this. The word "square" is a useful term, of course, because to say something is square distinguishes it from other objects that are non-squares. But if a square can also be a "non-square," say, a circle, at the same time, then our ability to conceive of, and thus to identify and discuss, squares is at an end. In short, the term "square" no longer remains from our point of view a meaningful term. And the same is true of the term "circle" in this context. But what if God were to inform us – and this is only a hypothetical – that the concept of a square circle is not contradictory from *his* perspective and that to him it is meaningful. Would this help us? Would this clarify anything for us? Well, it would certainly tell us something about God: that he is thinking in other than rational categories. But it would not make the concept of a square circle any more meaningful. Given the categories of meaning with which God created us, the concept itself would remain just as meaningless from *our* perspective as before. In the same way the alleged irreconcilable theological contradictories in the Bible, even though their advocates assure us that they are only apparently contradictory, are meaningless to us.

Third, if actually non-contradictory truths can *appear* as real contradictions that no amount of study or reflection on our part can harmonize, then there is no available means to distinguish between an apparent contradiction and a real contradiction. Since both will *appear* to us in precisely the same form, and since neither will yield up its contradiction to study and reflection, the human existent can never know at any given moment whether he is embracing only a seeming contradiction and not a real one. Accordingly, as Gordon Clark often said to his students, anyone who says that he *can* believe that contrary propositions can both be true at the same time simply has, without realizing it, a "charley horse between his ears."

Fourth and finally – and this point should deliver the *coup de grace* to the entire notion that irreconcilable contradictions exist in Scripture – once one asserts that biblical truths may legitimately assume the form of irreconcilable contradictions, *he has given up all possibility of ever detecting a real falsehood*. Every time he rejects some proposition as false because it contradicts the Bible or because it is illogical, the proposition's sponsor only needs to point out that it only "appears" to contradict the Bible or to be illogical, that it is just one more of those paradoxes that the theologians of paradox have acknowledged have their rightful place in our man-made "little systems," to borrow a phrase from Alfred, Lord Tennyson. But this means the end of Christianity's uniqueness as the revealed religion of God since it is then liable to, indeed, must be open to, the assimilation of any and every truth claim of whatever kind, as well as the end of all rational theology.

The only solution to this dreadful muddleheadedness is to deny to paradox, understood as *irreconcilable* contradictions that are actually only apparently so to us, a legitimate place in the Christian understanding of truth, recognizing it for what it is – "truth decay," the offspring of an irrational age. This view of paradox is destructive of Christianity for, by positing that the Bible contains such irreconcilable contradictions, it makes God the author of confusion, attacks the unity, inerrancy, and perspicuity of Scripture, and renders forever impossible a *rational* faith and a *systematic* theology. And any Bible-believing theologian who claims to have found such irreconcilable truths in the Bible pridefully speaks logical nonsense and deserves to be ignored by the Christian world, for his is not theology but *anti*-theology.

If there is to be (and there is) an offense in Christianity's truth claims, it should be the *soteric* and *ethical* implications of the cross of Christ as the only means of salvation and not the irrationality of alleged irreconcilable contradictories being proclaimed to mankind as being both true. Certainly there are biblical concepts that we cannot fully understand. We may never be able to explain how God created the universe out of nothing, how he can raise the dead, or how the Spirit of

God can quicken the unregenerate soul. But such concepts are *mysteries* to us; they are *not* contradictions. And certainly God himself upon occasion employed in his written Word paradoxes, understood however as *reconcilable* contradictories, for example, "Whoever wants to save his life will lose it, but whoever loses his life for me will find it" (Matt. 16:25) or "So the last will be first, and the first will be last" (Matt. 20:16). But he did so for the same reason we employ them – as rhetorical or literary devices to invigorate the thought being expressed, to awaken human interest, to intrigue and to challenge the intellect, and to shock and to frustrate the lazy mind. But the notion that God's propositional statements will often, if not always, finally appear to the human existent as contradictions must be rejected. Specifically, the contention that the cardinal doctrines of the Faith – the Trinity, the person of Christ, the doctrines of grace, and the doctrine of justification – when proclaimed aright will contain irreconcilable contradictories is a travesty of Scripture interpretation. To affirm otherwise, that is, to affirm that Holy Scripture when properly interpreted can and does teach that which for the human existent is both irreconcilably contradictory and yet still be true, is to make Christianity and the propositional revelation upon which it is grounded for its teaching irrational and absurd. And this strikes at the rational character of the God who speaks throughout its pages. God is Truth itself; he is not the author of confusion. Christ is the Reason of God. The Spirit is the Spirit of truth. None of them can lie. And what they say is internally consistent and non-contradictory. And none of their truth statements were in any way distorted in or by either the revelatory or inspired inscripturation processes. Hence, the Bible, as God's inspired revelation of his mind to man, is true – unqualifiedly and univocally so – and it contains no irreconcilable contradictions!

Let no one conclude from my rejection of paradox, understood as irreconcilable contradictories that are only apparently so, that I am urging upon the church a Cartesian rationalism that presupposes the autonomy of human reason and freedom from divine revelation, a rationalism that asserts that it must begin with itself in its build-up of knowledge. But make no mistake about it: I *am* calling for a *Christian* rationalism that forthrightly affirms that the God of truth is rational, that his promises in Christ are not both "Yes" and "No" (2 Cor. 1:19-20), that he does not, indeed, cannot lie (Titus 1:2; Heb. 6:18), that he is therefore always necessarily truthful, and that his propositional inscripturated revelation that the true church has made the bed-rock of all its theological predications is internally self-consistent and non-contradictory in what it teaches.

That this view of Holy Scripture is a common Christian conviction is borne out, I would remind you, in the consentient willingness by Christians everywhere to affirm that there are no contradictions in the Bible. I quite frankly cannot understand people who tell me on the one hand that the Bible is God's inspired Word and on the other that it contains irreconcilable contradictions. It is simply unthinkable to me that God, who is Truth itself, could ever reveal irreconcilable contradictions and ask men to believe them. The church as a whole has properly seen that the truthfulness and rational character of the one living and true God would necessarily have to be reflected in any propositional self-revelation that he determined to give to mankind. And for the Christian not to set for himself the goal of quarrying from Scripture its *harmonious* "big picture" theology devoid of paradoxes is to sound the death knell not only to *systematic* theology but also to *all* theology that would commend itself to thinking men as the truth of the one living, true, and rational God. We must be dogged in our efforts to harmonize the so-called contradictions that some theologians allege are present in Scripture,[18] and we may encounter difficulties as we do so. But

---

[18]By this assertion I am simply following the Reformation commitment to the logical nature of truth. In *What Luther Says*, compiled by Ewald M. Plass (St. Louis, MO: Concordia, 1959), Martin Luther declares: "…we are certain that the Holy Spirit cannot oppose and contradict Himself" (216). Therefore, "Passages of Scripture that are opposed to one another must, of course, be reconciled, and to one must be given a meaning which agrees

this effort and these difficulties are infinitely to be preferred to the epistemological difficulties that confront the theologians of paradox in their pursuit of biblical truth. So much then for God's Word as logical and rational.

2. In regard to the ethical steadfastness of God's Word, I want to call your attention to the following passages of Scripture:

Psalm 19:7-11:
The law of the Lord is perfect, reviving the soul.
The statutes of the Lord are trustworthy, making wise the simple.
The precepts of the Lord are right, giving joy to the heart.
The commands of the Lord are radiant, giving light to the eyes.
The fear of the Lord is pure, enduring forever.
The ordinances of the Lord are sure and altogether righteous.
They are more precious than gold, than much pure gold;
They are sweeter than honey, than honey from the comb.
By them is your servant warned; in keeping them there is great reward.

Psalm 119:86, 89, 138, 142, 144, 151, 160; Psalm 31:5:
All your commands are trustworthy;
Your word, O Lord, is eternal; it stands firm in the heavens.
The statutes you have laid down are righteous; they are fully trustworthy.
Your righteousness is everlasting, and your law is true.
Your statutes are forever right;…all your commands are true.
All your words are true; all your righteous laws are eternal.

Isaiah 40:8:
The grass withers and the flowers fall, but *the word of our God stands forever*.

---

with the sense of the other; for it is certain that Scripture cannot disagree with itself" (220).

2 Corinthians 1:18, 20:
...*as surely as God is faithful*, our message to you is not "Yes" and "No.".…For no matter how many promises God has made, *they are "Yes" in Christ Jesus*. And so through him the "Amen" is spoken by us to the glory of God.

Titus 1:2:
[Our hope of eternal life]...God, *who does not lie*, promised before the beginning of time.

Hebrews 6:17-19:
Because God wanted to make the *unchanging* nature of his purpose very clear to the heirs of what was promised, he confirmed it with an oath. God did this so that, *by two unchangeable things in which it is impossible for God to lie*, we who have fled to take hold of the hope offered to us may be greatly encouraged. We have this hope as an anchor for the soul, firm and secure....

These verses make it clear that there has always been and always will be a precise equivalence between *what God thinks* and *what God says*. In other words, we may believe that what he is thinking is *infallibly* reflected in what he says and what he says *infallibly* reflects what he is thinking. Since he cannot lie, when he declares things to be of a certain nature, we may be sure that that is what they are. When he makes a promise, we may be sure that he will keep his word. If he were ever to break his promise to me that he will save forever all who trust his Son, all I would lose is my sinful, miserable soul. But he would be the far greater loser for he would lose his honor and thus cease in that moment to be the God of truth. But that can never happen, he being the eternally immutable God that he is, for he cannot and will not go back on his eternal and immutably determined purpose. We may be sure then that he and his Word are *ethically* steadfast. Therefore,

Ye fearful saints, fresh courage take; the clouds ye so much dread
are big with mercy, and shall break in blessings on your head.
Judge not the Lord by feeble sense, but trust him for his grace;
behind a frowning providence he hides a smiling face.

His purposes will ripen fast, unfolding ev'ry hour;
the bud may have a bitter taste, but sweet will be the flow'r.
Blind unbelief is sure to err, and scan his work in vain;
God is his own interpreter, and he will make it plain.

3. *In regard to God's covenantal faithfulness*, I want to call your attention to the following ten Scripture verses:

Deuteronomy 7:9: "...the Lord your God is God; he is the *faithful* God, keeping his covenant of love to a thousand generations of those who love him...."

Psalm 89:8, 33: "You are mighty, O Lord, and *your faithfulness surrounds you*...[The Lord says] I will not take my love from him, nor will I ever betray *my faithfulness*."

Lamentations 3:22-23: "Because of the Lord's great love we are not consumed, for his compassions never fail. They are new every morning; great is *your faithfulness*."

1 Corinthians 1:9: "God, who has called you into fellowship with his Son Jesus Christ our Lord, is *faithful*."

1 Corinthians 10:13: "God is *faithful*; he will not let you be tempted beyond what you can bear."

1 Thessalonians 5:24: "The one who calls you is *faithful*, and he will [keep you blameless, body and soul, at the coming of our Lord Jesus Christ]."

2 Thessalonians 3:3: "...the Lord is *faithful*, and he will strengthen and protect you from the evil one."

2 Timothy 2:13: "If we are faithless, he will remain *faithful*, for he cannot deny himself."

Hebrews 10:23: "Let us hold unswervingly to the hope we profess, for he who promised *is faithful*."

1 John 1:9: "If we confess our sins, he is *faithful*...and will forgive us our sins...."

How is it that the righteous Judge of all the earth can be just and yet faithfully forgive and show compassion toward sinners? His steadfast mercies toward his people must be traced to the fact that he is governed by his covenant faithfulness, particularly as that covenant faithfulness came to expression in the terms of the Abrahamic covenant. Unlike the gods of the nations round about it who were capricious and unpredictable and whose devotees lived in constant dread of their malevolent and irrational intrusion into their daily lives, Israel's God was reliable – one may even say predictable – who stood in a stable relationship both with the world and with Israel, all this resulting from the fact that he had deigned to enter into and commit himself to covenantal stipulations with Israel's patriarchs and with the true Israel. And because of God's covenant faithfulness he will never turn against his elect. Because the covenant threat exhausted itself in Christ's suffering at Calvary, God's people are immune from eternal harm, and his irrevocable rectitude in covenant-keeping leads him to save and to vindicate his people.[19]

In sum, because God's Word is ethically steadfast he is *covenantally faithful*. Because there is an exact equivalence on the one hand between that which God the Father covenantally promised his Son in the eternal covenant of redemption and that which he covenantally promised Abraham and his seed, who is Christ, in the covenant of grace, and on the other hand that which he declares he will actually achieve in history (history is simply God acting) we may be certain that he will actually give to them that which he covenantally promised them.

To see this, all one need do is to recall that the Bible sweeps across the thousands of years between the creation of man and Abraham in only eleven chapters, with the call of Abraham coming in Genesis 12. This suggests that the information given in the first eleven chapters of Genesis was intended as preparatory "background" to the revelation of the Abrahamic covenant. Revelation subsequent to the Abrahamic covenant discloses that everything that God has done savingly in grace since then is the

---

[19]A paraphrase of Donald Macleod, *Behold Your God*, 41.

result and product of that covenant. In other words, once the covenant of grace had come to expression in the salvific promises of the Abrahamic covenant that God would be the God of Abraham and of his descendants and that in Abraham and his seed, even the Christ, all the nations of the world would be blessed, *everything that God has done since then to this present moment he has done in order to fulfill his covenant promises to Abraham*. If you had asked Mary the reason for Christ's first coming, she would have told you that the "Christmas miracle" was a vital constituent part of the fulfillment of God's gracious covenant promise to Abraham: "He has helped his servant Israel, remembering to be merciful to Abraham and his descendants forever, even as he said to our fathers" (Luke 1:54-55). Zechariah, John the Baptist's father, would have told you the same thing. When John was born Zechariah declared: "Praise be to the Lord, the God of Israel, because he has come...to remember his holy covenant, the oath he swore to our father Abraham" (Luke 1:68-73). If you were to inquire of Paul the reason even for Christ's death at Calvary he would tell you that Jesus died "in order that the blessing given to Abraham might come to the Gentiles in Christ Jesus" (Gal. 3:13). He also declared that Abraham is the "father of all who believe" among both Jews and Gentiles (Rom. 4:11-12), and that all who belong to Christ "are Abraham's seed, and heirs according to the promise" that God gave to Abraham (Gal. 3:29). In light of such New Testament data I would urge that Christians should celebrate at Christmas time and on Good Friday far more than they do the great truth and metanarrative ("big picture") theology of God's covenant faithfulness to his people, for that is why God sent his Son into the world and that is why Christ died at Calvary. And if you ask me, "What in the world is God primarily doing this very moment?" I would say, "He is in the process primarily of fulfilling his covenant with Abraham by building his church."

What did God the Father promise his Son in the eternal covenant of redemption? He promised his Son, whom he appointed the Head of his elect, that he would give him as the reward for his work of redemption an elect seed redeemed out of every tribe and race on the face of the earth for his "bride." In Psalm 2:8 the enthroned Son on Zion informs us that his Father said to him: "Ask of me and I will make the nations your inheritance, the ends of the earth your possession." And we can be certain that he asked. In his high-priestly prayer in John 17:1 Jesus speaks of the authority his Father had given him over all people in order that he might give eternal life to all those whom the Father had given him (see also 17:6, 9, 24).

And what did God promise Abraham and his seed in the covenant of grace? He promised that he would be their God and that they would be his people (Gen. 17:7). He promised that his people would become heirs of the world (Rom. 4:13). He promised that he would justify them through his gift to them of faith (Gen. 15:6; see Hab. 2:4). He promised that they would become members of the body of Christ. Therefore the psalmist sings: "All the ways of the Lord are loving and faithful…" (Ps. 25:10). Thus God's covenantal faithfulness is the saint's ground of confidence, the foundation of his hope, the cause of his rejoicing, and the source of his courage.

That God is infinite, eternal, and unchangeable in his truth highlights, then, the ground of our only hope in life and in death, namely, the Word of God that stands eternally firm in the heavens. Nothing is more pertinent today for this silly, fickle, inane world in this irrational age of non-reason than the fact that the one living and true God is infinite, eternal, and unchangeable in his truth.

> How firm a foundation, ye saints of the Lord,
> is laid for your faith in his excellent Word!
> What more can he say than to you he hath said,
> You who unto Jesus for refuge have fled?

So let us love his Word of truth more than we ever loved it before, more than life itself; let us cast ourselves wholly upon its promises, proclaim every time we are given the opportunity its amazing message of grace concerning the "wondrous cross on which the Prince of glory died," and be willing to defend its truthfulness to the death. And let us also never forget that the God of truth hates liars (Prov. 6:16-17) and that all liars will have their part in the lake of burning sulphur (Rev. 21:8).

Chapter Twelve

Faith's Reasons for Believing in the Apologetic Value of Christian Theistic Ethics

According to *Merriam-Webster's Collegiate Dictionary, Eleventh Edition*, ethics is "the discipline dealing with what is good and bad and with moral duty and obligation." Granted that this definition needs some refinement since there are non-moral as well as moral uses of the terms "good" and "bad" it is sufficiently accurate as a starting point to elicit the observation that Christian presuppositions require that ethics be undertaken as an integral part of Christian theology and its apologetic effort.

In contrast to morality that is primarily *descriptive* in that morality describes the behavioral patterns (the moral "isness") of a given person or society at any one time, ethics as a *normative* science, seeks to determine the foundations that prescribe obligations or the "oughtness" of moral behavior. Ethics then is concerned not primarily with the description of human behavior but with the determination of both the proper *imperatives* for human behavior and the ground of these imperatives.

Sometimes the term "theological ethics" is used as a descriptive title for this discipline but this seems to imply that there is also a legitimate autonomous philosophical approach to the subject. "Christian theistic ethics" describes our position more accurately. Christian theistic ethicists insist that their ethical system is the only sound alternative to unproductive secular philosophical ethics that is essentially humanistic in its ground.[1]

---

[1]I do not include in Christian theistic ethics the moral theology of Roman Catholicism. Grounded as the latter is on the authority of reason, natural

Henry Sidgwick (1838–1900), noted Cambridge moral philosopher, affirmed the distinctiveness of Christian theistic ethics in his widely circulated *Outlines of the History of Ethics* (1886). He observed that Christianity brought to the Graeco-Roman world a new moral consciousness not only in the area of practice but also and more fundamentally in "the conception of morality as the positive law of a theocratic community, possessing a written code imposed by divine revelation, and sanctioned by express divine promises and threatenings."[2] The method that Christian theistic ethicists follow assumes the fact of divine guidance for all of life and that moral commands "are to be ascertained in particular cases by application of the general rules obtained from texts of Scripture, and by analogical inference from scriptural examples."[3]

For the sake of clarity it is useful to make the distinction between personal, interpersonal, and social ethics: *personal ethics* focuses on the moral agent, his character and motivation, self-discipline, the dynamic of change, and use of the means of grace; *interpersonal ethics* concerns itself with the attitude and action of the individual toward his neighbors who are immediately present to him and who require his direct and personal attention; and *social ethics* concerns itself with the structures and relationships of human existence, especially the major institutions ordained by God, namely, family, church, and state. All three branches of the subject from the Christian perspective presuppose an ultimate biblical ground for their predications. To the justification of that stance I will now turn, beginning with a discussion of the failure of all secular ethical systems.[4]

---

law, canon law, and the tradition and authority of the Roman church and its *magisterium*, it is preoccupied with providing the priest with guidance in determining appropriate penance for various individual sins confessed in the confessional.

[2]Henry Sidgwick, *Outlines of the History of Ethics* (New York: Macmillan, 1902, fifth edition), 110.

[3]Sidgwick, *Outlines of the History of Ethics*, 111.

[4]David C. Jones was my teacher here. I have relied heavily upon his insights.

The Failure of Secular Ethical Systems

The most obvious question that a theory of ethics is supposed to answer is, "Which actions are right and which are wrong and why?" Closely related is the question, "What goals in life are worthwhile?" The former questions concern judgments of *obligation* (although "right" can mean "lawful" as well as "obligatory"), while the last question is concerned with judgments of *value*, particularly in light of an ultimate goal that is to be valued above everything else. These questions assume choice and responsibility, and any ethical system to be complete must give some account of these. But for now the main point is that an ethical theory is expected to provide *guidance* for human activity by setting forth *normative* principles of duty and of value. As Gordon H. Clark states: "...a theory of ethics that gives no specific guidance in the actual circumstances of life can hardly be called a theory of ethics at all.... Again, a theory of ethics that failed to identify the aim of life is even more obviously no theory of ethics at all."[5]

Questions of practical ethical guidance also raise a more fundamental issue, the issue of ground, for one can hardly say that the guidance issue has been answered unless one is able to explain *why* certain actions are right and others wrong. The judgment that an action is right or wrong presupposes some criterion by which it is so judged. What *makes* right actions right and wrong actions wrong? Accordingly, the questions of ethical guidance pursued logically lead to some more ultimate first principle or ground on the basis and truthfulness of which the correctness of all other ethical judgments depends. And, one might add, "Unless some such ultimate moral principles can be shown to be justifiable, no other moral judgments can be shown to be justifiable."[6] Thus *the question of justification takes precedence over all others*, the more so in view of the

---

[5]Gordon H. Clark, *Religion, Reason and Revelation* (Reprint; Jefferson, Maryland: Trinity Foundation, 1986), 159.

[6]A. Phillips Griffiths, "Ultimate Moral Principles" in *The Encyclopedia of Philosophy* (New York: Macmillan, 1967), VIII: 177-82.

widespread moral skepticism in our time. How do we know what is right? "The complete failure of moral philosophers to give a satisfactory answer to this fundamental epistemological question is probably the main reason for continued skepticism in ethics."[7] Against this background a Christian theistic ethic that is able to answer common objections will be of great apologetical as well as ethical significance, for if there is any crucial point at which both Christianity and secular humanism are obligated to present a convincing and, indeed, an unanswerable argument, it is with respect to the field of ethics.

Different ideas as to what constitutes rightness can and do lead to conflicting moral judgments. For example, the question of the morality of sexual intercourse outside marriage may be answered in different ways, depending on whether the criterion of rightness is "tendency to give pleasure," "promotion of personhood," or "obedience to God's law." It is no secret that people differ radically in their judgments regarding sexual conduct. Some people condemn group sex as disgraceful orgy; others commend it as a "shared experience" of interpersonal relationship. Who is right? How can we know? The following excerpt from *Humanist Manifesto II* is an illuminating indication of the trend of our post-Christian age:

> In the area of sexuality, we believe that intolerant attitudes, often cultivated by orthodox religions and puritanical cultures, unduly repress sexual conduct. The right to birth control, abortion, and divorce should be recognized. While we do not approve of exploitative, denigrating forms of sexual expression [Such as, and why not?], neither do we wish to prohibit, by law or social sanction, sexual behavior between consenting adults. The many varieties of sexual exploration should not in themselves be considered "evil" [But wait: Many would regard the acts that these authors regard as "exploitative, denigrating forms of sexual expression" as just "varieties of sexual exploration" between consenting adults,

---

[7]Kurt Maier, *The Moral Point of View* (New York: Random House, 1958), 18.

which acts they endorse]. Without countenancing mindless permissiveness or unbridled promiscuity [Such as, and why not?], a civilized society should be a *tolerant* one [Of course, these authors will not themselves tolerate what they regard as "exploitative, denigrating forms of sexual expression" even though others might regard these acts as "varieties of sexual exploration" between consenting adults]. Short of harming others or compelling them to do likewise [but who determines when harm is being done?], individuals should be permitted to express their sexual proclivities and pursue their life-styles as they desire.

Behind these judgments in the sphere of human sexuality lies a view of ethics obviously and radically at odds with that of Christian theism. What is the *Manifesto*'s justification for these judgments?

We affirm that moral values derive their source from human experience. Ethics is *autonomous* and *situational*, needing no theological or ideological sanction [where is the detailed argument for this position?]. Ethics stems from human need and interest. To deny this destroys the whole basis of life. Human life has meaning [what does the *Manifesto* mean by "meaning"?] because we create and develop our futures. Happiness and the creative realization of human needs and desires, individually and in shared enjoyment, are continuous themes of humanism. We strive for the good life [what is the "good life," who determines it, and how is it determined?], here and now. The goal is to pursue life's enrichment despite debasing forces of vulgarization, commercialization, bureaucratization, and dehumanization.

These statements bristle with unvarnished presuppositions, brute assertions, and dogmatic assumptions. I offer the above, however, not as a basis for present discussion (this I will do later in this chapter), but as a matter-of-fact example of an ethical system that is antithetical to Christian ethics with implications that affect the whole of society. It is ironic that the *Manifesto* protests against bureaucratization and yet undermines the one social institution that forms the basic safeguard against state interference and control, namely, the family. If marriage is no longer intended to create a permanent social unit, the family yields its social function to the state that must then become the guardian and educator of the children. Christopher Dawson put his finger on this result about seventy-five years ago. If the advocates of the new morality prevail, he wrote, "society will no longer consist of a number of organisms, each of which possesses a limited autonomy, but will be one vast unit which controls the whole life of the individual citizen from the cradle to the grave."[8]

Today skepticism in ethics, that is, denial of the possibility of justifying any objective truths of moral obligation, would appear to be more common than skepticism in general. It is commonly supposed that the diversity of moral opinion in the world means skepticism is unavoidable but this does not follow. Some view may, after all, be true. *What is needed to overcome skepticism, of course, is an irrefragable theory of justification of moral norms.* As I see it, Christian apologetics should make this its chief task in the area of morals rather than the empirical establishment of the moral consciousness of mankind as some apologists are wont to do.

I will now lay out in turn the major efforts to erect a secular ethical theory and show their inability to be of any assistance in providing ethic guidance and goals for mankind.

Utilitarianism

Utilitarianism, associated with the name of Oxford-trained Jeremy Bentham (1748–1832), is the hedonistic theory of ethics that urges that one ought to seek, not only his own pleasure, but also *the greatest pleasure of the greatest number*, this pleasure to be measured by the seven parameters of intensity, duration, certainty, propinquity (nearness of blood), fecundity

---

[8]Christopher Dawson, *Enquiries into Religion and Culture* (New York: Sheed & Ward, 1933), 262f.

(fruitfulness), purity, and extent (so Bentham). As has been often pointed out, however, to suppose that anyone can calculate the sum total of pleasures accruing to the whole human race by each and every ethical choice is utterly impossible. Gordon Clark asks: "…how much pleasure or pain will my action today produce for a Chinese peasant a few hundred years from now?" Clark's question underscores that only omniscient mathematicians could be moral, for one would have to estimate the intensity, the duration, the certainty, the propinquity, the fecundity, the purity, and the extent of each pleasure and then calculate how many units of pleasure X line of action would produce for x number of people and how many units of pleasure Y, the opposing line of action, would produce for y number of people and do this for every ethical choice. Moreover, this principle of determining choices is one by which dictators can justify any cruelty. It fails to protect the minority. And as a theory it can offer no reason why anyone should aim for the good of all society. In fact, no descriptive science, which is what Bentham's utilitarianism purports to be, can justify why anyone should govern his actions by the good of others.

Intuitionism

Intuitionism generally refers to the ethical theory that asserts man's innate knowledge or awareness of duty, but it may be also applied to the teleological theory in which right is defined in terms of good, and this good is intuited.

Henry Sidgwick in his *Methods of Ethics* tried to ground his utilitarian ethic on intuitions. He urged men to look at ethical considerations "from the point of view…of the Universe." Unfortunately, no one man is the universe and therefore no one man can see things from its point of view. Nor is it easy to discern why anyone ought to adopt any point of view other than his own. Why should another person's enjoyment or good take precedence for me over my enjoyment or good? Sidgwick was honest enough to admit that the compatibility of all individual goods is incapable of empirical proof, and therefore admitted into his discussion, much to his chagrin, the question of whether a theory of ethics can be constructed on an empirical base at all or whether after all it is not forced to borrow its ground principle from theology.[9]

In his *Principia Ethica* (1903) G. E. Moore (1873–1958), noted Cambridge professor of philosophy and logic from 1925 to 1939, insisted that an action is said to be right if it is productive of more good (shades of utilitarianism!) than would have been produced by any other action open to the agent. However, Moore seems to be more aware than the earlier utilitarians of the uncertainty that this principle brings to the question of what we ought to do: "…indeed, so many different considerations are relevant to its truth or falsehood, as to make the attainment of probability very difficult, and the attainment of certainty impossible."[10] His admission that there can be no certainty attached to moral rules is significant, for it means that practical knowledge cannot be derived from the theory. To put it another way, Moore was content in practical matters to rely on the borrowed capital of Christendom. But the weakness of his theory is exposed when prevailing social conventions are challenged. The main objection to Moore's theory is that the principle of utility within it (what action will lead to the greatest good?) can lead to no knowledge of what is right in concrete circumstances. In sum, Moore's intuitionism offers no criterion by which differences of opinion may be settled. It is useless therefore as a moral theory of value.

Ethical intuitionism by its own account only tells us what we already think we know. But if others should disagree with us there is no way within the theory to resolve fundamental differences on moral issues. The theory is unable to overcome "the difficulty of convincing an opponent that such and such a proposition is axiomatic and self-evident, when he does not

---

[9]Henry Sidgwick, *Methods of Ethics*, 506-09.

[10]Moore, *Principia Ethica* (First edition; Cambridge: University Press, 1959, 1903), 64.

'see' it."[11] This fault may be glossed over in a unified cultural situation, but it cannot remain hidden for long in any situation of social change where there are significant differences of opinion such as exist in western society today.

Emotivism

Ethical emotivism is the view that there are no meaningful concepts in normative ethics but only factually meaningless ejaculations used to express or arouse emotions (hence the name). The utterance "Stealing is wrong," for example, functions primarily not as a statement-making sentence but rather as a vehicle for expressing one's attitude or feeling about stealing (A. J. Ayer) and also as an evocative expression intended to generate a similar attitude in the hearer (C. L. Stevenson). In any case, the question of truth or falsity does not and cannot arise because ethical utterances, being composed of terms such as "right" or "good" (which have no factual import), express feelings without stating anything at all.

Clearly, such outright denial regarding absolute ethical norms renders emotivism a "non-theory" of ethics in so far as answering the question "Which actions are always right and which are always wrong?" is concerned. Any theory of ethics that gives no special guidance for human action in the actual circumstances of life, that fails to identify the aim of life, and that denies the possibility of knowing such things has no right as a theory to claim anyone's allegiance at all and can be ignored with no further discussion.

Existentialism

Gordon H. Clark argues that the subjectivist epistemology of existentialism is fatal for ethics.[12] Existentialists (Heidegger, Sartre) argue that to act on the basis that some things ought always to be done or that there is some value at which it is

---

[11]Gordon H. Clark, "Intuition" in *Baker's Dictionary of Christian Ethics*, 338.

[12]See Gordon H. Clark, *The Philosophy of Gordon H. Clark*, 52-54

always right to aim is a manifestation of "bad faith." If one would live *authentically* one should *choose freely* what is to be done or sought in every situation; to choose, and therefore to be oneself, is the human existent's one single value. *Only then* is one a fully responsible moral agent. In effect, the sole principle of conduct is: "Whatever you do, do it because *you* choose to do it and for no other reason."

The problem with "living authentically" is that it does not entail any values or goals beyond itself. "If choosing freely for oneself is the highest value, the free choice to wear red socks is as valuable as the free choice to murder one's father or sacrifice oneself for one's friend."[13] There is literally nothing that is not morally commendable so long as it is freely chosen, including suicide. The possibility of suicide raises another consideration, for existentialists continue to live by choice and as long as they do so *must* make, that is, are obligated to make, other choices as well. Clark presses the point:

> If these choices do not fall under some general norm, if no choice is similar to any other, if every situation exists as an utterly lonely individual, if there is no hierarchy of desirable or even desired ends, if *no reason* supports one in preference to another, then the lives of these men are irrational and they are insane.[14]

Clark never wrote anything more factually true than that. And, as has often been pointed out, when Sartre opted to remain with the human race and joined the Communist Party, he effectively abandoned his "insane" existentialist position.

Instrumentalism
Instrumentalism as an ethical theory is usually associated with the name of John Dewey (1859–1952). As an atheist, pragmatist, and behaviorist, Dewey believed that "intelligent action is the

---

[13]Mary Warnock, *Existentialist Ethics* (New York: St. Martin's, 1967), 54.
[14]Clark, *The Philosophy of Gordon H. Clark*, 423.

sole ultimate resource of mankind in every field whatsoever." Man has only himself. Dewey did not believe in fixed ethical principles any more than he believed in fixed truths of any kind:

> We institute standards of justice, truth, esthetic quality, etc.... exactly as we set up a platinum bar as a standard measurer of lengths. The standard is just as much subject to modification and revision in the one case as in the other on the basis of the consequences of its operational application....The superiority of one conception of justice to another is of the same order as the superiority of the metric system.[15]

He employs another analogy. Moral standards, he says, are like rules of grammar. They are both the result of custom. Language evolved from unintelligent babblings; then came grammar. But language continues to change to meet new situations and new needs. Words change their forms and meaning, new expressions are invented, and the old rules become archaic. So too, the rules of morality change with changing customs. In consonance with this, Dewey held that nothing is intrinsically good or bad; nothing is intrinsically valuable in and of itself alone; all beliefs, all actions, and all values are *instrumental* (hence the theory's name). And they are to be judged by their consequences. If they solve human problems, they are good instruments. If they do not, they are bad.

But is it true that there is no activity that is valuable for itself alone? Are all values merely instrumental? Is there no final end whatever? If nothing is intrinsically valuable, how can one distinguish between the serious and the trivial? If everything is chosen merely as a means to something else and never because of its intrinsic qualities, does it make any difference what we choose? Why follow one causal series rather than another if all activities are valueless means to other valueless means? If means have no end, why is not all choice irrational or at

---

[15]John Dewey, *Logic, The Theory of Inquiry* (New York: H. Holt, 1938), 216.

best simply personal preference? And as Clark points out,[16] if the rules of morality change, like the rules of grammar, with changing customs, this would suggest that if cannibalism and teenage rape, both of which are on the rise in Africa as nations gain their independence from colonial rule, occurred frequently enough, they would become moral. In response to such queries, Dewey appealed to *common opinion* and declared that no honest person can think that murder or rape is instrumental to anything good and that everybody resents acts of wanton cruelty. But the plausibility that a normal person will condemn murder and rape and resent wanton cruelty lies in the fact that the statement is true in the Western World at the present time because of our Christian heritage. But it is well known that Communists, the Islamic Jihad, and other radical groups today use assassinations, terrorist bombings, and all kinds of brutal means as political devices because they judge these acts as having very beneficial consequences. And many Latins, to the dismay of members of the Society for the Prevention of Cruelty to Animals, enjoy the wanton cruelty of bullfights. How then does one decide the "rightness" of incompatible ideals? If nothing is intrinsically right or valuable, how could anyone, even Dewey, choose? In fact, how does Dewey choose to do anything?

If there are no intrinsic values, if there is no final goal, if man has no chief end, by which alone subordinate means become worthwhile, the *ultimate* ethical question now arises in full force: Why continue living; why not commit suicide? Christianity with its revelational base asserts that life is from God and that suicide is immoral, but what can be said against suicide by an empirical, descriptive philosophy? Most modern secular moralists refuse to face this question even though they are obliged to defend their optimistic attitude toward life. Those who do recognize the logical possibility of a pessimism that holds life to be too dreary and boring to be worth the trouble offer no argument against such pessimism. This failure to

---

[16]Gordon H. Clark, *Essays on Ethics and Politics* (Jefferson, Maryland: Trinity Foundation, 1992), 82. I am indebted to Clark for this critique of Dewey's ethic.

give a rational refutation of pessimism is the final refutation of instrumentalistic ethics, for to choose an action as a means to another *ad infinitum*, and to find value nowhere, resembles nothing so much as the frustration of Sisyphus.

Evolutionary ethics

Antony Flew holds that ethics should be seen from an "evolutionary perspective." This involves a more fundamental contention:

> The case for urging the need to see morality – or anything else – in an evolutionary perspective must, of course, start from the contention that an evolutionary account of its genesis and future is in fact correct.[17]

The truth of this "surely not very seriously disputatious scientific contention" is taken for granted against the massive evidence for a Creator. The evolutionary perspective presupposes as factual truth "the claim that the history of mankind is a continuation of the general evolutionary process, and the claim that the future of this entire process – the future of all other living things as well as of mankind – lies largely or wholly in human hands."[18] Are these propositions beyond serious scientific disputation? The question is critical, because unless these propositions are demonstrable the evolutionary perspective is without foundation. Is Flew's confidence in the soundness of the theory of evolution justified? A question even more fundamental is whether knowledge is possible at all on a purely empirical basis.

Flew understands Darwin to have *deduced* natural selection, given as premises (1) the occurrence of individual differences in living organisms, and (2) the struggle for existence due to their rate of geometric increase. This is followed by a "massive case" (conducted inductively or empirically) for the evolution of the species, with natural selection as the main instrument.

---

[17]Flew, *Evolutionary Ethics*, 59.
[18]Flew, *Evolutionary Ethics*, 53f.

In Flew's view, "the greatest philosophical significance of Darwin's work...lies precisely in the fact that Darwin [by his discovery of natural selection] showed how the *appearance* of design among living things might come about without *actual* design."[19] Flew stresses the deductive core of Darwin's theory by which this is established.

In the selection from the *Origin of Species* that Flew quotes to bear out his view, the key sentence is the following: "But if variations useful to any organic being do occur, assuredly individuals thus characterized will have the best chance of being preserved in the struggle for life."[20] Darwin goes on to say: "This principle of preservation, or the survival of the fittest, I have called natural selection." The key sentence, however, turns out on closer inspection to be a mere tautology in terms of the theory in which the only criterion for *useful* is *survival*. All the sentence really says is that if variations *with survival value* occur, the individuals thus affected will survive. All that is warranted by the premises is that variations may have some bearing on survival. Whether and to what extent are matters for empirical investigation. In fact, Flew himself says that Darwin's argument with respect to the fact that some natural selection occurs "leaves open such theoretical possibilities as that there might turn out to be comparatively narrow limits on the amount of change which would in practice come about in this sort of way, or that a Creator might have chosen to create some or all species specially."[21] But he dismisses these possibilities as "arbitrary suppositions." Still, the admission of them as "theoretical possibilities" means that the basis for an evolutionary perspective is not irrefragable. To be that, a theory has to exclude other theoretical possibilities – the process in which I am presently engaged in making the case for Christian theistic ethics.

Moreover, it is far from clear that these possibilities are arbitrary suppositions to be rejected out of hand. After all, Luther

---

[19]Flew, *Evolutionary Ethics*, 15, emphasis supplied.
[20]Flew, *Evolutionary Ethics*, 11.
[21]Flew, *Evolutionary Ethics*, 11.

Burbank concluded after extensive experimentation that "there is undoubtedly a pull toward the mean which keeps all living things within some more or less fixed limitations."[22] One might also recall the fruitless experimentation with *drosophilia* that drove Richard B. Goldschmidt to despair of micromutations as the mechanism of evolution.[23] Combine a thousand variations in a fruit-fly – it remains a fruit-fly to the end.

These objections do not necessarily prove that evolutionary theory is wrong, but they do bring into question Flew's confident generalizations. It ought to be remembered that the burden of proof rests with the proponents of a theory. There is a vast difference between the proposition, "It might have been this way," and the proposition, "This is the way it was." Flew's evolutionary perspective, by his own insistence, requires that he be able to say the latter. But is the latter proposition warranted? Ernst Mayr in *Animal Species and Evolution* writes: "The basic theory is in many instances hardly more than a postulate and its application raises numerous questions in almost every concrete case."[24]

As for the idea that "the future not only of mankind but of the entire evolutionary process on this planet is in our hands,"[25] indeed the process "in the whole solar system,"[26] this contention neglects the lack of a guarantee by the theory that man will even survive. The point is not the possibility of *self*-destruction (since this would still be human agency), but the possibility of destruction by, let us say, microorganisms beyond human control. In this situation that cannot be disallowed by the theory, man is still subject to non-rational natural selection. Accordingly, if his own future is not in his hands, how can the future of all other living things in the cosmos be there? Until man achieves omnipotence such claims are, to say the least, premature.

---

[22]Cited by Norman MacBeth, *Darwin Retried* (New York: Dell, 1971), 36.

[23]Richard B. Goldschmidt, *The Material Basis of Evolution* (1940).

[24]Cited by MacBeth, *Darwin Retried*, 124.

[25]Flew, *Evolutionary Ethics*, 27.

[26]Flew, *Evolutionary Ethics*, 28.

Finally, Flew contends that the theory of evolution as applied to ethics implies that "all moral ideas and ideals have originated in the world," being "rooted in human needs and inclinations," and this in turn undermines "any assumption of an authoritative finality in principle beyond all criticism and reappraisal."[27] Besides the inherent contradiction in the latter statement (there is no finality, and that is final), it presupposes that there is some criterion of criticism and reappraisal. But if *all* moral ideas and ideals have originated in the world by evolution and are therefore subject to change, there is no possible criterion that is exempt, and hence no basis for criticism. A quite different conception of "morality" ensues.

The ethical ground of *Humanist Manifesto II*
At the beginning of this chapter I cited *Humanist Manifesto II*'s ground for its humanistic ethic: "We affirm that moral values derive their source from human experience. Ethics is *autonomous* and *situational*, needing no theological or ideological sanction. Ethics stems from human need and interest." Edwin A. Burtt, one such humanist, in his *Types of Religious Philosophy* repudiates biblical morality, stating, for example, that humanists regard "sex as an essentially harmless pleasure which should be regulated only by personal taste and preference." It is clear from both of these statements that secular humanism grounds its ethics in an empirical assessment of *human experience*.

The problem that all secular humanism must face, however, is this: Can an empirical, *purely descriptive* philosophy, a philosophy that repudiates theology and concerns itself only with a description of what *is* in human experience, provide a ground for the *oughts* of universal moral prescriptions, indeed, for any moral prescriptions whatsoever? A negative response is obviously the only response: One can never derive "oughtness" from "is-ness." For would not the same arguments that place sexual practice in the sphere of purely personal preference also imply that *all* the choices of life are equally a matter of private

---

[27]Flew, *Evolutionary Ethics*, 55, 58, 13.

taste? No doubt many humanists disapprove of the brutality and murder perpetrated by Soviet Communism, urging that the world should "make love, not war," but Joseph Stalin showed a personal preference for murder when he thought it appropriate and contributory to the propagation of worldwide communism, as did Chairman Mao. And many moderns have a personal preference for adultery over monogamy and for theft over labor. Thus murder, adultery, and theft, as much as friendship, fidelity, and honest labor and private property, have on empirical, descriptive grounds a claim as values because they have been discovered as values in human experience. How then can a theory of ethics that restricts itself to descriptive facts provide a ground for normative prescriptions? There is no empirical knowledge sufficient to brand murder as wrong and private property as right. Even if it could be demonstrated as true that murder and adultery frequently result in pain to the perpetrator, it is clear that this is not universally true. Stalin lived to a ripe old age, as did Chairman Mao, enjoying almost perfect fruition of his vengeful plans. Unless there is an Almighty God to impose inescapable penalties on transgressors after death, why should we not praise the rich, full, stimulating, dangerous life of a communist dictator and, to the degree that we can learn from him, the art of murder and massacre?

Probably most humanists today attempt to avoid this problem by speaking of moral obligation as a social demand. Instead of looking to theology for the imposition of moral sanctions, they look to society for the imposition of such. Apart from the fact that this appeal does not really avoid the problem of ground (where is the argument to establish an individual's obligation to any society?), it must address this question: If morality is a demand of society, which society? Is it the demand of the family, the church, the nation, or all humanity? Humanity as such can hardly demand morality since there are no demands that are clearly demands of humanity. If humanity speaks at all it speaks in such diverse, indistinct, and ambiguous language that no specific obligation can be proved. An ethical theory based on social demand must appeal then either to family, church, or nation. And since humanists repudiate the church out of hand as a legitimate ground of morality, they are left with the family and the nation. Of these two, the nation is most able to impose sanctions against "immorality." But then morality becomes loyalty to the State, and we are right back where we began – with murder, adultery, and theft becoming moral obligations when Nazism, Fascism, and Communism demand them.

On purely empirical grounds how can society obligate any man to sacrifice his personal preference and ease for the improvement of others? If there is no God and men are simply products of an impersonal beginning plus time plus chance, why should not every man say as the student said to Francis Schaeffer, "I want to destroy."[28] If there is no God why should not every man step out of the line and join the student in his bent to destroy or, at least, in his "dropping out" of society. And if humanism can do no better than to call such people social sponges, social misfits, and other derogatory names, it has abandoned rational argument and can provide no ground for moral education.

I have sufficiently demonstrated that secular ethics cannot serve as a ground for morality, nor can it serve as a ground even for the inculcation of the personal preferences of its exponents. In an empirical philosophy, one may find the verb *is*, but the verb *ought* has no logical standing. So much then for secular philosophical attempts to provide a theory of ethics that will commend itself to thinking people. The entire enterprise has been and is a failure at the three critical points of providing moral guidance for actions, goals for life, and the ground for ethical predication. This fact alone should commend a biblical theistic ethic if it can provide practical guidance, identify appropriate goals for life, and justify both.

---

[28]Francis Schaeffer, *The God Who Is There* (Downers Grove, Ill.: Inter-Varsity, 1968), 89.

Christian Theistic Ethics

What makes right acts right? Every secular philosophical or non-theistic view, as we have seen, tends to skepticism and the failure to answer pessimism. After well over two millennia of secular philosophizing on ethics and morality G. J. Warnock concedes that "this is a subject in which there is still almost everything to be done."[29] How do we know what is right? The history of secular attempts to answer this question is far from encouraging. The Christian theistic view, on the other hand, not only answers the question but also provides an explanation of the moral agency of those who are unable to provide a satisfactory solution: "Indeed, when Gentiles, who do not have the law, do by nature things required by the law, they are a law for themselves, even though they do not have the law, since they show that the requirements of the law are written on their hearts" (Rom. 2:14-15a). To the extent that fallen man retains knowledge of right and wrong it is because morality, instituted by God, is indelibly impressed on man's nature. The ground of rightness or oughtness, even here, is God's law, though it is not recognized as such.

These two facts – the fact that secular ethics tends toward skepticism and has "still almost everything to do" while Christian theistic ethics has available answers to the questions of right and wrong – ought, as I have already said, to commend Christian theistic ethics to the thinking person. For without concrete unchangeable ethical norms men are at the mercy of the ethical opinion of either the fifty-one percent majority of any society or of an elite oligarchy such as the majority opinion of a Supreme Court somewhere.

What makes right acts right? Gordon Clark states precisely the fundamental principle of Christian ethics: "God's precepts define morality."[30] So also Charles Hodge: "All moral obligation...resolves itself into the obligation of conformity to

---

[29]G. J. Warnock, *Contemporary Moral Philosophy* (New York: St. Martin's, 1967), 77.

[30]Clark, *The Philosophy of Gordon H. Clark*, 422.

the will of God."[31] John Murray writes: "From whatever angle this question [of the governing principle of ethics] is viewed, it is reducible to the insistence that jealousy for compliance with and conformity to the revealed will of God is the governing principle of life set forth in Scripture."[32] Carl F. H. Henry states: "Morality is what God commands."[33] Finally, in the words of the Westminster catechisms: "The duty which God requireth of man, is obedience to his revealed will" (*Larger Catechism*, Question 91; *Shorter Catechism*, Question 39). This fundamental principle presupposes that "God is there and he has spoken," that he is sovereign (his will being the highest rule of justice so that what he wills is just) and immutable (his moral requirements are permanent and unchanging), and that he is man's ultimate moral authority. Morality and theology, then, are inseparable!

The basic relationship between God and man entails obedience as the fundamental ethical category. God is the sole ultimate Lawgiver and Judge.

- Isaiah 33:22: "Yahweh is our Judge; Yahweh is our Lawgiver; Yahweh is our King: He will save us."

- James 4:12: "There is only one Lawgiver and Judge, the one who is able to save and destroy."

Furthermore, obedience, which is the basic principle of morality, God promises to reward in the covenant that he made with man "wherein life was promised to Adam; and in him to his posterity, upon condition of perfect and personal obedience" (*Westminster Confession of Faith*, VII.2). This covenant, man's disobedience to it, and its renewal in Christ, constitute the theme of the Bible

---

[31]Charles Hodge, *Systematic Theology* (Grand Rapids: Eerdmans, n. d.), II, 260.

[32]John Murray, "Ethics, Biblical" in *New Bible Dictionary* (Grand Rapids: Eerdmans, 1962), 397.

[33]Carl F. H. Henry, *Christian Personal Ethics* (Grand Rapids: Baker, 1977), 242.

and is summed up in the following contrast: "For just as through the *disobedience* of the one man the many were made sinners, so also through the *obedience* of the one man the many will be made righteous" (Rom. 5:19). The work of Christ as Mediator, especially in his estate of humiliation, is characterized above all as obedience to his Father's will. He is the Servant of the Lord and the suffering Servant of Isaiah 53. Christ is indeed also a Servant in the sense that he was the "man for others" who came not to be ministered to but to minister and to give his life a ransom for many. But back of this loving service to others was his obedience to his Father:

- Matthew 26:39: "My Father, if it is possible, let this cup pass from me; nevertheless, not as I will, but as you will."

- John 4:34: "My food is to do the will of him who sent me and to accomplish his work."

- John 6:38: "For I have come down from heaven, not to do my own will but the will of him who sent me."

- Philippians 2:7f: "[He] made himself nothing, taking the form of a servant, being born in the likeness of men. And being found in human form, he humbled himself by beoming obedient to the point of death – even death on a cross."

He is the living embodiment of what is written in Psalm 40:8: "I desire to do your will, O my God; your law is within my heart" (see Heb. 10:5-7). There is no moral principle more fundamental than this (see 1 Sam. 15:22-23). Sacrifice without obedience is the epitome of hypocrisy, for disobedience is the sure and certain evidence of a heart that is not right with God (see Isa. 1:10-20; Jer. 6:16-21; 7:22f.; Amos 5:21-24; Micah 6:6-8). The motive in obedience is simply to be pleasing to God in all manner of conduct.

- Romans 14:18: "Whoever thus serves Christ in this way is acceptable to God."

- 2 Corinthians 5:9: "So...we make it our aim to please him."

- Ephesians 5:8-10, 17: "Walk as children of light...and find out what is pleasing to the Lord...do not be foolish, but understand what the will of the Lord is."

- Colossians 1:10: "[We pray for you] that you may be filled with a knowledge of his will...so as to walk in a manner worthy of the Lord, and fully pleasing to him."

- 1 Thessalonians 4:1: "Finally, brothers,...you received from us how you ought to live and to please God."

In 1 Peter 1:14-16 believers are described as "children of obedience." The genitive is likely Hebraistic, that is to say, obedience to God is an essential characteristic of believers in times of crisis, as Peter earlier affirmed (Acts 5:29; see also Matt. 7:21 in its context). The covenant renewed brings justification and new life and creates the possibility of obedience.

The Norm of Christian Theistic Ethics

The single ethical principle that God's precepts govern ethical statements is dependent upon a still more fundamental axiom, namely, that the Bible is the Word of God.[34] From this it follows that God's precepts are immutably, infallibly, and sufficiently set forth in the Old and New Testament Scriptures, the only rule of faith and obedience. The Bible reveals man's chief end and all the means of its fulfillment including the whole duty that God requires of man.

Having made the case for a Christian theistic ethic by demonstrating that this system of ethics answers the questions of morality, namely, the questions of guidance, the aim and goals of life, and the ground for ethical predications, which secular humanistic ethics cannot provide, I now want to address the

---

[34]See Chapters Two and Three for the evidence for this fact.

question of what it is in the Bible that specifically serves as the norm of ethical behavior.

One consistent biblical ethic?

Is there one consistent ethic in the Bible? I would answer in the affirmative. Some Bible students, however, ask: "Are there not at least two ethical systems in the Scripture? As just one example of ethical discontinuity between the Testaments, does not the Old Testament sanction polygamy and divorce for light causes while the New Testament endorses only monogamy and legitimates divorce on only two grounds, namely, sexual infidelity and desertion?"

A Christian theistic response

John Murray in his *Principles of Conduct* responds to these questions in the following way:

> The only thesis that appears to me to be compatible with [the revelatory data of the Old Testament as interpreted by the New] is that polygamy and divorce (for light cause) were permitted or tolerated under the Old Testament, tolerated in such a way that regulatory provisions were enacted to prevent some of the grosser evils and abuses attendant upon them, and tolerated in the sense that they were not openly condemned and censured with civil and ecclesiastical penalties, but that nevertheless they were not legitimated. That is to say, these practices were basically wrong; they were violations of a creation ordinance, even of an ordinance which had been revealed to man at the beginning. Therefore they were inconsistent with the standards and criteria of holy living which had been established by God at the beginning. They were really contrary to the revealed will of God and rested under his judgment.
>
> The insistent question immediately arises: How could this be? How could God allow his people, in some cases the most eminent of Old Testament saints, to practice what was a violation of his preceptive will? It is a difficult question. Yet the position taken is the only one that satisfies the authoritative deliverance of our Lord in reference to divorce. He tells us

explicitly that for the hardness of their hearts Moses suffered the Israelites to put away their wives, but that from the beginning it was not so (Matt. 19:3-8; Mark 10:2-9). If Jesus could enunciate this position in reference to divorce, there is no good reason why the same principle should not be applied to polygamy. The position would then be that because of perversity they were permitted to take more wives than one. Polygamy was not penalized by civil or ecclesiastical censures, even though in terms of the creation ordinance it was a violation of the divine institution. Men were permitted to take more wives than one, but from the beginning it was not so. Sufferance there indeed was, but no legitimation or sanction of the practice.[35]

From these remarks we discover that Murray grounds the divine willingness to "endure" in his saints moral practices that violated his ordinances simply in the fact of human perversity. I concur with Murray. James Orr in his *The Problem of the Old Testament* offers an additional – I think very helpful – insight when he points out that special revelation, being progressive in nature, in its efforts to raise fallen man's ethical standards and to make them what they should be, "takes man up at the stage at which it finds him," that is, in sin, and is responsible "only for the new element which it introduces."[36] That is to say, God came to men, as any wise pedagogue would have done, and began his ethical instruction of them where he found them, adapting himself and his ethical standards to their lower ethical standards always *only* in form and always *only* temporarily, *never* principially and *never* permanently, and ever moved upon them, by means of the prophetic promise of weal and threat of woe and by his Holy Spirit's power, both to elevate their ethical standards to conform to his own and to raise the level of their ethical and moral expectations of one another.

Given then the fact that God is the Primary Author of both Testaments, we can safely conclude that ultimately there is

---

[35]John Murray, *Principles of Conduct* (Reprint; Grand Rapids: Eerdmans, 1957), 16-17.

[36]James Orr, *The Problem of the Old Testament* (New York: Scribner, 1907), 472-73.

only one biblical ethic in spite of surface appearances to the contrary.

What about Christian intuitionism?

What should be the ultimate norm of ethical behavior in a Christian theistic ethics? Should such an ethic be grounded in an objective norm such as the moral law of God (the Ten Commandments) as the canon of approved behavior? A proposal one often hears is that the renewed consciousness of the Christian has an intuitive sense of what is right and wrong (hence the name Christian intuitionism). Since the heart of the believer is renewed after the image of God in knowledge, righteousness, and holiness, the renewed person will spontaneously respond in the only way that bespeaks the divine exemplar after which the heart has been renewed. Of course, since the same renewal occurs over time in the hearts of a great number of individuals, which renewal dictates similar responses to similar situations, these common responses produce a moral "convention" that can and has become codified and systematized. If there are any objective norms of acceptable behavior, this is the explanation for their appearance. That is to say, they are human conventions that flow out of the renewed spirit, not objective norms revealed by God that exist objectively prior to the *palingenesis* to which the renewed spirit must give heed. In sum, the renewed heart does not require objective laws in order to know what to do or not to do.

A Christian theistic response

There is a surface appearance of truth in this position on two grounds: (1) Paul does teach that even in the hearts of those who have never received special revelation the works of the law are written so that Gentiles (sometimes) do by nature[37] the things of the law (Rom. 2:14-15). How much more significant, powerful,

---

[37]Paul is very careful not to say that Gentiles *always* conform to the demands of the law. He says: "*When* Gentiles…do by nature things required by the law…."

and intuitive then should we assume that inner inscription of the law to be in the hearts of those who have been regenerated. (2) Moreover, the requirements of the entire law admittedly are fulfilled in the outflowing of one's love toward God and his neighbor (Matt. 22:37-40). It would seem to follow then that to the extent to which love governs one, just to that same extent he fulfills the demands of the biblical ethic, and where love is perfected, there ethical behavior is perfected. It could be argued then that the intuited "readings" of love's dictates are all the "norms" that one needs in order to have a Christian ethic.

At this point I want to insist that the "law written inwardly" and the outflow of love toward God and one's neighbor that springs naturally from every renewed heart do not do away with the need for objective norms for approved behavior. I say this for the following reasons.

With respect to the first of these two points (the fact of the "law written inwardly"), the first question that must be addressed is whether natural law theory is sufficient to ground ethical behavior. Natural law theory contends that "there is, by the very virtue of human nature, an order or a disposition which human reason can discover.... The unwritten law, or Natural Law, is nothing more than that" (J. Maritain). This law of nature is considered superior to the statutes of the state; it is a norm for civil legislation; and a state is under obligation to confine its legislation within the limits prescribed by nature. But can human reason discover in human nature an order of morality that sets the norms for statutory law? Are Thomas Jefferson's "unalienable rights" self-evident? (He himself owned slaves, and the United States Constitution, as originally written, did not recognize slaves as persons.) Can limitations on governments, can the protection of minorities against majority action, can individual rights and liberties all be maintained on natural law? Can these things all be maintained by an observation of nature?

It is interesting to note that political theorists who were untouched by Christian revelation, almost without exception advocated some form of totalitarianism. If Plato was a communist,

Aristotle was a fascist. Private parental education was to be forbidden because education has as its aim the production of citizens for the good of the state. The number of children a family may have was to be controlled by the government, and surplus children were to be fed to the wolves. And everybody must profess the state religion. Jean Jacques Rousseau is equally totalitarian: "There is therefore a purely civil profession of faith of which the Sovereign should fix the articles...," he writes. "If anyone, after recognizing these dogmas, behaves as if he does not believe them, let him be punished by death." If individual liberties were as self-evident as Jefferson supposed, would not Rousseau have recognized them? If they can be learned by nature, would Aristotle have missed them? And in any case, would there not be a fairly widespread agreement on what these laws are in detail? Aquinas argued that all things to which men have a natural inclination are naturally apprehended by reason as being good, but Duns Scotus replied that this leaves no method for determining whether an inclination is natural or unnatural. Hume, in his criticism, based upon the existence of injustices in the world, of the argument for God's existence, throws doubt on the theory and demonstrates the difficulty, or rather the impossibility, of discovering by human reason any perfect justice in nature.

Now no orthodox Christian wants to deny that God at creation wrote the basic moral law on man's heart and that remnants of that law still remain stamped on human nature. But man fell into sin, corrupting his entire psyche thereby, and even though conscience still acts after a fashion, experiences of guilt occur too infrequently and self-commendation occurs all too frequently, and both are often improperly assigned (Clark). Caesar, Napoleon, and Stalin took pride in their crimes, and looking carefully at nature and seeing it red in tooth and claw, they could conclude that the universe is indifferent to the fate of the individual and that it is the law of nature for the brutal to rule the meek. There is evidence on every hand in nature of inclinations for domination and a will to power.

These brief considerations indicate that the theory of natural law is not a satisfactory theoretical defense of minority or individual rights. Human observation of nature (that includes the behavior of men), leads more naturally to totalitarian conclusions than to anything else other than anarchy. When, therefore, natural law advocates try to deduce normative conclusions from descriptive premises they commit a major logical blunder, for no matter how carefully or how intricately one describes what men do, or what the provisions of nature are, or how natural inclinations function, it is a logical impossibility to conclude that this is or is not what men ought to do. The moral *is* never implies the ethical *ought*. When the Thomist argues that it is a natural law to seek what is good because as a matter of fact everybody seeks what is good, he reduces the term good to the several objects of human desire, which is hardly the biblical definition of the good. When he further states: "No one calls in doubt the need for doing good, avoiding evil, acquiring knowledge, dispelling ignorance,"[38] he simply shuts his eyes to the massacre of the Huguenots and the massacre of the Covenanters by the Catholic Stuarts, Nietzsche's "will to power," the beatniks, the Mafia, the tribes of the Congo, and Stalin and his Communist regime.

I recognize, of course, that what I have been describing is the attitudes and actions, by and large, of the unregenerate heart and of fallen men in general. And has not the regenerate heart been delivered from sin's mastery? Of course it has. But does it follow that the regenerate heart instinctively knows, in its regenerate state, what to do? Those who think so must not merely assert the fact; they must demonstrate it to be so.

I would urge that the thought of the passages where the law is said to be written on the heart of the renewed person (Jer. 31:33; Heb. 8:10; 10:16) is not that we come to know what the law is by reading the inscription upon the heart. The thought is rather that there is generated in the sinful heart a new affinity with and

---

[38]Etienne Gilson, *The Christian Philosophy of St. Thomas Aquinas* (New York: Random House, 1956), 329.

a love for the law of God to the end that it may be cheerfully and spontaneously fulfilled. Surely Adam in the state of original integrity had the law of God inscribed upon his heart, but "this inscription did not obviate the necessity of God's giving to Adam positive directions respecting the activity that was to engage interest, occupation, and life in this world."[39] Murray continues:

> The procreative mandate, for example, had respect to the exercise of one of his fundamental instincts. Adam as created must have been endowed with the sex impulse which would have sought satisfaction and outlet in the sex act. But he was not left to the dictates of the sex impulse and of the procreative instinct; these were not a sufficient index to God's will for him. The exercise of this instinct was expressly commanded and its exercise directed to the achievement of a well-defined purpose. Furthermore, there was the marital ordinance within which alone the sex act was legitimate.
>
> These original mandates...show unmistakably that native endowment or instinct is not sufficient for man's direction even in the state of original integrity. The exercise of native instincts, the institutions within which they are to be exercised, and the ends to be promoted by their exercise are prescribed by specially revealed commandments. If all this is true in a state of sinless integrity, when there was no sin to blind vision or depravity to pervert desire, how much more must expressly prescribed directions be necessary in a state of sin in which intelligence is blinded, feeling depraved, conscience defiled, and will perverted![40]

With respect to the second argument – that the intuited "readings" of love's dictates are all the "norms" that one needs to develop a Christian ethic – I would say three things: *First*, that while it is true that love is the fulfillment of the law (Matt. 22:37-40; Rom. 13:10), it must never be forgotten that love to God with

---

[39]Murray, *Principles of Conduct*, 25-26; see also Gen. 1:27, 28; 2:2, 3, 15, 24.

[40]Murray, *Principles of Conduct*, 26.

all our heart, soul, mind, and strength and love to our neighbor as ourselves are themselves revealed *commandments*. We are *commanded* to love God and our neighbor. The antithesis often drawn between love as the only proper norm and commands as a sub-Christian norm for biblical ethics overlooks this elementary fact. Love itself is exercised in obedience to the divine command: "Thou shalt love." Love then is not ultimate but is dictated by a divine command that is prior to it. Love is itself obedience to a commandment that comes from a source (namely, God) other than itself, and not to love is sin because it is the transgression of this commandment of God. We do not, by taking refuge in love as the only proper "norm" of biblical ethics, totally escape thereby the norm of law.

I would say, *second*, that while again it is true that Jesus declares that on the two commandments of love hang all the law and the prophets (Matt. 22:37-40) and Paul affirms that love is the fulfillment of the law (Gal. 5:14), these very statements distinguish between love and the law that hangs upon it and between love and the law that love fulfills. In neither case do love and law have the same denotation. Love *per se* is not then the law. Hence there must be content to the law that is not defined by love itself.

I would say, finally, in harmony with the last conclusion, that the consistent witness of Scripture itself is to the effect that love is never allowed to discover or dictate its own standards of conduct. The renewed heart is simply never allowed spontaneously to define the ethic of the saints of God. Never is even the most committed saint permitted to chart for himself the path he would take. And never has the love that is the fulfillment of the law ever existed in a situation that is absent the revelation of God respecting his will. To think so amounts to an abstraction that has never been true of the human experience. Rather, from the beginning, even from the state of innocence, into the New Testament era itself, the norms of human behavior have come in the form of divinely revealed objective precepts and commandments. After setting forth the doctrinal bases for the Christian life, the New Testament letters are filled with ethical imperatives addressed to the Christian mind and heart (see, for example, the extended treatments of ethical behavior in Romans 12–16 and Ephesians 4–6). The conclusion of the matter, then, is that the notion that love is its own law and the renewed consciousness its own monitor is a fantasy that has no warrant from Scripture and runs counter to the entire witness of biblical teaching. The uniform biblical witness is that the Decalogue is the summary covenant norm for all human behavior.

I have said enough to demonstrate that Christian theistic ethics has much to say to fallen mankind in general and much to say to professional ethicists in particular. It alone is able to provide moral guidance, aims and goals for life, and the ground for its ethical predications where secular ethical systems cannot. This alone should warrant its acceptance by thinking men, and this alone provides yet another aspect of Christian apologetics that warrants the conclusion that Christianity is true.

Addendum: Immanuel Kant's "Categorical Imperative"

Because my discussion in this chapter focused primarily on secular ethical theory in the twentieth century, I said nothing directly about Immanuel Kant (1724–1804) whose "Categorical Imperative," developed in his *Critique of Practical Reason*, marked a milestone in humanistic ethics.

Unlike Sidgwick in his utilitarianism and Dewey in his instrumentalism, Kant a century and a half earlier insisted that the morality of any act is entirely independent of actual consequences. In opposition to all empirical ethical theory (because it results in skepticism), Kant argued that moral precept must not be degraded into the hypothetical imperative of prudence or of calculation but is of the nature of an *a priori* categorical imperative, that is to say, one ought to be honest and tell the truth regardless of consequences and apart from any motive such as the obtaining of a good reputation thereby. A moral act must be motivated only by reverence for duty.

Kant had one and only one test of morality. For him the test of any moral law is necessity and universality: *Handle so, dass die Maxime deines Willens jederzeit zugleich als Prinzip einer allgemeinen Gesetzgebung gelten koenne* ("Act in conformity with that maxim and that maxim alone which you can at the same time will to be a universal law.").

Kant's categorical imperative runs into difficulty, however, both as a principle and in its application. Gordon H. Clark points out, with respect to its character as an ideal for determining morality, that

> ...the maxim, "Be a miser," can be universalized; so also "Be a spendthrift." Neither of these requires the agent to be an exception to the general rule; neither is self-destructive. Similarly the maxim, "Commit suicide," contains no self-contradictions. Or, if the maxim applied to children so that the human race would become extinct, in which case suicides would no longer be possible, the maxim can be replaced: "Commit suicide on your forty-fifth birthday." Kant tried his best to show that suicide is immoral, but if he succeeded it is because of an appeal to God and not because of a categorical imperative. Kant's ethics can be saved, then, only by an admission that suicide is right and that a miser and a spendthrift are morally equal.[41]

Kant did appeal to God. In fact, he believed that the transcendental presuppositions of God, immortality, and freedom were necessary for his system of morality and that duty and the categorical imperative particularly depend on freedom. But while he could explain how God and immortality were required (only God can guarantee the coincidence of virtue and happiness; moral progress to the goal of perfection is an infinite process), Kant had more difficulty justifying his presupposition of human freedom since, though certain as he was that his categorical imperative was undeniable and the insurer of human freedom, his *a priori*

---

[41]Gordon H. Clark, "Ethics" in *Essays on Ethics and Politics* (Jefferson, Maryland: Trinity, 1992), 79-80.

category of causality in the mind equally compels men to construct a world in which every temporal event is the effect of a cause. Where then is a place for human freedom?

Kant solved his problem by positing two worlds: the mechanical world of phenomena ("appearances") in which world of pure science there is no freedom and the noumenal world of "things in themselves" in which he placed both the idea of God (not as a constitutive idea, that is, an existent component of the universe, but as a regulative idea or rule of conduct) and the transcendental or noumenal self which, he contended, is free.

But while this removes the formal contradiction, difficulty in understanding how all this applies to individual moral acts still remains. Clark explains:

> Consider a particular act of theft. A man breaks the lock on a door, enters a house, and steals some cash and jewelry. All these actions are physical actions in time and space. Now Kant is adamant. There can be no freedom, he says, for bodies or actions in time; all temporal factors are mechanically determined. Some moralists have tried to preserve freedom by denying that the motions of the theft are physically necessitated, by asserting that they are produced by some sort of psychological causation. The thief is said to be free because he acts according to his own character. Kant calls this theory a wretched subterfuge. Psychological states are as much necessitated as physical motions. Logically, it follows therefore that the theft itself could have been avoided in the higher world, although the motions of the theft could not have been avoided in this world.

In other words, the theft "is a mechanical necessity of the causal world. It is inevitable; it cannot be otherwise; it is devoid of freedom. This, however, is only the appearance or phenomenon of theft. The theft-in-itself, the noumenal theft, could occur only in the noumenal world where we are free. Hence the theft-in-itself could have been avoided, but the appearance of the theft could not have been avoided."[42] Clark continues:

---

[42]Clark, "Immanuel Kant" in *Essays on Ethics and Politics*, 136.

This conclusion is paradoxical, to say the least; and Kant refused to explain it. He wrote: "Reason would…completely transcend its proper limits, if it should undertake to explain how pure reason can be practical, or what is the same thing, to explain how freedom is possible…. While therefore it is true that we cannot comprehend this practical unconditioned necessity of the moral imperative, it is also true that we can comprehend its incomprehensibility; and this is all that can be fairly demanded of a philosophy which seeks to reach the principles which determine the limits of human reason.[43]

We are left then, not with a justifying argument, but only with Kant's mere assertion that his two worlds are the way it is – hardly sufficient ground for the determination of the morality of human actions. We see once again, then, that moral theory grounded in human ratiocination fails to provide the arguments necessary for a theory of ethics worthy of the name. And once again by implication Christian theistic ethics, grounded as it is in divine law, receives full vindication.

---

[43]Clark, "Ethics" in *Essays on Ethics and Politics*, 80-81.

Chapter Thirteen

Faith's Reasons for Believing in the Pauline Apologetic for Reaching This Postmodern Generation

As long as Christianity was a dominant influence in Western culture so that a general Christian consensus prevailed among the populace concerning the nature of truth and values the presuppositional apologetic, presupposing as it did the full truthfulness and trustworthiness of the Bible, was practiced in many quarters of the church. But in light of the fact that this postmodern generation of mankind has for the most part rejected the Bible as God's Word and Christianity's concepts of absolute truth and rationality as essential requisites for the acquisition of knowledge, particularly in the religious realm, and has adopted in their stead the *scientific* approach to the acquisition of truth and values, the church is faced with a new situation. And the questions might be asked, Must not the Christian apologist committed to the presuppositionalist or scripturalist apologetic now modify his approach, if not abandon it altogether, in order to meet the scientific demands of this postmodern world? Must he not at least make some major adjustments in his apologetic methodology and be willing to confront men today with evidentialist arguments that will pass scientific muster if he expects to reach this generation? I would answer these questions with an unqualified "No!" Indeed, I believe that the scripturalist apologetic is as necessary in reaching this postmodern generation as it ever was. In this concluding chapter I will give my reasons for saying this. But as I do so I will also argue that we must be wiser, given the new situation, about how we go about making our case for the truthfulness of Christian theism. I will begin by narrating a story.

For a good many years during my tenure at Covenant Theological Seminary I had the great privilege of knowing and laboring with Dr. Francis Schaeffer, founder of L'Abri ("The Shelter") in Huemoz, Switzerland, as a faculty colleague. Holding adjunct faculty status at Covenant Seminary he came each year and taught for about a month, taking the student body through his understanding of Western culture and how to reach it for Christ. One evening we who were on-site faculty invited Dr. Schaeffer to supper at a local restaurant – the Flaming Pit, if I recall correctly (What a strange place for a bunch of orthodox theologians to gather – the Flaming Pit!). Among other things we chatted about that evening he informed us that after he completed his assignment with us he would be going to Yale University to speak in the chapel there. Sitting directly across from him, I asked: "How did you get that invitation, Dr. Schaeffer?" He informed us that the very active Inter-Varsity Christian Fellowship chapter on campus had gone to the university chaplain, William Sloan Coffin, and had said: "You bring all kinds of kooks to speak to the students in chapel. How about inviting one of our evangelical kooks to speak?" So, he said, Coffin invited him. I then asked Dr. Schaeffer: "You know that you will probably not be invited back any time soon. What are you going to preach?" Ever the teacher Dr.Schaeffer immediately asked me: "What would *you* suggest I preach, Bob?" "I'm not sure," I replied. "How about a sermon on John 3:16?" "No," he said, "the Yale students by and large would not properly understand a thing I said if I did that. They have no frame of reference in which to place the teaching of John 3:16. So I intend to ask them to open their pew Bibles and to turn to Genesis 1. I will read the creation account to them, and inform them who they really are." "Dr. Schaeffer," I declared, "when you announce that text you will be able almost audibly to hear minds clicking off all over that chapel." "Perhaps," Dr. Schaeffer said, "but that's the very reason I have to take them to Genesis 1." "You won't have time to preach the gospel if you do that," I responded. "True," he said, "but the Inter-Varsity chapter can do that after I'm gone. But, Bob, students whose minds have been raped their entire lives by evolutionary teaching, existentialism, and the secular humanism of their public school education, must be reminded about what they already know in their hearts is true about themselves, that they are people created by God in his image, in which fact resides their true worth, who therefore are responsible to him, who therefore make responsible decisions, and who therefore will answer to him someday if they are not living for him. Only when they acknowledge their creaturehood will the 'good news' of John 3:16 mean anything to them." This exchange took place over thirty years ago. If Schaeffer's words were on target then they are even more so today.

D. A. Carson would have concurred with Schaeffer, for in his article, "Athens Revisited," he writes:

> In the recent past, at least in North America and Europe, evangelism consisted of a fairly aggressive presentation of one small part of the Bible's story line. Most non-Christians to whom we presented the gospel shared enough common language and outlook with us that we did not find it necessary to unpack the entire plot line of the Bible. A mere quarter of a century ago, if we were dealing with an atheist, he or she was not a generic atheist but a Christian atheist – that is, the God he or she did not believe in was more or less a god of discernible Judeo-Christian provenance. The atheist was not particularly denying the existence of Hindu gods – Krishna, perhaps – but the God of the Bible. But that meant that the categories were still ours. The domain of discourse was ours.
>
> When I was a child [he continues]…evangelism presupposed that most unbelievers, whether they were atheists or agnostics or deists or theists, nevertheless knew that the Bible begins with God, that this God is both personal and transcendent, that he made the universe and made it good, and that the Fall introduced sin and attracted the curse. Virtually everyone knew that the Bible has two Testaments, [that] history moves in a straight line, [that] there is a difference between good and evil, right and wrong, truth and error, fact and fiction. They knew that Christians believe there is a heaven to be gained and a hell to be feared, [that] Christmas is bound up with

Jesus' birth; Good Friday and Easter, with Jesus' death and resurrection. Those were the givens. So what we pushed in evangelism was the seriousness of sin, the freedom of grace, who Jesus really is, what his death is about, and the urgency of faith and repentance. That was evangelism. ... For most of us, evangelism was connected with the articulating and pressing home of a very small part of the Bible's plot line.[1]

What happened that has changed all this? Why must American evangelical Christians not presume that the generation of people to whom they speak today can be evangelized as in the past? There are several reasons for this but the five most basic reasons are the following:[2]

- The *first* reason is that the Immigration and Naturalization Act of 1965 abolished the earlier quota systems of the Immigration Act of 1924 that had excluded non-westerners from becoming citizens and established new ones, giving significant immigration slots to Asians. This later included Hispanics and Mid-Easterners as well. While nearly 90% of immigrants in the nineteenth century came from Europe and as such still had some semblance of Christianity (Roman Catholicism primarily) about them, from 1981–1990, of the 1,031,620 immigrants who migrated to these shores only 15% were Europeans while 70% of these immigrants were Asians and Mid-Easterners who brought with them their Eastern religions and Islam. In the 1990s 43% of immigrants were Asian and 39% were Hispanic, the latter bringing their corrupt forms of Roman Catholicism with them. Hispanics are now the largest minority in the United States, and there are now more Muslims than Jews in the United States. As a result the United States now has more than 1500 different religions within its borders and the public schools of America

---

[1]D. A. Carson, "Athens Revisited" in *Telling the Truth: Evangelizing Postmoderns*, edited by D. A. Carson (Grand Rapids: Zondervan, 2000), 384-85.

[2]These five reasons apply equally *mutatis mutandis* to Western evangelical Christendom in general.

teach their students that they must be tolerant of all of these religions and not believe that any one of them should be given any special preference or consideration. Immigration has so impacted American life that *today America is the most religiously diverse nation in the world*, with the United States now being as much a mission field as any to which churches now send missionaries.

- The *second* reason is that for a generation now Western students have been fed, and in turn have imbibed, massive doses of scientific naturalism (evolution),[3] philosophical existentialism (the denial of antithetical truth and the acceptance of the relativity of truth[4]), Eastern mysticism (this but not Christianity can be taught in the public schools of America), and broad secular humanism (the toleration of every religious view) in their public schools[5] and at their universities, all this fortified by the sexual revolution of the sixties to the present.

---

[3]Lee Stobel's *The Case for a Creator* (Grand Rapids: Zondervan, 2004) is very helpful in the acquisition of scientific arguments for Intelligent Design.

[4]Christians hold to a "correspondence view of truth" but *not* the classic correspondence view of truth, most famously linked with John Locke, that naturalistic philosophers espouse. These philosophers state that truth is what corresponds to reality. But the question then arises: "Reality as perceived and determined by whom?" And these philosophers answer: "Reality as perceived and determined by man and his sciences!" Thus man becomes the standard of truth and the measure of all things. But we say that truth is that which corresponds to reality *as God defines it*, for just as God is love so also is he the source of all truth. His truth is firmly rooted and grounded in his immutable nature. It is not a construction of men; it is not variable, not relative, and not dependent upon social or cultural conditions. Thus that which God knows and tells us in his Word is the perfect standard of absolute truth.

[5]Christian Smith and Melinda Lundquist Denton, conducting the most comprehensive research ever done on American teenagers (ages 13-17) and their attitude toward religion, state in *Soul Searching: The Religious and Spiritual Lives of American Teenagers* (Oxford: University Press) that today's teenagers generally believe that, while religion is "good for lots of people," it is "not worth fighting about." They consider religion to be of marginal

- The *third* reason is the advent of the internet that has added an entirely new dimension to the way in which information is disseminated, obtained, and processed. The average person tends no longer to feel that he must look to authority figures in his geographic and cultural circle for what he needs or wants to know. If he needs or wants to know something he tends to believe that he can obtain the information for himself from almost an endless choice of internet sources. In short, the average person tends to feel that he is now his own authority.

- The *fourth* reason is the constraints that our nation's highest court has placed on Christian public school teachers who would, if permitted, give religious instruction to their pupils.

- The *fifth* reason is the Evangelical Church's almost total failure to understand what has been going on in these areas for a generation and to erect effectual countermeasures against them. In fact, instead of the church furnishing this generation with Christian soldiers who are "well-taught, sturdy in faith, animated by love for God and man, sophisticated in the ways of the world, the flesh, and the Devil, polished in the manners of genuine Christian brotherhood, overshadowed by the specter of the Last Day, and nerved to deny themselves and to take up their cross so as to accomplish great exploits for Christ and Kingdom" (Robert S. Rayburn) – instead, I say,

---

importance and are inarticulate regarding the content of their faith. According to Smith and Denton: "The *de facto* dominant religion among contemporary U. S. teenagers is what we might well call 'Moralistic Therapeutic Deism,'" the creed of which religion is as follows:

a. A God exists who created and orders the world and watches over human life on earth.
b. God wants people to be good, nice and fair to each other, as taught in the Bible and by most world religions.
c. The central goal of life is to be happy and to feel good about oneself.
d. God does not need to be involved in one's life except when he is needed to resolve a problem.
e. Good people go to heaven when they die.

of the church furnishing such "other-worldly" and resolute Christians who are superbly prepared for spiritual warfare it has for a generation now been hemorrhaging its children into the world, with large numbers of them abandoning the faith in exchange for what the world has to offer. Why this has happened Tom Wolfe's novel, *I am Charlotte Simmons*, documents. It is the story of a brilliant, beautiful, chaste but naïve young woman who leaves her Appalachian Mountain home to obtain an "elite" education at one of America's "finest" universities. His novel, he tells us, is based on research he did at five well-known university campuses (Stanford, Michigan at Ann Arbor, North Carolina at Chapel Hill, Alabama in Huntsville, and Florida at Gainesville), but to concentrate on them would miss Wolfe's point: Choose *any* five secular universities at random and the results will be the same. Wolfe's lurid descriptions are neither a caricature nor fiction but rather reality. His novel documents the pervasive reality of the vileness, vulgarity, and corruption that

"...fills classroom after classroom in both content and style of teaching. It affects the ethics of the faculty. It fills the social life of the students, which for most of them tends to make their academic and intellectual lives irrelevant. The corruption fills the residence halls, whose filth of every kind Mr. Wolfe makes repulsively vivid. The corruption fills the athletic program. It reaches to the nation's politicians who come to speak on campus and the businesses that come to recruit the university's graduates. But mostly the corruption pervades the students themselves – their ambitions, their daily morals, and their language. The young men are so corrupt you don't want a young woman near them. But the young women are so corrupt they are no longer worth protecting or defending...."[6]

As for Charlotte, while her churchgoing mother is satisfied that she had prepared her daughter to confront all this simply by pulling herself together and saying: "I won't believe that. I won't do that. After all, I am Charlotte Simmons. I know who

---

[6]Joel Belz, "Vile and vulgar," *World*, Vol. 21, Num. 24 (June 17, 2006), 3.

I am, and I don't need to go there," we soon discover that "not by a country mile does she have the resources within herself to withstand…all that seeks to corrupt her" – not by half. 'Nuf said! Now, asks Joel Belz,

"…if the contemporary secular university scene is even half as corrosive and Sodom-like as Tom Wolfe portrays it, why is that scene patronized by even a few Christian families, much less by the hundreds and thousands [of Christian parents] who send [their] sons and daughters there to be "educated" by such powerful forces?"

The answer: Because they want their children to be "successful," to get the best jobs, and to make lots of money in order to afford the "good life." Most would be horrified to learn that their child was contemplating Christian service on the mission field.

As a result of these five influences on Western society the church has virtually lost an entire generation of people. The baby boomer generation and many high school and university students today no longer know even the most basic Bible facts such as facts about Abraham, David, Solomon, and Paul, much less Hosea, Zephaniah, or Haggai. Moreover, they are

not clean slates waiting for us to write on them. They are not empty hard drives waiting for us to download our Christian files onto them. Rather, they have inevitably developed an array of alternative worldviews. They are hard drives full of many other files that collectively constitute various non-Christian frames of reference.[7]

They no longer believe that this is a purposeful universe. Rather, they believe that it is a "mysterious universe" filled with chance oddities that could include even a bodily resurrection. They no longer believe that history reflects the Bible's "big picture" or "metanarrative" or that it is "going somewhere." This is true for increasing numbers of contemporary theologians as well, as I stated in my *A New Systematic Theology*:

---

[7]Carson, "Athens Revisited," 386.

The so-called postmodern theologians for some time now have been urging that the church should respect ambiguity and shun all attempts to formulate a synoptic or "systematic" vision of things; in other words, [the church should] acknowledge that there is no predetermined Big Picture of anything to be discovered. Therefore, they say: "Just draw your own Picture for there is no Big Picture to be discovered." Of course, these scholars refuse to recognize that their declamation: "There is no Big Picture," is itself a Big Picture with its own theology, cosmology, anthropology, Christology, soteriology, and eschatology. The problem with their Big Picture, however, is its fragmentation, incoherence, and failure to come to grips even with how the world really works.[8]

The implications for apologetics and evangelism in all this are immense and obvious. Consider three such implications:

First, we must take more seriously than we have in the past the fact that the people we are attempting to reach hold some fundamental positions that they are going to have to abandon in order to become Christians.

To continue [the] computer analogy, they retain numerous files that are going to have to be erased or revised, because as presently written, those files are going to clash formidably with Christian files. [Of course, this has always been true to some extent but not as much as now.] But the less there is of a common, shared worldview between "evangelizer" and "evangelee," between the biblically informed Christian and the biblically illiterate postmodern, the more traumatic the transition, the more decisive the change, the more stuff [that] has to be unlearned.[9]

Second, because this is so, we who would evangelize our generation must be prepared to start farther back with it. Cornelius Van Til correctly observes

---

[8]Robert L. Reymond, *A New Systematic Theology of the Christian Faith* (Second edition; Nashville, TN: Thomas Nelson, 2004), xx, fn. 2.

[9]Carson, "Athens Revisited," 386.

We must set the message of the cross into the framework [of Scripture as a whole]. If we do not do this, then we are not really and fully preaching Jesus and the resurrection. The facts of Jesus and the resurrection are what they are only in the framework of the doctrines of creation, providence and the consummation of history in the final judgment.[10]

The gospel will be incoherent unless certain theological structures are in place that will provide the frame of reference that makes our words sensible. The gospel's larger setting is all-important; it is that which gives meaning to the individual facts. Without its biblical setting the gospel's facts will be chance oddities in "a mysterious universe."

> You cannot make heads or tails of the real Jesus unless you have categories for the personal/transcendent God of the Bible; the nature of human beings made in the image of God; the sheer odium of rebellion against him; the curse that our rebellion has attracted; the spiritual, personal, familial, and social effects of our transgressions; the nature of salvation; the holiness and wrath and love of God. One cannot make sense of the Bible's plot line without such basic ingredients; one cannot make sense of the Bible's portrayal of Jesus without such blocks in place. We cannot possibly agree on the solution that Jesus provides if we cannot agree on the problem he confronts.[11]

This is the reason that one often sees the world responding to the Christian's bumper sticker: "Christ is the Answer," with its own sticker, "What's the question?" That is to say, the world quite simply does not know the plotline within which the Bible places the gospel. Accordingly, the world does not understand why or how Jesus is or can be the answer to anything.

Third, the evangelist must find ways into the hearts, the value systems, and the thought patterns – in sum, the worldviews – of

---

[10]Cornelius Van Til, *Paul at Athens* (pamphlet published by Lewis J. Grotenhuis; Phillipsburg, N. J., n. d.), 13.

[11]Carson, "Athens Revisited," 386.

those being evangelized. He "must find bridges into the…frame of reference [of those being evangelized], or no communication is possible; the evangelist will remain ghettoized."[12]

I should say parenthetically that no one was better at getting into the mind of the postmodern than Francis Schaeffer who, by insisting first that the postmodern live consistently with his worldview, forced him by what he called his pre-evangelistic method to experience and acknowledge the futility and despair inherent within it.

All this the apostle Paul well understood: In a synagogue setting he could and would cite Old Testament passages just as we today can still cite Scripture to non-Christian members of the older generation, but in Acts 17:16-34 we find him evangelizing intellectual people who were completely biblically illiterate. In the latter case he evangelized differently – remarkably so – and this passage has much to teach us as we attempt to evangelize this generation of biblical illiterates. Indeed, one would not be far from the truth, in my opinion, were he to conclude that the Holy Spirit led Luke to record Paul's *Areopagitica*, that is, Paul's address on Mars' Hill, in his Acts for just such a time as this! So I intend to spend some time considering his address with you now.

In Athens Paul became "greatly distressed to see that the city was full of idols." Indeed, Athens was so full of sculpted statues of the Greek pantheon that one ancient writer said there were more statues of the gods in Athens than in all the rest of Greece put together. Petronius, the Roman satirist, said it was easier to meet a statue there than a man.[13] They had even erected altars to an "unknown god" (*agnōstō theō*) (Acts 17:23), which altars they doubtless intended as expressions of religious *devotion* but which Paul more correctly perceived, as these altars acknowledged, as acts of religious *ignorance*.

If Paul entered the city from the south through the Piraeic gate leading to the harbor, he would have been confronted

---

[12]Carson, "Athens Revisited," 387.

[13]See the excursus on Athens in my *Paul, Missionary Theologian* (Ross-shire, Scotland: Mentor, 2000), 159-61.

immediately with the sculpture of Neptune seated on a horse
and hurling his trident. Nearby was the Temple of Ceres
within which stood the sculptured forms of Minerva, Jupiter,
and Apollo, with statues of Mercury and the Muses near a
sanctuary to Bacchus. Entering the Agora, the center of the
city's public life, that contained statues dedicated to Apollo,
the patron deity of the city, and the Altar of the Twelve Gods
(Zeus, Hera, Poseidon, Hades, Apollo, Artemis, Hephaestus,
Athena, Ares, Aphrodite, Hermes, and Hestia), Paul would
have seen the craggy promontory of the Areopagus to the north
on which rested the Temple to Mars, and looking toward the
east he would have seen the Acropolis on the rising ledges of
which were shrines to Bacchus, Aesculapius, Venus, Earth, and
Ceres, ending with the Temple of Unwinged Victory. On the
Acropolis itself, the whole of which was one vast composition
of architecture and sculptures dedicated to the nation's glory
and the worship of its gods, stood the Temple of Victory that
contained statues of Venus and the Graces. It also housed an
edifice dedicated to Minerva and a shrine to the goddess Diana.
Also sculptures could be found there of Theseus, Hercules, and
Earth. Of course, the most magnificent edifice of all on top of the
Acropolis was the Parthenon ("the Virgin's House") dedicated
to Minerva. A colossal statue of this goddess in ivory and gold
stood within its columns. Two other statues of Minerva stood
in the temple precincts, the most venerated of the three statues
called the *Erectheium* while the *Minerva Promachus* with spear
and shield rose in gigantic proportions above all the buildings
of the Acropolis as the tutelary divinity of Athens and Attica.
Paul would also have observed that every public building in
the Agora itself was a sanctuary for some god or goddess. The
Record House was a temple of the Mother of the Gods and the
Council House enshrined statues of Apollo and Jupiter and an
altar to Vesta. The theater was consecrated to Bacchus, and
altars were erected everywhere to the gods of Fame, Modesty,
Energy, Persuasion, Pity, along with altars, as I just said, even
to an "unknown god."

Paul would also have known that Athens occupied the chief place among the cities of the ancient world for great philosophers. It was the native city of Socrates and Plato and the adopted home of Aristotle. So while Paul first evangelized Athens' Jews and God-fearing Gentiles who would have known something about the Old Testament (17:17a), he realized that he was dealing in the main in Athens with biblically illiterate people who had various and competing religious worldviews. Two such worldviews are mentioned in Acts 17:18: Epicureanism and Stoicism. The ideal of the Epicurean worldview was an undisturbed life. The Epicureans taught that the chief end of life is pleasure, the highest of such pleasure being a life of tranquility free from pain, disturbing passions, and superstitious fears, including the fear of death. They did not deny the existence of the Greek pantheon; indeed, they believed in the Greek gods as "blessed and immortal beings." But they maintained that the gods took no interest in the affairs of men. The Stoics taught a pantheistic religious materialism: all that was real, including the gods, was material. They aimed at a life consistent with nature, their over-arching question being: "How can the wise man live in harmony with nature?" The life lived in harmony with nature is the life lived rationally, they taught, which life also included accepting one's fate from the gods that was inevitable anyway. The virtuous life, according to them, was the only absolute "good." All else, including health, wealth, beauty, even life and death, was termed "indifferent" because such things made no difference to virtue or to happiness. They laid great stress on the primacy of man's rational faculty and on the individual's self-centered pursuit of "virtue" which emphasis, though marked by great moral earnestness and a high sense of duty, was marked also by great spiritual pride. This pride displayed itself in the comment of some of the Athenian philosophers that Paul was just a *spermologos*, translated by the NIV as "babbler" but meaning literally "seed picker," that is, a "gutter sparrow," one who picks up and retails scraps of information for money. Others thought, because he preached about "Jesus and the resurrection," that he was advocating "strange divinities" (*zenōn daimoniōn*). In the latter case, since the word "divinities" is in the plural, these Greek thinkers may have associated *Iēsous* ("Jesus"), the Greek transliteration of the Hebrew proper name *Yᵉhōshua*ʿ (Joshua), with *iasis* ("healing") and *Iēsō*, the Ionic form of the name of the goddess of health, and the noun *anastasis* ("resurrection"), because it is a feminine noun, with Jesus' paramour or consort. If so, they may have viewed the expression "Jesus and the resurrection" as denoting the personified and deified powers of "healing" and "restoration."[14] So they brought Paul to a meeting of the Areopagus, the town council that owed its name to the fact that in antiquity it had convened on "Mars' Hill" but in Roman times it met mainly in the Royal Portico in the Agora. There they requested that Paul tell them more about this "new teaching" and these "strange ideas" (Acts 17:18-21), not because they had any interest in the gospel as such but because, as Luke notes: "All the Athenians and the foreigners who live there spent their time doing nothing but talking about and listening to the latest ideas" (Acts 17:21).

Being not only a Christian apostle but also a *Jewish* Christian apostle, Paul was not impressed by Athens' reputation as the Oxford or Harvard of the ancient world. Rather, he was horrified by the city's terrible idolatry! So he "reasoned in the marketplace day by day with those who happened to be there," most if not all of whom would have been biblical illiterates. He did not wait for the city fathers to invite him to do so. He simply got on with his evangelistic labors, and the Areopagus invitation came as a result. Paul's priorities included then, first, a God-centered cultural analysis (he saw Athens not as a city of great learning but as a city wholly given over to idolatry and in great spiritual need), and second, a persistent evangelism of both biblical literates and biblical illiterates in that order (see Rom. 1:16).[15]

---

[14]See F. C. Chase, *The Credibility of Acts* (London: Macmillan, 1902), 205ff.

[15]Carson, "Athens Revisited," 390-91.

Paul delivered his *Areopagitica* before these biblically illiterate philosophers in terms they could understand. Carson notes: "It has often been shown that many of the expressions in this address, especially in the early parts, are the sorts of things one would have found in Stoic circles... In other words, the vocabulary is linguistically appropriate to his hearers."[16] His *Anknüpfungspunct* – Don't you love German words? – that is, his "point of contact," with them was the city's altars that had the inscription: "To an unknown god." *This* deity whom they acknowledged they worshiped in ignorance, Paul said, "I am going to proclaim to you." How could these philosophers object to that? Their own altars acknowledged that they did not know all of the gods, so they had to be open to learning about Paul's God. In his masterful theological summary of the plot line of biblical history that followed, presented with evangelistic and apologetic sensitivity, Paul contextualized the following ten truths of revelation without ever citing the Hebrew Scriptures in so many words:[17]

First, Paul declared that the God about whom they acknowledged they were ignorant is the Creator of "the world and everything in it" (17:24). This means that God is other than the created order, ruling out Stoicism's pantheism. God's creatorship also established the basis of human responsibility: Man owes his Creator everything, and to defy him and to set oneself up as the center of the universe is the heart of sin. Worse, to cherish and worship anything in the creation instead of the Creator is the essence of idolatry.

Second, Paul declared that the Creator God was "the Lord of heaven and earth and does not live in temples made with hands (17:24). He is sovereign over everything; he cannot be assigned to any lesser domain such as the sea (Neptune). "He cannot be domesticated – not even by temples" (Carson).

Third, the Creator God is *a se*, that is, "from himself" or "self-existent": "He is not served by human hands, as if he needed

---

[16]Carson, "Athens Revisited," 392.
[17]Here I am following Carson's outline in the main.

anything" (17:25). This means that he is dependent upon nothing outside of himself for his existence; God does not need man for anything. This grounds his doctrine of divine providence that he later explicated in Acts 17:26-28.

Fourth, while this God, the living and true triune God, does not need us, just the opposite is true for mankind: We are utterly dependent upon him for "he himself gives all men life and breath and everything else" (17:25b). This fact strips mankind of its vaunted independence.

I pause here to ask a question: How would Paul's teaching about this Creator God have struck the Greek mind? Well, his teaching would have been totally foreign to it, convinced as the Greeks were of the eternality of form and matter. Gordon H. Clark states:

> Even those [philosophers] who eventually came to the notion of an incorporeal reality never thought of reducing the multiplicity of the universe to the creative act of an almighty, personal God. *This Hebraic concept was first introduced into the Greco-Roman civilization by the spread of Christianity.* Of course, the Greeks thought of gods; in fact, Thales is reported to have said that all things are full of gods; but these gods, sometimes scientifically but unhistorically interpreted as personifications of natural powers, were corporeal beings who like other hylozoistic persons had come into existence through natural processes. They were not eternal, but had been born; they could be overthrown and possibly destroyed. *The idea of Almighty God was entirely foreign to the Greeks. All the more so was the concept of creation. That an Almighty God could call the world into being from nothing was not a thesis that they had rejected; it was something they had never thought of. Creation is an idea found only in Hebrew thought.*[18]

So clearly Paul was not "trimming his doctrinal sails" to fit the worldview of his "foolish" auditors. Quite plainly he was confronting them with *his* Hebrew/Christian worldview.

---

[18]Gordon H. Clark, *Thales to Dewey* (Reprint; Grand Rapids: Baker, 1980), 14-15.

Fifth, turning to the area of anthropology, Paul asserted that all nations descended from one man (7:26). It was important for Paul to stress the unity of the race through natural descent from the first man because his gospel addressed a problem that was universal – universal because the first man introduced sin and death into the entire race (see Rom. 5:12-19).

Sixth, Paul then intimated, without saying so in so many words, that something was terribly wrong in the universe that God has created. His providential rule now had as one of its purposes that men would reach out for him and find him (17:27), the implication being that, unlike the "ox who knows his master, the donkey, his owner's manger" (Isa. 1:3), the human race as a whole – not just the Athenians – did not know the God who created it. Something had gone profoundly wrong.

Seventh, while it was very important that Paul should establish God's transcendence, it was equally important that he should establish God's immanence. Paul did not want these people to think for a moment that the transcendent God is indifferent to men's needs. So Paul declared: "He is not far from any of us." "We live and move and have our being in him, and we are his offspring."

Eighth, all this being so, Paul then implied that sin is essentially idolatry – the worship of anyone or anything other than this God – and went on to make idolatry utterly reprehensible (17:29). Upon this theology, this anthropology, this hamartiology, Paul grounded mankind's problem. He knew he could not introduce Jesus as mankind's Savior to them until he had established what mankind's real condition was. He knew that his gospel was "good news" only against the backdrop of the bad news of universal sin from which Jesus alone can rescue us.

Ninth, Paul then introduced his philosophy of history or time, the so-called "fourth dimension." Against Greek thought in general that history or time was cyclical, just going around and around and nowhere in particular forever, he stressed that earth history was linear, that is, that it had a beginning, that a long period of time had elapsed during which "God overlooked man's ignorance" of him – the ignorance that the Athenians had expressed in their altars' inscriptions to him – in the sense that he had done very little in a *direct* way to missionarize the nations during Old Testament times (17:30),[19] and that mankind is on its way to a future Final Judgment because of its idolatry.

Tenth, Paul then drove his ninth point home by informing the Athenian *intelligentsia* that while God permitted men in times past to remain in ignorance he *now* commands all men everywhere to repent. Why this change in God's dealings with mankind *now*? Paul's "now" obviously rested both upon the stupendous fact that Jesus Christ, God's Messiah, had in their generation come into the world and upon the "good news" embodied in him that he was explaining to them at that very moment. God *now* commands men to repent, declared Paul, because he has fixed a day in which he will judge the world in righteousness by that man whom he has chosen, and he has given proof of this fact by raising that man from the dead!

When and because Paul asserted that God had raised Jesus bodily from the dead the council immediately stopped him. Against their own claim to openness they could take no more of this. This means that we do not have Paul's address in completion. Some sneered at what he had to say, others more politely said that they would invite him to speak to them again sometime, but some immediately followed him away from that venue to whom he doubtless completed his sermon and who then believed as a result.

This then is the worldview that Paul presented to these philosophers. He did not do this simply for the pleasure of creating a worldview. He did so in order to provide the only framework within which Jesus' cross work makes sense. And

---

[19]See also Acts 14:16-17a: "In the past, he let all nations go their own way. Yet he has not left himself without testimony," and Ephesians 2:12-13: The Gentiles of the Old Testament age, Paul declares, were "excluded from citizenship in Israel and [were] foreigners to the covenants of the promise, without hope and without God in the world…[and] were far away" from these blessings.

it is highly important that Christians recognize that, without any accommodation of his message to what these thinkers were prepared to believe, he confronted the "foolish" errors of Greek thought directly at crucial points. He taught the doctrine of creation over against the eternality of form and matter; he taught divine providence – that his God was in control of all things – over against human freedom; he taught man's sinfulness and the truth that God would someday punish it; he taught that history had a beginning and was linearly moving toward the Last Judgment over against their cyclical view of history; he taught that God raised Jesus bodily from the dead over against the view that matter was evil; and he taught the need for men to repent and to turn to God; and he taught all this without citing in so many words *one* Bible verse. But what he did do was to set forth the larger biblical metanarrative within which alone the gospel story makes sense.

Now it is very important to see that Paul laid out the biblical metanarrative *before* he introduced Jesus. And we must be prepared to do the same in our apologetic approach to this postmodern generation, sensitively and winsomely, but with no compromise of the biblical story and its gospel doctrine. This is precisely what Schaeffer was doing when he preached to the Yale students about God as their Creator, terming his approach "pre-evangelism." I prefer to designate this approach "scripturalistic evangelism," or with Carson, simply "worldview evangelism." Carson explains:

> If metaphysics is a sort of big physics that explains all the other branches of physics, similarly metanarrative is the big story that explains all the other stories…what Paul provides is the biblical metanarrative. This is the big story in the Bible that frames and explains all the little stories. Without this big story, the accounts of Jesus will not make any sense – and Paul knew it…without the big story, without the metanarrative, the little story [in the Bible about Jesus' cross work and resurrection]…becomes either incoherent or positively misleading. Paul understood this point.

...What is striking is that Paul does not flinch from affirming the resurrection of Jesus from the dead. And that is what causes so much offense that Paul is cut off, and the Areopagus address comes to an end. Paul was thoroughly aware, of course, that most Greeks adopted some form of dualism. Matter is bad, or at least relatively bad; spirit is good. To imagine someone coming back from the dead in bodily form was not saying anything desirable, still less believable. Bodily resurrection from the dead was irrational.... So some of Paul's hearers have had enough, and they openly sneer and end the meeting (v. 32). If Paul had spoken instead of Jesus' immortality, his eternal spiritual longevity quite apart from any body, he would have caused no umbrage. But Paul does not flinch. Elsewhere he argues that if Christ has not been raised from the dead, then the apostles are liars, and we are still dead in our trespasses and sins (1 Cor. 15). He remains faithful to that vision here. Paul does not trim the gospel to make it acceptable to the worldview of his listeners.

For Paul, then, there is some irreducible and nonnegotiable content to the gospel, content that must not be abandoned, no matter how unacceptable it is to some other worldview. It follows that especially when we are trying hard to connect wisely with some worldview other than our own, we must give no less careful attention to the nonnegotiables of the gospel, lest in our effort to communicate wisely and with relevance, we unwittingly sacrifice what we mean to communicate.[20]

In his *Areopagitica* Paul employed the truth of Jesus' bodily resurrection from the dead as the "doorway" into the gospel although his auditors in this case "slammed the door" – not on Paul but really on themselves – before they walked through it. Was Paul's choice of "doorways" an anomaly? A survey of the sermons in Acts 2:14-39; 3:13-26; 4:10-12; 5:30-32; 10:36-43; 13:17-41; 17:22-31 and the teachings in the New Testament letters (Rom. 1:2-4; 2:16; 8:34; 9:5; 10:8-9; 1 Cor. 15:3-4) make it clear that Paul's use of Jesus' bodily resurrection as the "doorway" into the gospel was not an anomaly at

---

[20]Carson, "Athens Revisited," 394-96.

all. He used it for its shock value! Indeed, the stress in the primitive *kērugma* ("proclamation") was *always on Christ's bodily resurrection from the dead.* In none of these recorded preachments does the preacher stop to elucidate for his auditors the saving significance of the death of Christ. Rather, they all stress that God reversed the verdict of men by raising bodily from the dead a certain man – even Jesus of Nazareth – who had been crucified as a criminal by the Roman authorities at the instigation of the Jewish Sanhedrin. As Wilbur M. Smith asserts: "The Book of Acts testifies to the fact that it was by the preaching of the resurrection of Christ [not the cross, that] the world was turned upside down."[21] More accurately, as I said earlier in Chapter Four but it bears repeating, it was the *implications* that the Apostles drew from that momentous event that stirred the first-century Roman world to its very roots, namely, that

- Christ's bodily resurrection from the dead showed him to be divine (Rom. 1:3-4);[22]

- Christ's bodily resurrection from the dead was the means to his enthronement in heaven as the Lord of men (Acts 2:36; 10:42);

- Christ's bodily resurrection from the dead showed him to be the only Savior of men (Acts 4:12) and by implication gave

---

[21]Wilbur M. Smith, "Resurrection" in *Baker's Dictionary of Theology* (Grand Rapids: Baker, 1960), 453. I gave this data in the chapter on the bodily resurrection of Christ but it bears repeating: In Luke's Acts Christ's "blood" is mentioned once and that to the Ephesian elders (20:28). The fact that Christ was "killed" is mentioned only once (3:15). The fact that he was "crucified" is mentioned twice (2:36; 4:10). The "tree" upon which he died is mentioned three times (5:30; 10:39; 13:29) while his "cross" is not mentioned at all! But his "resurrection" is mentioned ten times. The fact that he had been bodily "raised" from the dead is mentioned fourteen times. And the apostolic witness to the fact of his bodily resurrection is mentioned ten times. The emphasis in the primitive *kērugma* is clearly on the fact of Christ's bodily resurrection from the dead and its implications.

[22]See my exposition of this passage in my *Jesus, Divine Messiah: the New and Old Testament Witness* (Ross-shire, Scotland: Mentor, 2003), 372-84.

evidence that all the other religions of the world are false and
unworthy of men's devotion;

- Christ's bodily resurrection from the dead showed that
  God had set his seal of approval on Christ's atoning work
  (Rom. 4:25; Heb. 24-25);

- Christ's bodily resurrection from the dead made him the
  true "temple site" at which men are to find and worship God
  (John 2:19, 21; Mark 14:58);

- Christ's bodily resurrection from the dead is a necessary
  aspect of the faith that saves sinners (Rom. 10:9);

- Christ's bodily resurrection from the dead assures Christians
  of the truthfulness of his teaching (Matt. 16:21) and becomes
  their encouragement to be faithful to him when persecuted
  for their faith (2 Tim. 2:8);

- Christ's bodily resurrection from the dead, as the "first-fruits of
  those who sleep," assures both Christians and by implication
  all other people that the eschatological resurrection of the
  dead has already begun and therefore that someday they too
  will be raised bodily from death, some to weal and some to
  woe (John 5:28-29; Acts 24:15; Rom. 8:19ff.; 1 Cor. 15:20ff.;
  1 Thess. 4:14; 1 Pet. 1:3-4);

- Christ's bodily resurrection from the dead and subsequent
  ascension to Lordship has established him as the Judge of
  all men (Acts 17:31); and

- The church was to celebrate the fact of Christ's bodily
  resurrection from the dead by assembling together every first
  day of the week throughout the year until the end of the world!
  The church must never allow mankind to forget the reason for
  the shift of the Sabbath from the seventh to the first day.

You see, while one might legitimately remain unimpressed
by the announcement that someone claiming to be the Jewish

Messiah had been crucified on a Roman cross since thousands of people had so died, one cannot remain neutral regarding the announcement that God had raised this Jesus bodily from the dead. One cannot yawn and say, "How nice," and shake the apologist's hand and turn away with impunity! Christ's resurrection was a miracle! It either occurred or it did not occur! There is no room for neutrality here! This aspect of the primitive proclamation arrested the hearer's attention and demanded that he submit to Christianity's truthfulness. If he rejected it, he did so at the peril of his soul for he was denying the exalted Lord who would someday judge him. If he accepted it he was in the process of turning to the only Savior of mankind who had died for his sins. And when Paul explained that "good news" to him he explained it, I would submit, in terms of justification by faith alone!

Some Bible students, basing their opinion upon Paul's later statement in 1 Corinthians 2:2, "I resolved to know nothing while I was with you [Corinthians] except Jesus Christ and him crucified," argue that he concluded from his "poor showing" in Athens that his mission strategy there had been unwise, and they therefore contend that Paul's entire approach in the *Areopagitica* was a mistake, that he had substituted a "natural theology" for gospel theology and a "theology of glory" for the "theology of the cross," that he goofed when he set forth the Bible's metanarrative before he "preached Jesus," and that he should have stuck with simply "preaching Jesus." Merrill C. Tenney, former dean of the graduate school at Wheaton College, for example, comments: "...the unusual dismissal which Athens gave him unnerved him and caused him to rethink his whole procedure in apologetics."[23] But Paul's *Areopagitica* had not compromised in any way the gospel and his stated resolve in

---

[23]Merrill C. Tenney, *New Testament Survey* (Grand Rapids: Eerdmans, 1961), 287. See also William M. Ramsay in his *St. Paul, The Traveller and the Roman Citizen* (New York: G. P. Putnam's Sons, 1896), 252, and Jack Finegan in his *Light from the Ancient Past* (Princeton: University Press, 1959), 358.

1 Corinthians 2:2 he did *not* intend as a mid-course correction that he planned to make to his ministry to correct a perceived earlier failure on his part at Athens. F. F. Bruce, with rich insight, declares:

> At Athens, as formerly at Lystra, the Paul of Acts does not expressly quote Old Testament prophecies which would be quite unknown to his audience.... But he does not argue from "first principles" of the kind that formed the basis of various systems of Greek philosophy; [rather,] his exposition and defence of his message are founded on the biblical revelation and they echo the thought, and at times the very language, of the Old Testament writings. Like the biblical revelation itself, his speech begins with God the creator of all, continues with God the sustainer of all, and concludes with God the judge of all [all three concepts being offensive to the Greek mind – RLR].[24]

Besides, what is the evidence that Paul's *Areopagitica* resulted in a "poor showing"? Luke does not say in Acts 17:34 that only a "few" people believed. He says rather that "certain people, following [Paul], believed," naming two of them specifically (Dionysius and Damaris) apparently because of their civil importance, and then he informs us that there were "others *with them.*" We simply have no way of knowing what percentage of the audience this number represented. Finally, when one bears in mind, first, that Paul's address was interrupted by the Council when he mentioned the resurrection of Jesus so that what Luke reported of it in Acts is not all that Paul would have said if he had been allowed to continue (and we know from what he proclaimed elsewhere what he would have said if he had been allowed to continue), and second, that Paul "by this time was no novice in Gentile evangelization, experimenting with this approach and that to discover what was effective,"[25] Paul will have been

---

[24]F. F. Bruce, *Paul: Apostle of the Heart Set Free* (Grand Rapids: Eerdmans, 1996), 239.

[25]Bruce, *Paul: Apostle of the Heart Set Free*, 246.

sufficiently absolved of any and all missiological wrongdoing in the eyes of all but his most antagonistic interpreters.

Developing for biblical illiterates the Bible's historical metanarrative does not make matters more complicated for them; to the contrary, it makes the meaning and intention of the "lesser narrative" of the gospel clearer to them. Developing for biblical illiterates the Bible's historical metanarrative makes it evident that the gospel also has content about the *historical* Jesus and what he said and did that must be taken seriously. Developing for biblical illiterates the Bible's historical metanarrative goes a long way in determining the *direction* the discussion will take between the evangelist and the "evangelee." And developing for biblical illiterates the Bible's historical metanarrative will enable the evangelee to understand better the gospel's truthfulness, relevance, beauty, and life-changing power.[26] In sum, while *we will never improve on telling men what God tells us to tell them*, namely, that they are his creatures, that they stand under his condemnation because of their sins against him, that God himself has provided mankind a way to escape his wrath, which is grounded in the cross work of his divine Son, Jesus Christ our Lord, and that by believing in him one is "freed from everything from which [he] could not be freed" (Acts 13:39) in any other way, we must be wise and therefore willing today, as was Paul in his day, to place that message, when necessary, without compromising that message, within the metanarrative of Scripture as a whole.

May God help us all more wisely to evangelize this generation by providing by our witness, when necessary, the metanarrative that alone gives the gospel of Jesus its meaning. And may this be done as well on the mission fields of the world as the church seeks there to fulfill its Lord's Great Commission.

---

[26]These thoughts are from Carson, "Athens Revisited," 398.

Epilogue

In 1962 Cornelius Van Til was a visiting professor at Fuller Theological Seminary where I took two courses from him. In his opening comments in the very first class (it was supposed to be a course in systematic theology but it quickly became a course in apologetics, a shift that all of his students know well), he declared that he wanted to accomplish basically one goal by his instruction and that was to challenge us to become "epistemologically self-conscious" in all our thinking and in all our predications. What did he mean? We quickly learned that he meant that he wanted us to learn "to think things whole and to think things through" *in the light of who we were by grace*, namely, the Christians that we were by grace. That is to say, he wanted us as Christians to learn to think *as Christians* and he wanted us never to think in any other way. This is essentially what I have tried to do in this book and what I have been urging you my readers also to do.

Accordingly, when it comes to the theology that Holy Scripture teaches, I believe that the Reformed Faith with its five great *solas*, as set forth in the Reformed creeds, is the most consistent expression of biblical Christianity ever confessed by sinful men. And I believe the need of the hour is both a method of communicating that Faith to a fallen world and an apologetic method of defending that Faith that are consistent with that Faith. I also believe that when the Reformed Faith is properly communicated it will in the same process be properly defended, and when it is properly defended it will in the same process be properly communicated. This is due to the fact that, conceived as it is in the foregoing pages, both the proclamation and the defense of the Reformed Faith take seriously all that the self-attesting Scriptures declare concerning the nature of fallen man. The Bible teaches that

- "the wickedness of [antediluvian man] was great on the earth, and that every intention of the thoughts of his heart was only evil continually" (Gen. 6:5);

- mankind "drinks iniquity like water" (Job 15:16);

- Foolish men (the Bible's description of every man outside of Christ) "are corrupt, their deeds are vile; there is no one who does good. The Lord looks down from heaven on the sons of men to see if there are any who understand, any who seek God. All have turned aside, they have together become corrupt; there is no one who does good, not even one" (Ps. 14:1-3);

- every person is "conceived and born in iniquity" (Ps. 51:5);

- "...the wicked are estranged [from God] from the womb; they go astray from birth, speaking lies. They have venom like the venom of a serpent, like the deaf adder that stops its ear" (Ps. 58:3-4);

- "No one living is righteous before you" (Ps. 143:2);

- "There is not a righteous man on earth who does what is right and never sins" (Eccles. 7:20);

- "...there is no one who does not sin" against God (1 Kings 8:46);

- "The heart is deceitful above all things and beyond [human] cure" (Jer. 17:9);

- mankind is "filled with all manner of unrighteousness, evil, covetousness, malice. They are full of envy, murder, strife, deceit, maliciousness. They are gossips, slanderers, haters of God, insolent, haughty, boastful, inventors of evil, disobedient to parents, foolish, faithless, heartless, ruthless. Though they know God's decree that those who practice such things deserve to die, they not only do them but give approval to those who practice them" (Rom. 1:29-32);

- all mankind, excluding Jesus Christ, sinned in Adam and are born corrupt (Rom. 5:12-20);

- the Ephesian Christians had been "dead in the trespasses and sins in which you once walked, following the course of this world, following the prince of the power of the air, the spirit that is now at work in the sons of disobedience – among whom we all once lived in the passions of our flesh, carrying out the desires of the body and the mind, and were by nature children of wrath, like the rest of mankind" (Eph. 2:1-3);

- the nations "walk...in the futility of their minds. They are darkened in their understanding, alienated from the life of God because of the ignorance that is in them, due to their hardness of heart. They have become callous and have given themselves over to every kind of sensuality, greedy to practice every kind of impurity" (Eph. 4:17-20);

- people are by nature "bad trees," and according to Jesus "...a bad tree *cannot bear* good fruit" (Matt. 7:18);

- unless a person is born from above, he "*cannot see*," much less "*enter* the kingdom of God" (John 3:3, 5);

- "*no one can come* to [Jesus Christ] unless the Father draws him" and "enables him" to come (John 6:44, 45);

- people "*cannot accept* the Spirit of truth [this is what theologians call moral inability], because they neither see him nor know him [this is what theologians call moral depravity]" (John 14:17);

- people *cannot* bear any true moral fruit *on their own*, for according to Jesus: "No branch can bear fruit by itself; it must remain in the vine. *Neither can you bear fruit unless you remain in me*. I am the vine...apart from me *you can do nothing*" (John 15:4-5);

- "...the sinful mind...*does not submit* to God's law [there it is again, moral depravity]; nor *can it do so* [there it is again, moral inability]. Those controlled by the sinful nature *cannot please* God" (Rom. 8:7-8);

- "...the person without the Spirit *does not accept* the things that come from the Spirit of God, for they are foolishness to him [there it is again, moral depravity], and he *cannot understand* them [there it is again, moral inability], because they are discernable only through the Spirit's enabling" (1 Cor. 2:14);

- "...*no one can say*, 'Jesus is Lord,'" and mean it in the sense that Paul intended it, that is, savingly, "except by the Holy Spirit" (1 Cor. 12:3);

- people "*cannot [even] tame* their [own] tongues" – the bodily organs that are "restless evils, full of deadly poison" (James 3:8);

- *no one can learn* the "new song" that is sung around the throne of God except he be redeemed (Rev. 14:3);

- "The whole world lies in the power of the evil one" (1 John 5:19); in sum,

- it is as impossible for people to improve their character or act in a way that is distinct from their native corruption as it is for "the Ethiopian to change his skin or the leopard to change his spots" (Jer. 13:23).

Clearly, in its raw *natural* state the entire human race is incapable of the understanding, the affections, and the will to act that, taken together, would enable it apart from *supernatural* aid coming to it *ab extra* ("from outside") and *anōthen* ("from above") to be subject to the law of God, to respond to the gospel of God, and to love God as people ought. Accordingly, fallen mankind has an anti-theistic bias, an apostate *pou stō* from which it launches all its religious and scientific predications.

If the fallen human being cannot believe the gospel prior to a gracious operation of the Holy Spirit in his heart because he is dead in trespasses and sins (John 6:44-45, 65; Eph. 2:1), then the Christian apologist must not imply that he can do so by granting him the right prior to faith to test the Scriptures with regard to their truthfulness by applying to them the test of "systematic consistency." When the unbeliever tests the Scriptures by this test of the "foolish" mind he will conclude – indeed, he must conclude if he is true to himself – that the Scriptures are not the Word of God because the things of the Holy Spirit are foolishness to him and he cannot understand them. Only the man whom the Holy Spirit enlightens can understand spiritual truth (1 Cor. 2:14).

Consequently, the instructed Christian apologist will never invite, by suggestion or implication, the unbeliever to examine the biblical revelation and the evidence for the truthfulness of the Christian faith (which is manifestly present everywhere) *from the latter's perspective.* To do so is to deny what Scripture declares about him and implies that he is not the covenant breaker that he is. It is to suggest that he has already been able to bring meaning, reasoning from his apostate *pou stō,* to much of the universe already without assistance from the divine *pou stō.* Such an invitation permits the unbeliever to extend his authority into the domain of Christian theism and to determine there what is and is not true and what is and is not possible.

Furthermore, it is to imply that the unbeliever, as "normal," as "neutral," and as "capable" man, is able to judge the evidence for the veracity of the God of Christian theism. Indeed, it is to imply that the unbeliever has the right to demand that the Creator provide him sufficient credentials before he will permit him a place in his universe.

The result, at best, will be the apostate conclusion that what in actuality is revelational data is only possibly true. He may very well conclude that some propositions in the Bible are true, but even such a conclusion by the very nature of such an invitation will be reached on the unbeliever's authority and not because of the inherent authority of God's Word. Furthermore, he will permit God access to his cosmos, at best, only as an "expert" in religion (because even experts may be wrong at times) but not as the true and living God whose sovereign authority is a threat to human autonomy. In this matrix fallen man remains the ultimate authority in determining truth and his apostate autonomy remains intact.

Rather than making his appeal to the apostate reason of autonomous man, the instructed Christian apologist will appeal to the man who is *really* standing before him – the man the Bible says he is – the man made in the image of God who "knows God" (Rom. 1:20) but who is suppressing his innate awareness of him, the man whose very nature requires that he worship and whose need to worship will never be rightly met until he worships the triune God who created him through Jesus Christ. The Christian apologist will give him the reasons why he must forsake his autonomy in repentance toward God and faith in Jesus Christ. In short, he will tell the "image of God" standing before him the good news of the gospel and pray that God's Spirit will open his blind eyes. If and when he appeals to the natural man's understanding of things he will do so only to show him where it will lead if he would be consistent with his *pou stō*. When he includes in his apologetic effort an appeal to the biblical evidence he will do so by presenting it *not* as data in a probability argument but as certain proof that the biblical God is the one living and true God. All the while he will pray that God, if he is pleased to do so, will grant to his fallen creature grace to believe and to receive the *pou stō* of the self-attesting Christ who speaks throughout Scripture. Christ's Word is the light in which we see light (Ps. 36:9). In him are hidden *all* the treasures of wisdom and knowledge (Col. 2:3). Why should we close our eyes, as it were, to Christ's light and to his wisdom and knowledge when we talk to the non-believer? To do otherwise and to begin with the "flashlight" of apostate human reason in order to see the brilliant blazing sun of Christ's divine wisdom is – let me say it frankly – ludicrous.

When unbelieving people challenge the Faith, as they most certainly will do (see Ps. 2:1-3), we must muster in its defense all the knowledge we have acquired and must address their objections. But in our defense we must not water down the gospel message that is the real offense of our Faith to the natural man just as Christ was unwilling to water down his demand when he refused to call the rich young ruler back to tell him that he did not really mean it – that he was just kidding – when he told him: "If you would be perfect…sell what you possess…and come, follow me" (Matt. 19:21), and just as we saw in the last chapter that Paul was unwilling to do in his *Areopagitica*. Too radically committed to God's truth were both of them – the Master and his disciple – to compromise the truth of the gospel. So when these unbelievers perceive that we will not water down the gospel message and they turn away from us in disgust we must resist the impulse, I say again, to run after them and to water down our message. We must not assume a stance of neutrality – a "nobody knows as yet" attitude – with them. Rather, we must inform them that we understand why they resist our message. When with surprise they ask us how that can be, we should tell them that we understand their resistance to the gospel because we too were at one time where they are now and we resisted the gospel as well when we were unbelievers and we would still do so were it not for the illuminating grace of God. Should they leave our presence still in unbelief, we should tell them that we will pray for their salvation, and we should do so with the confidence that in his sovereignty the Holy Spirit, using the biblical truth we gave them, can remove the spiritual scales from their unbelieving eyes in order that they may see the error of their autonomy and the beauty of Christ who is their king and the only Savior of the world. We should do this because the truth of God's Word, the Bible, when proclaimed and taught in the power of the Holy Spirit, is able to create its own reformation in the hearts of unbelievers. And when in repentance and faith they bow before him, confessing Christ's name as exalted above every name, we should be able to say with the apostle Paul that our witness was not with persuasive words of human wisdom but with words demonstrating the Spirit's power. Then, and only then, will their faith rest on God's power and not on human wisdom (see 1 Cor. 2:1-5). Then they too can become "epistemologically self-conscious" Christians.

The Christian's life should be one grand doxology to God. This means that his intellectual life should be lived under the Lordship of Christ, which means in turn that he should take seriously the fact that "in Christ are hidden all the treasures of wisdom and knowledge" (Col. 2:3) and that the fear of the Lord is the beginning of knowledge and the beginning of wisdom (Prov. 1:7; 9:10). Therefore, the Christian should make Christ's Word the *pou stō* not only for his theology but also for all of his sciences and his ethics. Not to place Christ's Word at the base of all of his thinking is to be untrue to his Savior who died for his sins and rose for his justification. Accordingly, both when he propagates his faith and when he defends his faith he should do so as the epistemologically self-conscious Christian that he is. This means that he should make Christ's Word the base for, and the circle from which emerges, all of his apologetic predications. The apologetic methodology outlined in the foregoing pages seems to me to be most in accord with the doxological character of the life that Scripture requires one to live before the God of all grace. It calls upon the Christian apologist to take seriously the self-authenticating Word of Christ in the Scripture he has given us and to challenge the self-acclaimed autonomy of the so-called "rational man" in terms of *that* revelation and in Christ's name. It demands that the so-called "rational man," in order to save his own rationality, both recognize Christ's epistemic Lordship over him as the ground for the very possibility of knowing anything for sure and acknowledge his sinful autonomous motive that controls his thinking in all of his intellectual pursuits by which he reduces to "brute" (that is, uninterpreted) fact every "theistic" datum in this theistic universe, including even Christ's Word.

At the risk of wearying my readers I want to say again that it should be apparent by now that any argument for Christianity that begins with fallen man's own "creatively constructed" facts, that is, with facts constructed and interpreted by the natural man, and with fallen man's "test of truth" will yield at best only possibilities that permit him to believe that he can reject what are actually God-created, God-revealing data and still be an honest man, true to his own best insights. At worst, it is an argument that represents the universe as one governed by Chance in which there can never be a unified world of knowledge inasmuch as every datum in it is a unique contingency that means nothing. J. I. Packer needs to be heard when he states that

> ...the apologetic strategy that would attract converts by the flattery of accommodating the gospel to the "wisdom" of sinful man was condemned by Paul nineteen centuries ago, and the past hundred years have provided a fresh demonstration of its bankruptcy."[1]

The Church cannot expect to know the fullest blessing of God upon its apologetic endeavors until it sets aside all accommodations to the autonomy of unbelieving people and insists, in conjunction with the proclamation of the Reformed gospel, that the authority of the word and knowledge of the self-attesting Christ of Scripture is the only *pou stō* sufficiently capable of justifying human truth claims. Therefore, the church

---

[1]J. I. Packer, *"Fundamentalism" and the Word of God* (Grand Rapids: Eerdmans, 1958), 168.

should insist and must be able to show that until Christ's authority is acknowledged and placed at the base of the non-Christian's knowledge systems those systems will remain unjustified and no truth assertion within them can be shown to have any significant meaning at all.

Before I conclude I want to address one final objection that someone might raise concerning this entire apologetic enterprise. It is this: that I have written the "story line" so poorly if not incorrectly throughout that I had to introduce the Christian God as my *Deus ex machina* to save the argument. *Deus ex machina* literally means "a god out of a machine." The expression had its origin in ancient Greece, particularly in the plays of Euripides, when the complexities of the plot became so incapable of resolution that a god was set down on stage by a mechanical crane (the "machine") to sort things out and make them right. Today the expression is usually applied to narrative works, especially the works of playwrights and novelists who find themselves so enmeshed in complexities of their own devising in the plot line that they are incapable of bringing their plot to a close without resorting to a highly unlikely or very improbable coincidence (the impoverished widow facing eviction suddenly receives a legacy; the Cavalry suddenly and unexpectedly appears to save the wagon train). Admittedly, this is the stuff that bad fiction is made of. But, as Gordon H. Clark declares:

> ...it is not the dogmatist who has tangled up the plot.... It was not the dogmatist who made [empiricism] chaotic and inferences from it fallacious. These difficulties were first written out by people who were not dogmatists. Hence by the fixed truth of literary criticism a *Deus ex machina* is a rational solution. Yet dogmatism is not precisely a *Deus ex m.* In the eyes of its opponents it is worse. The literary devise is used just once at the end of the play. But in dogmatism God and his revelation are invoked at every step of the way. Is this worse, or is it better? Do not logic, consistency, and System require God's actions to be pervasive rather than restricted to Act V Scene IX? The

> God of dogmatism is a sovereign Deity who determines all his creatures and all their actions.[2]

I concur. As the reader must acknowledge I have not introduced the God of Christian theism at the end of the story to save my argument. I introduced him at the beginning and have argued throughout that he must be placed at the beginning of all intellectual activity because "the fear of the Lord is the beginning of wisdom" (Prov. 1:7), because "in Christ are hidden all the treasures of wisdom and knowledge" (Col. 2:3), and because not to do so is to commit intellectual suicide.

---

[2]Gordon H. Clark, *Three Types of Religious Philosophy* (Nutley, N. J.: Craig, 1973), 103.

Subject Index

Act of worship, theology as 60-61
Areopagitica, Paul's, provides ten-point "metanarrative" method
    to reach postmoderns .... 445-48.
Apologetics, Christian:
    aspects of task of 22-26
    major issues confronting 26-27
    major systems of 27-28
    place of in theological encyclopedia 21-22
    significance of 1 Peter 3:15-16a for 19-20
    what it is .... 17-32.
Apologetic,
    Carnell's 280-84
    Ligonier's 275-80
    St. Paul's 431-55
    Pinnock's 285-86
    Schaeffer's 284-85
    Warfield's 244-67
    Westminster's .... 273, 287.
Ascension, Jesus':
    biblical data concerning 157-62
    significance of .... 162-65.
Auburn Affirmation of 1924: .... 131-34.
Augustine, view of on biblical inerrancy .... 123.

Being, Christian view of 44-45
Bible
    as man's only *pou   stō* for knowledge and personal
    significance...343-70
    as the Word of God: faith's reasons for believing in....69-112
    Holy Spirit's witness to 95-103
Biblical "fool," answering the..62-68
Biblical inerrancy,
    Augustine on 123
    Calvin on 123-30
    Gaussen on 111-12
Biblical miracles in general 197-203
    faith's reasons for believing in 197-207
Bodily resurrection of Jesus Christ:
    apostles' proclamatory "doorway" into the gospel 450
    critical views against answered................................148-54
    faith's reasons for believing in 134-57
    implications of for evangelism................................450-52
    significance of..154-57
    two great strands of evidence for 136-45
Book's title, explanation of..10-15

Calvin's advocacy of inerrancy............................. 126, 128
    Briggs on 126
    Dowey on 124
    Kantzer on 125
    McKim on 126
    McNeill on ....126, 127 fn 65, 128, fn 66
    Murray on...125, 130
    Packer on... 126
    Rogers on 126
    Warfield on 124
Canonicity
    of Hebrews 114-17
    of James.. 113-14

of Jude 118
of Revelation 122
of Second John 121
of Second Peter 119-21
of Third John 121-22
Canonization process, God's providence the ultimate guiding
    force behind 103-10
Christian theology as an intellectual discipline:
    faith's reasons for believing in 33-61
    five supporting pillars of 39-58
    justification of 39-61
Clark's argument for biblical inspiration 92-95
Conversion, Paul's 227-42
    arguments showing improbability of other explanations for
    238-41
    biblical material concerning 228-29
    rationalizing explanations of 229-33
    his own argument for 233-38

Design, intelligent: *ad hominem* addendum on for the biblical
    "fool" 334-42
"Disputed books," canonicity of 113-23

Emotivism, failure of as an ethical system 405
Epilogue 457-67
    Reformed apologetics not a *Deus ex machina* in classical
    sense 466
    summation of the Reformed apologetic method 457-65
Ethics, Christian theistic:
    a consistent ethic 418-20
    Christ the living embodiment of 417
    faith's reasons for believing in the apologetic value of 397-426
    God's law the ground of 415-16
    God's law the norm for guidance 415-16
Ethics, secular
    failure of to provide guidance, goals, and ground for 399-414

Ethics, evolutionary
    failure of as a system of ethics 409-11
Evidentialism
    faith's reasons for rejecting 243-92
    Jonathan Edwards on 317-18, 324, 329-30
    ten problems with 315-32
Evidentialist school of apologetics 267-85
Existentialism, failure of as an ethical system 405-6

F irst day worship: 145-47;
    church's shift to as evidence for Christ's resurrection . 145 fn 8
Five supporting pillars of Christian theology 39-58
    apostolic model 51-54
    Christ's mandate to his church 43-51
    Christ's own theological method 39-47
    example and activity of the New Testament church ... 54-57
    nature of Holy Scripture as revealed Word of God 57-59

G od of Christian theism,
    faith's reasons for believing in 293-334
    biblical description of 293-306
    empirical arguments for 313-32
    ontological argument for 307-12
    why Christians believe in 306-7

H umanist Manifesto II, failure of as an ethical system .. 405-14

I nerrancy, scriptural: Calvin's view of 123-30
Instrumentalism, failure of as an ethical system 406-9.
Intuitionism,
    Christian, inadequacy of 420-26
    secular, failure of as an ethical system .... 403-4.
Isaiah 7:14, exposition of: historical setting of 167-70;
    meaning of 'almāh 170-78

problem of relevance 178-80
solution to the problem of relevance 180-86

Kant's "categorical imperative" 427-30
Knowing, Christian view of 345-49
justification of 349-55
non-analogical between God and man 375-81

Miracles, Jesus':
biblical data concerning 203-8
critical responses to 208-11
evangelical responses to 211-13
faith's reasons for believing in 203-13
significance of 214-17

Nature of biblical truth, faith's reasons for believing in 371-96.

Passages on inspiration and inerrancy, exposition of .. 71-92
1 Corinthians 2:16-14 71-73
2 Timothy 3:16 74-78
1 Peter 1:10-12 79-80
2 Peter 1:20-21 80-88
2 Peter *3:15-16* 73-74
Pauline apologetic for the postmodern 431-48
Personal significance, justification of 354-70
Post-crucifixion appearances of Jesus 141-45 ....
Pou stō, meaning of .... 7-8.

Realism, Scottish common sense .... 246 fn 3.

Stolen body theory .... 137-39.
Swoon theory .... 139-40.

Transfiguration, Jesus'...217-26
   its background 217-20
   its historicity..220-22
   its meaning 223-26
Testimony of the Holy Spirit: what it is and what it is not.. 289-91
Truth: faithfulness of God's...393-96
   God's logically rational..381-91
   not paradoxical...383-91
   univocal for God and man..375-81
   ethical steadfastness of..391-93

Utilitarianism, failure of as an ethical system..............402-3

Virgin birth, Christ's:
   faith's reasons for believing in 167-96
   Isaiah 7:14 on 167-86
   New Testament teaching on 186-87
   purpose of...190-96
   testimony from church history on ....188-90.

Warfield apologetic 244-67
   argument for inspiration...248-53
   diagram of 253
   difficulties with..264-67
   his larger view of...253-59
   nature and degree of certainty in.............................259-63.

Other books of interest
in the
Mentor Imprint

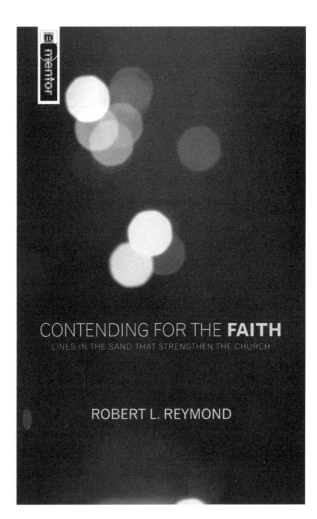

CONTENDING FOR THE **FAITH**

LINES IN THE SAND THAT STRENGTHEN THE CHURCH

ROBERT L. REYMOND

Contending for the Faith:

Lines in the sand that strengthen me

Robert L. Reymond

'Contending for the Faith' offers a selection of Reymond's papers in the areas of Systematic Theology and Apologetics. The one thing these articles generally have in common is their apologetic flavour, that is to say, each in its own way contends for the Biblical and Reformed Faith. Many of these papers have never been previously published.

Robert offers them to a broader readership as they address topics that are, in many cases, being debated within the Church at large today. We are given unique insights into a huge range of subjects from Creation to Lord's Day Observance, from the Trinity to Islam. This is a hugely significant contribution to the defence of the Christian Faith that makes points that are difficult to ignore.

'With customary thoroughness and exacting exegesis, Professor Reymond leads us through a maze of theological topics which call out for a clear biblical perspective in our day. His guiding principle is that God can be glorified in our theological reflection only as we listen to the teaching of his authoritative Word. Reymond is a much-needed prophetic voice in our day, calling us to pay attention to 'Thus says the Lord.'
Dr. Iain D. Campbell, Back Free Church of Scotland

ISBN 978-1-84550-045-8

ENTOR

An investigation of the
perfections of God's nature

WHAT IS
GOD
?

ROBERT L. REYMOND